Religious Perspectives
in
College Teaching

By

HOXIE N. FAIRCHILD

ALFRED R. BELLINGER   DOROTHY D. LEE
KENNETH E. BOULDING   EDWARD MC CRADY
JOSEPH S. DALTRY   ROBERT B. MAC LEOD
THEODORE M. GREENE   TALCOTT PARSONS
JOHN H. HALLOWELL   HUGH S. TAYLOR
E. HARRIS HARBISON   GEORGE F. THOMAS

ROBERT ULICH

THE RONALD PRESS COMPANY , NEW YORK

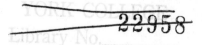

Library of Congress Catalog Card Number: 52-9464

PRINTED IN THE UNITED STATES OF AMERICA

PREFACE

This volume completes an undertaking which originated in a letter written in 1947 by Professor George F. Thomas of Princeton University to The Edward W. Hazen Foundation. In it he urged the need for careful studies by natural scientists, social scientists, and humanistic scholars concerning the religious issues, implications, and responsibilities involved in the college teaching of their respective disciplines. At that time The Foundation, jointly with the Committee on Religion and Education of the American Council on Education, was conducting a survey of the quantity and quality of the religious facts and ideas provided by college textbooks in the principal academic fields. The results of this investigation were published in 1948 in a book entitled *College Reading and Religion*. Several contributors to the volume emphasized the fact that although much could be learned about the status of religion in the American college from an examination of textbooks, a more important factor was the attitude of the teacher toward religion and his willingness to express that attitude in the classroom.

As regards the problem of the teacher, what seemed to be required was not a statistical survey but the presentation of a body of constructive ideas by scholars whose opinions would command respect even when they aroused disagreement. The Hazen Foundation therefore decided to evolve a new project from Professor Thomas' suggestion and approved a grant for this purpose. In the spring of 1949 the following were appointed a committee to develop a plan and project: Bruce M. Bigelow of Brown University, Paul J. Braisted of The Hazen Foundation, Hoxie N. Fairchild of Hunter College, Albert C.

Outler, then of Yale University and now of Southern Metho-
dist University, Edmund W. Sinnott of Yale University,
George F. Thomas of Princeton University, and Robert Ulich
of Harvard University.

Under the sponsorship of The Foundation, this Committee
enlisted the aid of scholars who were not only deeply interested in the relations between religion and higher education
but who had made substantial contributions to their respective
fields of learning. Each of these scholars was invited to discuss the problem as it pertains to his own discipline and to his
conception of his intellectual and spiritual responsibilities to
his students, to the institution which he serves, and to society
in general. The original plan was to secure essays on the religious implications of almost every subject usually offered to
college students. It soon became apparent, however, that such
exhaustiveness would make the project unwieldy and would
entail too much overlapping and repetition. The Table of
Contents will show that the policy arrived at after a short
period of initial groping was to present discussions of selected
subjects important both for religion and for education and
representing the recognized divisions of the liberal arts curriculum. An essay on the Preparation of Teachers was also included
because of the obvious importance of the topic. In addition
one essay, which now forms the introductory chapter of this
volume, was prepared on college teaching as a whole, dealing
specifically with what constitutes a religious perspective and
the relationships of the professor and his students.

These essays do not reflect the views of any one school of
religious thought. On such matters the members of the Committee themselves vary all the way from Anglo-Catholicism to
a theistic type of transcendentalism. Yet although they wished
to avoid dogmatism, they were no less anxious to avoid a
vagueness which would produce nothing but meaningless generalities. For their own guidance they drew up a statement of
principles which they shared and which they hoped would be

accepted as a sort of common denominator by the scholars whom they invited to participate:

> Religion is not nature-worship, or man-worship, or science-worship. It is not the totality of human value. Although it is metaphysical, ethical, and humanitarian, it cannot be equated with metaphysics, or ethics, or humanitarianism. Religion is man's quest for communion with an ultimate spiritual reality completely independent of human desires and imaginings. Religion apprehends this Absolute Reality and Value in faith, and seeks to give concrete embodiment to the ineffable in creed, cult, and conduct. The creative power of the universe is not an intellectual abstraction but an objective entity, a Divine Being. Although God infinitely transcends our human nature and understanding, He most potently reveals Himself to those who conceive of Him in personal terms. Thus symbolized, He becomes for us not merely Cosmic Mind, but Creator, Judge, and Redeemer of mankind.

Within this broad but positive consensus the authors of the essays were encouraged to exercise complete freedom in expressing their personal standpoints, and it will be obvious to the reader that they have done so. In reviewing the tentative draft of a given manuscript, the Committee sometimes made editorial comments pointing, in their opinion, toward a more effective presentation of the contributor's own views or toward more complete consistency with the general purpose of the project. Occasionally an individual member would question the validity of some particular assertion or plead for the inclusion of a point which the author had intentionally or unintentionally omitted. But all such suggestions were thoroughly undogmatic and tentative, and once it was clear that the author had said precisely what he wanted to say in the way in which he wanted to say it, not the slightest attempt was made to interfere with his thoughts or words.

Even in these days of general education, the scholar continues to know much more about *something* than he knows about anything else. Many college teachers are by no means oblivious of the importance of religion for higher education in general but hesitate to grapple with the more specific problem of how religion pertains to the study and teaching of their particular subjects. The Committee felt that this more specialized aspect of the question deserved closer study than it had usually received. Originally, therefore, these essays were issued at intervals as separate pamphlets on "Religious Perspectives of College Teaching" in various subjects so that each might appeal directly to those professionally concerned with the discipline which it discussed.

From the first, however, the Committee had foreseen the possibility that the series of essays might later be published in a book. The response to the separate pamphlets was abundant and almost wholly favorable. It indicated that college administrators and religious workers found the essays even more significant for what they implied as a whole than for what they said as discussions of particular topics. Also many teachers, after reading the pamphlet pertaining to their own field, expressed a desire to read those on related fields or even to possess the entire series. Quite naturally and properly, their interests as members of a college faculty were broader than their interests as scholarly specialists. It seemed clear, then, that if there had been one kind of advantage in keeping the essays separate, there would be another kind of advantage in bringing them together.

In their present collected form, these studies contribute not only to an understanding of the religious perspectives of particular topics but to a realization of the unity which underlies the heterogeneity of intellectual endeavor. Despite their theological divergencies, they similarly bear witness to a corresponding spiritual coherence. The essays represent the earnest convictions of reputable intellectual workers in a free society. All of these scholars believe that religion, as defined in the Committee's statement of basic principles, is of cardinal importance for higher education. All of them believe that the cleavage which divides intellectual from spiritual life is probably the most ominous defect of modern civilization. All of them believe that college teachers should think more deeply and speak more boldly as regards the religious bearings of their respective disciplines. If this much unity should become generally prevalent in academic circles the American college would be transformed.

THE COMMITTEE

Hoxie N. Fairchild, *Chairman*
Bruce M. Bigelow
Paul J. Braisted
Albert C. Outler
Edmund W. Sinnott
George F. Thomas
Robert Ulich

New Haven, Connecticut
July, 1952

CONTENTS

RELIGIOUS PERSPECTIVES
IN COLLEGE TEACHING

RELIGIOUS PERSPECTIVES IN COLLEGE TEACHING: PROBLEMS AND PRINCIPLES

By GEORGE F. THOMAS

Any inquiry into the problem of religious perspectives in college or university teaching must begin with the recognition that since the First World War there has been a moral breakdown in Western civilization. In our generation, we have witnessed violence and cruelty on a scale unparalleled in modern history. Paradoxically, the European nation which had reached the highest point in intellectual development was captured in the thirties by a highly irrational ideology and surrendered its freedom to lawless and desperate men. The generation that discovered the secret of how to split the atom used it to produce the most appalling weapon of mass destruction. The economic, political, and international conflicts which threaten the very existence of our civilization are in large measure results of this moral breakdown.

The moral crisis, however, is only an expression of a deeper spiritual and cultural crisis. " 'Mores,' ways of life, the recognition of binding obligations," says Sir Walter Moberly, "are bound up with some accepted view of the nature of man and of the world, though this may take the form less of a doctrine embraced by the mind than of a picture dominating the imagination. But it is just this common picture or framework that has now so largely disappeared . . . Over a large part of Europe and Asia [he might well have added America] binding convictions are lacking and there is confusion, bewilderment, and discord. The whole complex of traditional belief, habit, and sentiment, on which convictions are founded, has collapsed. All over the world indeed the cake of custom is broken, the old gods are dethroned and none have taken their places." [1]

Higher education during the twentieth century has been deeply affected by this spiritual and cultural crisis. It has also helped to produce the crisis. In a striking article in the *American Scholar* some years ago, Walter Lippmann pointed out that the Founding Fathers of America were educated in schools and colleges where the classics of Western religious and classical culture formed "the substance of the curriculum." "Modern education, however," he asserted, "is based on a denial that it is necessary or useful or desirable for the schools and colleges to continue to transmit from generation to generation the religious and classical culture of the Western world." What has been the result of this denial? In the first place, a "cultural vacuum." "There is no common faith, no common body of principle, no common body of knowledge, no common moral and intellectual discipline." In the second place, "progressive disorder" due to the fact that, lacking a social goal, education has become the servant of egoistic aims. "So when parents and taxpayers in a democracy ask whether education is useful for life they tend by and large to mean by useful that which equips the pupil for a career which will bring him money and place and power." [2]

THE SECULARIZATION OF EDUCATION

What has brought us to this pass in liberal education? Everyone knows that colleges were established in the Colonial period largely from religious motives. During most of the nine-

[1] Sir Walter Moberly, *The Crisis of the University* (London: Student Christian Movement Press, Ltd., 1949), p. 16.
[2] Walter Lippmann, "Education vs. Western Civilization," *American Scholar* (1941), pp. 187, 190.

teenth century, privately supported as well as church colleges continued to teach the religious heritage of the West and were to a large extent religious in their outlook. Dean Christian Gauss has recently pointed out that even the new state universities were far from indifferent to the claims of religion.[3] During the latter part of the nineteenth century, however, powerful forces were beginning to make themselves felt and by the turn of the century they had effected a radical change in liberal colleges and universities. What were these forces?

The strife between Protestant sects and denominations was undoubtedly one of them. In the early part of the nineteenth century, the narrow zeal of Protestant groups turned Christian education in schools and colleges into little more than indoctrination in denominational beliefs and practices. It is well known that this sectarianism had much to do with the exclusion of religious instruction from the newly established public schools. In colleges also educators insisted more and more that there was no place in liberal education for indoctrination. The unfortunate results of this narrow denominationalism may be illustrated by the fact that many college administrators and faculty members are still opposed to the teaching of religion on the ground that it is necessarily sectarian.

More important was the rapid expansion of knowledge and the growth of specialization. This led to the establishment of many new subjects and departments of study. The new departments, organized along the same lines as the older ones, claimed equality with them. Since they were in many cases more "practical" in the sense that they were more closely related to vocational interests, they attracted large numbers of students to their courses. Those who wished to do their "major" work in one of the new departments often resented the necessity of taking required courses in classics, philosophy, and religion. The result was that these traditional subjects

[3] Christian Gauss, *The Teaching of Religion in American Higher Education* (New York: The Ronald Press Co., 1951), chap. i.

gradually lost their privileged status. The fact that they provided a broader perspective than more specialized studies and were concerned with the values of our Western cultural heritage made little impression upon those whose motive in acquiring an education was frankly utilitarian.

But the strongest force making for radical change in liberal education was the growth of secularism. Secularism consists of a preoccupation with the interests and values of the world of the senses, with the here and now, with time to the exclusion of eternity. Though it may not be based upon a formal rejection of religious beliefs, it relegates religion to a peripheral place in life. It is an attitude towards life, not a philosophy. But it rests, explicitly or implicitly, upon the philosophy of Naturalism. According to this philosophy, reality is identical with nature as the totality of things and events in space and time. There is no eternal, supersensible, spiritual world that transcends the natural order. Man is part and parcel of nature. His values are wholly subjective and relative to desire and feeling. Since his spiritual aspirations and moral efforts are supported by no cosmic will or purpose, he must depend entirely upon himself for his fulfillment. Though this naturalistic world view is incompatible with traditional religion, it has often been accompanied by a religious or ethical humanism which consists of devotion to ideal ends and values. But it owes most of its appeal to the fact that the only kind of reality with which the scientific method concerns itself is that of natural phenomena in space and time. It is easy to infer from this fact that there *is* no other kind of reality, and that whatever *seems* to be different from natural phenomena, e.g., the human spirit and its values, is only apparently so. Thus, secularism is in part a product of the naturalistic philosophy which many have thought to be required by modern science. It is, of course, even more a product of the optimism about the future and the practical materialism that dominated America in the age of economic expansion following the Civil War.

However, our main concern is not with the theoretical and practical causes of secularism, but with its effect upon religion in the liberal colleges. Usually, secularism has manifested itself not in open opposition to religion but in indifference to it. Its strategy has been to insist that the colleges must maintain strict impartiality or neutrality on ultimate religious or philosophical issues. According to its spokesmen, liberal education should not commit itself to any religion or philosophy, because it can accept no authority but that of truth and must at all costs keep an open mind. Furthermore, secular educators point out that there is no agreement in our society on religious and philosophical beliefs and that democracy requires the toleration of different beliefs. It is not too much to say that secularism, based upon "scientism" and in the guise of "neutralism," has been the dominant factor in liberal education during the last two generations.

The Turn of the Tide

We have seen how sectarian narrowness, specialization of knowledge, secularism, and neutrality on ultimate issues combined in the early twentieth century virtually to exclude religion from the curriculum of liberal colleges. However, there has been another remarkable swing of the pendulum during the last decade. This has involved, on the one hand, a growing recognition of the need for adequate religious instruction, and, on the other hand, an attempt to overcome the evils of specialization and fragmentation of knowledge. With respect to religious instruction, one of the reasons for the change has been the decline of sectarianism and the growth of the ecumenical movement in the Protestant churches. The result is that the teaching of religion, even in most church colleges, has ceased to emphasize denominational differences and has become less dogmatic. Moreover, in the early twenties The National Council on Religion in Higher Education was founded and since that time has provided fellowships for several hundred men and women to enable them to prepare themselves for college teaching in all departments and all divisions by the best graduate training available. As a result of these changes, the charge that the teaching of religion is nothing more than sectarian indoctrination is no longer valid, and courses in religion are now taught by men and women whose scholarship is equal to that of their colleagues in other departments.

With respect to the specialization and fragmentation of knowledge, the most striking change is the attempt in recent years to get rid of the excesses of the "free elective" system. This system had led to the disunity and disorder described by Walter Lippmann in the article to which we have already referred, and the demand for "integration" became increasingly insistent before and during the Second World War. As a result, many institutions made a thorough revision of their curricula. The great majority of them sought to bring about an increased emphasis on "general education," involving a larger proportion of required subjects and the distribution of study among all the divisions of knowledge. "The major purpose behind all of these new schemes," says President Van Dusen, "is to introduce larger unity, coherence, and therefore meaning, into the undergraduate's course of study . . . The college must undertake responsibility to determine, in considerable measure, his choices. And in an age lacking coherence and in a culture crying for cohesion but under the sway of specialized interests and fragmentary loyalties, it must introduce him to the great disciplines of learning which together constitute the foundations of an educated mind." [4]

Above all, secularism has begun to lose its appeal. Part of its attraction was derived from the optimism of modern man about his capacity to fulfill his aspirations within the limits of

[4] Henry P. Van Dusen, *God in Education* (New York: Charles Scribner's Sons, 1951), pp. 60, 61.

earthly history, an optimism that reflected itself in the nine-teenth-century belief in inevitable progress and in the utopian-ism associated with that belief. But a generation which has suffered from two world wars and is haunted by fears of a third has not been able to maintain this optimism. It begins to suspect that the this-worldliness of secularism ignores the sin and frustration of human existence. Moreover, the philosophi-cal naturalism which is the main theoretical basis of secularism has been vigorously challenged in recent years. Since the prestige of naturalism is largely the result of the illegitimate claims made on behalf of the scientific method, the growing recognition of the limitations of science, especially in the realm of the spiritual life and its values, is beginning to weaken the hold of naturalism upon the academic mind.

Finally, there has been a sharp reaction during the last decade against the assumption that open-mindedness requires neutrality on ultimate issues. It has become more and more clear that the attitude of neutrality has been producing thou-sands of college graduates each year without religious com-mitments, without ethical and political convictions, without any clear purpose or sense of direction. As a result, their lives are empty and meaningless, with no higher aim than pleasure or material success. How can we expect it to be otherwise? Without loyalty to values like truth and goodness which are regarded as absolute, how can our college graduates be ex-pected to devote their energies and talents to the common good? Without belief in a purpose that transcends their own personal happiness, how can they be expected willingly to risk their lives to defend the cause of democracy or to spend their lives unselfishly in some other worthy cause?

Considerations like these have led many liberal colleges during the last decade to change their requirements in order to help their students attain "binding convictions." Realizing that they had neglected to teach any "common faith," they have established "core" courses in philosophy and religion which introduce Freshmen to the fundamental ideas and ideals of our Western heritage. Other colleges have grouped religion with one or two other subjects as one way of meeting a basic requirement. Still other colleges have added elective courses in the Division of the Humanities, in which students are offered the opportunity to read parts of the Bible and other religious classics.[5]

Equally significant is the fact that a number of privately supported and state universities have established new departments of religion during or since the end of the Second World War. Among these are Princeton, Columbia, Pennsylvania, the University of North Carolina, and the University of Florida. Another indication of the growing recognition of the importance of religion in the curriculum is a number of books which have been published in America in recent years, e.g., Howard Lowry's *The Mind's Adventure*; Henry P. Van Dusen's *God in Education*; and three symposia: *The Teaching of Religion in American Higher Education*, edited by Christian Gauss; *Liberal Learning and Religion*, edited by Amos M. Wilder; and *College Teaching and Christian Values*, edited by Paul M. Limbert.

IS A DEPARTMENT OF RELIGION ENOUGH?

There can be no doubt, therefore, that the tide is turning and that liberal colleges are acknowledging more fully their responsibility for religious instruction. But there is a danger here. It is the danger that colleges which have established small departments of religion or have added a religious philosopher to the department of philosophy will think they have done

[5] At Princeton University, for example, a humanities course entitled "Man and His Freedom in the Western Tradition" has been offered since 1942, in which half of the readings and lectures during the first semester are from the Bible and from medieval Christian thinkers. Several modern Christian thinkers like Luther, Pascal, and Reinhold Niebuhr are studied during the second semester.

enough. Even church colleges are subject to this danger of assuming only "limited liability." Unless there is a genuine and deep religious concern on the part of the administration and faculty, it is all too easy to meet the demands from religiously minded alumni, parents, and students for religious instruction by establishing a department of religion with one or two members and then forgetting about the problem.

We are convinced that, while a department of religion is a vital part of any program of religious instruction, it should never be the whole. Indeed, a strong case can be made out for the thesis that it is not even the most important part of such a program. The reasons are obvious to anyone who reflects a little upon the problem. In the first place, in a privately supported or state university where no courses in religion are required, it is unlikely that more than a sizable minority of students will elect any courses in religion. Consequently, if religion is never discussed in any other department than the department of religion, most students will receive an education as completely secular as if there were no department of religion at all. In the second place, those who do elect courses in the department of religion normally find time for only one or two semester courses in the subject, because of the pressure of general and departmental requirements. If all the courses they elect in other departments are taught from a purely secular point of view, the few courses they take in the department of religion are likely to have little lasting effect upon them. An uncritical student, who is taught in a course in social psychology that religion is a product of ignorance and wishful thinking, may be so deeply affected that he will pay no attention to what is said in a course in Bible. If he hears in a course in history that religion has always been a reactionary force in society, is he very likely to listen to what is told him in a course in Christian ethics about love as a powerful motive for social reform?

There is a third factor that is even more important: the student who is not shaken by open attacks upon religion may be affected deeply by the complete silence about religion he meets everywhere. Rightly or wrongly, he interprets silence as meaning indifference. If religion is completely ignored everywhere in the curriculum except the department of religion, can it be important? The fact the the college supports a chapel is hardly a sufficient proof to the student that the administration regards religion as important. He knows that often a service of worship is maintained by an institution mainly to please parents and alumni of the last generation. Therefore, it is natural for him to infer that, since religion is never mentioned except by a chaplain and a few professors paid to teach it, it must be of real interest to only a few people. The fact that many professors who never speak of religion in the classroom are members of churches is usually unknown to him. Even if it were known, would it make much difference to him? Since he has observed that people who care deeply about something usually reveal it sooner or later in what they say, why should he not think that a person who has never said anything about religion cares nothing about it?

A fourth consideration of an entirely different kind must also be mentioned. If religion is important, the liberal college should help the student to think clearly and coherently about it, to evaluate carefully the beliefs he brought with him to college and to enlarge his religious horizon by sympathetic study of the beliefs of others. For this purpose, he needs guidance not only from the department of religion but also from other departments. He cannot understand fully the meaning and significance of religion by studying it in and by itself alone; he must also investigate the way it has shaped the thinking and conduct of those who have come under its influence. Now, the study of religion, in and by itself as a distinct reality, is the function of the department of religion. But the study of religion in its relations with other human interests and in its impact upon social institutions and cultural activities belongs largely to other departments. The professor of religion may speak in a general way of the contribution of Christianity to democracy, but who can speak with authority upon that subject except the historian and the political scientist? The professor of religion may know that Buddhism has given rise to important schools of sculpture and landscape painting, but who can do justice to these schools except the art historian? The professor of religion can teach the student about the Reformation as a religious movement, but does he have either the time or the knowledge of the professor of European history to deal with its political, economic, and cultural aspects? Thus, if a liberal college has the responsibility to teach religion not merely as a distinct kind of human experience but also as a formative force which has helped to shape the whole life of culture and society, many other departments must share that responsibility with the department of religion. If they refuse to do so, the student will get a very narrow and inadequate view of religion, because he will not have learned to see it in its wider relations and ramifications.

The Nature of a Religious Perspective

For all of these reasons, it is not enough for a liberal college to offer courses in a department of religion. *Religious facts, issues, and implications should be dealt with in every division, department, and course where they arise naturally.* If the significance of the essays included in this volume is to be fully understood, however, it is essential to have a clear idea of *what* a "religious perspective" in teaching is, and *how* such a perspective should affect the teaching of a professor in his field.

It must not be thought that professors with a religious faith teach from the perspective of that faith merely "as a favor" to their colleagues in the department of religion, or "to support the work" of the chaplain and others serving the cause of religion on the campus, or primarily "to bear witness" to their faith. Whatever the validity of these motives may be, the primary motive of any professor of physics or history is to *teach his subject* as fully and adequately as possible. The religious issues and implications of his subject should be dealt with because they are part of his task as a teacher of that subject. The professor of physics, for example, discusses the religious issues and implications of his subject only if and when it is necessary for him to do so in order to teach physics in an adequate way, i.e., in its wider relations and ultimate significance. He is a professor of physics, not a preacher of religion. Therefore, he does not "drag in" religion when it is not relevant to a full understanding of the facts he is interpreting or the problems he is trying to solve.

To put it in positive terms, my thesis is that, if a professor is a Christian theist, he has a perspective from which he can interpret the facts and deal with the issues in his field more adequately. If Christian theism is true, it asserts the ultimate Truth about reality as a whole. Therefore, it provides the key for the interpretation of all the truths in special fields of knowledge which deal with particular aspects of reality. God is not only the absolute Light; He is the Source of the imperfect light which illuminates every field of reality we explore.

But religious truth is truth about God and His relation to the world. As such, it is not truth of the same order and at the same level as other truths. The failure to understand this is at the root of the "conflict" between science (or history) and religion. For if religious truth is regarded as truth of the same kind as other truths, it is bound at times to come into conflict with them. For example, if the great myth of the Creation in the book of Genesis is interpreted as asserting a scientific rather than a religious truth, it obviously conflicts with the theory of evolution. But if it is interpreted as asserting a religious truth, a truth about the relation of the world to God,

it embodies a profound truth about another dimension of
reality than that described by the scientist. This implies that
the religious perspective on physics does not add *new* facts to
the subject, in the usual sense of the word "facts"; it provides
an interpretation to *all* the facts of the subject by indicating
their relation to God as the ultimate Being upon whom they
depend. Similarly, the religious perspective on politics or
aesthetics does not add *new* values of the same order as the
human "values" dealt with by these disciplines; it offers values
of a higher order and another way of evaluating all human
"values" by reference to the Good which God wills for man.

One or two examples may help to make this point clear. If
the existence of nature is grounded in and sustained by God's
will and if its order is a product of His wisdom, it cannot be
a self-explanatory system as naturalistic philosophers think.
Therefore, the laws of physics, chemistry, and biology must be
interpreted, not as final explanations, but as descriptions
of natural phenomena. If so, the natural scientist who is
a Christian will see in nature all that his secular colleague sees;
but he will look upon it with eyes filled with wonder and awe,
because he believes that it is the product of divine power and
wisdom rather than blind chance and that it is a manifestation
of divine goodness. As a scientist, he cannot allow his wonder
and awe to affect his descriptions of a natural phenomenon;
but in so far as he is a man, they are bound to affect his
thoughts and feelings about nature. Again, the Christian
political scientist must describe the structures and functions
of different branches of the American government in the same
way as his secular colleague. But his Christian belief that man
is not merely an animal struggling to survive and exercise
power, but also a spiritual being created in the image of God,
will give deeper meaning and stronger conviction to his treatment of the dignity and rights of man in American democracy.
Finally, the Christian historian will investigate the events of
a period and trace their causal relationships, using the estab-

lished method of all careful historians. But his conception of man and his belief that God has a purpose for history will lead him to look for a pattern of meaning in them, however impossible it may be to discover that pattern with certainty in the tangled skein of events.

Thus, the religious perspective of the Christian theist does not contribute new facts in any of these fields; it contributes an interpretation of the facts that deepens one's understanding of their ultimate significance. Obviously, this interpretation is bound to affect one's view of the facts themselves. Indeed, that is one of the main reasons it is important. But a genuinely religious interpretation of the facts can never lead us to deny or distort any of them, since God is Truth and wills that we should acknowledge every truth. Moreover, our religious perspective does not allow us to abandon or abridge any of the established methods of dealing with the facts in a field. The Christian physicist, political scientist, or historian must use precisely the same methods as his secular colleagues and he must use them with the same thoroughness. This is what is meant when it is said, "There is no such thing as 'Christian' physics, economics, politics, or logic; there is only physics, economics, politics, or logic." For the technical work of a scholar in any field is the same whether he is a Christian or not. He must gather, classify, and describe the facts by the methods which have proved most successful in his field. He must develop and test hypotheses for the interpretation of them according to the established procedures in the field. There is no way to avoid or shorten the task if one is to be faithful to the demands of scholarship. Obviously, the same principle applies to teaching in the field.

Therefore, the Christian scholar and teacher must not succumb to the temptation to bring in God when there is a gap in his knowledge or a confusion in his thinking. If he yields to this temptation, he evades the responsibility of filling the gap or clearing up the confusion by hard work. One of the reasons why modern science and philosophy have asserted their independence of theology is that Christians have sometimes substituted an appeal to God or to the authority of the church or the Bible for patient and independent study of the facts and thinking about the problems. If he was speaking only as an astronomer, Laplace was surely right when, in reply to a question about the role of God in his science, he replied, "Sire, I have no need of that hypothesis." For the appeal to a "First Cause," though essential in theology and (ultimately) in philosophy, cannot take the place of description of "second causes" in natural science. Laplace was wrong, then, only if he implied that scientific description did not need to be supplemented by theological and philosophical explanation.

The conclusion we should draw from all of this is that the Christian professor must never allow his religious perspective to become a substitute for the careful establishment of facts and development of theories appropriate to his field. The role of his religious perspective is to enable him to see the facts in *a deeper dimension* and to relate the descriptions of them by the methods used in his field to *a more ultimate and inclusive interpretation.*

"Christian" or "Liberal" University?

At this point, it is necessary to guard ourselves against a possible misunderstanding of our argument. If religious issues and implications are to be dealt with in every division and department where they are relevant, someone may think it will be necessary to return to the "Christian university" of the Middle Ages or of seventeenth-century Puritanism and this will be the end of intellectual liberty. But this is far from our meaning and intention. A "Christian university" which would impose religious uniformity upon its faculty and its curriculum would be neither possible nor desirable. It would be impossible because our society is not a "Christian society" in the sense of a "society in which the great majority of people accept the Christian faith and way of life." Broadly speaking, at least half of the citizens of the United States are not Christians. Consequently, whatever may be said of our church colleges, it is unrealistic to think that in the foreseeable future our privately supported or state universities can become "Christian" in the traditional sense. As long as administrations, faculties, student bodies, and parents are only partially Christian, our universities cannot be expected to be wholly Christian. Even if it were possible, however, it would not be desirable for us to return to the medieval or Puritan pattern. Modern democracy is committed to the principle of religious and intellectual liberty. Certainly, Americans do not believe that religious uniformity should be imposed by the state and they would be equally opposed to any attempt to impose it by any church or educational system. They believe that each person, when he reaches maturity, should have the right to determine his religious belief for himself. Thus, a "Christian university" in the traditional sense would be inconsistent with both the religious realities and the religious and political ideals of our people. Moberly adds that an "all-Christian" university might be dangerous to the Christian cause itself. While Christians believe, he says, that "the whole truth is in Christ, we have to recognize that it is not in possession of Christians, either individually or collectively." "Domination by theologians," he adds, "is no less objectionable than domination by any other group. Any implied claim to infallibility is unchristian, since it clashes with Christian insight into human creatureliness and human corruption . . . But it is still more essential to recognize that God may speak, and often does speak, through what we should have thought very improbable voices, through men who do not consciously know Him and who are disastrously wrong in their main contentions. As of old the heathen peoples might be instruments of His judgments on Israel, so Marx or Nietzsche or Freud may have a word for our generation, to refuse to hear which would be to be deaf to the voice of God." [6]

What is possible and desirable is something quite different from the traditional "all-Christian" university: a university which would be genuinely liberal in the sense that it would permit and encourage the open expression of convictions on ultimate issues by both Christians and others. As we have seen, secular educators have held that to be "liberal" required one to be "neutral" on ultimate philosophical and religious questions. But this profession of neutrality has been little more than a pretense. Though they have claimed to be neutral with respect to religion, they have actually had a religion of their own, consciously or unconsciously, and have inculcated it in their students. It is the religion of Scientific Humanism. The majority of faculty members of our liberal colleges, including many of our "church-related" colleges, have believed firmly that there is no higher end for man than his earthly fulfillment ("humanism") and that science provides the only dependable knowledge of the means to this end ("scientism"). Though it has been weakened during the last decade, as we have said, this Scientific Humanism is still a powerful force.

What we propose, therefore, is that Christian professors should do what their secular colleagues who believe in scientific humanism have been doing all along, i.e., teach freely and openly from their perspective. In this way, they would make clear to their students the presuppositions with which they approach their subjects. If they were as open in expressing their convictions as their humanistic colleagues now are, there would be a more lively ferment of ideas. Students would be confronted with various alternative positions on ultimate issues and would be challenged to decide among them. They would no longer be misled into thinking that the position one takes on ultimate issues is unimportant; indeed, they would

[6] Moberly, *op. cit.*, pp. 104, 105.

see that it is the most important thing in life. Under these conditions, if they decided against Christian theism and in favor of scientific humanism, it would be only after they had faced the issue between the two positions. At present, the decision often goes by default against Christian theism because the issue is simply ignored.

Thus, we are not arguing for a "Christian university" in the traditional sense; we are arguing for a genuinely "liberal university" which would not in the name of a spurious neutrality evade the ultimate issues but would bring them into the open. In such a university, the perspective and presuppositions from which each professor does his teaching would be freely acknowledged by him, and his students would be encouraged to evaluate them for themselves. Of course, the distinction between teaching and propaganda would have to be carefully guarded. The primary concern of the university teacher in any field, including religion, is not to make proselytes. "His immediate task is to aid understanding rather than to impel his pupils towards, or away from, any prescribed type of action, to supply them with data for forming intelligent judgments of their own rather than to enlist them as disciples. But among those data should be his own conclusions and the reasons which have led him to them." [7]

The administration of a university has the responsibility to promote and encourage the discussion of ultimate issues. By doing so, it can help to create the conditions for a vital university. But if a university is to become throughout a genuinely "liberal university" in the sense we have described, it must be primarily as the result of a radical change of mind on the part of professors. They must begin to take ultimate issues more seriously in both their thinking and their teaching. As this change of mind is not likely to occur on a large scale all at once, such a university cannot be expected to come into being quickly. But each professor can help to bring it into being by

[7] *Ibid.*, pp. 110, 111.

beginning to be more concerned about the perspective and presuppositions from which he does his own thinking and teaching.

THREE OBJECTIONS

1. *The Illusion of Neutrality.* We must now consider the major objections to our proposal which are likely to be offered. The first and most fundamental one is that liberal education must be neutral on ultimate issues. In so far as this objection is not an expression of secular indifference or hostility of religion, it is due to the influence of the positivistic view that all knowledge of ultimate reality is unattainable. According to the philosophy of positivism, the only genuine knowledge is that which is discovered by the use of the scientific method. Therefore, the propositions of metaphysics, religion, and ethics are meaningless.

This is not the place to refute positivism, except to point out that it rests upon an unjustifiably narrow view of knowledge. What concerns us here is the effect of positivism on education. Positivism leads men to substitute the accumulation of facts for the pursuit of wisdom. Many half-educated people today admire the possession of a vast mass of unrelated information about many subjects more than deep insight and broad vision. This is one of the main reasons, of course, for the decline of the prestige of philosophy. Another result of positivism in the field of education is an almost complete skepticism about the validity of all judgments of value. This skepticism shows itself above all in ethical relativism, according to which moral judgments and practices are wholly relative to a particular society (or even individual) at a particular time. The lack of moral and political convictions which was so wide-spread among students before the Second World War was one expression of this skepticism. The uncritical acceptance by some Americans of the moral practices of the majority, e.g., of the sexual behavior described by the Kinsey Report, is also in part a product of ethical skepticism. If dependable knowledge of moral standards is thought to be unattainable, it is natural to conform to the moral practices of the majority, to determine what men *ought* to do from what they actually *do*. Thus, positivism leads to a corrosive skepticism about philosophical wisdom and moral standards.

But even if the neutrality fostered by positivism were desirable, it would be impossible. The idea of teaching without presuppositions is an illusion. If a professor does not base his interpretation of his field upon presuppositions derived from Christian theism, he will base it upon presuppositions derived from some other perspective. The positivist, for example, usually accepts the presuppositions of scientific humanism. Thus, the real issue is not whether a professor shall teach from a religious perspective or from no perspective at all, but whether he shall teach from a religious perspective or from a humanistic perspective.

Why is it impossible to teach without presuppositions? It is because facts are meaningless unless they are interpreted, and any interpretation is based upon presuppositions. The human reason cannot think about phenomena of any kind without organizing and synthesizing them by means of principles of interpretation.[8] It is impossible to do away with all philosophical presuppositions and continue to think at all. In effect, those who urge us to "dispense with presuppositions and simply teach the facts" are inviting us to stop thinking

[8] Kant's dictum that "precepts without concepts are blind" is profoundly true, and it has a wider application than he gave to it. Kant meant by it that sense experience must be synthesized by the understanding with the help of categories and principles furnished by the understanding itself. But the same truth applies to the religious and philosophical interpretation of experience as a whole. On the positivistic view, as we have seen, religious and philosophical interpretation is useless because knowledge is unattainable beyond the realm of sense experience. But positivism itself is a philosophy and makes its assertions on the basis of philosophical presuppositions about knowledge. It is possible to attack one set of philosophical presuppositions only from the point of view of another set of such presuppositions.

altogether. Of course, we *cannot* stop thinking, because we are rational beings. When one tries to do so, the results are disastrous. A historian becomes a mere chronicler, industriously gathering the materials of history but evading the task of history itself. A teacher of literature describes in great detail the facts about a writer and the style of his books, but refuses to make a critical judgment about them. A social scientist accumulates masses of statistics about social institutions and processes, but has no insight into their significance and no capacity for evaluating them. Are such men fulfilling their responsibility as professors? If they refuse to interpret the facts from the perspective of a considered world view and ethical ideal, from whom will their students learn to interpret the facts? The answer is all too clear: if they cannot learn from trained and responsible scholars, they will have to learn from politicians, generals, newspaper reporters, radio commentators, popular preachers and, in general, "public opinion."

Of course, some presuppositions are false and exert a distorting influence upon thought. For man is a finite and fallible being whose mind is conditioned by his limited ability, his social backround, his interests, and the dominant way of thinking of his time.[9] Therefore, education must put us on our guard against the arbitrary presuppositions of others and make us critical of our own. For uncriticized presuppositions can do as much harm as the lack of presuppositions. "What is essential to honest thinking," says Moberly, "is not that all presuppositions be discarded, but that they should be uncovered, clearly expressed and thoroughly scrutinized . . . The most dangerous preconceptions are those which are unrecognized and uncriticized. The most pernicious kind of bias consists in falsely supposing yourself to have none . . . Once our presuppositions are brought into the open, they are relatively harmless. We can discount them ourselves and so can other people."[10]

[9] Moberly, *op. cit.*, pp. 62, 63.   [10] *Ibid.*, pp. 64, 67.

2. *The Lack of Special Knowledge.* There is a second objection to our argument—perhaps it would be better to call it a difficulty—which is of a more practical nature. Frequently, when a specialist in one field is urged to deal with the relation of his field to another field, he replies that he is not competent to do so. Even if the fields to be related are as close to one another as economics and politics, this difficulty is present. But if a physicist or economist is asked a question about the religious issues and implications of his subject, he is likely to feel the difficulty more acutely. In so far as he is conscientious and well-trained in his own field, he will be keenly aware of the contrast between what he knows in that field and what he does not know about religion. Nor is it simply his lack of knowledge that will trouble him; it is also his lack of skill in dealing with facts and problems very different from those with which he is accustomed to deal. As a result, he usually concludes that he would do well not to consider questions with which he is not qualified to deal but to leave them to the department of religion or philosophy.

One must respect the feelings of a physicist or economist who comes to this conclusion. He has probably had little or no religious instruction since he left Sunday School at twelve or thirteen. He has specialized in natural or social sciences since his college days if not earlier. He has never been taught in high school, college, or graduate school even the essential facts about his own religion; much less has he learned to cope with the religious issues and implications of his field. Trained as a specialist and working in a society that prizes specialized knowledge above wisdom, he is not prepared to do something quite different from what he has always done.

Nevertheless, his refusal to venture out beyond the field of his special competence is tragically wrong, for himself and for his students alike. For himself, because he loses the opportunity to become something more than a specialist; for his students, because he fails them where they need help most, where the ultimate meaning of their existence is at stake. Moreover, the refusal is not necessary, as he seems to think. He is not being asked to do something that would require lengthy specialized training like that which he has undergone in his own field. For he does not have to be an expert in religion to express his convictions about the religious implications of his subject. We have argued that religion does not contribute new facts to a subject like physics or economics; it brings a new dimension or perspective to the interpretation of the facts. To speak about that dimension or perspective, what is required is not specialized knowledge of religion but religious experience and convictions. Of course, if one is to interpret the facts and think about the issues in his field from the perspective of his religious experience and convictions, he must have some understanding of them. But it is not necessary that he should be an expert in religious history or ideas. For example, the Christian political scientist may believe in the reality and universality of sin and may be helped by that belief to be more realistic about the necessity of curbs upon power and about the limitations of law. But he does not need to know the history of theological thinking about the origin and nature of sin.

Of course, if he has no understanding at all of the religious convictions which provide him with his perspective, he will not be able to use them effectively in interpreting the facts or thinking about the problems in his field. Therefore, he has the responsibility of making up for this deficiency, as far as time permits, by means of reading and discussion with others. This is what is meant by saying that a Christian professor must become a "lay theologian," though this is misleading in that it suggests a degree of knowledge in theology which is not likely to be possible for most busy professors. The objection that a professor who is already burdened with work cannot find time to do even as much as we have suggested is a flimsy one. Anyone who will not take a little time to make his re-

ligious convictions clear to himself can hardly be taking those
convictions very seriously in his life.

3. *The Fear of Dogmatism.* A third possible objection to
our argument is that religious perspectives and presuppositions
are held with a dogmatism and inflexibility which do not permit critical examination of them or further inquiry into their
meaning and implications. This objection rests upon a misunderstanding. It is true that some religious people hold their
beliefs in a dogmatic way. But the beliefs of Christian theism
do not need to be held in this way. The divine revelation
which is the source of Christian beliefs came to the prophets
and apostles not in the form of propositions but in the form
of historical events in which God confronted men. Dogmas
are only attempts to formulate the meaning of this encounter
with God for men who have responded to it with faith. Indispensable as they are to clear thinking, they can never exhaust
the meaning of the events. The finiteness of men's minds
and the transcendence of God make that certain. Thus, the
Christian faith is not faith in dogmas *about* God and Christ,
but faith *in* God as manifested in Christ. If so, commitment
to that faith does not require the Christian to close his mind
about it, but allows him to remain open to new light on the
meaning and implications of his faith. For example, faith in
God as Creator affirms only that nature is the product of
divine wisdom and power rather than chance or necessity,
but it leaves the method and details of the creative process
open and is thus quite compatible with the theory of evolution or any other new discovery about the way God works in
the Creation.

Thus, teaching from the perspective of Christian theism is
consistent with inquiry into the nature of that perspective
and reformulation of the convictions it implies. Consequently,
it is not opposed to the spirit of liberal education. As W. A.
Christian has recently pointed out, liberalism is incompatible

with a dogmatism that closes the mind to further inquiry, but it is also incompatible with a skepticism which makes all belief impossible.[11] It accepts the necessity both of belief or commitment and of inquiry into new truth. If religious belief is held in such a way that it is possible to question any particular formulation of it, further inquiry is not excluded. "The liberal," says Christian, "believes and questions at the same time, in contrast to the dogmatist who believes and does not question, and in contrast to the skeptic, who questions and does not believe. The dogmatist is the child who wakes in the dark and clings to his mother. The skeptic is the child who has burned his fingers and stays away from the fire . . . To the liberal it seems that each is in danger or in process of evading one or the other of those demands on the human spirit, for thought and for decision, which he accepts as responsibilities."[12] If this is the case it is possible for a professor to *teach* from the perspective of Christian belief and at the same time to avoid the pitfalls of dogmatism by continuing to *learn* from every possible source.

This is particularly important in view of the fact that any professor who expresses his convictions in the classroom is under a strong obligation not to impose them upon his students. Teaching from a religious perspective is not indoctrination. Anyone who attempts to force students to accept his own convictions by rewarding those who agree and penalizing those who disagree with him serves the ends neither of spiritual religion nor of liberal education. As to the former, a public profession of religious belief and an outward observance of religious practices can usually be secured by coercion of one kind or another, but genuine religious faith or worship cannot be enforced because it is an inner act and must be free. As to the latter, the attempt to force students to conform to one's

[11] W. A. Christian: "Belief, Inquiry, and the 'Dilemma' of the Liberal," *Journal of Religion*, April, 1951.
[12] *Ibid.*, p. 90.

own convictions does violence to their intellectual freedom and to the development of their personality.

The Professor and His Students

It is not enough for a Christian professor to teach from his religious perspective; he must also seek to establish and maintain a truly personal relationship with his students. One of the crying needs of liberal education today is to overcome the impersonal relationship between professor and student which has developed during the last generation. There are many institutions today where the typical student comes to know well none of his professors, and where he is on a speaking acquaintance with only a few of them. The main reason for this, of course, is the rapid increase during the last generation in the number of men and women enrolled in the universities. In the large classes that have resulted from this increase in enrollment, there is little or no opportunity for discussion and professors must use the lecture method almost exclusively. Since professor and student are not brought together by the process of education, they seldom come to know one another as persons inside or outside the classrooms. Friendship on a basis of equality is out of the question and personal counselling is rare.

One of the main duties of the Christian professor is to combat this state of things in every possible way. A Christian must seek, wherever he is and whatever vocation he follows, to establish a community of persons based upon mutual respect and love. He cannot be satisfied with a university community which is *not* a community. He cannot be happy in a situation where he sees his students only as a crowd of faces in a lecture room, where he is known by them only as a specialist in a field and they are known to him only as passive recipients of facts and ideas. He must seek to be related to each of them, not merely as mind to mind, but also as person to person. He must be interested not only in what he says, but also in the way they respond. For education has to do with the development of the whole personality, with the will and the feelings as well as the intellect.

When viewed in this way, his religious perspective in teaching requires of him more than the interpretation of his subject in the light of his convictions; it requires that he do everything that will make it easier for his students to approach him as a person, whether to discuss a point of disagreement with him or to ask his advice about a vocational decision. As often as possible, his office door should be open to them and he should take the initiative in getting to know personally as many of them as he can. Of course, in the largest institutions where the method of education does everything to discourage personal relationships, where individual instruction is almost unknown even in the upper-class years, he may not be able to do as much as a professor in a smaller institution. But he should do what he can. He will find that he can express his Christian perspective in his office, on the campus, or in his home at least as well as in the classroom.

However, he should never yield to the temptation to substitute a friendly attitude toward his students for a religious perspective in his teaching. If he does so, he will only confirm the student in the fallacy that, while religion may have value in practical life, it is irrelevant to the intellectual life. The main thesis of this essay has been that religion is not only relevant but indispensable to a full understanding of nature and human life as a whole.

TEACHING FROM A RELIGIOUS PERSPECTIVE

In reading the essays included in this volume, one is impressed by their breadth of view, their penetration, and their sanity. They have obviously been written by professors who are at home in their own special fields but are also able to see the wider relations of their fields in the whole of which they are parts. It is because they combine respect for scholarship in their own subjects with loyalty to truth as a whole that they see the necessity of teaching from a wider perspective than that of the specialized scholar.

Their attitude toward religion is as healthy as their attitude toward scholarship. Despite their religious concern, they do not attempt to defend everything that has been said or done in the name of religion. Dean Taylor acknowledges that the church has not always been wise in its attitude toward new discoveries in science. Professor Ulich points out that much of the appeal of Communism to the poor and oppressed has been due to the failure of Christians to deal with social evils. Professor Greene makes a sharp distinction between "high" or "developed" religion and "low" religion and argues that "the only type of religion wholly compatible with philosophy at its best is high religion." Professor Parsons rightly insists that religion has been involved in the complexity, tragedy, and sin of human existence. For example, the success of a new religion brings with it power and wealth and involves it in the temptations of the world. It tends to establish a system of orthodoxy and to persecute those who challenge that system. It becomes a defender of things as they are. It may even come to regard the world as radically evil and seek salvation exclusively in a transcendental world. Consequently, students who desire to be mature in their thinking and living should not refuse to face the "seamy side" of religion. Indeed, one may infer that a major task of the sociologist is to help students to discriminate between the good and the bad in organized religions and that teachers in other fields can hardly evade a similar responsibility. Certainly, the Protestant churches of America have little reason for complacency when they consider their involvement in the secularism, the social inequality, and the racial discrimination of our society.

Thus, the point of view from which the essays are written is that of broad scholarship, on the one hand, and reasoned faith, on the other. In general terms, it is the point of view of Christian humanism which seeks to do justice to the claims of both faith and reason. However, it would be misleading to stress the unity of the authors at the expense of their diversity. A few of them are not explicit about their personal religious convictions. They are content to stress the importance of study of the religious facts and problems in their fields. Their approach is tentative and exploratory, as if they were unwilling to prejudge the results of further investigation. What they seem to emphasize most is that religious facts and issues should not be neglected or slighted by the scholar and teacher, whatever his own personal beliefs about religion may be.

Most of the essays, however, go well beyond this point to defend the thesis that Christian theism provides a more adequate perspective for teaching than the secularism which is its chief rival in our time. There is diversity, of course, among the authors of these essays, which are written from an explicitly Christian point of view. Their Christianity ranges from Roman Catholicism through Anglo-Catholicism to a chastened Liberalism and Quakerism. At times these differences are quite noticeable and they should not be minimized. They remind us that Christianity, though it is essentially one, has been interpreted in many different ways throughout its history. They also serve as a warning not to suppose that all Christians apply their faith in precisely the same way in their thinking and teaching.

However, the unity of these authors is far more impressive than their differences. They are all attempting to show how their Christian perspective contributes to a broader and deeper interpretation of their fields of study. It may be worth while to call attention briefly to some of the ways in which they conceive of this contribution.

First, a religious perspective requires the teacher to give due weight to the *religious facts* which are relevant in his field. Professor Fairchild and Professor Daltry point out that in English literature and in music it is impossible to deal intelligently with many, perhaps most, of the great writers and composers without an understanding of their religious background, experience, and belief. Professor Harbison argues that, while every historian recognizes that religion was a primary factor in medieval history, many historians do not realize that it has also been important in the "secular" modern period. Professor Hallowell and Professor Boulding show that the history of political theory and economic history cannot be understood without some knowledge of the impact of religion in different periods.

Of course, religious facts show themselves differently in different subjects. They are more inescapable in English literature, for example, than in economics or physics. Professor Fairchild asserts that, with the exception of the departments of religion and philosophy which are usually small, "English is probably the department for which religious knowledge is most important." In view of the fact that religion has been a major concern of so many English and American writers, who would dispute his claim? On the other hand, Professor Boulding points out that in economics religion has little relevance to pure economic theory or to the analysis of economic institutions but has an important bearing upon economic history and upon decisions of economic policy. Similarly, Dean Taylor says that "in many areas of scientific instruction the religious aspect will seldom if ever intrude itself," e.g., geometry, trigonometry, or the calculus, but that in other areas it is necessary to deal with it, e.g., in interpreting the evolutionary theory. But these differences between various fields of study do not affect the main point that, wherever they are relevant, religious facts and issues should be given adequate consideration.

Second, a religious perspective enables the teacher to recognize the *limitations of the method* used in his field. This is particularly important with respect to the scientific method which enjoys such great prestige at the present time that it is often uncritically accepted as the sole method of attaining truth. Dean Taylor speaks of the "too current illusion that the paths of scientific research are the only reliable avenues to truth, an illusion which increasingly imposes itself upon the unthinking." He points out how science abstracts a "particular set of data from the whole complex" and "does not lead to knowledge of the *intrinsic nature* of things." In addition, "the whole area of ethical judgments or conclusions lies outside the province of these sciences." Again, Professor MacLeod shows how modern psychology has been increasingly dominated by materialistic ways of thinking which represent man as only a biological organism. He holds that it is impossible to deal adequately with religious phenomena and other aspects of experience by means of the categories of physics and biology. "Values, goals, purposes, intentions, the self, are facts," he says. "It is a fact that behavior is directive . . . To deny these facts because an interest in them might make one look like a teleologist is to fail in one's duty as a scientist." "What we must do," he concludes, "is to broaden the concept of causality and ultimately our notion of science." Thus, the limitations of the scientific method require us to use other methods outside the field of the sciences and also to enlarge the conception of science itself in the sciences of man.

In addition to these limitations, there are *dangers* in the evil or uncritical use of the scientific method. "We are apt today to think of the natural sciences," says Professor Boulding, "with their ominous threat of atomic or bacteriological destruction as the greatest danger to mankind . . . But whereas the natural sciences lead mainly to power over nature, the social sciences lead directly to power over man . . . A greater nightmare than that of atomic destruction is that of a world tyranny resting on the unshakable foundation of social-scientific knowledge of the manipulation of men—the 'Brave New Worlds' of Aldous Huxley or George Orwell." Professor Ulich is concerned about a more subtle danger. Scientific descriptions seem to be more adequate to deal with "the regularities and laws of matter" than with "the overwhelming wealth of human reality." "We may be further away from its center," he says, "than the genius with his profound intuitions or the so-called common man. For in spite of all contrasts, both of these men rely on their immediate experience in the great adventure of an active and striving life, and if they need some explanation or contemplation, they rely upon the great intuitive revelations of human wisdom and experience, more than on analytical discourse."

The authors we have quoted are not tempted by these and other dangers to reject science or minimize its benefits; but they would all agree, I think, with Dean Taylor's assertion that precise scientific knowledge must be *supplemented* by art, literature, philosophy, and religion if we are to attain wisdom. We must recognize the need for a unity of "scientific techniques" and "moral idealism and religious faith," says Dean Taylor. "Unless we can ennoble the material realities that are available to us with the spiritual realities that are even more fundamental the outlook is dark indeed. It is the age-long struggle for primacy between the material and the spiritual. Now, when Man's capacity for control over the material through science is becoming ever more potent, it is even more essential that he pursue with equal intensity the principles of a spiritual order."

In the third place, a religious perspective affects profoundly the *interpretation of facts* in a field of study. It is not enough to give due weight to the religious facts in the field; it is necessary to interpret *all* the facts from a religious perspective. Naturally, this has to be done differently in different fields. In biology, President McCrady thinks that, while the fact

of evolution must be accepted, the explanation of it by the
theory of natural selection is inadequate. "It (natural selection) influences the course of evolution," he says, "by preventing it in certain directions and allowing it in others,
but it does not *cause* it in any direction." He also offers
evidence that random variations cannot account for evolution and that design is present throughout the process. He
concludes from an examination of the scientific data that
the world was created by a supernatural cause that could
not have been "less than a mind." Thus, while religion is
not dependent upon scientific support for its foundation,
it may be enhanced and enriched by scientific knowledge.
Professor Harbison is as suspicious of philosophies of history
as he is of the skeptical denial that there is any meaning in history. That which is distinctive of a Christian historian he
argues, is "his attitude toward history, the quality of his concern about it, the sense of reverence and responsibility with
which he approaches his subject." "Where materialists may
see mere blind process, where rationalists may see evident
progress, he will see providence—a divine *providing* in both the
conscious decisions and the unintended results of history, a
purpose partly revealed and partly concealed, a destiny which
is religious in the deepest meaning of the word, in which
human freedom and divine guidance complete each other in
some mysterious way." Professor Hallowell seems to think
that Christianity provides, if not a political philosophy, principles for political action. For example, it enables us to avoid
the errors of Liberalism, especially its optimism about man
and his future possibilities. "Christianity provides us with a
realistic conception of man which neither overrates man's
motives nor underestimates his potentialities. If man is a
sinner, he is also, potentially, a saint. The Christian understanding of man helps us to avoid the extremes both of illusive
optimism and of hopeless despair." Again, "the Christian
insists that the only genuine and solid basis of community is

love and justice." Professor Fairchild suggests still another way in which a religious perspective may be used. In the concluding section of his essay, he offers a "negative and astringent" criticism of modern English literature from the point of view of Christian orthodoxy. "The story," he says, "includes much beauty, much high aspiration, many broken recollections of primal truth and therefore many glimpses of hope for the future. Nevertheless its central theme is the inflation and collapse of a human pride which has either forsaken Christianity or transformed it into a delusive caricature of the historic faith."

Thus, the Christian perspective can be used as the basis of an *attitude* toward a subject, the source of *principles* for dealing with the problems that arise in a subject, or a norm for *criticism* in a subject. Doubtless, there are still other ways in which a Christian perspective can be used, but these will serve to illustrate the ways in which it can make a radical difference in the interpretation of a subject.

In the fourth place, more than one of the writers point out that a religious perspective may often be expressed more effectively through the *personal qualities and attitudes* of the teacher than through anything he says. For example, Professor Greene stresses the fact that philosophers should exemplify in their own persons "a sympathetic receptivity to all insights," "genuine open-mindedness, humility, and tolerance," and "an attitude of reflective and critical religious commitment." "Our basic attitude and our personalities and actions will influence our students as profoundly as will our philosophical discourse." Professor Daltry stresses the same point in a somewhat different way. "Unless the teacher shows by his daily conduct that he has access to a source of strength and serenity, students are not likely to treat his religious pronouncements with much respect. But if, in addition to professional competence, he displays good humor and kindliness, respect for the undergraduate as an individual and concern for his development

. . . he can now and then say something that will arouse in this or that young woman or young man a religious interest that has been dormant."

Finally, one cannot read the essays of this book without being convinced of the *vital importance of religion* in Western civilization. Professor Parsons asserts that a scientific study of religion gives rise to "an overwhelming impression of the fundamental importance of religion in human affairs." Religion, he says, has often been a "source of creative innovation" and of the "moral patterns of value" upon which a society depends. Christianity has contributed to Western civilization the "activism" which tries to overcome obstacles instead of accepting things as they are and the "universalism" which asserts the validity of fundamental principles for all times and places. From "activism" has come the effort of Western man to master his environment and actively to investigate nature by means of the scientific method. As a result of Christian "universalism," Roman law was preserved and universalistic systems of law were gradually created in the West. The "universalistic individualism" of Christianity, by asserting the equal worth of all men in the religious sphere, has also been one of the main sources of the concern for political and social equality in the Western world.

In the light of these facts, Professor Ulich's analysis of teaching in relation to *American democracy* raises serious questions. He is disturbed by the fact that, in our preoccupation with techniques and with scientific description, we have tended to lose the religious attitude, the sense of an Infinite and Transcendental Reality. Religion involves a "longing for wholeness" through the relation of the individual to the ultimate. Since we have lost our vision of this ultimate Reality that overarches and gives meaning to all human life, the ethical convictions upon which democracy rests are in serious danger. For example, it is not enough for us to boast of our progress in the development of new types of airplanes, for "true historical progress is *total* progress, a continual integration of achievements of the mind, the heart, and the hand." Moreover, progress is not automatic; it is largely "a decision of the spirit." "Progress, freedom, and security are accomplishments and not gifts of nature. Those who take them for granted will lose them." Similarly, the value of the individual must not be regarded as a justification of rugged individualism, since "the strength of each nation depends on its capacity to combine individual freedom, which in isolation easily turns into egotism, with the cooperative spirit of brotherly love." In short, if there is a "fading away of transcendental convictions" in our democracy, it will fail.

Thus, the issues at stake are great. If the moral breakdown and spiritual crisis of our time are not to destroy our Western civilization, if the secularism which has dominated our education is not to rob our American democracy of its higher meaning and to stunt and dehumanize the lives of our children and their children, we must renew our religious faith and make it the basis of all our teaching. "The choice," says Professor Ulich, "is still before us."

2

ENGLISH LITERATURE

By HOXIE N. FAIRCHILD

I

This essay will discuss the part which religion may legitimately play in the teaching of English literature in colleges and universities. It is addressed primarily to my fellow-teachers and to those who are preparing to enter our profession, but undergraduates and members of the general public who wish to overhear a little academic shoptalk on a theme of more than academic importance are heartily welcome.

My remarks apply to nondenominational institutions both public and private. In the teaching of religion as a separate academic discipline, most privately endowed colleges are freer from restrictions than most tax-supported ones, though there are too many exceptions in both groups to permit a rigid dichotomy. But as regards the treatment of religion in English courses, the individual teacher is probably no more restricted in a public than in a private college, provided the institution is a decent specimen of its kind. The special advantages and disadvantages of colleges committed to a particular religious position will not be examined, but the inquiry would pertain to "remote-control" denominational colleges which impose no doctrinal uniformity upon faculty or students.

Treatment of the subject will be focussed mainly upon the teaching of English (not excluding American) literature in the advanced undergraduate courses usually elected by Juniors and Seniors, but the general principles involved would be about

equally applicable to the Sophomore Survey and even to the
sort of Freshman English which teaches composition through
the study of literature. At the other extreme, graduate courses
intended to fill gaps left by undergraduate education need
not be excluded, but students who have reached the level of
specialized research are here regarded as junior colleagues
rather than as objects of instruction. I believe also that
teachers of any of the modern European literatures could
easily adapt the fundamental ideas of this essay to the material
of their fields.

Our own discipline cannot be discussed in complete isolation from the liberal arts curriculum as a whole. Both within
and without academic walls, American higher education is
accused of having aggravated, rather than corrected, the aimless, fragmentary, centrifugal character of modern intellectual
life. In a shamefaced endeavor to expiate the sin of specialization, a reaction toward breadth and inclusiveness is at work.
"Integration" has become the educator's shibboleth; orientation courses and interdepartmental areas are the order of the
day.

The new movement is not wholly untinged by the great
American fallacy that any crisis in civilization can be sur-
mounted by substituting new machinery for old. What society has a right to expect from institutions of higher learning
is a perennial crop of graduates who possess some rational conception of what it means to be a man. Teachers have failed
to satisfy this demand not because their courses have been too
broad or too narrow, but because they have so persistently
dodged the fundamental issues of human life.

It would be absurd to advocate the indoctrination of all
students with a single official philosophy. The necessary consensus does not exist, and even if it did exist it should not be
imposed arbitrarily. The college should be a community of
inquirers—some called students, some called teachers—each
of whom is striving to arrive at a philosophy. What the indi-

vidual discovers may be very new or very old; it may be congenial or repugnant to the majority of his fellows. The far-away goal is unity, but it must be sought in and through the diversity which now actually exists. The quest entails historical investigation and critical evaluation, in an atmosphere of complete freedom, candor, and disinterestedness, of all the great normative hypotheses now available for thinking men.

No one will deny that religion has been the supreme integrator of intellectual and emotional experience, or that the subsidence of religious faith and the consequent chasm between intellectual and spiritual life are largely responsible for the predicament of modern man. Those who hold that it has become desirable or necessary to do without religion must at least be prepared to describe what it is they are abandoning and what they propose to substitute for it. At present there is a marked revival of religion among members of the intellectual class. Whether this is a retreat from reason or a reassertion of the possibility of reason is a debatable question. By all means, then, let it be debated. Certainly our students are seeking, in larger numbers and more urgently than for many years, some rational basis for interpreting human existence in other than merely mechanical terms. If the final aim of all disciplines is to contribute to the development of a philosophy, the bearing of religious facts and problems upon those disciplines must be recognized as vitally important for higher education.

II

The *immediate* pertinence of religion, however, varies with the work of different academic departments. What of our own discipline in this connection? The teaching of English literature on the college level has two main objectives: (1) ability to criticize works of literary art; (2) knowledge of the history of literature as man's expression of response to his environment in successive stages of culture. Fortunately this essay need not grapple with the disputed question as to which of these purposes is the more important. In my opinion neither of them can be achieved without paying considerable attention to the other, though in any course, either the critical or the historical approach may properly be emphasized in accordance with the interests and the abilities of the instructor. On the one hand, the historical teacher will become submerged in nonliterary considerations unless he constantly reminds himself that his subject is the history of an *art*. On the other hand, literary criticism requires historical imagination, which in turn depends upon historical knowledge. The teacher of literature must remember, furthermore, that his discipline is not an autonomous and isolated activity, but one of the chief unifying factors in liberal education. To study the work of art as a reflection of many different aspects of the age in which it was produced is not only a prerequisite for appreciating its nontemporal uniqueness but a valuable means of giving the student a sense of the connectedness of knowledge. Hence historical considerations which in extra-academic criticism might be secondary though never negligible may assume primary importance in college teaching of English literature.

But no matter whether the individual teacher's approach be aesthetic or historical he must recognize the importance of religion as a factor in the author's choice of subject-matter, his intellectual and emotional response to the subject, his background of allusion, his imagery and style. One may also observe analogies between poetic and religious experience even in works not ostensibly concerned with religion. For poetry, like religion, apprehends reality through the entire man— sensuous, emotional, intellectual, and spiritual—integrated in a creative act. In essential respects, too, poetic form is comparable to forms of worship in its struggle to achieve equilibrium between passion and pattern. Coleridge's description of metre as "more than usual emotion under more than usual control" applies equally to religious ceremonial.

When we say that we are discussing a poet's "philosophy," what we are usually discussing is his religion. Every serious work of literature is directly or indirectly an expression of the writer's personal religious experience. Essentially religious, therefore, is the reader's reconstruction of the creative process within himself. Despite the Abbé Brémond's well-known contention, the religious implications of poetry, both for writer and reader, are sacramental rather than mystical—not the concrete made ineffable, but the ineffable made concrete.

We must add that the author's religious experience, though never identical with that of anyone else, is never merely personal. Both his experience and the language in which he expresses it are strongly conditioned by religious traditions which he shares with other men. Whatever loftier results may be expected from the study of literature can hardly be attained by students who do not understand what the author is saying. It is not, of course, necessary to know everything that he knows. But to be wholly ignorant of matters which are vitally important for the content and style of the work—still worse, to have erroneous or prejudiced notions concerning such matters—is assuredly something of a handicap. The teacher can hardly get through a single class period without being reminded how deeply English literature is saturated in the language and thought of the Scriptures and in theological ideas, ecclesiastical history, liturgical imagery, the lives and opinions of religious leaders, the technical terminology and *realia* of religious thinking and living.

Let us ask an imaginary English major a few questions pertinent both to religion and to the field in which he has chosen to specialize. What parallels between Old Testament history and English history are involved in Dryden's *Absalom and Achitophel?* Tell the story of Susanna and the Elders. What is a "Job's comforter," a "doubting Thomas," a "Magdalene"? What are the connotations of "the voice of the turtle," "barren fig-tree," "went by on the other side"? What

are the "two massy keys" of St. Peter in *Lycidas*? Explain
Wordsworth's line, "Thou liest in Abraham's bosom all the
year," and the titles of Swinburne's *Super Flumina Babylonis*,
Ruskin's *Unto This Last*, Aldous Huxley's *Eyeless in Gaza*.
List, without "editorializing," the chief doctrinal differences
between Roman Catholicism and Calvinistic Protestantism.
Define "predestination," "transubstantiation," "puritanism,"
"deism," "theism," "pantheism," "atonement," "school-
men," "Dissenter," "Puseyite," "Higher Criticism," "ritual,"
"agnostic," "Papal Infallibility." Account for Chaucer's treatment of the Prioress, Monk, Friar, Parson, and Summoner
respectively. What does he mean by a "Loller"? Does his
criticism of ecclesiastical abuses establish him as a precursor
of the Protestant Reformation? Discuss the interdependence
of theology and politics in Spenser's *Faerie Queene*. Wherein
does Crashaw represent the Counter-Reformation? What does
Donne mean by "The new philosophy puts all in doubt"? Is
there anything curious about the fact that the main theme of
Paradise Regained is not the Crucifixion and Resurrection,
but the Temptation in the Wildnerness? To what extent is
the *Essay on Man* consistent with Pope's Catholicism? Show
how the Evangelical Revival is reflected in the poems of Cow-
per, and how the conflict between "Auld Licht" and "New
Licht" helps to motivate Burns's satires. In Browning's *Christmas-Eve*, why is infidelity represented by a Goettingen professor, and why may we suppose that his name is Strauss?
Why does George Eliot display all the moral urgency, but
none of the religious beliefs, of a Puritan? Explain Hopkins'
line, "And you unhouse and house the Lord," in relation to
the Catholic liturgy. To what seventeenth-century religious
community does T. S. Eliot allude in *Little Gidding*?

One could expand the quiz endlessly, but these questions
would be sufficient to remind us, if any reminder were necessary, that the advanced student of English literature needs to
know a good deal about religion in general and Christianity in

particular. This fact exists quite independently of what we may happen to believe or disbelieve. Religious knowledge may be meaningless in our private lives, but it is important for us as teachers of literature.

With rare exceptions, our students enter college knowing nothing about the Bible and less than nothing about normative religious books such as *The Imitation of Christ* and *Pilgrim's Progress*. They are usually ignorant of the fundamental Christian doctrines, and they suppose that "theology" is an exact synonym for "bigotry." They are unaware of the fact that the Christian Church embraces a philosophy, a history, a sociology, a psychology, and a literature, all of which have been profoundly influential in the shaping of Western civilization. Their religion, when they possess any at all, is likely to be some vestigial remnant of nineteenth-century sentimentalism. It seems never to have occurred to them that precise thinking in matters of religion is either possible or desirable. These generalizations must be qualified as regards Roman Catholics, Anglo-Catholics, Orthodox Jews, and a considerable number of well-informed Protestants. But too many members of these groups turn out to be glib little bigots who rattle off the proper formulas without understanding them.

By the time they graduate, some students have acquired a modicum of religious knowledge from courses in the Bible, History of Religion, Comparative Religion, History of Christian Thought, and the like. Teachers of English should welcome the lightening of their burdens which is promised by the growing readiness of educational administrators to encourage the study of religion as an independent humanistic discipline. For many years to come, however, the total registration for courses in religion will probably remain smaller than for courses in English. At most institutions, a definite requirement in religion would raise difficulties, while one year of English is a practically universal and two years a not very uncommon prescription. Excluding the small department of religion when it exists at all, and the not much larger department of philosophy when it offers instruction in religion, English is probably the department for which religious knowledge is most important. This by no means implies that the teacher of English literature should assume responsibility for teaching religion as a subject in itself. It does imply, however, that he must still rely largely on his own efforts in giving his students such religious knowledge as is necessary for their comprehension of literature.

It may be presumptuous to ask whether the teacher of English is always fully equipped for this task; but some professors, to judge from their books and articles, must be telling their classes some astonishing things. Whether those who possess adequate religious knowledge sufficiently emphasize its importance is a still more dubious question. In most cases, naturally enough, religious backgrounds are treated more amply and zestfully by believers than by unbelievers; but one knows agnostics who discuss the religious thought of periods and individual authors fully, expertly, and with meticulous fairness. They give religious knowledge an emphasis proportionate not to their own opinions but to the interests of the writers whom they interpret. This is the spirit of the genuine scholar. If it were universal among us, more of our English majors would discover that religion is an essential factor in the history of literature and in the creative process.

III

It is not enough to say that tradition and environment have given the author religious materials with which the student should possess some acquaintance. What of the author's *response* to those materials as a man and an artist? Inseparable from the total meaning of his work is a religious experience in which intellectual concepts and emotional states are interwoven. In the classroom, furthermore, this experience must be described and discussed by teachers and students who have religious ideas, beliefs, and feelings of their own. If the study of literature aimed only at collecting ponderable facts and discussing their causal relationships it would be merely an inferior imitation of natural science. But ours is a value-subject, or what might more cynically be termed an opinion-subject: it concerns itself with higher and lower degrees of technical skill, imaginative power, and intellectual validity.

At this point teachers who have espoused the cause of the "new criticism" may urge that only aesthetic values should be considered in studying a work of literature, and that the reader's agreement or disagreement with the writer's thought is totally irrelevant for criticism. But if it is true that the thought-content of a work cannot be isolated from its form, it is equally true—if not a little truer—that the form cannot be isolated from the thought-content. From Homer to T. S. Eliot, every great literary artist has desired to speak truth to men. The current tendency to ignore this fact is no less excessive for being a natural reaction against the overt didacticism of the Victorians. Professor Bush represents the necessary counter-reaction when he writes:

> The common reader might go so far as to think that poetry deals with life, that for the serious poet life embraces morality and religion, and that it seems very strange for a serious critic to retreat into technical problems. One might ask how many of the world's great critics have done so. However valuable the processes and results of the new criticism, for some readers its preoccupation with technique, its aloof intellectuality, its fear of emotion and action, its avoidance of moral values, its dislike of "impure" poetry (which includes much of the greatest poetry we have), all this suggests the dangers of a timid aestheticism. . . . Technical aesthetic criticism is of course very important, but if it becomes a circumscribed end in itself, it is the equivalent of the scientist's escape from life into the laboratory. . . . Poetry is not read, any more than it is written, with the aesthetic intelligence only, and I think the new criticism denies and evades some of its chief responsibilities.

The critics, some of whom are also poets, have bemoaned the failure of belief, the loss of traditional values, the excessive nihilism of the scientific positivists, but they themselves have been doing all they could to create a moral vacuum.[1]

In short a work of literature says something, and the reader must come to grips with what it says. Criticism is talk about literature, and literature is talk about the whole of life—the thoughts, feelings, and actions of human beings. It is studied in our colleges by young men and women who are trying to form lives of their own by discovering their personal centers. Not only expository and argumentative writings but novels, plays, and poems teem with ideas—suggested through action and metaphor when not directly expressed—concerning religion, metaphysics, ethics, history, science, psychology, social relations of every sort. Young people in search of a philosophy want to see ideas at work in forms of life to which their own natures can actually or imaginatively be related. Hence the special importance of creative literature as a means of drawing ideas from many other subjects in the curriculum, blending them as they are blended in the stream of life, and vividly displaying them in a setting of human personality and experience. Ideas as expressed in imaginative literature therefore have a peculiar potency. They possess the superior teachability of the concrete. They mingle reason and emotion in a way which reflects, and which in turn powerfully stimulates, the natural workings of the mind. They gain persuasiveness from beauty of form, sharpness of image, the power of the illuminating phrase. Since ideas appear in literature not as abstract propositions but as human responses to specific stimuli they strongly impress the minds of young people who are trying to formulate responses of their own. Literature displays not merely pictures of life, but the efforts of exceptionally perceptive, intelligent, and articulate persons to make sense of those

[1] Douglas Bush, "The New Criticism: Some Old-Fashioned Queries," *PMLA*, LXIV (Supplement, Part 2), pp. 20–21.

pictures. Thus it helps the student to think through vicarious living and to live through vicarious thinking.

In my opinion, then, the teacher of English who does not encourage discussion of the ideas expressed or implied in books is depriving the study of literature of precisely those elements which constitute its principal value for a liberal education. But as a matter of fact the students, if they deserve to be in college at all, will indulge in such discussion whether the instructor encourages it or not. This recalcitrancy need not be lamented by the teacher who desires to emphasize the formal beauty of the work. Students are usually more willing to proceed from content to form than from form to content. Once they are convinced that the author is saying something relevant to their lives they will gladly analyze the skill with which he says it. They will, of course, frequently need to be reminded that they are supposed to be talking about Milton and not about themselves. Nevertheless their discovery of what they think of Milton's thought is an important part of their education, and in order to make this discovery they will need to organize and express their own notions about "the ways of God to man." After a little free discursive philosophizing they can be led back to *Paradise Lost* with a better chance of understanding the masterpiece both as a separate work of art and as a factor in the history of culture.

The religious ideas and insights in which literature abounds deserve discussion no less than the author's opinions on other subjects. A large proportion of any class will be eager to discuss them, for most of our religious illiterates are groping toward some sort of spiritual reliance in a world of unprecedented confusion and insecurity. So strong is their curiosity about religion that the teacher who performs his duty of giving them religious *facts* will inevitably become involved in the discussion of religious *ideas*. He may, for example, tell the class that Swinburne's *Hymn of Man* was suggested by the Oecumenical Council of 1870, and that the concluding line, "Glory to Man in the highest, for Man is the master of things," reflects, either directly or through Mazzini, the influence of Auguste Comte's Religion of Humanity. These facts are worth knowing, for they help us to experience the poem in the way Swinburne wrote it—as a response to a specific stimulus. But if the teacher and his students have any life in them, they will soon find themselves considering something more interesting and important: namely, the question of the *truth or falsity* of Swinburne's deification of man in this and other poems. This question is germane to the study of literature if, as I believe, it is part of the critic's business to ask whether Swinburne was wise or foolish in these matters.

In examining such questions, of course, the inevitable subjectivity of all value-judgments comes into play. It does not follow, however, that discussion of an author's religious thought is a waste of time. Rigorous application of the same skepticism to the humanities, to the social sciences, and even to some areas of the laboratory sciences would brand two-thirds of the curriculum with the stigma of futility. If talk about religion is unprofitable, what justification can be found for talk about aesthetic judgments? Surely we cannot *prove* that this poem by Keats is superior to that poem by Longfellow.

In my opinion all valid intellectual discourse assumes, first, that absolute objective truth exists; secondly, that the relation between that truth and our own mental impressions can never be determined with certitude in this mortal life; thirdly, that the life of reason is each man's struggle to move away from crude solipsistic subjectivity toward a personally refracted but not wilfully self-centered apprehension of the unknown suprapersonal truth. The success of these individual gropings cannot be estimated by any individual mind, but that some of our guesses come closer to the mark than others is at least a fair human guess. Man is condemned to live pragmatically in an absolutistic universe, judging the validity of ideas mainly in terms of their survival value. His endeavor to be intelligent about religion rests on the same basis as his endeavor to be intelligent about anything else. Hence the attempt to evaluate a writer's religious thought is not futile unless the whole of intellectual life is futile. The certainty of incertitude merely warns us against the futility of dogmatism. What one may expect from discussion of a religious idea is not proof or disproof, but comprehension of its meaning, knowledge of its background, presuppositions, implications, and historical consequences, along with the opportunity to clarify one's notions through comparison with the notions of others. Even though no generally acceptable findings are achieved, the free clash of opinion may help the student to discover his philosophy of life, and that is what liberal education is for.

IV

In these discussions the teacher of English literature should himself play an active part. Students' talk about religion is liable to be ignorant, aimless, inconsistent, sentimental, and prejudiced. Applied to such topics, a chaotically "democratic" classroom procedure may have the undemocratic effect of aggravating the bewilderment of already bewildered minds and hurting the sensibilities of students who hold minority opinions. In the investigation of a religious as of any other problem, the teacher's duty is to *teach*. His relation to his students should, of course, be that of leadership in a common inquiry. He should think *with* the class, not *at* them. But since he is a better-equipped, more experienced inquirer than they, his students will look to him for knowledge and perhaps even for a little wisdom. Hence the term "discussion" includes the ideas of the teacher himself, whether woven informally into the give-and-take of the classroom or expressed in more systematic disquisitions. If the professor can talk like a human being and if the student can listen actively rather than passively, the lecture can still be a useful pedagogical device.

If there exists a teacher who has formed no opinions about the subject which he teaches, he may charitably be ignored in these pages. Of course, when we say that every good teacher has ideas of his own we do not mean that they are absolutely unique: even in the twentieth century, intellectual life is not quite so chaotic as that. Usually his position is a more or less individualized version of the doctrine of some established academic party. Such groupings are not necessarily the result of stereotyped thinking. A thoroughly independent and original mind may conclude that some already existent theory, just as it stands, is superior to other theories. Once this conclusion has been reached, however, there is danger that loyalty to it may load the dice of the scholar's subsequent thinking.

To whatever extent the individual teacher succeeds or fails in avoiding this danger, his view of the truth about a given subject will inevitably condition his selection of material and his emphasis on this or that aspect of the field. It will also influence what he says and the way in which he says it. No teacher can keep his mind, his words, and his voice so colorless as to conceal from an intelligent student his most deeply cherished opinions. Even if complete intellectual neutrality were possible it would be pedagogically disastrous. No teaching is surer to win the deserved contempt of the class than that of the instructor who pretends to have no opinions. Students like and respect the teacher who sets forth his own ideas freely and frankly, not in order to force them upon the class but in order to encourage them to form ideas of their own. Higher education can never achieve a philosophy if the faculty refuses to philosophize.

The reader may urge that the teacher's opinionatedness should be confined to his special field. But it would require a bold man to declare precisely on what topics the philosopher, the sociologist, the historian, or the literary scholar may or may not venture to express opinions. Consciously or unconsciously, the teacher's views about his own subject stem from fundamental presuppositions about the universe and human life which are not the private property of any one department. Beneath his professional theories lies his philosophy of life, of which a positive or negative attitude toward religion is an essential part. He is not only a learned specialist but a human being. Where no one can pretend to speak as an authority he may speak as a man.

Since the religious hypothesis is ultimately relevant to every subject of inquiry, there is no academic discipline in which expression of the teacher's religious opinions will not sometimes be justifiable. But this applies *a fortiori* to literary studies, where the author's religion forms an essential part of the subject-matter. The teacher of English must often lead his students in their discussion of religious topics, and this he cannot do effectively or honestly without revealing what he himself thinks.

V

The teacher's opinions need not be favorable to any particular creed or even to religion in the broadest, haziest sense. Here I dissociate myself most emphatically from those bigots who wish all the "godless professors" to be thrown out of their jobs or silenced by the administration. Such obscurantism has done more than anything else to create the present cleavage between intellectual and spiritual life. In the long run the position of religion in higher education will be solidified rather than weakened by encouraging both the unbelieving and the believing professor to speak their minds in complete liberty. The religious-minded teacher often has reason to complain that his skeptical colleagues are ignorant, prejudiced, and crudely dogmatic in their treatment of religious questions. Unfortunately—one remembers the adage concerning pot and kettle—these faults are not monopolized by the unbelievers.

No matter how positive or negative the teacher's religious views may be, his obligations are simply those entailed by the general principles of academic freedom. All the cards should be laid on the table: the student should know his instructor's basic presuppositions and commitments just as the soldier should know that his rifle, measured against an abstract norm of mechanical accuracy, tends to shoot a little to the right or to the left. Let there be no lugging in of religious questions extraneous to the material under consideration. Our business is not to make pious Christians or stout atheists, but to impart understanding and appreciation of English literature. Opinions should be distinguished from facts and expressed without proselytizing insinuation or authoritarian bluster. Evidence should be stated fully and without distortion. Contrary views should be given a fair hearing, with honest recognition of their merits and honest criticism of their defects. When full discussion of some religious problem would lead the class too far beyond the scope of the course, interested students should be shown how they may investigate the problem for themselves.

A course in literature governed by these principles will provide as good a lesson in "character-building" as secular education can be expected to furnish. If we taught literature with the primary purpose of making young people more religious or democratic or "global," our discipline would become one huge amiable corruption. Let us rather give them, day by day, the example of a free and honest mind at work among books. In the present state of the world, of course, the teacher who is interested in his students as human beings will do what he can to direct the discussion of books toward normative principles which, whether religious or nonreligious, seem to offer at least a tentative solution of the predicament of modern man. As professors of a discipline which deals with man's intellectual and emotional responses to life's ultimate problems, we hardly do our full duty when we plunge the student into the depths of the contemporary chaos and then just leave him there with a smiling, "Some say this and some say that. Think it out for yourself." Nevertheless if the teacher sincerely believes that nothing is left for man but despair it is his right and his duty to say so. For this also is a philosophy.

The number of aggressively unbelieving professors of English is small in proportion to the general state of academic opinion. Mere indifference—refusal to think about the author's thought—is much more common among us than active irreligion. The occasional combination of indifference with some enthusiasm for the aesthetic trappings of traditional Christianity provides a recognizable type. But what especially characterizes our guild is an amorphous religiosity arising from the notion that literature—especially of course poetry—is itself a superior kind of substitute-religion. It is not merely from self-interest that so many teachers of English are active in the "save the humanities" movement: they sincerely believe that the spiritual reintegration of our bewildered young men and women will be furthered by studying those subjects which most fully display the joy and dignity of being human.

My own position in this matter may seem paradoxical: I am an antihumanistic humanist. Unquestionably the wisdom and beauty of great literature exerts a civilizing and even a morally elevating effect upon some students, though by no means upon all. Nevertheless I fear that a revival of the humanities without a revival of the superhumanities would merely entail a repetition of the tragedy of modern history—the rise and collapse of the gospel of human self-sufficiency. One thinks of the little boy who, having seen his father tumble downstairs, ecstatically cries, "Do it again, Daddy! Do it again!"

Some professors of English support the "save the humanities" campaign from crypto-Christian rather than from purely humanistic motives, hoping that students who read Blake and Browning will acquire a little grace without knowing it. I respect their intentions but question the wisdom of their strategy. One of Screwtape's favorite tricks is to encourage emotional experiences which enable one to feel religious without believing in a religion. Religion will produce an edifying humanism, but humanistic studies in themselves will never produce a valid religion. The result of these efforts is likely to be a cult which employs literature as a means of convincing men that they are independently strong, wise, good, and creative. This is the illusion which arose in the Renaissance, inflated itself into a pseudo-religion in the nineteenth century, and burst in the twentieth.

But although for me the notion that Shelley was a profound spiritual seer is ultimately far more detrimental to religion than honest atheism, I cordially recognize the right of my colleagues to say what they please about such matters. All I demand is that they grant me the same privilege. My basic contention is that all good teaching of literature arises from a philosophy and points toward a philosophy. Whatever that philosophy may be—naturalistic, humanistic, or religious—it is the right and the duty of the teacher to set it forth with no restrictions other than those imposed by the accepted standards of sound scholarship and intellectual probity.

VI

But all this is rather too abstract. Let us imagine a teacher who "professes" both English literature and Christianity and ask how these two professions may be combined without disloyalty to either and with advantage to both. Inevitably our hypothetical professor will bear a rather close resemblance to the author of this essay. Hence the illustrative examples will be drawn mainly from the eighteenth and nineteenth centuries, the fields to which most of my teaching and my private studies have been devoted.

The Christian professor will naturally give due emphasis to those matters of religious knowledge which, as we have reminded ourselves, are often essential for an understanding of the work. Scriptural influence on subject-matter, style, and imagery will be pointed out; pertinent theological concepts and terms will be explained. The class will consider religious trends and movements as conditioning not merely the opinions but the feeling-tone and expression of various writers: Pope and Deism; Richardson and sentimentalized Puritanism; Shelley and romanticized Neoplatonism; Tennyson and Victorian Broad Churchmanship; Browning and liberalized Nonconformity; Kingsley and Christian Socialism; D. G. Rossetti and the ritualistic phase of the Catholic Revival. These and similar relationships will be used not merely in studying particular writers and their works, but also in tracing the general history of the human spirit as it is reflected in literature.

The Christian teacher will be tempted to overemphasize such knowledge, just as teachers with different interests will be tempted to overemphasize prosody, or biography, or social history. He may avoid lopsidedness by trying to give religion all the importance, but no more than the importance, which it possessed for the writer under consideration. This principle cannot be applied with complete objectivity, but it provides a control within which the Christian teacher, like any other teacher, remains free to set up his chosen frame of reference. He will not, of course, stultify the usefulness of his approach by isolating religion from the philosophical, scientific, and sociological trends which blend with it to form the intellectual matrix of English literature. On the contrary, he will devote considerable attention to the politico-ecclesiastical ferment of the Queen Anne period as reflected in the writings of Defoe, Swift, and Steele; to the aesthetic implications of Shaftesbury's doctrine of the "moral sense"; to the respective influences of German transcendental idealism and of Comtian positivism upon various nineteenth-century writers; to the impact of evolutionary science upon the beliefs and disbeliefs of Tennyson, Arnold, Clough, and Meredith.

Interpretation of such topics as those mentioned in the preceding paragraph involves not only the religious views of the writers who are being studied but those of the teacher and the class. Precisely in proportion to the definiteness of his religious commitments, the teacher will endeavor to break the traditional association, which for many of his students will seem axiomatic, between orthodoxy and intolerance. He will welcome any chance to show that valuable religious insights are not the exclusive property of Christianity, still less of any particular interpretation of the Christian faith. Robinson Crusoe, that stout Presbyterian, learns much from Man Friday. Newman first discovered the fundamentals of Christian dogma in the writings of eighteenth-century Evangelicals. Furthermore, the Christian professor will accept the obligation to show how largely the spiritual shortcomings of organized Christianity are to blame for the deviation of many writers from the historic faith. If he prefers the poetic fruits of the Catholic Revival to those of Broad Churchism, he should preserve a just critical balance by recognizing the morbid escapism which often tinges the former and the sincere struggle of the latter to reconcile traditional religion with modern thought.

In classroom discussion of any religious idea, the Christian professor will carefully avoid offending the susceptibilities of Jewish students. To deny or ignore the important differences between Judaism and Christianity is to falsify both religions, but especially in the present state of the world the unifying elements of the Judaeo-Christian tradition deserve strong emphasis. Let us show how closely the atmosphere of *The Cotter's Saturday Night* resembles that of a Jewish Sabbath, and that in *Michael* Wordsworth discards the neoclassical pastoralism of the eighteenth century for the pastoralism of the Old Testament. No belief which is precious to any student, no matter how absurd it may seem to the instructor, should be attacked with anger or mockery. Students who are indifferent or hostile to supernaturalistic religion of any sort should be

treated with a friendly courtesy which will make it impossible
for them to suppose that they must pretend to agree with the
professor's views in order to pass the course. By observing him
they may gradually discover that it is possible for a learned,
intelligent, and honest man to be a Christian; but what they
infer from that discovery is a private matter which has no
bearing upon the teaching of literature. If the student of his
own volition chooses to visit the professor's study for a man-
to-man discussion of his personal religious difficulties, he must
expect to be dealt with in a way which goes beyond the for-
mality of the classroom teacher-pupil relationship. The professor should not, however, unfairly exploit such occasions by
trying to force his views upon a bewildered, suggestible boy.
It will be better to remind the student of the values inherent
in the religious tradition of his own family background. If he
has not merely drifted away from this tradition but rejected
it after serious thought, the existence of some other solution
for his problem may quietly be indicated without any evan-
gelistic urgency. Perhaps he will read a few books or investigate a mode of worship which is unfamiliar to him.

In teaching any period of English literature, the Christian
will often find it easier to refute a fallacy than to enforce a
truth. Students like polemics, but they detest preachment and
they loathe unction. The surest way of making them reject a
religious idea is to urge them to accept it. Approaching a poem
of deep spiritual insight, the teacher will do well to remember
that the poet has already said what the teacher himself would
wish to say much better than he could say it. A great thought
beautifully expressed seldom needs to be underscored: it can
be trusted to exert its own power. The competent reading of
a poem to the class will often be more convincing than any
overt attempt to make the students agree with its thought.
Sometimes, however, it will be necessary to point out the
specifically Christian elements in the words which have moved
them. They will probably interpret George Herbert's *Love*

bade me enter in terms of modern sentimentalism unless they
are shown that it is a poem about the Eucharist. This is not
proselytizing: it is simply making sure that the student shares
the poet's experience. A legitimate remedy for spiritual tone-
deafness is to contrast non-Christian and Christian treatments
of the same theme—the concluding passages of Epistle I of
Pope's *Essay on Man* and of Dr. Johnson's *Vanity of Human
Wishes,* or Wordsworth's *The World Is Too Much With Us*
and Hopkins' *God's Grandeur.*

VII

Although the culture of eighteenth- and nineteenth-century
England remains nominally Christian, the most representative
creative literature of the period diverges markedly from traditional Christianity. The poetry of the Catholic Revival provides an interesting exception, but one can hardly call it a part
of the dominant historical trend which leads from the nineteenth century into the twentieth. The attempt to describe
and evaluate these deviations from the Christian norm will confront the teacher with some difficult problems.

In the critical study of particular works the Christian professor cannot assume any fixed positive correlation between
orthodoxy and literary merit. The devout Tupper is unbear-
able; the blasphemous Swinburne is a very good though hardly
a great poet. Pope's deistic *Essay on Man* is better poetry than
his *Messiah*; Wordsworth's pantheistic *Tintern Abbey* better
than his *Ecclesiastical Sonnets.* But the teacher may be openly
skeptical of the opposite assumption that the "greatness" of a
poem varies with the poet's ability to spout misty aspirations
which not only the rational unbeliever but the rational believer
must repudiate as noble nonsense. It is fair to suggest that
Tennyson's *The Ancient Sage* does not triumphantly soar
above "man-made creeds," but merely expresses the modern
hankering to feel religious without making any religious com-

mitments. People do not begin to debilitate their minds with valedictorian gush about gleams, goals, ideals, torches, horizons, and quests until they have ceased to believe in Christianity and have almost, though perhaps not quite, ceased to believe in God. The sentimental pantheon created by beginning words like Nature, Love, Beauty, and Man with a capital letter is spurious not only for religion but for art. To the subsidence of positive religious belief may be ascribed much of the vagueness and softness, the verbosity and didacticism which contemporary critics object to in nineteenth-century poetry. *The Hound of Heaven* is a better poem than *Merlin and the Gleam*. But so also, the Christian teacher must freely grant, are *Dover Beach* and *The City of Dreadful Night*. Not only passionate belief, but passionate sorrow over the loss of faith and passionate unbelief are poetically stimulating because they produce the concentrated vitality of utterance and the sharpness of image which arise from centripetal rather than centrifugal emotion. Granting the possession of literary talent, genuine religion is favorable to poetry. The same is true of genuine irreligion so long as it retains vivid images of what it denies. But the substitute-religions—the amorphous naturalisms and humanisms and idealisms which spawn from the decay of Christianity—resist by their very nature the creation of a satisfying aesthetic form. A supremely gifted artist may surmount this handicap, but only with great difficulty.

Such critical considerations cannot be isolated from the question of the inherent truth or falsity of the writer's assertions. Here the free expression of personal opinion, both by the instructor and by the members of the class, provides a valuable means of relating the study of the work to the general aims of liberal education. In supporting his own views, however, the teacher should be very careful not to force upon his students the *a priori* assumption that a writer's position is false because it departs from this or that Christian doctrine. The divergency should be noted as an historical fact, not as a

moral error. The only authority to be invoked is that of
natural reason, of personal experience, and above all of history.
The agreement of Christianity with these criteria is by no
means the obligatory starting-point of the argument, but a
conclusion which may be arrived at inductively. The teacher
should make it clear to his students that he is a Christian because he holds certain opinions, not that he holds certain
opinions because he is a Christian.

Tintern Abbey, for example, expresses in noble language
an authentic spiritual experience. That this experience is
basically un-Christian is an objective fact important for an understanding of romantic ideology, but the poet's thought is
not to be condemned because pantheism is a heresy. The instructor may, however, draw from other poems of Wordsworth
and from the works of his contemporaries evidence for asserting
that when the romantic poet appears to be worshipping the
divinity of nature he is mainly worshipping the exploits of his
own imaginative power. Hence, if religion is anything more
than a man-worship which is a cloak for self-worship, the
Wordsworth of 1798 is not so religious as he sounds. It is fair
to note that he himself soon began to realize the inadequacy
of the position on which his best poetry is grounded. And
looking forward into the nineteenth century the teacher may
ask his students to observe how utterly the romantic nature-
cult was smashed by an evolutionary concept of nature which
left the foundations of non-romantic Christian supernatural-
ism completely unshaken.

As the foregoing example indicates, the limitations of an
idea will often be most fruitfully exposed not by frontal attack,
but by showing what finally emerges from it. As expressed in
Sartor Resartus, Carlyle's conception of sense-impressions as
the garment of supersensuous spiritual reality seems favorable
to religion in general and by no means hostile to Christianity
in particular. We scent danger, however, when in *Heroes and
Hero-Worship* the masterful man emerges as he who can re-

veal to weaker spirits the eternal truths enshrouded in the phenomenal "clothes." My readers need not be reminded how, step by step through successive works, Carlyle the seer betrays himself as a forerunner of Fascism.

The Christian professor may legitimately suggest that Carlyle's abandonment of his ancestral religion for German transcendentalism is a factor in his spiritual tragedy. He may, however, find it necessary to add that Carlyle's Calvinistic background included implications of individualism, subjectivity, and energy-worship which prepared him only too well for reception of the post-Kantian gospel. For if the teacher believes that certain areas of Christianity have proved less resistant to decay than others, it will sometimes be his duty to say so. Emerson's "No law can be sacred to me but that of my own nature" is radically anti-Christian. It represents a cult of human self-sufficiency which would have been no less repugnant to Calvin than to Aquinas. Nevertheless, this collapse of Christian objectivity into romantic solipsism is much more obviously an outgrowth of the Protestant than of the Catholic tradition, which of course has its own very different snares of authoritarianism and mechanical formalism. Emerson's career in itself epitomizes the shift from Puritanism to Unitarianism and from Unitarianism to romantic transcendentalism. This fact exists quite independently of the teacher's personal religious commitments, although his desire to *express* the fact will certainly vary with those commitments. The point may be stated in precisely the same tone as would be used in explaining the qualities of Pope's couplets, and whatever fundamental implications it may suggest had better be left to the student.

Similarly many utterances of Victorian writers cannot be discussed profitably without observing their relationship to a general trend moving from evangelicalism or noncomformity to a vague theism and thence to nothing at all. Browning's career exhibits the first two phases of this movement: contrast

Christmas-Eve and *La Saisiaz*. The class may wish to discuss
the central thought of *The Statue and the Bust*:

> Let a man contend to the uttermost
> For his life's set prize, be what it will.

These lines embody the courage, the vitality, the omnivorous
lack of discrimination, the hearty optimistic muddle-headed-
ness which characterize both the art and the "philosophy" of
this poet. Intelligent students will see that some of the prizes
for which man strives are worthier of pursuit than others. The
teacher need not underscore the alertness of Christianity to
the moral danger of Browning's position; but he should feel
free to say that it becomes natural to glorify mere activity for
its own sake in a period when men grow increasingly uncertain
as to the objectivity of religious truth and hence increasingly
uncertain as to the aim of their striving. Perhaps Tennyson's
Ulysses would be an even finer poem if the courageous old
wanderer had some faint idea of where he wanted to go. The
class may well consider the ultimate fruits of this wide-spread
gospel of "I don't know where I'm going, but I'm on my way,"
this "inspirational" notion that it is somehow nobler to miss
a bus than to catch it. That such fallacies are utterly opposed
to Christian realism may be profitably surprising to students
who have come to identify Christianity with *Schwärmerei*.
Objections of this kind may be raised without blaming the
writer for saying precisely what he would be expected to say
at a particular stage in the history of ideas. With rare exceptions, poets do not make the thought of their time: they
simply respond to it with especial sensitiveness. It would be
ungrateful to scold at men who reveal so clearly and movingly
the spiritual struggles of the age in which they lived.

Some readers of this essay will feel that such teaching is unnecessarily negative and astringent. They will assert that the
highest office of the Christian teacher is not to encourage
habits of spiritual discrimination but to bring inspiring

thoughts to the attention of the student. Speaking now wholly for myself, I admire and envy, though I cannot fully understand, those religious-minded colleagues who are able to treat their material in a bracing and optimistic spirit. Unfortunately the facts as I see them compel me to regard the history of the literary expression of religious thought mainly as a study in spiritual pathology. Perhaps the accurate description of a disease too clearly indicates the remedy to be a source of despair. Inevitably, however, the story which I must tell my students, up to the point where it leaves off unfinished in our own day, is not a cheerful one. Looking back upon the past, I cannot describe English literature from the sixteenth century onward as the record of an ever increasing enlightenment. The story includes much beauty, much high aspiration, many broken recollections of primal truth and therefore many glimpses of hope for the future. Nevertheless its central theme is the inflation and collapse of a human pride which has either forsaken Christianity or transformed it into a delusive caricature of the historic faith. To trace the course of this tragedy, showing the relation of individual authors and their works to the development of the plot, must be my task as a Christian teacher and scholar.

I need hardly say, however, that this theme does not constantly occupy the foreground of my instruction. A course in English literature devoted exclusively to religious considerations would be absurdly disproportionate. There are many hours when an observer who visited my classroom would not infer that I believed anything at all except that Keats was a great master of fresh-minted metaphor. One must also remember that the student who is exposed to the sort of teaching which I have described will also be exposed to quite different points of view championed by other professors of English and by members of other departments. The consequent confusion at least eliminates the danger of illegitimate indoctrination. The student will discover what any scholar must grant—that

3

HISTORY

By E. HARRIS HARBISON

I

A theologian who had written an eloquent history of the Reformation is said to have met the historian Ranke in Berlin and embraced him effusively as one would a confrere. "Ah please," said the father of scientific history, drawing himself away, "there is a great difference between us: you are first of all a Christian, and I am first of all a historian."

It was with this anecdote that Lord Acton introduced the central argument of his inaugural lecture on "The Study of History." [1] The story dramatizes vividly the nineteenth-century belief that history is a "science," and that science is knowledge of an utterly different order from religion. The "great difference" which Ranke saw between Christian and historian has undoubtedly narrowed in our own day as historians have grown more conscious of the subjectivity of their interpretation and more uneasy about calling history a "science." But a difference still exists in the academic mind between one who would call himself "first of all a Christian" and one who would call himself "first of all a historian."

Many years ago men would have looked at the same difference from the other side of the gulf. Imagine Acton's anecdote

[1] A Lecture on the Study of History (London and New York: The Macmillan Co., 1895), p. 50 and p. 115 n. Acton quotes an article of Victor Cherbuliez in Revue des deux mondes, Vol. XCVII (1872), p. 537, in which the historian is not identified.

in reverse: Ranke (in a previous incarnation) enthusiastically embraces a great medieval saint, let us say Bernard, as a comrade; but the saint draws himself away, saying, "You are a chronicler of the City of Man, I am a citizen of the City of God; between us there is a great gulf fixed." The point is simply that in the Middle Ages the tables would have been turned. Sainthood once had the prestige which science (and "scientific" history) was to attain in the nineteenth century. St. Bernard, in the position in which we have imagined him, would have sensed the danger in Ranke's desire to clothe his secular scholarship with the aura of Christian sanctity. "You are first of all a historian," he might conclude, "I am first of all a Christian."

In letting the imagination play upon the apparent difference between professing Christian and professional historian, however, it is easy to oversimplify. We know, for instance, that Ranke himself was a deeply religious person. "In all history," he wrote at one time, "God dwells, lives, is to be seen. Every deed demonstrates Him, every moment preaches His name." [2] I can find little information about the effusive theologian in the story, but I am sure that if Ranke thought his history of the Reformation a bad job, it *was* a bad job. Assuming that what Ranke objected to was the distortion of events "as they actually happened" to fit the demands of sectarian prejudice, the cause of Christian truth certainly did not suffer through his rebuke. The eager quest from Bayle to Voltaire to cleanse the historical record of superstition and priestly distortion, the passion for accuracy, objectivity, and exhaustiveness in the nineteenth-century German school of "scientific" historiography—these things were certainly not anti-Christian in and of themselves. It is far too simple to say that in our anecdote Ranke represents something called "history" and the theologian something called "Christianity." Each in a different

[2] James Westfall Thompson and B. J. Holm, A *History of Historical Writing* (New York: The Macmillan Co., 1943), Vol. II, p. 171.

sense was a *Christian historian.* The question as Ranke stated it was which comes "first of all," a man's vocation as Christian or his profession as historian.

II

There is a false sharpness in this apparent contradiction between "Christian" and "historian," which results from the survival of a naïve nineteenth-century conception of "objectivity." Deep at the heart of the American academic world is the belief that the word "scholar" cannot tolerate any qualifying adjective like "Christian." Has not the scholar had to battle the priest at every step of the way in his fight for freedom of inquiry? Did not the Church burn Bruno and humiliate Galileo? And in the search for historical truth, were not the real heroes those who (like Valla) exposed the arrogant forgeries of Popes or (like Bayle) laid bare the superstitions on which Christians had been nourished for centuries? Once a man allows himself to be *anything* before he is "scholar" or "scientist," so the argument runs, truth flies out the window and prejudice fills the classroom. The adjectives most feared today are of course not religious, but pseudoreligious—not "Christian" and "Jewish" but "Communist" and "Fascist." Fascist, Nazi, and Bolshevist regimes have attacked the disinterested pursuit of truth for its own sake as not only dangerous but fundamentally immoral, and it is no wonder that older convictions about the incompatibility of science and religion should be reinforced by the present-day evidence that disinterested scholarship cannot survive under the shadow of our great pseudo-religions. Such convictions are particularly strong among historians because they know what happens to the historical profession and the historical record in the hands of totalitarian governments. In any discussion of the hackneyed problem of "academic objectivity" it is important to remember that American academic communities are keenly aware of the overwhelming threat to the disinterested pursuit of truth which has driven a throng of scholarly exiles to our shores and onto our campuses. The jealous fear of coupling any adjective implying zealous faith with "scholar" is not altogether unjustified.

This was borne in upon me vividly at Bossey near Geneva during the summer of 1949, at a conference of professional historians and graduate students on "The Meaning of History." Years of totalitarian tyranny or war regimentation on the Continent have sapped any vitality which might have been left in the nineteenth-century belief in "objectivity." Historians who lived under "thought control" learned to use "objectivity" as an escape from publicly committing themselves to the dominant political philosophy. Today their students have only contempt for the tendency they notice in the older academic generation to avoid commitment of any kind, on or off the lecture platform. On the other hand, they warm to teachers who believe something, even though it be a Communism which most of them would reject. To most of them "objectivity" is either a hypocritical dodge designed to cover up unspoken assumptions or an immoral escape from the necessity of taking a stand on the vital issues of the day. Many European historians are so saturated in existential thinking as to deny the possibility of objectivity in any sense of the word. The only attainable objectivity, one member of the conference argued, is a frank and detailed confession of all subjective prejudices in the preface of a historical work. In other words, the dominant opinion in many European academic communities appears to be the opposite of the dominant American opinion. You must proclaim openly what sort of a historian you are—Communist, bourgeois, or Christian. Words like "scholar" and "historian" must always and inevitably have qualifying adjectives attached to them or they have no meaning.

Contact with such thinking has a dual effect upon an American. On the one hand, it gives him a sense of pride and gratitude that belief in the possibility of disinterested inquiry is still alive and vigorous in American universities. On the other hand, it makes him sensitive to the naïveté and hypocrisy in much American talk about impartial objectivity. There is a sense in which "impartiality" has become a luxury which only those nations can afford which remained neutral or happened to avoid the worst physical and moral destruction during the late war. Swedish students at the conference mentioned were insistent that they and their friends were not a bit interested in the personal beliefs of their professors but solely in what they *knew*. Any teacher of history this side of the water will remember the same disposition in many students he has known. Faith in the possibility of "objective" knowledge is evidently still strong in these two parts of the world at least. But to most Europeans, and even to many Americans, teachers and students alike, impartiality is simply a pose adopted by fearful academicians with desensitized social consciences and dried-up emotions. Even in the United States all of us who face students in the college classrooms have at one time or another sensed the utter seriousness with which undergraduates ask, "But what is *your* relation to what you know? What is *your* concern with it? What do *you* think it's all about?" This is not the place to spell out what has happened to the concept of "objectivity" in recent epistemology—and only a philosopher would do the job well. It is enough to point out that the contemporary teacher and writer of history is confronted in fact by an audience which includes an increasing number who think that Ranke was not necessarily any more "objective" than his theological friend. Europeans are simply a few steps ahead of Americans in popular awareness of the truth that the knower is intimately involved in the process of knowing.

III

The question which haunts any historian today who is at all sensitive to the deeper currents of the age in which he lives, the question his students constantly ask of him by implication even when they do not put it into words, is the question of the meaning of history. A great many of the veterans who flocked into courses in history and the social studies in such swollen numbers after the war made it clear to advisers and teachers that they were looking for answers they thought neither the arts and letters nor the natural sciences could give. Somewhere in history, many of them thought, the answer to how it all came about was to be found. This search is still on on many campuses, at least so far as history courses are concerned. Students who would hardly think of asking "What is the meaning of nuclear energy?" or "What is the meaning of the artistic impulse?," will ask in some way "What is the meaning of human history?" What they mean is "Where are we headed?"

Questions like this are not fashionable among professional historians, but when a man reaches the top of the profession and no longer has reason to fear the sneers of his colleagues, it is a well-established custom to reflect upon such matters. Kenneth Scott Latourette, delivering the presidential address before the American Historical Association in 1948 on "The Christian Understanding of History," pointed out that "a survey of the presidential addresses made before this Association reveals the fact that no one single topic has so attracted those who have been chosen to head this honorable body as have the possible patterns and meanings of history." [3] In a recent discussion with a fellow historian Arnold J. Toynbee remarked, "This job of making sense of history is one of the crying needs of our day—I beg of you believe me." [4] The philos-

[3] *American Historical Review*, LIV (January, 1949), p. 261.
[4] *Can We Know the Pattern of the Past?* Discussion between P. Geyl . . . and A. J. Toynbee (Bussum, Holland: 1948), p. 30.

ophers and above all the theologians have been even more eager than the historians in recent years to make sense of history. Books on "The Meaning of History," "Meaning in History," "Faith and History," "Christianity and the Nature of History" have poured from the presses in fairly steady succession, patricularly since the close of the war.[5] The historian may perhaps be pardoned for thinking that this question of the whole meaning of his subject is pressed upon *him* more insistently these days by students and fellow scholars than it is upon any of his colleagues in other departments of higher learning.

There are two easy answers to this question of the meaning of history. One is to say that meaning is so woven into the texture of history that the pattern is self-evident to any interested and careful observer. All that is necessary is to study the historical record "objectively" and impartially, and a design of meaningful progress will become evident. The other is to say that there is no meaning in history and that the search for design is futile and stupid. The first is an attitude of assurance which is closely affiliated to the nineteenth-century faith that if the facts are only heaped high enough they will amount to something. The second is an attitude of doubt which is generally born of disillusionment about the failure of exactly this kind of assurance.

It is not the purpose of this essay to present and preach a Christian "interpretation" of history. Rather it is to suggest that the question of meaning must be faced by every professional historian whether he likes it or not, both in his teaching and writing; that current secular answers generally end up either in a too easy assurance or a too abject doubt; and that there is a Christian way of looking at history which is something less than a philosophy of history but something more than a mere frame of mind and which constitutes the only really adequate alternative to either dogmatism or skepticism.

[5] See the bibliographical references at the close of this chapter.

The men of assurance in the historical profession are perhaps not so numerous as they once were, but they are still an impressive group. They are generally the "social scientists" among historians, the heirs of a great hope, that science will save society. The study of history has always had its statistical side and the areas of it which are capable of semiscientific treatment have received increasing attention during the past two centuries: geography, climate, demography, production and exchange, class struggle and social displacement. Historical study has profited immensely from this statistical emphasis, and the hard-boiled statisticians who keep reminding their colleagues of prices and wages, food production and population fluctuation, "forces" and "trends," are stimulating and indispensable members of any department of history. But the perception of trends and the drawing of graphs appear to exercise a fatal fascination on the academic mind. The trends become animated, and before we know it we are confronted with mechanisms and determinisms which "explain" history. Any practising historian knows how deliciously seductive these magnificent simplicities can be to students who for the first time encounter the historical interpretations of Marx, for instance, or Spengler, or Sorokin.

If the men of assurance seize upon one of the emotional attitudes of modern science—its self-confidence and optimism —the men of doubt seize upon another—its tentative, skeptical, inquiring attitude, Descartes' *de omnibus dubitandum*. History to them is an unintelligible and meaningless process. Any meaning ascribed to the course of history is totally subjective; any determination of cause and effect is difficult and dubious; even the concept of cause itself, many of them maintain, is best dispensed with. There is an intellectual honesty about these people, a refusal to be taken in, an ascetic renunciation of wishful thinking, which are altogether admirable. But in the classroom this second attitude too often ends in a philosophy which proclaims that life is a mess, history a farce, and historical study a kind of intellectual game, interesting in a gruesome sort of way, but not enlightening and certainly not ennobling. All this is particularly appealing to a bewildered, disillusioned, and fearful postwar generation of students. In times of trouble, pessimism is a surer balm than optimism. Men can enjoy misery if they know they have company in it. I have often seen students gain real emotional release through the discovery that a professor of history was more cynical and despairing about the state of the universe than they were themselves. But the anodyne is not permanent. And although doubt may be the beginning of wisdom, I know of no guarantee that it must end in wisdom. It is hard to nourish vigorous and creative historical thinking on the thin gruel of thoroughgoing skepticism.

IV

It should be the mark of a Christian attitude toward history that it resolves the antinomy of assurance and doubt about the meaning of the historical process on a higher plane. St. Augustine was the first Christian thinker to wrestle long and hard with the problem of how the Christian must look upon history, and it was Augustine who first saw clearly that to the Christian, history is *neither* a deterministic system *nor* a meaningless chaos. The determinists of his day believed that history moved in cycles and that if historians only studied the process of recurrence carefully enough they could describe and predict the movements of history almost as they could predict the motions of the planets. Origen had seen that if this were true, then

> Adam and Eve will do once more exactly what they have already done; the same deluge will be repeated; the same Moses will bring the same six hundred thousand people out of Egypt; Judas will again betray his Lord; and Paul a second time will hold the coats of those who stone Stephen.

"God forbid that we should believe this," Augustine wrote, "for Christ died once for our sins, and rising again, dies no more."[6] In other words, there is a decisiveness and unpredictability about history which is falsely annihilated in any view of history as mechanical recurrence, scientifically intelligible and predictable.

Augustine saw with equal clarity that history is not chaos. The rise and fall of states and civilizations is not meaningless process.

> We do not attribute the power of giving kingdoms and empires to any save to the true God . . . He who is the true God . . . gave a kingdom to the Romans when He would, and as great as He would, as He did also to the Assyrians and even the Persians . . . And the same is true in respect of men as well as nations . . . He who gave power to Augustus gave it also to Nero . . . He who gave it to the Christian Constantine gave it also to the apostate Julian . . . Manifestly these things are ruled and governed by the one God according as He pleases; *and if His motives are hid, are they therefore unjust?*[7]

The very essence of a Christian understanding of history, despite the many sectarian forms it may take, is in this last sentence. The Hebrew Prophets and the Christian Fathers agreed in believing the strange paradox that God both *reveals* and *conceals* Himself in history. There is too much revelation for a Christian to think that there is no judgment or mercy in history, no moral meaning, no spiritual significance. On the other hand, the divine concealment is of such a character that no Christian may think that the judgment or meaning or significance is unambiguously clear to him as a human being. To Luther, who wrote eloquently about this "hiddenness of God" in history, there is mystery as well as majestic purpose

---

[6] Augustine, *De Civitate Dei*, Book XII, chap. xiii. The passage from Origen (*Peri Archon*, II, chap. iii) is quoted by Lynn White, Jr., "Christian Myth and Christian History," *Journal of The History of Ideas*, Vol. III (1942), p. 147.
[7] *De Civitate Dei*, Book V, chap. xxi.

in the historical pageant; and the one is meaningless without the other. God is Lord of history to Luther, but He does not work openly and visibly in the historical process. In typically extravagant imagery, he speaks of history as God's "play," God's "mummery," God's "joust and tourney." The actual course of secular history cannot be identified with God's will—nor can it be wholly divorced from His will. God wills to conceal as well as to reveal Himself in the fate of empires, and above all in the unplumbed depths of two central events, the Birth and Passion of Christ. In a famous comparison of God's grace to a passing shower of rain, Luther suggested in a single brief passage the simultaneous revelation and concealment of the divine will, the unity-within-diversity of human history, the uniqueness of events, and the decisiveness of the present moment in history for the individual:

> For this shall you know, that God's word and grace are a passing shower of rain, which never comes again where it has once been. It was with the Jews, but what is gone is gone, they have nothing now. Paul brought it into Grecian land. What is gone is gone again, now they have the Turks. Rome and Latin land had it also. What is gone is gone, they now have the Pope. And you Germans must not think that you will always have it. So grasp on and hold to, whoever can grasp and hold.[8]

V

In developing the implications of these basic Christian insights into history, Christian thinkers and Christian sects have not escaped the danger of falling into one or the other of precisely the same attitudes which we have described in the case of secular historians. We might say that in the Christian case these are the "heresies" of overassurance and overdiffidence about the meaning of history, the one closely parallel to the sin of pride, the other to that of sloth.

[8] Luther, *Werke* (Weimar ed.), Vol. XV, p. 32.

To Christian historians the Biblical record has always appeared to reveal a broad pattern of the divine activity in history. A Swiss scholar, Oscar Cullmann, has recently sketched this pattern with brilliant strokes as he believes it to appear in the New Testament.[9] As he sees it, the God who created the universe is the Lord of redemption and so of history. By the dual process of "calling" and "substitution," he directs the drama of salvation through its various stages to triumphant conclusion beyond the historical vision of mankind. He first calls or chooses mankind to stand for creation; then calls a nation, the Hebrews, to substitute for man in general; then summons a remnant to represent that nation when it falls away; and finally fixes upon one man, the Christ, to stand for all humanity and creation. The progressive reduction then gives way to progressive expansion and the process reverses itself. Through Christ the apostles are won, through the apostles the Church is founded, through the Church all mankind will be reconciled to God, and the new heaven and earth will complete the first creation. The fact that the Western world divides time into "A.D." and "B.C." is the most obvious evidence of the incalculable influence which this broad pattern of meaning envisioned by the early Christians has had upon historical understanding.

The point at which this pattern becomes controversial for Christian groups is naturally the concrete meaning given to the age in which we live, the age of the Church from the Resurrection to the present. Is the gradual unfolding of this age a significant part of the drama or not? Is God's hand still evident in every turn of events? If so, how and where and in what?

The answer has been clearest through the ages for the Roman Christian. For him, God's hand has been clearly evident in history since Pentecost in the Roman Catholic Church.

[9] See Oscar Cullmann, *Christus und die Zeit* (Zürich, 1946). French translation: *Christ et le temps* (Neuchâtel and Paris: Delachaux et Niestlé, 1947), particularly Part I, chap. viii.

There is a real progress in history: progressive unfolding of doctrines which were only implicit in New Testament times, progressive winning of the pagan, the infidel, and the schismatic in spite of all appearances of defeat. History has a central thread in Church history, in the growth of a visible divine institution—what Sir Thomas More called "the common, known church"—changeless in goal but constantly changing in its temporal position in relation to this goal. In different times and in different ways, such a conviction that God's hand in history is unmistakably revealed in a visible historical institution has been shared by Eastern Orthodox Christians as well as by Lutherans, Anglicans, and early Calvinists. Its remote source is undoubtedly the Old Testament Covenant of Jehovah with his chosen people.

Another form taken by Christian assurance about the meaning of history is the belief that God's hand is evident not so much in *institutions* as in *events*. In the Middle Ages, the most significant events were visions and miracles. To readers of the lives of the saints, God's love and power were constantly breaking in upon the ordinary course of human affairs in a direct and self-evident way. The successor to this belief in more sophisticated early modern times was the conviction, particularly evident in Oliver Cromwell and his Puritan contemporaries, that God's hand appears not so much in miracle as in the outcome of historical events like battles. This conviction that God guides men not by mystical vision or miraculous breaking of natural law but by his shaping of secular history, by what Cromwell called "dispensations," was rooted in the Hebrew prophets and widely prevalent among our seventeenth-century American ancestors.

Among Protestants today assurance about the meaning of history is certainly not a besetting sin. Christians have never entirely recovered from the eighteenth-century attack on the "theological interpretation" of history which had been dominant from Augustine to Bossuet. Nor should they, perhaps.

Many of the things which Voltaire assailed in Christian historiography needed to be assailed: the narrow parochialism which funneled all ancient history into the story of "that miserable little people," the Jews; the neglect of non-Christian civilizations; the partisanship and axe-grinding so characteristic of monkish and priestly chronicle; the easy recourse to miracle as a short-circuit of causal explanation. Voltaire and his fellow philosophers destroyed the older Christian pattern of meaning in history only to substitute another, that of secular progress. But the shattering experience of two world wars and the cold shadow of a third have effectually destroyed the naïve belief in inevitable progress, and most Protestant leaders today are concerned to extirpate the last traces of nineteenth-century optimism about the course of secular history.

The result is a strong tendency on the part of Christian intellectuals today to adopt a kind of Christian skepticism about the meaning of history. Among Protestant theologians this group is clearly in the ascendancy today, in terms of prestige if not also of numbers. There is sound historical reason for this. Primitive Protestantism had at its center a passionate protest against identifying the will of God with any visible institution such as the Roman Church. Too often the result was simply to substitute the church of Wittenberg, Geneva, or England, for that of Rome. But it is impossible in the long run for a Protestant to rest content with any theory of history in which a visible institution is the sole channel of God's grace. This is why Protestants turned so easily to something like Cromwell's doctrine of "dispensations." They soon abused this doctrine, to be sure, by seeing God's will in secular events or movements which pleased them, all the way from parliamentary government and democracy to liberalism and socialism. Led by Karl Barth, Protestant theologians today are moving in strong reaction to such tendencies. In spite of the widespread current interest in history among theologians, the deepest currents in Protestant theology, particularly in Europe, can only be described as *antihistorical*. These currents find their source in Kierkegaard, in Barth, in Berdyaev, and in secular philosophers of the existentialist school. Diverse as they are in their sources and present courses, they have some things in common: a deep distrust of everything associated with "progress"; a sense that God is the "wholly Other" and hence not to be identified with any historical institution or movement, whether it stem from Rome or Geneva or Moscow; a radical Christian relativism in viewing all historical achievements.

This Christian skepticism about the possibility of discerning any pattern of meaning in secular history bulks large in recent theological works. "There never has been and never will be," a recent writer concludes, "an immanent solution of the problem of history, for man's historical experience is one of steady failure . . . History is, through all the ages, a story of action and suffering, of power and pride, of sin and death . . . The importance of secular history decreases *in direct proportion to* the intensity of man's concern with God and himself . . . A 'Christian history' is non-sense." [10] I have heard a similar view eloquently expressed by a deeply spiritual Danish professor of church history who was arguing "the impossibility of a Christian conception of history." Since real knowledge presupposes simultaneity, he maintained that we can never actually know the past and the past can never have real significance for us. The mere unrolling of history has no visible meaning for a converted Christian. "Christian belief," he concluded, "is to trust God in the uncertainty of life. It is the most abominable arrogance to make false certainties by interpreting history in a Christian way." [11] The trend toward a Christian agnosticism with respect to any self-evident meaning in the course of history is very strong indeed, particularly in

[10] Karl Löwith, *Meaning in History* (Chicago: University of Chicago Press, 1949), pp. 190–97. Italics mine.
[11] P. G. Lindhardt, of the University of Aarhus, Denmark, at the conference at Bossey mentioned above.

Europe. Evidently the Christian historian does not avoid the twin dangers of dogmatism and doubt simply by being a Christian.

VI

The historian who happens also to be a Christian is thus besieged, as it were, by four attacking armies of colleagues, students, and friends who come at him from the four points of the compass. His secular colleagues who have all the answers, tell him to put aside childish things like religion now that he has become a man and to open his eyes to the great material mechanisms which determine history. A few of his Christian friends are perhaps equally dogmatic on the other side of the matter, exposing the naïve assumptions of the materialists and pointing out with equal assurance just where the hand of God is to be discerned in history. The agnostics among his colleagues both in history and in theology come at him from two different and opposite quarters—each with *Nescio* inscribed on their banners, but for quite different reasons. Each group maintains that history has nothing much to do with Christianity, the first because Christianity is nothing, the second because history is nothing. In this plight I think the Christian historian may well stand up and make a brief speech which might run something like this:

"I am neither a philosopher nor a theologian. I am interested as any educated man is in philosophy and theology, but as a professional historian you must not expect of me a fully rounded philosophy or theology of history. Thanks to my training, I am suspicious of big words and big ideas. I believe that Marx was wrong in his interpretation of history for the same reason that the authors of saints' legends were wrong— that human history cannot be reduced to magnificent simplicities, either material or spiritual. I have a feeling that agnosticism, not assurance, is the first step toward wisdom, provided that it does not sink away into cynicism and despair. But I cannot agree that history has nothing to do with the religious insights of Christianity, or that Christianity has nothing to do with secular history. I could not long remain either a believing Christian or a practising historian with my convictions about Christianity and history in watertight compartments. I believe, in spite of secular skeptics, that Christianity offers a profound insight into the general nature of the historical process, even though both as historian and Christian I am too diffident to think that I can discern a clear-cut pattern. I believe, in spite of the theological skeptics, that secular history is important to the Christian and that Christianity always suffers when its historical character is minimized, because the immediate result is always a loss of ethical vigor among Christians. I think I see a fine traditional ambiguity in the word 'vocation' as the call of God both to religious commitment and to service in a job. I see no reason why I cannot find a reconciliation between my two 'vocations' on the practical working level of teaching and writing history, if not on the loftier levels of philosophy and theology."

VII

To the professional historian, much of what has been discussed thus far may seem highly theoretical and only very tenuously related to the practical work-a-day problems of the classroom. It is my conviction, however, that in any discussion of religious perspectives in teaching history—whatever may be true of other subjects—it is impossible to separate the theoretical and the practical, just as it is impossible to split apart the historian's dual function as teacher and writer. The real problem is to find a practical working form of Augustine's or Luther's understanding of history which takes account of the immense recent progress of historical knowledge and technique, which conforms to the idiom of twentieth-century thought in general, but which remains true to the basic insights of Christianity into the nature of man, of God, and of time.

On this level the first illusion to be got rid of is the idea which I have heard expressed by enthusiastic theologians that being a Christian will make a man a better professional historian—nay, that it is the very condition of being a true historian at all, since it was Christianity which nurtured the modern historical sense of unique events happening in irreversible sequence in straight-line time. Christian belief is obviously no substitute for competent scholarship at the technical level, and it would be intolerable pride in a Christian to suggest that on this level his religion gives him an advantage over the nonreligious historians. I cannot see how Christian belief contributes anything significant to the careful study of matters like the laws of Solon, medieval land-tenure, or the impact of gunpowder on the history of military tactics. Furthermore, sectarian prejudice has long been a notorious obstacle in the path of historical understanding.

There is an important truth, however, at the basis of this illusion, a truth most eloquently developed in Herbert Butterfield's penetrating and exciting recent lectures on *Christianity and History*. It is that the Christian understanding of the nature and destiny of man—created, yet free, fallen, yet redeemable, bounded by history, yet able to transcend it by his imagination and creativity—cannot fail to deepen and enrich any historian's understanding of his subject. It cannot be said too often that historical understanding is never merely a matter of reading documents. A child cannot comprehend Luther's experience in the monastery until his own human experience and powers of imagination are mature enough to provide at least some common ground of understanding. A student cannot understand the complexities of the movement Luther started, its contradictions and confusions, the mixture in it of

lofty ideals and base motives, until he has absorbed something at least of how the politics and mass movements of his
own day operate. In the same way, the truly great historian
cannot afford to ignore the thinking about human nature and
the problem of evil which has been done by the most sensitive
and intelligent observers. To the Christian, the profoundest
view is the Hebraic-Christian as it has been developed from
the prophets and Christ through the apostles and later teachers
of the church.

There is an opposite illusion which may also be dismissed
briefly. This is that a man will be a better Christian for being
a historian. Stated in this form, the proposition is of course
absurd. Learning of any sort has never been a condition of
Christian perfection. But again there is a truth at the basis of
the illusion. The Christian faith was born among a people
which had developed a relatively strong historical sense, and
the New Testament is saturated with temporal terminology
used naïvely: "then," "straightway," "when the time was
fulfilled," "in the fullness of time." At the Last Judgment men
are judged by what they have done in history, even though
their righteousness or unrighteousness is not evident to them
during their historical existence. The Apostles' Creed is a
statement of belief about events which happened in time, not
a statement of truths which are eternally true apart from time.
To Augustine, as to the Hebrew prophets before him, there
was significant development in time of God's purpose; and to
Dante, the destiny of Rome was linked firmly and surely to the
destiny of the church.[12]   In other words, the Hebraic-Christian
tradition, unlike others which arose in India and China, is a
history-valuing tradition; and it is no accident that when it
became partially secularized, the result was the modern idea

[12] The most significant passages for the study of the general problem seem
to me the following: Acts II, III, X, XI; Romans VI; Galatians IV; I Corinthians XV; Augustine, *De Civitate Dei*, Book V, chap. xxi; Book XII, chap.
xiii; Book XVIII, chap. xlvi; Dante, *De Monarchia*, and *Purgatorio*, cantos xvi
and xx.

of progress. Except when Greek or Oriental influences have become dominant, Christians have never looked upon time as something to be fled or annihilated. There is a sense in which a man must be historically-minded in an elementary way in order to be a Christian.

Let us grant that Christian belief will not improve a historian's standing with his fellow scholars, nor professional historical knowledge a Christian's standing among the saints. On the practical level the gulf between Christian and historian is, nevertheless, by no means so wide as Ranke implied it was. There are some qualities and attitudes which are equally admired by Christians and by professional historians, and which may serve as guide-posts for the man who wishes he were both a better Christian and a better historian.

One of these is *universality* or catholicity of outlook. The best historians are not satisfied until by a rigorous intellectual asceticism they have risen as far as humanly possible above all parochialism of both time and place which narrows or distorts their historical vision. It was part of Ranke's greatness that he strove so hard and so self-consciously to rise above sectarian and national prejudice and to judge past ages by their own standards rather than by those of a later day. The most obvious source of this rationalistic universalism was the stoic conception of the natural equality of all men and the eighteenth-century cosmopolitanism so akin to it. This outlook blended easily with the catholicity preached by a religion which insisted from the beginning upon the fatherhood of God and the brotherhood of all men. The monotheism of the Hebrew prophets and the belief in the universal fatherhood of the Christian God formed the basis upon which the first clear conception of the *unity of history* was built in the West. Christian historiography, with all its failings, constituted a notable step beyond the parochialism and nationalism of Greek and Roman historical writing; and even if it developed a new parochialism of its own, it never entirely lost the belief that all local histories are really one history. The Christian believed that though one nation may be "chosen," the mission of a chosen people is world-wide, more is demanded of it than of others, and if it falters, its mission may pass to the Gentiles. Amid all the welter of histories written in the interests of class, nation, race, or sect, this ideal of universality of perspective still stands as that of professional historian and Christian alike.

Closely related to universality is the difficult matter of *judgment*. The secular historian would dislike any theological terminology here, but a reading of the ablest contemporary historians I think would suggest that they believe in something very close to the Christian belief in a justice completed, though never annihilated, by mercy. Most historians are aware that they cannot avoid judgment of men and movements, either in their writing or their teaching. Monographs and textbooks which simply "give the facts," betray underlying judgments in the very choice and arrangement of such facts—especially when they are read after the lapse of a generation or so. Students are quick to sense the judgment implicit not only in the conscious choice of material for presentation but even more in the unplanned and half-conscious tone of voice or facial expression which betrays the teacher. Granted the necessity of making judgments, the real question is on what basis they are to be made, and here the historian and the Christian are in general agreement. Justice requires that all the relevant data be used and fairly weighed before judgment is given. The usual result of a long and honest attempt to get at all the historical evidence about any disputed event or personality is an overwhelming sense of the complexity and relativity of the issues, a sense of *tout comprendre, c'est tout pardonner*. The desire to be fair ends often enough in the desire to extend mercy, even on the level of purely secular historical labor. In the Gospels "Woe unto you, Scribes and Pharisees . . ." is balanced by "Judge not that ye be not judged." The historian knows—or should know—that the limits of judgment lie for him too

between these same two extremes, between a sense of righteousness which refuses to blink the fact of evil, and a sense of
mercy which follows from the complexity of human affairs
and the frailty of human judgment.

To take a concrete case, any historian who writes, lectures,
or talks with students about Luther is sooner or later forced to
take up an attitude toward him. A Roman Catholic teacher
may vent his righteous indignation upon the reformer; a
pious Lutheran may make a spotless prophet of him; a Marxian
may point out that Luther was a mere puppet in the grip of
irresistible economic forces. It may be suggested, without any
intent to blaspheme, that the best professional historian's ideal
here is theoretically the same as the Christian's: to see Luther
as nearly as possible as his own Lord saw him, in all his weakness and strength, his compromises and triumphs, his freedom
and his compulsion, so that in the resulting judgment, justice
is perfectly tempered with mercy. As a matter of fact, close
and persistent study of Luther and his whole age by professional historians, has brought us closer at least to the possibility
of such a judgment than was conceivable a century ago, simply
because we knew too little then. Mere knowledge is no guarantee of sound judgment of men and movements, either in historical study or in ordinary Christian living, but it is often the
beginning of true understanding. The kind of judgment the
best historians strive for is not, so far as some may think, from
the kind of judgment the truest followers of Christ have
striven for.

A third quality or attitude which is characteristic of both
historians and Christians on different levels is best described
as *realism*. Generally it is the "humanists" among historians,
not the traditional Christians, who are shocked by the realities
of human nature as they are encountered in history. The historian and the social scientist habitually deal with human
nature at its lowest level, the level at which "moral man" is
absorbed in "immoral society." Much of the time they are

concerned with the competition of groups for wealth and power, the game of power politics, the awful destruction of revolution and war. My guess is that the ratio of cynicism among historians is higher than that among, say, professors of literature or of physics. At any rate the historian is not apt to be a Pollyanna at the present moment of world history. Nor is the Christian. Both succumbed for a time to the eighteenth-century belief in the goodness of human nature and the inevitability of progress, but a good many non-Christian historians today would be impelled to agree with Herbert Butterfield when he writes, "We have gambled very highly on what was an over-optimistic view of the character of man. . . . It is essential not to have faith in human nature. Such faith is a comparatively recent heresy and a very disastrous one." [13] The tough-mindedness about which many professional historians pride themselves is not so far from a Christian attitude toward human nature as is a soft and idealistic optimism.

Tough-mindedness must be balanced, however, both with the historian and the Christian, by *open-mindedness*. By this I mean openness to unforeseen possibilities in human nature and history. The historian who is merely cynical is obviously going to be blind to the unexpected and unexplainable good in human nature, the movements which turn out better than their sordid origins would lead one to expect. "Good" events in history have a disconcerting way of producing unlovely results. But many of the results which we later call "good" have been the by-product of selfish conflicts—civil liberties in English history, for instance, were partly the product of self-interested squabbles over privilege by social or religious groups. The great historians have invariably had a certain open-mindedness to the infinite possibilities in human nature which is certainly akin to, though it is not identical with, the Christian's sensitivity to the redemptive possibilities in any human

[13] Herbert Butterfield, *Christianity and History* (London: George Bell & Sons, 1949), pp. 34, 47.

situation. In the mental make-up of a historian, realism must be balanced by a certain naïveté and wonder, a sense of the kindliness in human beings that is the ultimate foundation of societies and of the resilience which human beings keep demonstrating in the face of disaster and evil. On a different level the Christian would call this kindliness and resilience evidence of the workings of grace. Luther's warning that to talk of the Law and forget the Gospel is "to wound and not to bind up, to smite and not to heal, to lead down into Hell and not to bring back again," has its clear implications for the historian as well as for the Christian.

Finally there is a sense in which both historians and Christians are *relativists*. One of the major counts brought against teachers of history by moralists in our day is that they instill into the minds of our youth a corrosive relativism, a feeling that there are no universal and unchanging standards and that moral codes are always relative to time and place. In this view, for instance, there is no justification for saying that Democracy is any better than Nazism, or "civilization" any better than "barbarism." Undoubtedly there are radical skeptics among historians (as we have already pointed out) who appear to enjoy fostering the amoral relativism they find ready-made among their students. But the Protestant Christian at least will find some common ground more readily with one of these relativists than he will with an absolutist who deifies some historical institution or movement or individual. The Christian is too deeply rooted in history to be unconcerned about the strivings and achievements of his own class, nation, or civilization in history. But his nature and destiny can never be understood from the historical perspective alone since man transcends history in addition to being immersed in it. In other words, the prospect of the collapse of our civilization is important (as it is not to a Buddhist), but not all-important (as it is to a humanistic believer in progress). If God is really Lord of history, then no man or group or idea is lord of it.

The Christian can never compromise with men who see the meaning of history exhausted, for instance, in the rise of the Aryan race to world empire under the leadership of a Fuehrer; but he can find a beginning of mutual understanding with men who refuse to deify any hero or cause in history.

In all this there is meant to be no implication that the attitudes of professional historians and of Christians are *necessarily* the same, or even that when parallel attitudes emerge they spring from the same underlying motives. It is simply to say that from the perspective of the mid-twentieth century, Ranke was wrong. There is no inherent and necessary contradiction between being a Christian believer and being a professional historian.

VIII

We are left with a final question. Is there anything *distinctive* about a historian who is also a Christian? What are his marks and how will he be known? How will he understand history and how will he attempt to teach others to understand it?

To many—students, colleagues, and friends—the chief test will be quantitative: the amount of time and attention a historian devotes in his writing and teaching to the place of religion in history. Important as this test undoubtedly is, I believe it is generally overemphasized. A good historian, whether he is a person of religious belief or not, should give religion its due just as he gives every other factor—economic, political, intellectual—its due in his study of the historical process. The current tendency is to ignore or minimize the role of religion in history as the story gets closer to the present. It is no particular surprise to most historians to learn that while the average college text in European history devotes about 30 per cent of its space to religious developments in the Middle Ages, only 2 per cent or less of its space is taken up with specifically religious movements after about 1800.[14] There is no question that a glib unexamined assumption that "religion is through" is often behind this progressive neglect of religious factors as the textbook writers skim over the modern centuries. In any truly impartial search (if such were possible) for what made the nineteenth century tick, religion would bulk much larger than it does in most of our texts. But this is a matter for historians in general to settle with their scholarly consciences. Naturally a historian of Christian leanings will be interested in the religious factors in history and he will probably give them due space. But being human, he will be in constant danger of giving them *too much* space, of "dragging religion in," like the Marxian who distorts the historical picture by overweighting the economic factors. The plain fact is that specifically religious ideas, religious images, religious institutions, and religious influences in general were nowhere near so dominant in the Europe of 1800 as they were in the Europe of 1300, and any historian who blurs this fundamental fact is not being honest. There is no simple quantitative test of a Christian historian. His mark is not the quantity of time he devotes to religious matters, but the quality of his treatment of his subject.

To follow out the example chosen, how will a Protestant Christian historian view the "secularization" of European society since the Middle Ages? How will his view differ, if at all, from the average textbook and classroom treatment? In terms of time and space devoted to religious movements it may differ very little, and yet I fancy there should be a profundity to it which is generally lacking in the ordinary treatment. "Secularization" is an extremely complex and subtle sort of historical process. In many ways people in the Middle Ages were as worldly and immoral as people in our own day,

[14] *College Reading and Religion: A Survey of College Reading Materials,* sponsored by the Edward W. Hazen Foundation (New Haven: Yale University Press, 1948), pp. 209–11.

and considerably more brutal and insensitive in some respects. True, the Church dominated their daily existence, their whole culture became infused with Christian ideals, and there was no real alternative to Christianity as a system of ultimate truth. But when we ask whether the hold of Christianity upon their lives was more or less "totalitarian" than the hold of Nazism upon Germans under Hitler or of Marxism upon Russians under Stalin, the answer is that the hold was probably less total. Nazism and Communism are not religions, but they appeal to the religious emotions of men; they organize themselves along lines strikingly similar to those of the medieval Church, and they make demands upon their followers that are best described as religious. If we grant that they are pseudo-religions, it could even be argued that we live in a more "religious" age than the Middle Ages. Christianity itself is more widely spread over the earth's surface than ever before, and even the economic and political philosophies of our day have to be given a "religious" dynamic in order to move great masses of men. This suggests that "religion," often in a bewildering variety of perverted and idolatrous forms, is still one of the major forces in the twentieth-century world, as it was in the thirteenth. This is an exaggeration, of course, but it may serve to suggest dimensions of the problem of "secularization" which generally remain unseen by "secular" historians and which should be evident to those of Christian belief. The latter should be aware that the concept of secularization is only one of many—and a crude and clumsy one at that—which historians need to describe the historical change which has taken place since 1300. The Western world has become more "worldly" since Dante's day, but to anyone who knows the history of the "Dark Ages," the present battle of the Christian churches with "worldliness" is surely nothing new. The "secularization of society" is a far more subtle affair than it appears to be in most textbooks.

The Christian who is also a historian, then, will be known neither by any fully rounded "philosophy of history" which is the necessary outcome of his Christian belief, nor by the amount of time he spends talking or writing about Christianity. He will be known by *his attitude toward history*, the quality of his concern about it, the sense of reverence and responsibility with which he approaches his subject. This attitude will of course be determined by the quality of his Christian faith and life. The intensity and character of Christian belief varies enormously. An indifferent Roman Catholic will differ a great deal in his attitude toward history from a recent convert, and a Calvinist will see things differently from a Quaker. But I believe it possible to sketch the characteristics of a sort of composite Christian historian, provided the reader remembers that the author of the sketch is a Protestant, and provided both remember that although it is given to all men to follow Christ in any profession, it is given to none to become like his Master.

The attitude of the Christian historian toward the past will be like that of the Christian toward his contemporary fellow beings. He may seldom mention the name of God, of Christ, or of the church, but in every remark he makes in the classroom and in every paragraph he writes in his study there will be a certain reverence and respect for his material, a certain feeling for human tragedy and human triumph in history which is closely parallel to the Christian's respect for human personality in general. He will try to understand before he condemns, and he will condemn with a sense that he too, being human, is involved in any judgment he may make. He will not bleach the moral color out of history by steeping it in corrosive skepticism. Nor on the other hand will he use history as a storehouse from which deceptively simple moral lessons may be drawn at random. He will admire Lord Acton's unquenchable moral fervor in urging historians "to suffer no man and no cause to escape the undying penalty which history

has the power to inflict on wrong," but he will not be impressed either by Acton's historical wisdom or by his Christian
humility in this famous passage. He will have too lively a
sense of his responsibility to his students, his community, and
his society, too deep a sense of the urgency and crisis of his
time, to dismiss the whole story of the past as a tale told by an
idiot, signifying nothing. He will know that to see any meaning at all in history is an act of faith, not a result of studying
documents, but he will not dodge the question for that reason.
He will be aware that every man in his beliefs belongs to *some*
school or party or church, and he will not be afraid to admit
that his own beliefs have their source in a church. He will say
that he thinks them to be far better beliefs than those which
stem, for instance, from the school of skepticism or the Communist party.

At the same time he will remember that he is a teacher, not
a preacher or a pastor; a layman rather than a clergyman. He
will remember that as a layman and a historian he has no more
right to pontificate about the ultimate meaning of history
than his students or his friends. If he is a Protestant, he will
not grant this right to any human being, whether priest or lay.
Where materialists may see mere blind process, where rationalists may see evident progress, he will see providence—a divine
providing in both the conscious decisions and the unintended
results of history, a purpose partly revealed and partly concealed, a destiny which is religious in the deepest meaning of
the word, in which human freedom and divine guidance complete each other in some mysterious way.

He will not blink the fact of evil in history. He will not be
so naïve as to relegate it to a past which is progressively being
left behind, or to an "environment" which can be changed
merely by a little human good will, or to some convenient historical scapegoat such as a "bad" nation, an "inferior" race,
or a "degenerate" class. But he will not leave his hearers or
readers to wallow in masochistic enjoyment of history's folly

and brutality. He will be sensitive to the unpredictable and sometimes unbelievable redemptive forces in history. He will not "know it all." He will neither sell his fellow human beings short, nor will he overrate them. Behind both the personal decisions and the vast impersonal forces of history he will see an inscrutable purpose. He will look for the working of God both in the whirlwinds and in the still small voices of history. He will give a sense of pondering and wondering more than of either dogmatizing or doubting. ". . . And if God's motives are hid, are they therefore unjust?"

There is a sense in which the Christian historian is justified by faith. No man can *know* the meaning of history, but his faith that there is meaning in history may perhaps be counted to him as knowledge in the same sense that faith is counted to the Protestant believer as righteousness. The Christian historian's faith may nourish, enrich, and deepen the faith of those about him for the very reason that it is *not* knowledge. Let us insist upon it again, that it is *an attitude toward history* which is neither assurance nor doubt—*an understanding of history* which is something less than a philosophy but more than a mere frame of mind—it is these that are the marks of a Christian historian. In the last analysis, the attitude a Christian takes toward the history of which he himself is a living part will determine his attitude toward the history which is past.

This will not be enough to some—to an Orthodox Jew, for instance, to a Roman Catholic, or to a fundamentalist Protestant. To many others it will be too much. A professing Christian member of the historical profession will be constantly aware that he is fighting a two-front war, against non-Christians who think he believes too much and super-Christians who think he believes not enough. From the subjective point of view, this consciousness that there is no wall for him to put his back to, may be the ultimate mark of his calling. Deep within him will be the faith, counted to him perhaps as righteousness, that in spite of the conviction of Ranke with which we began, a man may be "first of all a Christian *and* a historian."

BIBLIOGRAPHY

BERDYAEV, NICOLAS. *The Meaning of History*. New York: Charles Scribner's Sons, 1936.

BUTTERFIELD, HERBERT. *Christianity and History*. London: George Bell & Sons, Ltd., 1949.

CASE, SHIRLEY JACKSON. *The Christian Philosophy of History*. Chicago: University of Chicago Press, 1943.

COLLINGWOOD, R. G. *The Idea of History*. New York: Oxford University Press, 1946.

CROCE, BENEDETTO. *History, Its Theory and Practice*. New York: Harcourt, Brace & Co., 1921.

CULLMANN, OSCAR. *Christ et le temps*. Neuchâtel and Paris: Delachaux et Niestlé, 1947.

LÖWITH, KARL. *Meaning in History: The Theological Implications of the Philosophy of History*. Chicago: University of Chicago Press, 1949.

NIEBUHR, REINHOLD. *Faith and History: A Comparison of Christian and Modern Views of History*. New York: Charles Scribner's Sons, 1949.

ROSENSTOCK-HUESSY, EUGEN. *The Christian Future or the Modern Mind Outrun*. New York: Charles Scribner's Sons, 1946.

RUST, E. C. *The Christian Understanding of History*. London: Lutterworth Press, 1947.

TILLICH, PAUL. *The Protestant Era*. Chicago: University of Chicago Press, 1948.

TOYNBEE, ARNOLD J. *Civilization on Trial*. New York: Oxford University Press, 1948.

WOOD, H. G. *Christianity and the Nature of History*. New York: The Macmillan Co., 1934.

WOOD, H. G., *et al*. *The Kingdom of God and History*. Chicago: Willet, Clark & Co., 1938.

4

PHILOSOPHY

By THEODORE M. GREENE

THE PROBLEM

What are the "religious issues, implications, and responsibilities involved in the teaching of philosophy"? This is a highly controversial question today and one to which very different answers are being given by able philosophers and by responsible religious leaders.

Many contemporary philosophers, among them some of the most influential here in America and abroad, are convinced that all religious beliefs lack objective validity and that it is therefore one of the major tasks of philosophy to unmask religious pretension, discredit faith in any kind of a Deity, and develop a purely secular philosophy in which religion, at least in any of its traditional forms, has no place. This, they would say, is the intellectual responsibility of the honest and competent philosopher to his students, his institution, and his society.

A good many contemporary theologians entertain a suspicion of philosophy as profound as is the skeptical philosopher's suspicion of religion. This arises in some cases from their conception of God as a Being who is so mysterious that human reason is wholly incapable of apprehending Him; in other cases, from the conviction that reason is radically perverted and perverse unless it is made absolutely subservient to religious faith; and, very frequently, from the belief that the Truth has been proclaimed to man by God with such authority and finality, whether through an authoritative church or a verbally inerrant Bible, that reason's only function is to accept and elucidate what is already indubitably known to the devout believer. Any one of these conceptions suffices to arouse profound suspicion of, if not open hostility to, any philosophical inquiry which accepts the general reliability of human reason and the right of philosophy to examine critically all beliefs, even those hallowed by ecclesiastical authority and endorsed by an intense religious faith. Such critical inquiry is branded as "pagan rationalism" against which the orthodox believer must be protected at all costs.

It is unlikely that what I have to say will be congenial or convincing to the dogmatically antireligious philosopher or the dogmatically antirational believer. I must address myself to those who are at least willing to consider open-mindedly Professor Robert L. Calhoun's assertion, that "High religion and intellectual enterprise belong together. Each gains from close association with the other. The two in conjunction, but neither one by itself, can move with hope toward more effective conquest of the chaos that again and again threatens to engulf human living." [1] I shall attempt to show that a "liberal" Christianity and an equally "liberal" philosophy do, in fact, imply one another and are essential to the survival of a "liberal" cultural tradition. Let us start by examining the nature of philosophy at its best.

The Nature of Philosophical Inquiry

There are certain characteristics of the philosophical enterprise which all philosophers, of whatever persuasion, would agree are crucial, though they would not all formulate them in exactly the same way. These characteristics can conveniently be described in terms of a distinctly philosophical attitude, scope, orientation, and method.

[1] "The Place of Religion in Higher Education," Hazen Pamphlet No. 2, p. 10.

1. The *attitude* characteristic of a philosopher is one of radical inquiry into all human beliefs, however self-evident they may seem or however sanctified by secular or religious authority. It is the privilege and the duty of philosophy to analyze all experience and its data without predetermined conclusions. This critical temper extends itself to an examination of all institutions and their mores, to all social conventions and cultural heritages, and to the presuppositions, procedures and conclusions of all the other disciplines, including experimental science, historical research, the social studies, the criticism of literature and the fine arts, and the theological formulations of religious faith. It is also directed to the philosophical enterprise itself—to its own presuppositions, its own ways of knowing, and the reliability of its own conclusions. All philosophers would agree that to be credulous, uncritical, and dogmatic on *any* issue is, by definition, to be unphilosophical.

2. Philosophy can also be distinguished from the other disciplines by its *scope*. Its scope is all-embracing; its field of inquiry includes the whole of reality knowable to man and the sum-total of human experience. The other disciplines are, by comparison, limited in scope both "horizontally" and "vertically"—horizontally, in the sense that each focuses upon certain aspects of reality and certain types of experience to the exclusion of others; vertically in the sense that these disciplines do not normally examine their own basic presuppositions. Thus, physics restricts itself to a certain type of experimental exploration of the physical structure and behavior of the spatio-temporal world, ignoring, as irrelevant to its particular enterprise, the distinguishing characteristics of living organisms, of man as a moral agent, of works of art, and of the God of religious worship. Similar self-imposed restrictions characterize all other specialized inquiries. Each has its delimited subject matter and each makes various necessary assumptions which it, quite properly, does not pause to examine. Philosophy, in contrast, surveys the "horizontal" interrelation of all these fields

of inquiry and of all the resultant bodies of knowledge; it also accepts as its special task the "vertical" scrutiny of all the assumptions of all the special disciplines and of the nature and criteria of all human knowledge and evaluation.

This characterization of philosophy in terms of its greater scope is useful despite the fact that the "horizontal" boundaries of the specialized disciplines are by no means rigidly established, each discipline tending increasingly as it advances to overlap certain other disciplines. The growing interpenetration of physics and chemistry, chemistry and biology, biology and psychology, psychology and sociology indicates that these disciplines are concerned not with radically different realities but rather with different aspects of the same all-embracing reality, and that the chief generic types of experience are in fact interrelated phases of a single all-embracing human experience.

3. The "vertical" scope of philosophy can also be described as an *orientation* to "ultimates," if "ultimate" is defined not as an unconditioned Absolute, but as the limit of man's most penetrating insight at any given point in his cultural evolution. To be oriented to ultimates is to ask the most probing questions which the human mind can devise, however controversial the best available answers to these questions may be. The philosopher is forever in search of the most profound understanding of the physical world, of human history, of art and beauty, and of the goal of religious aspiration.

I have used the term "ultimate" in order to avoid the suggestion that philosophy can ever achieve absolute knowledge or absolute certainty. Reality itself can properly be said to be absolutely what it is, and its innermost and irreducible essence might be referred to as the Absolute with a capital A. Since the philosopher is continuously trying to discover what reality is in itself, he is in this sense searching for the Absolute. But unless we believe, as some philosophers do, in the possibility of indubitable human insights into the nature of this Absolute, we must insist on the partiality and fallibility of all human knowledge, and we must brand any claim to complete adequacy or certainty of comprehension as the fallacy of "misplaced absoluteness." This fallacy is incurred in all dogmatism, whether secular or religious; hence such dogmatism is fundamentally unphilosophical. Philosophy should strive for more and more penetrating insights into the nature of reality, but with the full realization that any attainable ultimate is still humanly finite and fallible and therefore not to be identified with an inerrant knowledge of the absolute nature of reality itself.

4. The relation of philosophy to the other disciplines can also be described by saying that the distinctive *method* of philosophy is "dialectical," that is, simultaneously inductive and deductive in its relation to the other disciplines. The philosopher generalizes from the inductive findings of his more specialized colleagues and, simultaneously, explores deductively the implications of his basic principles of interpretation for each of their more specialized fields.

Philosophy is, I believe, necessarily inductive in that it is obliged to take seriously into account our ever growing and ever changing body of empirical information regarding ourselves, our human experiences, and our total environment. This statement involves the assumption that philosophy has no distinctive subject-matter of its own which it alone seeks to investigate, and that every type of human experience and every aspect of reality available to human exploration are already being studied, or can in principle be studied, at closer range and in greater empirical detail by one or more of the specialized disciplines. This assumption would be challenged by certain philosophers and therefore requires a word of explanation.

Every discipline, including philosophy, has its distinctive approach, problems, and basic concepts. If "subject-matter" is defined to signify these, philosophy, like the other disciplines, does of course have a "subject-matter" of its own. But if "subject-matter" is defined to mean an aspect or area of our total environment, or a type of generic human experience, we must, I think, say that philosophy has no "subject-matter" which is not also the concern of one or more of the specialized disciplines. The philosopher is interested in the physical world, but so are the natural scientists; in art and beauty, but so are the critics of art and literature; in human history, but so is the historian; in the Absolute, but so is the theologian. The perspective of these specialists is more limited than that of the philosopher, but he and they are concerned with the same reality and the same human experiences. Philosophy differs from the other disciplines not in possessing a unique subject-matter, but merely in approaching all aspects of reality and types of experience in a distinctively synoptic manner.

This approach gives the philosopher a certain advantage over his more specialized colleagues, but this advantage is balanced by certain limitations. In metaphorical terms, he views the plain of human endeavor from the aerial perspective of the mountaintop, but from this vantage point he cannot study at short range the trees and fields, cities and houses, in all their detail. He will not, as philosopher, indulge in firsthand scientific experiment or sociological survey or literary criticism; he must depend upon the findings of his more empirically oriented co-workers, as they, in turn should rely on his help for a more inclusive and more ultimate interpretation of their methods and conclusions.

Such philosophical interpretation should, in turn, have its deductive repercussions in each of the empirical disciplines. Just as, within each of these disciplines, the "upward" or inductive movement of thought from particulars to wider and wider generalization is balanced by the "downward" or deductive movement from abstract generalizations or hypotheses to their observational implications, so too does philosophical dialectic involve a two-way movement—the "upward" inductive movement from the several empirical disciplines into the realm of maximum philosophical generality, and the "downward" deductive movement from basic philosophical prin ciples to their implications in the several empirical realms Thus, it is the physicists, not the philosophers, who discove new truths regarding the physical world, but it is the philoso pher who is best qualified to discuss the presuppositions o physics and the ways in which the truths of physics can bes be related to the truths issuing from man's other empirical in quiries. These philosophical analyses and assessments shoulc be of great interest and value to the physicist who would like to see his own enterprise in a wider setting.

This account of the relation of philosophy to the empirica disciplines is not meant to imply that only professional phi losophers philosophize. Actually, the boldest and most pro found thinkers in all the empirical realms must themselves be more or less philosophically oriented and skilled. The philoso pher who would shrewdly interpret the presuppositions methods, and conclusions of empirical research must, in turn be able to understand such research, and this understanding is greatly aided by some firsthand experience in the severa fields and particularly by a capacity for imaginative projection and assimilation. We must recognize, however, that the effec tive passage from one level of inquiry to another is becoming increasingly difficult because of the growing complexity of philosophical interpretation and of the several fields of em pirical knowledge. This partly explains the tendency of em pirical specialists to be somewhat naïve philosophically, and of professional philosophers either to specialize in some branch of philosophy, such as logic or aesthetics, to the partial neglect of other branches of philosophy and of the ultimate philo sophical task, or else to attempt a metaphysical synthesis with out adequate empirical orientation in one or more crucial direc tions. This lack of philosophical sophistication in empirical circles, and this lack of empirical rootage or proper balance in philosophical circles, are as deplorable as they are understand able, but a practical remedy is not easy to find. It must be ought, I believe, in closer cooperation between professional philosophers and the experts in the several major fields of empirical research, since no man can hope today to emulate the synoptic achievement of Plato or Aristotle, St. Thomas or Hegel.

The account here given of philosophy, or of the philosophical component or dimension of human knowledge, is based on an extension of the Kantian dictum that concepts without percepts are empty, percepts without concepts, blind. I am assuming, in short, that reason cannot spin a knowledge of reality out of itself by sole reliance upon logical noncontradiction, and that primary experiences, whatever their quality and intensity, can never in and of themselves constitute knowledge. All knowledge is the product of rational interpretation of empirical evidence. This is equally true of the more richly empirical reaches of knowledge and of the most abstract philosophical generalizations. To understand and evaluate any particular experience involves putting it in a wider empirical context; to understand any empirical discipline involves relating it to other empirical disciplines in a still wider philosophical context. In this sense it is meaningful to say that all knowledge is ultimately philosophical. But no philosophical generalization has any meaning save in relation to generic types of experience explored by the several specialized disciplines, and these generic types of experience and these empirical disciplines, in turn, mean nothing apart from the particular experiences which exemplify the genus, or apart from the specific observations on which all specialized knowledge must be based. Hence all knowledge, including the most universal philosophical insights, must be inductively rooted; a philosophy which is not finally anchored in primary human experiences is empty, meaningless verbiage.

Two conclusions follow from this conception of philosophy. The first is that a philosophy will itself be provincial in scope if its interpretations of "experience" are narrow, and will be truly synoptic only if it bases itself broadly on *all* the generic types of human experience without initial prejudice. Much contemporary philosophy must, it seems to me, be described as provincial because it so dogmatically rejects man's value experiences, and particularly his religious experiences, as being, by definition, unproductive of significant contacts with, and clues to, the existence and nature of the objectively real—in short, because it limits itself so exclusively, for its empirical anchorage, to man's sensory experiences. This, surely, is the opposite counterpart of a mystical type of provincialism which exhibits a corresponding prejudice against sensory evidence of a physical world and which bases itself exclusively upon certain mystical experiences. Both types of philosophy are one-sided for the same reason, namely, the unjustifiable repudiation of a whole area of human experience which may well be rich in empirical clues to the nature of the real.

The second conclusion follows from the inductive aspect of philosophical reflection. No philosophical interpretations of reality and human experience can be absolutely certain or rationally demonstrable beyond all possible doubt. In their own way, philosophical conclusions must be as tentative and hypothetical as are the conclusions of the empirical disciplines upon which philosophy must lean so heavily. Like them, philosophy is an on-going concern, a continual re-examination of evidence and an ever renewed interpretation of reality in the light of all available human experience. A philosopher dare not even assume that his most basic concepts and procedures are final and absolute. Philosophy affords no omniscient encounter with Reality, no privileged access to Absolute Truth. Such authority as it has derives entirely from its distinctive perspective, scope and orientation and method, and this authority carries with it the limitations of a distant, embracing view. It lacks the wealth of empirical particularity and the capacity for concrete experiment and verification of the empirical disciplines. Its authority is therefore not superior to theirs but complements theirs.

This conception of philosophy and its relation to the other disciplines will be disputed by some contemporary philosophers of differing persuasions. Some place greater reliance on pure philosophical reason and believe that the philosopher can arrive at some significant truths which are absolutely final and indubitable. These "rationalists" would claim for philosophy an authority greater and more absolute than I would claim. Others, who might be labeled "physical empiricists," base themselves exclusively on the physical sciences and sense perception and deny that value experiences are revelatory. Still others would validate man's moral and aesthetic insights but would on principle regard all religious beliefs as invalid, insisting that the convictions characteristic of a "high" religion are no more credible than are the crudest superstitions of a primitive religion. These might be called "antireligious humanists." Finally, there are many philosophers today who either repudiate or ignore metaphysical interpretations of reality as a whole and whose sole concern is highly specialized research in logic or semantics. In what follows, I shall use the term "philosophy" to signify the type of philosophy I have described, recognizing that the "rationalists," the "physical empiricists," the "antireligious humanists," and the antimetaphysical logicians and semanticists will all disagree in varying degrees and often for very different reasons.

THE NATURE OF RELIGION

The critical study of the complex phenomenon "religion" does not, of course, fall outside the domain of philosophy. A comprehensive philosophy will concern itself with all types of human experience and all claims to valid insight, and religion is not only a fact in human experience but, in addition, it makes claims of which philosophy must take serious account. Men of religion have always claimed that religion is, or involves, distinctive encounter with, and a response to, a real

Being or beings conceived of as not only dynamic and active, but as the source of whatever quality and meaning human existence can have. They have also claimed that their belief in this "saving" divine power, thus encountered, is a valid, not an erroneous, belief. This is a claim which a conscientious philosopher dare not ignore. He must first try to understand the experience in question and then seek to interpret and assess the alleged validity of the associated beliefs.

This generic religious experience is found to possess, in all its historical exemplifications, three basic components which can conveniently be designated by the terms "creed," "cult," and "conduct." These terms signify, for the individual, the beliefs which he himself holds, the religious acts which he performs, and his religiously motivated attitudes and actions towards his fellow men. The same components reappear in every institutionalized religion. The credal component is a more or less articulated body of traditional beliefs regarding the Deity or deities worshipped. In primitive religions these beliefs are normally expressed in story and myth; in a developed religion they are also formulated and interpreted systematically in a theology. As a cult, a religion prescribes various acts of public and private worship, involving the use of symbolism and ritual established under the disciplinary sanction of a continuing institution which, in Christianity, is the church. Every historical religion has also prescribed various social attitudes and patterns of moral conduct which are felt to be consonant with its beliefs.

Though each of these components is integral to a religion and is always present in some form and to some degree, the act of worship is, from the religious point of view, the most basic. For religion, even the most primitive, is first and foremost man's attempt to relate himself, in what he believes to be the most appropriate and effective way, to what he conceives to be an objectively real Deity or actually existing deities, and this relationship is what the generic term "worship" signifies. Such worship cannot be wholly divorced from some belief, however vague and inarticulate, in the objective reality of the Being or beings worshipped; it is psychologically impossible to "worship" what is believed to be merely a phantom of one's own imagination, or a mere social ideal. It is also psychologically necessary that the worshipper believe that the Deity or deities he worships be at least partially knowable; it is impossible to worship a wholly unknown and unknowable deity. No religion, therefore, can exist without a credal component. Such belief, in turn, whatever its specific content, invariably has certain implications regarding human nature and man's resultant obligations to his fellow men. It is true that some religions have become so stereotyped and religiously sterile that the moral implications of their professed beliefs have been largely ignored or forgotten, but this is not the case in any religion, primitive or advanced, which possesses religious vitality. The heart and center of this vitality, meanwhile, is the act of religious communion with what is judged to be the divine. It is this communion, interpreted as a real encounter, that constitutes the religious experiences in which the emergent beliefs are rooted and by reference to which they are tested and verified, modified or abandoned, and it is from this communion that the worshipper ultimately derives his sense of obligation to act in a manner pleasing to the divine and his motivation to make every effort so to act. In this crucial sense, cult, in the triad of creed, cult, and conduct, is *primus inter pares*.

The religions of mankind differ enormously, however, in respect to all three of these essential components—in content of belief, in institutionalized tradition and ritual, and in prescribed moral attitude and behavior. We cannot here review these differences; we can merely emphasize one differentiation which is crucial to our discussion, that, namely, between what is sometimes referred to as a "high" or "developed" religion and a "low" or "primitive" religion.

A religion can be said to be "low" or "primitive" in proportion as its beliefs are superstitious, its ritualistic practices magical, its basic orientation egocentric and anthropocentric rather than theocentric, its social precepts directed to conventional correctness rather than to inner spiritual righteousness, and its prevailing attitude arbitrarily authoritarian and dogmatic. A religion is "high," in contrast, in proportion as its beliefs are reflective and enlightened, its ritualistic practices expressive of a belief not in magic but in orderly processes, both natural and spiritual, its orientation theocentric, its moral precepts directed to inner spiritual purity, and its prevailing attitude one of reflective commitment, humility and tolerance. These criteria for the differentiation of "high" and "low" religion will not recommend themselves to those who believe that all religions are equally superstitious, magical, obscurantist, and arbitrarily authoritarian. But they are meaningful and useful for those who are able to accept the actuality, or even the possibility, of valid and enlightened religious belief and practice.

Superstition is partly the result of ignorance, but it cannot be identified with mere ignorance; we would hardly call a man superstitious who lacks certain information and acknowledges that lack, nor would we call him superstitious merely because he is mistaken. Superstition is also partly a function of credulity, yet it cannot be equated with a wholehearted acceptance of a belief; we would not call a man superstitious because he firmly believes in an orderly world of nature and in the validity of scientific inquiry. Superstition can better be defined as belief in arbitrariness rather than order, or as belief which is uncritical and dogmatic rather than critical and open-minded. Religious belief is superstitious, then, in proportion as it is a belief in a Deity or deities conceived to function in an arbitrary and irrational manner, and, further, in proportion as this belief is held in a spirit of blind and uncritical credulity. Religious belief in an objective spiritual order, in contrast, or in a Divine

Being who is the source of orderly processes and who conforms to them, may be mistaken, as any scientific or philosophical belief may be mistaken, but it should not be branded as superstitious merely on that account. Such a theistic belief may furthermore be held with great conviction without thereby becoming superstitious. It becomes superstitious only when it is regarded as final and indubitable, i.e., when it is divorced from a sense of human finitude and fallibility.

Superstition, so defined, almost inevitably involves a reliance in magic, that is, in the possibility of invoking and controlling irrational spiritual powers or forces by means of procedures which are correspondingly irrational. "Black" magic involves a belief in demonic forces and, normally, the attempt to make use of such forces to bring harm to others; "white" magic involves belief in beneficent forces and is normally used for beneficent purposes. In both cases the resort to magic involves the performance of essentially arbitrary acts in order to cajole or coerce essentially arbitrary spiritual forces to promote certain desired human ends. A belief in magic and an indulgence in magical practices, so defined, characterize "primitive" or "low" religions, whereas "high" religion condemns all such belief in, and resort to, magic, whether black or white.

A further characteristic of religious primitivism is its egocentric and anthropocentric orientation; the corresponding hallmark of a "high" religion is its theocentric orientation. By an egocentric orientation is meant a primary desire on the part of the worshipper to use the Deity or deities for his own advantage; by an anthropocentric orientation is meant a corresponding preoccupation with mankind, and the attempt to use the divine primarily to further human ends and human welfare. A religion is theocentric, in contrast, which ascribes ultimate value to the Deity and which therefore conceives of worship as consisting, first and foremost, in reverent adoration.

This attitude of reverence is frequently misinterpreted by the critics of religion as necessarily implying a sadistic indifference to human welfare and even a masochistic indifference of the pious worshipper to his own welfare. Such indifference has indeed on occasion characterized theistic belief, but it is certainly completely at variance with "high" religion, e.g., Judaism or Christianity. The conception of God as not only holy and righteous but as a loving Father means that reverence for God constitutes not only man's proper response to the Divine initiative but, in addition, man's own highest felicity; and the Hebraic-Christian exhortation to love our fellow men and to seek to promote their true welfare because we are all equally the children of the same loving Father is a perfectly logical corollary of the Hebraic-Christian conception of the Deity. The twofold commandment, to love God *and* to love our neighbor as we love ourselves, should be a conclusive answer to the oft-repeated charge that Judaism and Christianity are essentially committed to an otherworldly indifference to human needs or to a self-destructive asceticism.

Yet Judaism and Christianity, like other theistic religions, merit the designation "high" only in proportion as they insist that the sole proper object of religious reverence and ultimate loyalty is God Himself, not mankind, or any of man's self-generated ideals, or the self with all its egocentric proclivities. Within this theocentric orientation, mankind and the self fall into their proper place in the hierarchy of being and value. All men, however sinful, possess an inalienable God-given value which should elicit respect and love, but not reverence, and each individual, as an immortal God-created soul, is under similar obligation not to make an idol of himself but to respect himself and to promote his own welfare *through* devotion to the welfare of others and ultimate devotion to God.

The moral precepts of a "high" religion are all focused upon inner spiritual righteousness which reflects, so far as possible, the righteousness of God and which expresses itself in just and

beneficent human conduct, whereas the emphasis in "primi-
ive" religion is on strict conformity to conventional stereo-
.ypes of behavior which have the sanction of traditional ortho-
loxy. Here the contrast is between "purity of heart" and an
undeviating obedience to more and more particularized pat-
.erns of individual and social behavior. This emphasis of
"high" religion on inner attitude does not, as is sometimes
charged, imply an indifference to overt actions and their social
consequences. On the contrary, the pragmatic test of the
authenticity of inner attitude is asserted to be appropriate overt
behavior and a lively concern for the social results of one's
actions. What is condemned by "high" religion is the rigidifi-
cation of specific codes of behavior, the absolutizing of specific
actions as being not only always right but as satisfying, in and
of themselves, all the requirements of a religiously motivated
morality. The more "primitive" a religion, in contrast, the
more does it ignore inner attitude and spiritual self-discipline
and the more does it emphasize correctness of external behavior and the heinousness of deviation from the prevailing
orthodoxy.

It is inevitable that "high" religion, as here described, should
be dynamic rather than static, critical rather than dogmatic,
and productive of tolerance and humility rather than of intolerance and arrogance, whereas a "primitive" religion will tend
to be the precise opposite. Belief in arbitrariness must itself
be arbitrary and dogmatic, hostile to criticism and incapable of
reflective self-examination and reform. Belief in magic must
express itself in a concern for correct procedures, and the more
unintelligible and irrational these procedures are, the more
must their mechanical correctness be emphasized. Furthermore, since the object of religious concern is not here conceived
of as itself righteous or worthy of man's reverence, man is
inevitably tempted to exploit it for his own individual advantage or to elevate an ecclesiastical institution and the ritual
prescribed by it to a position of ultimate religious importance.

Hence the tendency of "primitive" religion to idolatry, whether the idol be a figure of stone or clay, a priest, a church, a sacred document, a theological system, or a saintly life; hence the claims to infallibility and absolute authority; hence also an inevitable intolerance and bigotry. "High" religion, in contrast, has within itself its own safeguards against all these "perversions" of religion. Its theocentric orientation enables it to recognize and condemn all idolatries as the substitution of humanity and human artifacts for the Deity himself. Its conception of God as alone omniscient and wholly righteous, and of man as intellectually and spiritually finite, enables it to unmask and condemn all human pretensions to infallibility and saintliness. Its belief in a God who, though mysterious, is partly knowable, and who, though transcendent, is also self-revelatory, invites an attitude of reflective commitment and tends to generate a progressively enlightened faith, rooted in an evolving religious experience and capable of increasing theological articulation, yet ever mindful of God's ultimate mystery and man's inescapable limitations. St. Paul's exclamation, "now we *see* through a glass *darkly*" well expresses this middle ground between blank ignorance and smug assurance. We do see, but only through the glass of mortal finitude; we do know, but not with complete clarity or certainty. Such a belief, if sincerely and intelligently held, is well calculated to generate humility and tolerance.

I have taken pains to describe "high" and "primitive" religion in such a way as not to suggest that any historical religion, past or present, is "high" or "primitive" without qualification. Certainly historical Christianity, in its present-day institutional expressions, is not unqualifiedly "high." All religions, as complex historical phenomena, reflect the strengths and the weaknesses of their adherents, and Christianity is no exception. In actual practice Christianity is today by no means devoid of dogmatic intolerance, of superstitious appeals to

nagic, of idolatries of various sorts, and of concern with ecclesiastical orthodoxy and correctness of prescribed behavior. It
is a "high" religion, I would urge, only in proportion as it
avoids these characteristics of primitivism and as it becomes
dynamic, reflective, tolerant, and mature.

This surely, is not an unreasonable way in which to analyze
and assess the religions of mankind. It is in fact the way in
which we analyze and assess all other human enterprises. The
science we praise is science at its dynamic evolving best, not
the stupidity, arrogance, or bigotry of those who have called
themselves scientists without exemplifying what we conceive
to be the true scientific spirit. The democracy we praise is the
ideal of democracy which our own and other democracies fall
short of in so many respects. In trying to understand and
evaluate any complex human enterprise we must be discriminating, recognizing its gradual historical evolution, and judging
its present-day achievements and failures by reference to some
norm. To identify science with its primitive beginnings and
its long record of mistakes would be as stupid as it would be
to identify it, as an actual historical phenomenon, with our
ideal of scientific objectivity, precision, and verification. It is
no less stupid to identify religion with its earliest manifestations in history or its present-day primitivisms, or, alternatively,
to regard any historical religion as the perfect exemplification
of all that a religion can and should be.

In any case, the only type of religion wholly compatible
with philosophy at *its* best is "high" religion, or, more accurately, a religion in proportion as it is "high," that is, reflective,
tolerant, and undogmatic; and, reversely, the only type of philosophy which is compatible with "high" religion is a philosophy which is true to itself in being open-minded and undogmatic. High religion and mature philosophy so defined are
equally critical both of religious primitivism and of philosophical antireligious dogmatism.

Philosophy and Religion—Rivals or Allies?

It is an historical fact that philosophy and religion have again and again complemented one another as allies; they have also repeatedly competed with one another as bitter rivals. They have been able to assist one another because of their complementary differences; they have competed with one another whenever they have generated conflicting beliefs and particularly when either has dogmatically repudiated the potential contributions of the other. It is therefore important to formulate as precisely as possible their crucial similarities and differences, and to examine somewhat more closely the major sources of mutual hostility and the conditions of friendly cooperation.

Both similarities and differences are briefly indicated in the statement of principles quoted in the Preface: "Although it [high religion] is metaphysical, ethical, and humanitarian, it cannot be equated with metaphysics, or ethics, or humanitarianism." This means that whereas philosophy is primarily a process of intellectual inquiry, issuing in a metaphysical interpretation of reality and an ethical analysis of human conduct, religion is primarily "man's quest for communion with an ultimate spiritual reality" and his attempt to live his life oriented to this reality. In short, philosophy is characteristically an intellectual pursuit; religion is first and foremost a distinctive type of experience and way of life.

Philosophy, however, is not merely a method of intellectual inquiry and a conceptual interpretation of reality and human behavior; its various accounts of man and the cosmos themselves suggest, and even dictate, appropriate ways of life. Religion, in turn, is not merely a quest for communion with the Divine and a way of life; it is a body of beliefs, varying from one religion to another, about the cosmos and man's place in it. Hence, philosophy and religion inevitably tend to overlap, both at the level of speculation and at the level of conduct. This overlapping, at both levels, is a source of potential and actual rivalry; but it also provides the opportunity for mutually helpful cooperation.

Particularly in a secular period such as ours, philosophy tends to become a self-sufficient "philosophy of life" and therefore a substitute for religion in its traditional forms. Contemporary philosophy, for instance, has set itself up as a rival to religion in at least three distinguishable ways: by deriving a system of ethics from a metaphysic, and a way of life from this system of ethics; by conceiving of ethics as an autonomous discipline, independent of metaphysics but prescriptive of moral conduct; and by transforming itself into a humanitarianism in making human welfare its highest good and in regarding "scientific method" as the only reliable guide for individual conduct and social reform. Each of these three procedures seems, to its adherents, to provide so satisfactory a "way of life" as to make religion unnecessary.

1. Metaphysical systems, whether they be "idealistic" or "materialistic," monistic or dualistic, etc., are bound to have certain implications regarding human nature and man's ability to adapt himself to the reality with which he is confronted. These implications, in turn, dictate certain attitudes toward the universe and toward oneself and one's fellows, as well as certain patterns of private life and social behavior. In short, every metaphysic tends to generate a system of ethics and to point to a "way of life" which is conformable to this system. A philosopher who takes his metaphysical thinking seriously will feel bound to develop a system of ethics conformable to it and, furthermore, to attempt to live up to the practical injunctions dictated by this system. Plato and Aristotle, the Stoics and the Epicureans, Lucretius and Spinoza, Kant and Hegel, Josiah Royce and Bertrand Russell, can all be cited as examples of philosophers who have followed this procedure and who have developed "philosophies of life" which can be said to be,

though in very different ways, substitutes for religiously oriented ways of life.

2. There are some philosophers who believe that ethics can and should be a relatively self-contained philosophical discipline which is capable, at least in principle, of being developed into an "exact" or rigorous "science," and, as such, can provide a thoughtful person with reliable guidance for his private life and his social behavior. These philosophers are either uninterested in metaphysical speculation and wholly preoccupied with ethical analysis and its practical applications, or else they regard metaphysics as so incorrigibly "speculative" and controversial that it can never serve as a reliable basis for ethics and therefore for a practical way of life. The British utilitarians, Bentham, J. S. Mill, and Sidgwick, and, more recently, philosophers as various as G. E. Moore and Brand Blanshard, may be cited as variant examples of this position. Their attitude to religion is not necessarily hostile; indeed, it can be sympathetic and friendly. But in their predominant concern with man's secular experiences of satisfaction and dissatisfaction, pleasure and pain, their "philosophies of life" tend to be divorced from any vital religious orientation.

3. The third philosophical rival to religion might be entitled "reflective humanitarianism." It differs from the position just described in its insistence that ethical analysis is valid and valuable only in proportion as it does in fact promote human welfare, and, further, in its emphasis on a method of inquiry and verification rather than on any explicit ethical doctrines or standards. It resembles the position of ethical autonomy in its suspicion of traditional metaphysics, though its adherents are usually sympathetic to some type of naturalism. American pragmatism or instrumentalism exemplifies this tendency to make human welfare the object of man's ultimate allegiance, to stress the importance of individual and corporate effort to promote this welfare, to rely on "scientific method" as the only reliable guide to responsible human conduct, and

to distrust metaphysical speculation. John Dewey's critical rejection of all traditional religions because of their belief in an "anterior" spiritual Being, and his desire to substitute for religion the "religious" attitude, that is, loyalty to man-made ideals and the cooperative effort to actualize these ideals, indicates the extent to which this program finds itself in opposition to traditional Christianity and to all other world religions. A "humanitarianism" of this type is so predominantly a way of life that it must be regarded as a secular substitute for religion.

In so far as the exponents of these three positions are *dogmatically* secular in outlook, the philosophies of life which they advocate will necessarily be irreligious if not antireligious on any traditional definition of religions. So long as they refuse a priori to take man's religious experiences seriously, that is, as possibly constituting "encounters" with an objectively real Deity and therefore as the empirical source of verifiable religious insight, their metaphysical accounts of reality must ignore the God of religious worship, their ethics must lack all religious orientation and motivation, and their ultimate loyalty must be to mankind. I can see no reason, however, why these three philosophical approaches need necessarily be indifferent or hostile to religion, if the philosophers who favor these approaches exemplify the philosophical objectivity which they profess. What is there to prevent a metaphysically minded philosopher from developing a metaphysic which takes the religious experience and its proper claims fully into account? This is precisely what religiously minded metaphysicians, whether non-Christian or Christian, Roman Catholic or Protestant, have done. Why should the attempt to develop a rigorous ethic necessarily ignore whatever is valid and verifiable in Christian ethics? Or why should an instrumentalist concern with a fruitful method of inquiry and vigorous social reform designed to promote human welfare necessarily reject whatever in our Hebraic-Christian tradition is experimentally verifiable and in fact productive of human welfare?

Such an open-minded, though critical, approach to religion at its best would undoubtedly dictate significant changes—metaphysical, ethical, and practical—in all three philosophical approaches, if religion is in fact found to be productive of valid insights and possessed of unique spiritual resources. But the realization that such changes would be required should not dismay a metaphysician whose chief concern is the truth rather than a defense of his particular formulation of it, or a student of ethics who wants his ethical system to be as adequate and useful to mankind as possible, or an instrumentalist who is really concerned with human welfare and unprejudiced experimentation. The obstacle to such a reconciliation of philosophy to religion is always, on the part of philosophy, some type of rationalistic, secular dogmatism which, I must repeat, is essentially unphilosophical.

Religion, meanwhile, must inevitably try to develop a more or less coherent system of beliefs regarding the Deity or deities which are worshipped, and regarding the cosmos and man's relation to it and to the divine. In their more developed forms, religions tend to articulate in great theological detail a full-blown metaphysics and a carefully worked-out system of ethics. In proportion as religion also lapses, as it continually does, into some form of dogmatic and authoritarian primitivism, it is bound to find itself in opposition to science and philosophy at their responsible best, both in doctrine and basic attitude. This primitivism may express itself in an idolatrous or superstitious ritualism in which a religious rite becomes an end in itself, or a magical device, instead of a spiritually helpful vehicle for religious communion. Or it may express itself in the form of ecclesiastical idolatry; here the church, with all its human limitations, becomes the object of highest veneration or the source of infallible wisdom. These perversions of man's religious quest are of course opposed to the spirit of scientific and philosophical inquiry. Religious authoritarianism may also express itself in a rigid theology and a code of ethics ad hered to with dogmatic finality and therefore necessarily hostile to scientific discovery and philosophical criticism.

But it is only such theological and ecclesiastical rigidity, based upon a pretension to infallibility, which is radically opposed to free and honest metaphysical interpretation, ethical analysis, and humane social movements at their secular best, and which is therefore reactionary rather than conservative, dictatorial rather than spiritually assured. "High" religion, as I have described it, is not only not hostile to secular discoveries and philosophical inquiry; it openly welcomes all such discoveries and all responsible destructive and constructive philosophical criticism. It explicitly repudiates obscurantism and superstition, and it disassociates itself from all magic. While recognizing the inability of the human mind to fathom exhaustively the deepest mysteries of reality, both in its spatio-temporal and its spiritual aspects, it none the less accepts the basic reliability of human reason. It therefore never fears responsible philosophical interpretation or scientific discovery. Though it asserts the reality of a Deity who transcends the spatio-temporal order of nature, it does not conceive of this Deity as irrational or arbitrary, either in His own nature or in His manifestation of Himself in nature and in human history. In short, "high" religion, to use the language of theology, is never fearful that any human truths will contradict God's Truth.

Philosophy and religion need not therefore be rivals or hostile to one another; it is only stubborn dogmatism, either secular or religious, which calls for radical opposition. They can, on the other hand, be allies partly because their distinctive emphases complement each other and partly because they inevitably overlap in important respects. Religion is most like philosophy in its credal component, and it is precisely here that it must turn to philosophy for help in achieving theological precision, scope, internal coherence, and orientation to secular discovery. Philosophy, in turn, in its quest for the most inclusive knowledge of reality as a whole and in its concern for the wisest and most realistically oriented philosophy of life, dare not ignore the religious claims to a unique type of insight productive of a unique type of spiritual power. It should base itself empirically upon man's religious experiences as well as his secular experiences and be prepared to help men avail themselves of whatever Divine power may be at their disposal in addition to natural forces and human effort.

Objections and Replies

There remain to be considered certain difficulties which philosophers and theologians are likely to regard as obstacles to the harmonious cooperation of these two disciplines. Let us examine some of these difficulties and see whether they can be weakened or eliminated by further analysis.

Philosophers are likely to ask three legitimate questions which concern (1) the nature and implications of religious faith, (2) the religious use of myth, and (3) the assumption, necessary to religion, that the Deity is at least as objectively real as is the physical spatio-temporal world.

1. The insistence of all religions on the importance of faith seems to many philosophers to differentiate religion so completely from philosophy, with its insistence on reason and critical inquiry, that it is impossible for one and the same person to be sincerely religious and at the same time truly philosophical. Contrast, for example, the typically religious utterance of Job, "I know that my Redeemer liveth," with the typically philosophical utterance of Socrates, "The unexamined life it not worth human living." Are not these two attitudes radically incompatible?

Our answer will depend entirely on how "faith" is defined. If by religious faith we mean sheer credulity which rests on no empirical evidence, is wholly irrational and arbitrary, and is literally indubitable, we must conclude that philosophy can have no traffic with such faith and must, indeed, oppose it as being completely obscurantist. We must further admit that religious believers in all the religious traditions have *tended* to conceive of religious faith in this way. In its authoritarian temper, religion has too often been inclined to defend the credibility of its prescribed beliefs by an appeal to an infallible church or Book rather than by appeal to individual and corporate religious experience which, rationally interpreted, would render these beliefs credible to a reflective person. It its preoccupation with human sinfulness and depravity vis-à-vis God's perfect righteousness and infinite majesty, religion has tended to emphasize the chasm between God and man and to insist on man's inability to fathom the Divine mystery, with the result that faith in Him has been made almost completely irrational and arbitrary. Finally, in its determination to differentiate a "living faith in a living God" from the purely intellectual entertainment of an hypothesis regarding the nature of the real, religion has tended to confuse reflective certitude with complete logical certainty and to regard religious faith as authentic only if its tenets are held to be absolutely indubitable. Philosophical suspicions of religious faith are therefore partly justified.

Yet in proportion as religion is truly "high," i.e., enlightened, it itself repudiates this conception of faith as ardently as does philosophy itself. It would define a mature religious faith as an attitude of assurance in the Deity which is based on reliable but not exhaustive evidence, and on rational reflection but not on incontrovertible demonstration—in short, as a "certitude" or "moral assurance" which can dictate and sustain resolute action but which can never be identified with absolute "certainty" in its strict philosophical sense. So defined, religious faith is not radically different from the faith which is the precondition and the product of scientific inquiry, political action, or moral endeavor, that is, from the faith which all intelligent and well-informed men must have in order to live and function as human beings and as thoughtful inquirers. Such religious faith is a variant, and from the religious point of view the most important variant, of faith as a generic human attitude.

We can clarify this conception of faith by distinguishing between what can be called "initial" faith from "resultant" faith. By "initial" faith is here meant that attitude of trust which is the precondition of any venture, whether intellectual or practical. Such initial faith is essential since, without it, man cannot hope to have the experiences which alone can provide the requisite empirical evidence in the light of which a more and more informed "resultant" faith can develop. For example, the entire scientific enterprise would be impossible without an initial act of faith on the part of scientific investigators that there exists a world of nature to be investigated, that observation and experiment can provide clues to its structure and functioning, and that rational interpretation of such clues will increase rather than diminish scientific comprehension. No friendship or business venture, political experiment or exploration of art, is possible save on the basis of a corresponding initial assurance. Initial faith is as necessary for religious as it is for secular pursuits. Without such an initial faith in a Deity who is objectively real and at least in some degree knowable by men, active participation in a religious tradition and the active sharing of corporate religious experiences, is quite impossible, and unless these experiences are thus participated in, there is obviously no way of knowing their quality, their urgency, or their fruits at first hand.

This is what is meant, or should be meant, by religious believers when they accuse their secular opponents of not knowing what they are talking about. The charge, often legitimate, is that such secular skeptics condemn themselves to a second-hand and superficial knowledge of what religious experience actually is because of their refusal, or their inability, to indulge in this initial act of faith precludes the possibility of their actually participating in the crucial religious experiences and therefore knowing them as "agents" rather than merely as external "observers." As mere spectators they apprehend so inadequately what the reflective believer regards as crucial evidence that their skeptical interpretations of this evidence are correspondingly untrustworthy. As a result, they and their religious opponents are literally talking about different things and in a different language. No wonder that communication between them becomes progressively difficult and finally impossible!

Such initial faith, whether secular or religious, is of necessity largely blind, though it is probably never completely blind, for it is at least possible to argue that a completely blind faith, based on no evidence whatever and possessing no initial plausibility, is psychologically impossible. It would perhaps be more accurate to say that initial faith is, at least in most cases, faith of the "second order," that is, faith based not on first-hand experience and reflection but on confidence in the integrity and insight of someone else. Thus, if I am unfamiliar with the writings of some author, I may well be induced to read them on the advice of someone who recommends them to me and whose recommendations I accept as both honest and informed, or if I am wholly ignorant of poetry I will hardly go to the trouble of trying to find out what it is like save on the advice of someone in whom I have great confidence.

Where no such advice is available, the initial faith requisite for a new venture must be even blinder and more hazardous. Its only basis is some actual or fancied similarity between the new venture, as it is rather blindly envisaged, and some other venture already participated in and at least partly understood at first hand.

All arguments from analogy derive whatever cogency they may have from an appeal to similarities of this type. Such is, in fact, my present plea to open-minded and honest religious skeptics. I am saying to them in effect: I fully admit that you cannot at present possess religious faith because you seem not to have had any of the relevant experiences and cannot, therefore, really understand the religious experiences of others. Nor can you at present be thoroughly convinced of the validity or value of such experiences. Your first step, if you are to take it, must indeed be pretty blind—all you have to go on is the conviction, which I hope you do possess, that at least *some* religious believers in *some* religious tradition are neither fools nor knaves, plus the recognition that your present predicament is similar to what my predicament would be if I were as lacking in first-hand scientific knowledge and experience as you are of first-hand religious knowledge and experience. Will you not, therefore, trust at least some professing believers in the long religious tradition of your own culture or of some other culture enough to venture wholeheartedly on that initial act of faith which, as you can surely see, is analogous to the initial act of faith which, were I as skeptical of science as you are of religion, I would have to make in order to get at the evidence and understand the reasoning which alone could convince me at first hand that your scientific method is a valid and reliable method of inquiry and that your scientific conclusions are credible?

"Resultant" faith, as the term implies, signifies the measure of assurance that is progressively achieved through the discovery of relevant evidence and the clarification of interpretive theory. Here again the analogy between science and religion can be helpful. On the basis of an initial act of faith the scientist formulates his first vague hypotheses and then proceeds to test their deducible empirical consequences. Subsequent observations will normally lead to a modification of the original hypotheses, which, in turn, will dictate new observations—and so the process of scientific inquiry proceeds, with the result that the scientist gets greater and greater assurance not only that he is on the right general track but that certain basic concepts and principles of interpretation are reliable. He never achieves, or can hope to achieve, complete certainty because he can never assume that all the possible relevant evidence is in, or that his interpretation of such evidence as is available is the most reasonable possible interpretation. But as he and his fellow scientists continue their work, generation after generation, in close cooperation, there develops in them all a growing assurance that amounts to "moral certainty" that they are facing in the right direction, that their methods of inquiry are basically sound, and that a steady advance is being made toward an understanding of the regularities of nature. This assurance is further strengthened by technological advance, for man's amazing control of nature, under the guidance of science, would be quite unintelligible save on the assumption that science is indeed on the right track in its dealings with phenomenal existence. Our resultant faith in science and in particular scientific laws and principles thus becomes more and more informed, reflective and mature, and less and less blind; yet it never wholly ceases to be tentative and partial, simply because man never achieves omniscience. In short, man is not omniscient or infallible, and he must therefore be content with a certitude or assurance involving faith. Finitude precludes certainty as completely as infinite wisdom precludes the possibility of, or necessity for, mere faith. Faith is as characteristic of man as absolute certainty is characteristic of an omniscient Deity.

Now this, I would urge, is the kind of resultant faith that characterizes "high" religion, or religion in proportion as it becomes "high." It rests on evidence which is spiritually relevant—on the experiences of the individual believer and of the countless other believers who, in sum, constitute the "assembly of all the faithful." It also rests on an honest and rigorous theological interpretation of this evidence. It results in greater and greater spiritual maturity and in a more and more informed and ardent religious faith, yet it remains faith to the end, since man is as finite and fallible in his religious search as he is in his scientific inquiries. Yet this faith is what the man of religion lives by, and the longer he lives by it and reflects upon it in the context of his own religious tradition and of other religious traditions, the greater is his reflective assurance or "certitude" that he is on the right track.

Such religious faith, both "initial" and "resultant," is, I submit, not hostile to honest philosophy. On the contrary, it alone makes philosophical sense. So interpreted, Job's confession of faith and Socrates' insistence that critical examination is essential to mature living are not at variance but actually complement each other.

2. The role of myth in religion opens up a large area which we cannot here hope to explore. I must confine myself to a few basic observations.

First of all, the distinction must be kept in mind between myth in the sense of pure literary fiction and myth in the sense of concretely and imaginatively expressed truth. A mermaid is a purely mythical creation in the first sense, with no objective counterpart in the real world. Plato's myths and the stories of creation in the Book of Genesis, in contrast, can be regarded as myths in the second sense, that is, as poetic, imagistic expressions of truths which could also be expressed in abstract conceptual terms.

Rationalists have always been inclined to regard myths in this second sense as agreeable and pedagogically useful devices for immature minds, but as essentially inferior to abstract philosophical and, in more recent times, scientific statements. It is at least possible to argue, however, that the mythical expression of insights having to do with values and value situations can articulate and communicate such insights more accurately than can abstract conceptual statements, because a myth can better enable us to participate imaginatively and emotionally in the evaluative experiences in question and therefore to apprehend their true meaning and significance.

Such apprehension depends, of course, on not making the crude mistake which is very commonly made, especially in regard to religious myths, of accepting them as true in a literal, prosaic sense or, alternatively, as merely the product of fancy and therefore quite untrue. The Protestant fundamentalist's reading of the stories of creation and the fall in Genesis illustrates the first error, and the religious skeptics' complete rejection of these stories as pure fiction illustrates the second. "High" religion adopts a middle position. It regards these myths not as literally accurate, since the truths which they express are spiritual in character, but as none the less expressing with great clarity and power the religious tenets, here accepted as basic truths, that God as a spiritual Being is the source and ground of the entire phenomenal world in space and time, and that all men are afflicted by a deep-seated idolatrous perversity entitled "original sin."

The term "myth" has a third meaning, allied to the second but not identical with it, which is of prime importance for all religions which assert that God has progressively revealed Himself to mankind in history. Both Judaism and Christianity are historically rooted in this sense, in contrast to Hinduism in at least some of its aspects, or to the more philosophical and mystical religion of Plato. Both Judaism and Christianity attach major importance to what they declare to have been God's successive appearances to Abraham, Isaac, and Jacob, and to the long line of major and minor prophets; the Christian would add that God has revealed Himself to men in Jesus Christ in a unique manner, and that He has continued to disclose Himself to His followers during the succeeding centuries. The reports of these events, as recorded in the Bible, are "myths" in this third sense. Regarded as *merely* historical records, they are incomplete and often in conflict with one another, somewhat in the way in which Plato's account of Socrates' life and sayings is far from being a wholly accurate biography or a stenographic report of what Socrates actually said. Yet the Gospels convey, it is reasonable to believe, a spiritually reliable report of the character of Jesus and of the main burden of his teachings, and they are reliable records of the events in question with respect to their spiritual significance. Their historical reliability, in this spiritual sense, is of prime importance to Judaism and Christianity. There is, for example, for the Christian, all the difference in the world between a fictitious Jesus who is merely the creation of man's literary imagination, however inspired, and the historical Jesus of Nazareth who lived and preached and died on the Cross for our sakes.

Lest the objection be raised that, in its anchorage in historical events, religion shows itself to be hopelessly antithetic to science and philosophy, an analogy in science to this historical anchorage should be briefly mentioned. In general, science is quite indifferent to history, but its concern with cosmic and biological evolution is a marked exception. Here the actual temporal order of events, an order that may well prove to be irreversible and in many respects unique, is of major importance to the scientist who wishes to learn how our particular universe evolved in time and when the main stage of its temporal evolution actually took place. This is so obvious that examples need not be given. Science is also compelled to recognize the uniqueness of this actual temporal series, though the entire process is conceived of as being obedient to certain abiding natural laws and regularities. It recognizes, for example, the great likelihood that our planet is in some respect unique among the planets, and that the actual course of biological and human evolution on this planet is similarly distinctive. These familiar scientific beliefs should make more plausible the Christian insistence on a similarly unique set of religious events in human history, and on the importance to religion of the Biblical "mythological" record of these events.

Whatever one's credal response to this claim may be, Judaism and Christianity cannot be understood unless the

Biblical record is regarded in this light and unless the appropriateness and validity of this kind of "myth" be admitted. Only on this basis can we then proceed critically, as philosophy quite properly demands that we should proceed, to examine the religious claim that these myths are in this sense true and that these events, so reported and so understood, provide Christian faith with an historical basis for which there is no substitute.

Closely associated with the religious use of myth, in both the second and the third senses, is the insistence, in all forms of theism, and especially in Judaism and Christianity, that the Deity can more adequately, or less inadequately, be apprehended in personal rather than impersonal terms. This, too, is a large and controversial problem to which we cannot here do justice.

We must start with the recognition that, since all human experiences and reflection are dependent, at least in part, upon our finite human faculties of apprehension and our limited human perspective, *all* human knowledge is in this sense and to this degree necessarily anthropomorphic, that is, the kind of knowledge that *men* can achieve. This recognition protects us, at the outset, against the danger of supposing that some types of human knowledge, either the scientific type or the religious type, for example, transcend these actually inescapable human limitations.

We must bear in mind, secondly, that *all* human languages are human artifacts which are only partially satisfactory for the purposes for which they have been invented and for which they are used. It is indeed true that, since the area of human experience most thoroughly explored by man is the area of man's sensuous experience of objects in space and time which invite quantitative apprehension, the languages which have been thus far most adequately developed and which permit of the greatest precision of expression and communication are the quantitative and descriptive languages of the mathematical and biological sciences, and of modern technology.

Next most adequate for their purposes may well be the languages of literature and the fine arts, and perhaps the languages employed in our practical pursuits. The languages available to us in our moral relations with our fellows and in our corporate political activities are certainly less satisfactory, as is our understanding of ourselves as moral agents and our knowledge of how to cooperate with one another socially and culturally in large groups.

If reality does have the spiritual dimension which religion insists it has it is certainly plausible to suppose that this dimension is the hardest for finite man to know, and that he has thus far made the least satisfactory progress in exploring its nature and in adapting himself to it. It is also surely understandable that the problem of how to devise a language which is as adequate to the task of spiritual comprehension as is the language of science to its task is the most difficult linguistic and semantic problem which man has ever had to confront.

It is in this context, I suggest, that we should consider the insistence of the theist that, for religious purposes, the language of persons and personal relations is superior to the impersonal language appropriate to things and our relation to them. God, he declares, is less inadequately, though certainly not wholly adequately, conceived of as a person than as a thing or as an impersonal force; and His relations to man are less inadequately described on the analogy of the relation of father and son than on the analogy of the relation of a man to a stone, or of a stone to the law of gravity. This linguistic usage, it must be admitted, does invite the crude anthropomorphism of regarding God as literally a person, that is, of forgetting that such language is properly used not literally but analogically; but this error is avoidable, and it is in fact, avoided by religion at its enlightened best. Such use of personal language in theology has also the merit of safeguarding us from what is a far worse error, at least from the Judaic-Christian point of view, that, namely, of identifying God with part or all of nature in all its impersonality. The cautious theologian, meanwhile, will use the language of personal relations with great circumspection, careful not to fall into crass anthropomorphic literalism. He will, for example, take pains to describe God's nature in terms of those divine attributes by virtue of which He infinitely transcends humanity in righteousness, power, and knowledge, and to qualify God's "love" for man in such a way as not wholly to identify His love with purely human love. He may even prefer to conceive of God not as a Person but as that Being (note the resort here to impersonal language!) whose nature it is to be the source and ground of all human personality and the objective condition of all human growth.

Our conclusion, then, is that religion is quite justified in accepting myth as poetic truth and as historical occurrence, and in using the language of personal relations, provided it does so with intelligence and caution, fully aware of the dangers and limitations of such usage. At the very least, this procedure does not automatically invalidate religious beliefs expressed in these ways.

3. The third philosophical objection referred to raises a problem which is even more controversial in contemporary philosophical circles than are the problems just dealt with. Both naturalists and instrumentalists today are very insistent that our universe is in itself neutral with respect to all values, aesthetic and moral values no less than religious, and this insistence must, of course, preclude the very possibility of taking religion seriously in any of its traditional forms. If nothing is in itself beautiful or ugly, right or wrong, good or bad, holy or profane; if everything depends upon human interest and man's creation of ideal standards and objectives; in short, if the ultimate basis of all evaluation is human need, desire, interest, and wish, it is indeed hard to see how religion can be taken seriously save in the radically transformed sense in which John Dewey regards what he calls the "religious" attitude.

Since this subjectivistic position with regard to all values has been criticized repeatedly by competent philosophers without much success in convincing naturalists and instrumentalists, I despair of saying anything further on the subject that is at all likely to be persuasive to them. All I will attempt to do is to point out one common misunderstanding which has certainly contributed to the confusion which now prevails.

It is often supposed that those who believe in objective values must necessarily believe that their own evaluation of them is final and definitive, and that any reference to Beauty, Goodness, or God, capitalized and accepted as absolutes, implies that at least some human interpretations of them are as absolute as they are in themselves. This supposition has, alas, been encouraged by authoritarian dogmatists, both secular and religious; indeed, these dogmatists have so frequently countenanced this belief, that subjectivistic philosophers can perhaps hardly be blamed for thinking that all believers in objective values are equally smug and dogmatic regarding their own evaluations of them.

There is an alternative position, however, which those who are skeptical of objective values should at least seriously consider. This position asserts that objective values are indeed the objects of man's progressive evaluative search; that all progress in this search is real discovery and not pure human creation or invention; *but* that all human evaluations are relative to human culture and personal temperament and are as finite and fallible as are man's judgments regarding physical fact or historical occurrence. This position, in short, carefully avoids what we have called the "fallacy of misplaced absoluteness" by asserting that, whereas Beauty, Goodness, and God are absolutely what they are, human understanding of them is finite, inadequate, and relative.

Once again, the analogy to science suggests itself, and may be of value to the naturalist. The latter would normally admit that "nature" is absolutely what it is and not the mere product of human interests, desires, needs, and wishes, but that no scientific understanding of nature has ever been, or ever will be, final, definitive, and infallible. Nature would thus be regarded as the continuing object of man's scientific inquiry, remaining what it is with a character of its own, whereas man's knowledge of it evolves, though never to the point of infallible omniscience.

No more than this, be it noted, is claimed by "high" religion for man's knowledge of God as holy and righteous. It is not claimed that man can know God completely, or that man's knowledge of Him is not culturally and temperamentally conditioned. It is claimed, however, that He is actually encountered in religious experience and in certain crucial historical events; that the evolution of a "high" religion like Christianity from its primitive superstitious beginnings to its highest stage of enlightenment is a record of progressive, if somewhat uneven, discovery; and that what is now believed to be known and understood of His nature is genuine and reliable, though certainly inadequate, partial, and fallible.

The man of religion must add that the objective reality of God in all His holiness and righteousness is really essential to the vitality of his religious faith. Without this assurance, prayer becomes impossible, as do all forms of communion and worship, and such experiences and concepts as those of sin, forgiveness, and redemption lose all meaning. Here, then, we are indeed confronted with a crucial issue which demands of us an either/or decision and a basic act of faith. I am *not* here arguing that the religious conviction on this score is "of course" or self-evidently correct; far from it! But I would urge that the opposing view is no more self-evident or inevitable. Both beliefs deserve sympathetic exploration and critical scrutiny.

Certain theologians may, in their turn, raise the following objections to my account of "high" religion and its relation to philosophy. They may ask (1) whether I have not denied the legitimate authority of Church and Scripture, (2) whether I have not arrogantly set man's judgment above God's, (3) whether I have not undermined vital religious assurance, and (4) whether I have not ignored the way in which the philosopher himself, in his ultimate concerns, may fairly be called religious. Let us briefly examine each of these charges.

1. The first objection hinges on the definition of the word "legitimate." I have, it is true, rejected as "primitivistic" the belief that any institution or document or person is divinely inspired in the sense that any pronouncements issuing from such a source and with such sanction are infallible and "above" critical evaluation. Such authority I must call arbitrary and therefore philosophically unwarranted. This does not, however, involve the denial of Revelation or authentic inspiration or spiritual authority. It does not deny that God has indeed revealed Himself to man, or that certain historical events are of special spiritual import, or that the historical Jesus was in fact the Incarnation of the Deity, or that His Church is the special vehicle of spiritual insight and power. Nor would I deny the impressive spiritual authority of the Bible, as a uniquely revealing document, or of the Christian tradition as the funded wisdom of centuries of Christian experience and reflection—a wisdom far greater and more profound than the wisdom of any individual, however spiritually gifted and devout. All that is here insisted is that, whereas God Himself is what He is, and His actual Revelation of Himself to man, in whatever form, is what it is, man's comprehension of His nature and of His Self-revelation to man is inescapably fallible, and that therefore all authoritarian dogmatism with regard to any belief or interpretation is wholly unjustified, not only in a critically philosophical but also in a devoutly religious perspective. To deny this is, I sincerely believe, to be guilty of the sin of intellectual and spiritual pride.

2. But, the theologian may retort, does this not involve setting our own fallible human judgment above the judgment of

the Almighty? My answer is, emphatically, "No!" God Himself, as the object of our search and our worship, is the absolute standard of all truth and righteousness. All apprehensions of Him must be judged by reference to their relative adequacy or inadequacy to His own nature. It is not we who judge God; it is God who judges us.

The crucial problem, of course, concerns the criterion whereby conflicting interpretations of the Deity are to be assessed. In one way or another, the authoritarian position claims that certain accounts of the Deity are divinely inspired in so unique a manner that they are indubitable and not subject, as are all strictly human judgments, to rational criticism. This is supported by the claim that certain human individuals have, on certain occasions, been so used by the Deity as the vehicles for His Self-revelation that their human finitude has, on these occasions, been inoperative—the claim, in short, that certain individuals have, at certain times, spoken infallibly. Authoritarians would insist that acceptance of this claim is part of the "initial" faith requisite for authentic religious experience and understanding.

It is, in the nature of the case, as impossible to prove that this claim is invalid as it is to prove that it is valid. No one can prove that God has not in fact operated upon certain men in this way. The trouble is that no one can prove that He has so operated. Even more serious, however, is the question as to whether an acceptance of this claim is in fact necessary to religious experience at its best, and further, whether it promotes the spiritual humility which believers are commanded by all "high" religions to exemplify. I can only record my own "liberal" conviction that such belief in the infallibility of *any* pronouncement is not necessary to religious faith, and that it almost inevitably produces spiritual pride, dogmatism, and intolerance. The rich and vital faith of those who repudiate this doctrine of infallibility shows, I believe, that its acceptance is not a *sine qua non* of "high" religion; and the long history of religious persecutions which have issued from the claim of infallibility provides impressive evidence that the claim is in fact productive not of humility but of pride.

3. At this point authoritarians may insist that the denial of religious infallibility must rob the believer of that religious assurance in the Deity which is essential to wholehearted religious faith and dedication. This raises the same issue in another way. Must faith in God be rooted in absolute certainty in the strict philosophical definition of that term, i.e., as signifying the utter inconceivability of the opposite? My answer to this question must also be an emphatic "No!" Indeed, it seems very clear to me that a mature faith differs from a childish faith precisely in its ability to rise above man's natural but immature craving for absolute certainty. A child's state and sense of insecurity necessarily produce in it a hunger for absolute assurance, but a mature adult can and should be able to face the fact of human finitude and of the precariousness of *all* human belief with courage and even zest. He can and should prefer reflective assurance or "certitude" to unreflective and necessarily dogmatic "certainty," and he should be able to live by such assurance and, if need be, suffer and die for it.

In any case, this is, so far as I can see, the only type of religious faith which is consistent with a wholehearted allegiance to philosophy at its best, and it is only this type of faith which I, for one, believe to be consonant with religion in its highest development. It is in this spirit, and only in this spirit, that I am able to "subscribe" to the theistic position briefly outlined in the statement of principles in the Preface. My acceptance of this position is not a profession of certainty or an inflexible adherence to a set of infallible dogmas which no philosophy dare challenge and to which I, as a philosopher, must blindly conform. The statement expresses beliefs to which I wholeheartedly subscribe, both as a professing Christian and as a reflective philosopher, but I hold these beliefs with full realization of human finitude, of the partiality of all human insight, and of the possibility and desirability of future clarification or modification. I do not fear such revisions of belief; rather I hope for them, and I am confident that on-going philosophy, as well as on-going religious experience and interpretation, will contribute to them.

4. Nothing is more likely to infuriate some philosophers than to be told that philosophy, regarded as a serious human enterprise, is itself an expression of man's religious aspirations, and that every philosopher is, at least in his ultimate concerns, religiously oriented. Yet it is hard to avoid this conclusion if religion is broadly and basically defined as man's perennial attempt to probe into reality as deeply as possible, to root himself in this reality as completely as possible, and to adapt himself to it as realistically and vitally as he can.

Philosophical analysis can, it is true, be conducted as a kind of intellectual game, more or less divorced from mankind's ultimate concerns. Some benefit can accrue from such an enterprise; definitions can be sharpened, concepts can be clarified, and procedures can be more clearly established. But unless these intellectual tools and operations are eventually put to use by application to man's basic search for reality and truth they will remain, however fascinating, mere rules and counters of an idle and irresponsible pastime.

Even the philosopher who engages in this pastime, however, is also a human being who, whether he likes it or not and whether he acknowledges it or not, is involved in an "existential" situation in which he must make vital decisions. Like all men, he is confronted with the brute facts of life and death, the alternatives of attempting to escape from reality or of facing it and seeking to adapt himself to it, and the choice, conscious or unconscious, between many alternative ways, some far more satisfactory than others, of living his own life. Defining religion, most inclusively, as man's attempt to relate himself to reality through comprehension and response, every human being can be said to be religious in this sense, and that which he is willing most resolutely to affirm and to which he gives his highest loyalty can be called his God. Since no one can fully comprehend the Absolute, or reality in its inmost essence, all men must indeed be said to worship idols, that is, more or less distorted images of that which at least partially eludes our grasp. It is reasonable to believe that some idols are far cruder than others, far worse distortions of reality in its actual inner essence. Yet each man's idol is his best approximation to the true object of human reverence, and each man's ultimate loyalty is his best approximation to an ideally enlightened and purified form of worship.

In this sense, then, even the philosopher who ignores or explicitly repudiates religion must be described as religious *malgré lui* because, as a human being, he must have concerns that transcend his technical philosophical inquiries. If in his thinking he fails to grapple with the major problems of human existence, his intellectual pursuits remain correspondingly irrelevant to the religious dimension of his own life and the lives of others. If, on the other hand, he does seek to interpret the crucial issues of human existence in his philosophy and finally develops a philosophy which is opposed to religion in any of its traditional orthodox forms, it is still meaningful to assert that, on a wider definition of man's religious quest, even his antireligious or unreligious philosophy has a religious dimension and relevance.

There remains, of course, the third possibility, that, in his search for all the wisdom available to man, the philosopher will draw upon whatever light and power he and others can discover in the major religious traditions, thereby deepening and enriching his own synoptic interpretation of reality and human destiny. It is obviously this third approach which the foregoing account of a comprehensive philosophy and a "high" religion would favor as most conducive to philosophic wisdom and religious enlightenment. On this approach, the quality of the philosopher's religious perspective will profoundly influence, consciously or unconsciously, his philosophical method and conclusions. The less adequate his religious insights, the less significantly and illuminatingly will they inform his philosophy; the richer and purer his religious experience and beliefs, the profounder and the more incisive will be his interpretation of reality and life.

This swift survey of a few objections raised in the philosophical or the religious camp is not, of course, exhaustive. Many other important questions, relating to the nature of so-called "religious experience" and to specific religious doctrines call for further and painstaking examination. My concern has not been primarily apologetic; I have not attempted to present the evidence in support of religious faith, or to expound the meaning of specific religious beliefs, or to argue for their cogency. I have merely tried to suggest in quite general terms that "high" religion and philosophy, conceived of as distinguishable but related enterprises, are and ought to be complementary and not in conflict or competition. As they have been here described, "high" religion offers men a tradition, a funded wisdom, a discipline, and, above all, a living community which, in conjunction, make available to him the illumination and the strength which he desperately needs at all times and especially in "times of trouble" such as ours. Even when philosophy generates a secular "way of life" it is no adequate substitute for a living religion which puts man into vital contact with a "living" God. Philosophy, in turn, is man's only safeguard against provincialism, blind credulity, and ultimate dogmatism, and religion, even when it is most critical within its own theological framework, cannot of itself provide this philosophical perspective or critique. Religion alone can provide man with authentic religious insight and spiritual power; philosophy alone can enable man to survey *all* his experiences and beliefs, including his most compelling religious experiences and his most inescapable religious convictions, judiciously and wisely in their relation to one another. Each, therefore, as Professor Calhoun has pointed out, "gains from close association with the other. The two in conjunction, but neither one by itself, can move with hope toward more effective conquest of the chaos that again and again threatens to engulf human living. That way lies whatever chance we may have for a more humane world." [2]

THE ACADEMIC RESPONSIBILITIES OF PHILOSOPHY TO RELIGION

A department of philosophy in a college or university can find many ways of discharging its responsibilities to religion within the framework of scholarly research and instruction. It must do so, of course, in terms of the concrete situation in which it finds itself, taking into account the abilities, interests, and available time of its departmental staff, the personnel and course offerings of allied disciplines, and the character and over-all policy of the institution of which it is a part. Thus the optimum procedure will differ in important aspects in small colleges and large universities, in church-affiliated and predominantly secular institutions, etc. It may be helpful, however, to mention a few of the ways in which a philosophy department might demonstrate an active concern for religion under relatively ideal conditions.

1. It could, in the first place, support or, if necessary, help to establish, a strong department of religion characterized by first-rate scholarly and pedagogical competence. It would do so in the conviction that religion is so vast, complex, and distinctive a subject for scholarly research, and so important a field for undergraduate and graduate study, that it merits full departmental status. One might perhaps argue, in opposition to this proposal, that religion would receive adequate academic recognition if historians did justice to religious movements and motivations, anthropologists and sociologists to the role

[2] *Loc. cit.*

of religious belief and practice in various societies, psychologists to religion as a complex and recurrent psychological phenomenon, the student of art to various artistic treatments of religious themes, and the philosopher to the content and validity of religious beliefs. All these complementary approaches to religion are not only possible but invaluable; without them, our understanding of religion would indeed be hopelessly provincial. Specific provision, however, should be made for their effective coordination, both scholarly and pedagogical, and such coordination can best be achieved on a campus by an enlightened department of religion. The chief function of such a department, however, is not to synthesize such tangential approaches; it is rather to provide the proper academic vehicle for the directly focussed study which religion, as a distinctive subject, demands as urgently as do other major aspects of human experience. Few people would be willing, for example, to leave the study of history exclusively in the hands of the historians of art, religion, philosophy, science, or political institutions; the pattern of human history must be the full-time concern of competent historians associated, academically, in a department dedicated specifically to this embracing and challenging discipline. The need for similar departmental responsibility for other major fields of knowledge is equally clear. Religion invites and requires no less; we can hope to achieve a sympathetic and critical understanding of it in all its complexity and human impact only if it is accorded the same academic privileges that are accorded other major aspects of human life.

An enlightened department of philosophy will realize this. It will be aware that its own proper activities will depend as much upon the informed study of religion as upon the several natural and social sciences and the several humanistic disciplines. For its own sake, therefore, as well as for the sake of religion in its own right, it will do all it can to encourage the establishment and growth of a department of religion comparable in scholarship and teaching to the strongest departments in its institution.

2. A department of philosophy properly concerned with religion will also try to include on its staff at least one philosopher whose special interest and competence lies in the field of the philosophy of religion, and it will provide him, so far as possible, with at least one undergraduate course in this field and, whenever feasible, additional courses at the graduate level. Such an undergraduate course would normally be focussed upon what is generally distinctive in man's religious experiences, upon what mainly distinguishes major religious traditions from one another, upon the pattern of development from primitive to "high" religion, upon the problem of the validity or invalidity of religious belief, and upon the proper place of religion in the life of the individual and of society. No two teachers will approach these aspects of the subject in the same way, but it is perhaps appropriate to suggest that, in view of the wealth of first-rate literature that is available, there is little excuse for too exclusive reliance on textbooks. It has been my own experience that nothing will dampen the student's interest more effectively than the average textbook, whereas nothing will arouse his interest and evoke his respect more effectively than carefully chosen books of the stature of Augustine's *City of God*, Hume's *Dialogues on Natural Religion*, Bergson's *Two Sources of Morality and Religion*, Dewey's *A Common Faith*, Dostoevsky's *Legend of the Grand Inquisitor*, T. S. Eliot's *Four Quartets*, or Richard Niebuhr's *The Meaning of Revelation*. If books like these are studied and discussed with imaginative sympathy *and* critical scrutiny, no question can possibly arise as to the academic propriety of such a course or of its value to the individual student. The same type of study, more detailed and technical, is obviously possible and desirable at the graduate level.

3. The members of a well-rounded department of philosophy will also have ample opportunity to discuss religion,

in one or another of its various aspects, in other courses normally included in the departmental curriculum; indeed, neglect of the religious factor frequently amounts to professional incompetence. Thus, the history of philosophy cannot ignore with impunity the variant concepts of God in the main philosophic tradition, from Socrates, Plato, and Aristotle, through the Middle Ages to Descartes, Leibniz, Spinoza, Kant, Hegel, and Whitehead. Similarly, a course in epistemology or metaphysics can hardly be competently synoptic which neglects various claims to religious insight, whether authoritarian or empirical, intuitive, mystical or speculative; a course on the nature of values and evaluation is bound to be lopsided if it ignores religious values and value judgments; a course in ethics can hardly afford to restrict itself entirely to secular ethical theories; a course in semantics should certainly include a consideration of religious discourse and its meaning; and even a course in logic might well consider the applicability of logical principles and operations to theological analysis and argument. Finally, empirically oriented courses in social and political philosophy, the philosophy of art, and even the philosophy of science can with complete propriety, concern themselves with religion as and when religious issues properly arise, as, for example, in a consideration of religious among other social institutions, or of works of art with religious subject-matter and content, or of the antipathy, neutrality, or sympathy of science to religion.

4. More important, however, than all these academic expressions of religious concern on the part of professional philosophers is their exemplification, in their own persons, of a sympathetic receptivity to all insights, secular *and* religious alike, coupled with responsible critical analysis and appraisal. It is not necessary that all the members of a department of philosophy be avowedly religious; indeed, it is to their mutual advantage, as well as to the great advantage of their students, that, between them, they represent several basic points of view, religious and secular, naturalistic and humanistic. In our pre-

dominantly secular society, however, such representation can normally be achieved only with special effort and careful planning.

Most important of all, since teaching never quite escapes the direct, crucial impact of one human being on another, is the individual philosopher's attitude to religion and the effect of his attitude, as it reveals itself in many ways, upon the attitude and understanding of his students. Here the minimum requirement would seem to be genuine open-mindedness, humility, and tolerance; most to be desired, if the claims of "high" religion have any validity at all, would be a spiritual dedication, an attitude of reflective and critical religious commitment, that reflects a firmly held and enlightened religious perspective. The religious commitments of many philosophers undoubtedly hamper their philosophical inquiries because these commitments are provincial and dogmatic, but the antireligious attitudes and commitments of many other philosophers are equally prejudicial to comprehensive and vital philosophical interpretation. The answer is not the avoidance of commitment but rather a commitment, both firm and reflective, which can give direction and meaning to a man's life and to his philosophical interpretations of it. What we professional philosophers are and do and believe, in short, is not irrelevant to our professional activities; on the contrary, our basic attitudes and our personalities and actions will influence our students as profoundly as will our philosophical discourse. We would do well, therefore, to reconsider our own attitudes toward and treatment of religious issues, not only in order to increase the depth and breadth of our philosophy, but also because of the effect of our attitudes upon our students. This will require of us a great effort to rise over traditional provincialism and to explore and express the free spirit of man in his search for whatever in the universe evokes and nourishes his freedom.

above is one aspect of the acute awareness of man's relation to the divine which is a vital aspect of the great works of Greek literary art.

Homer's goddess has no name, but she is a person nonetheless, as are all his gods. Everyone has remarked how much like men and women are the denizens of Olympus. They are immortal and they are much more powerful, but otherwise there is little to choose. Indeed it may be said that the gods are neither so reasonable nor so moral as men. If they staunchly support one loyal worshipper, they are ready enough to abandon another. Their enmity is without pity and their vengeance exceeds justice. It is impossible to fit them into any consistent theological scheme, and their part in the cosmos is not by any means clear. Zeus is the father of gods and men, and at times it appears that the supreme power is his; at other times it appears that he too is subservient to a Fate, most dimly suggested in the shadow behind the bright Olympians. It is obvious that these uncertainties and deficiencies do not trouble Homer at all. He is not writing cosmology but a story in which some of the characters are human and some divine. Both classes are portrayed by their acts. Neither class is analyzed or explained or accounted for. In both, the great virtue is power: Achilles is a hero because he is mighty, Odysseus, because he is astute. It is the success of the gods in turning human affairs to their liking that displays their divinity. Whether divinity was no more than that to Homer is an unanswerable question. In the creation of Hector he has given a wonderful suggestion that there may be human virtues independent of success and unassailable by defeat, but his tale has no place for a suffering or compassionate god, and we shall never know whether he conceived of such a thing. But, in spite of their inadequacy as embodiments of the divine, the gods of Homer have virtues of the greatest importance: they are real, they are interesting, and they are very beautiful. Their reality must be apparent to any reader of the *Iliad* and the *Odyssey*. Chryses prays to

Apollo in the assurance that he is addressing a person who can hear him and who will. Odysseus and Athena are companions. The gods are not forces or abstractions or symbols. They are individuals. As for their interest and their beauty, classical literature is full of these qualities and would be impoverished without them.

When life is portrayed not as a tale but as a drama the result may be more profound, but the simplicity and freshness of the epic is gone. The gods of the Athenian tragedy are still real, still interesting, and still beautiful, but they are no longer to be taken with the carefree delight with which one watches the angry Apollo striding down the ridges of Olympus. The problem of choice is essential to the drama, and if the gods are to participate in the situations they must be involved in the dilemma of destiny and free will. This dilemma Aeschylus faces courageously, relying not on any solution in detail, but on a basic faith in the cosmic plan which allows him to accept what he cannot explain. The problem of Orestes is one of the simplest and clearest of all tragic situations: he must avenge his father, whom his mother has killed, and he must not kill his mother. Action and inaction are both enjoined and both forbidden. He is not responsible for this situation, but he alone can resolve it. But behind the conflict within him is a conflict among the gods themselves, not now, however, such conflict of pride and jealousy as had produced the enmity between the Homeric Hera and Aphrodite but a moral conflict between essentially different aspects of the problem. The Furies, whose specific function was the punishment of matricide, are opposed by Apollo, by whose command Orestes does the awful deed, and by whose counsel and support he is eventually purged of his guilt. The vital question is not whether the course he may choose is punishable, for that is certain, but whether it is expiable. Athena judges that it is, and the Furies themselves are eventually appeased. But to the question why a man should suffer for a situation not of his making no answer is given. Here, as in Homer, gods and men are alike, the gods immortal and more powerful but individuals still, and not omniscient, so that they grasp the cosmic whole only in part. Both gods and men, however, have undergone a great change since Homer's day, and now think more than they act. And the ultimate power behind Olympus is now much more clearly discernible as the figure of Justice. Whether this be Zeus himself or not, Aeschylus does not quite explain and evidently is not quite sure, but it is immanent and omnipotent, and its operations, while mysterious in detail, are right and sure in the end. Faith in ultimate justice redeems a universe in which the gods, though real, are many and therefore less than perfect; and where man is confronted by conditions that he cannot understand, not the least torturing of which is the power and the necessity of exercising his will.

Without the support of this faith the old gods may be a very perplexing element in the drama, as they are in Euripides. For him they are real enough; his plays are full of them and most frequently it is they who control the action. They are also interesting enough. They are individuals, the best drawn of whom are quite as sharply differentiated as the human characters and scarcely less complicated in their actions and reactions. But their Homeric beauty is largely obscured by the emphasis laid upon their limitations. Their loves and hates are quite as trivial and unreasonable as in the epic, but the dramatist can no longer weave them unjustified into the texture of a decorative tale. He must consider them, and in so doing he is lost. He is not saved by the Aeschylean reliance on the final triumph of Good. In his view it is very often Evil that triumphs, and that triumphs as the will of the gods. Yet he cannot dismiss them as wholly evil, as St. Augustine was to do in another age. Unhappily for his peace of mind their virtues are as real as their vices, and through the plays there is a pathetic return to the suggestion that there must be some mistake about man's conception of the gods, who cannot really be the imperfect creatures of the legends. No new conception is achieved, however, and to the end the only gods Euripides knows are those against whom he brings the final indictment that they are like men and that the likeness is unworthy of deity.

Of course, many currents beside the artistic had flowed between Homer and Euripides, of which the most important is the current of speculation. Philosophy hardly belongs to the history of Greek literature until its flowering in Plato, but much of Greek literature can only be imperfectly understood without taking account of philosophy. It was not in Greece proper, where the mountains and the thin soil and the laborious harvesting of the sea gave man little leisure from the business of living, that speculation began, but in the richer cities of Asia Minor and of south Italy. There men could pause, having gained some security in the struggle for existence, to contemplate the universe in the midst of which they had been set and to seek to understand its plan and purpose. It was inevitable that the traditional gods should be subjected to the same kind of scrutiny that was applied to the physical world. Now scrutiny is just what the gods of Homer cannot bear. One may fear them and love them and believe in them but one cannot explain them. The attempt to include them in a consistent explanation of the cosmos is fatal. Doubtless the great mass of worshippers continued to believe and not to speculate at all, and we can see the effects of this conservatism in the comedy of Athens. Aristophanes presents to his audiences a startling contrast of burlesque and reverence very hard for a descendant of the Judaic tradition to accept. How can that be worshipped which is ridiculous? Yet that is what Aristophanes shows us. In *The Frogs* the protagonist is an absurd caricature of Dionysus, the great god of wine, in whose honor all the plays at Athens were produced. There is nothing godlike or even respectable about him; he is simply a clown. Yet it would be a complete misunderstanding to suppose that the play is an assault on the established religion. Inserted into the middle of the farce, in the very presence of the counterfeit Dionysus, comes one of the most beautiful and sincere of all pieces of Greek religious poetry, a hymn to Dionysus himself and to his two companions, the goddesses of Eleusis. The confronted pictures are impossible to reconcile rationally. But that does not mean that they were impossible for the audience to accept. The preposterous Dionysus is really only an exagger-ated relative of the lame Hephaestus of the *Iliad*, awkwardly serving the nectar while the gods laugh at his clumsy gait. The lameness, acquired when his father had tossed him out of heaven, will not bear consideration, but it is a part of him nonetheless, and if one is to believe in the Homeric Hephaestus one must accept him, limp and all. It is on this tolerance of irreconcilable elements of deity that Aristophanes relies, and it is evident that he did not overestimate the capacity of his audience to enjoy the incredible. In spite of all the penetrating thought which had been directed to cosmic problems, fifth century Athens was still full of people who could believe in defiance of reason. It would be a rash prophet who should say when some form of that capacity should cease to characterize man. There is no need to suppose that it was only the ignorant who enjoyed the comedy, however. The distinction between thinking and unthinking man is quite as much a difference of moods in one individual as a difference between one individual and another. Nothing that we know about Aristophanes him-self suggests that he was a skeptic; his plays show clearly enough that he was no fool. Just what he believed it is impossible to say, but his belief certainly was not confined to systematic theology.

Literature in general reflects the thinking rather than the unthinking man, whether the distinction be specific or tem-porary, and to the former the Olympians clearly presented a problem. The easiest way out was to avoid it altogether by turning the attention to things human to the practical exclusion of things divine, which is the course taken with perfect propriety by much literature. It is essentially the course of Pindar, whose magnificent odes in praise of mortal victors are full of pious references to divine power in which the problem of divine personality is constantly evaded. It is really the course followed by Sophocles, a dramatist as reticent as Shakespeare in exposing his own convictions. Though continually treating of situations for which the gods are in fact responsible, he steadily focuses the interest of the audience on the reaction of the human characters to those situations rather than on the divine machinery which produced them. Even in his last play, the *Oedipus at Colonus*, in which the ancient Oedipus, finally purged by his sufferings, is mysteriously translated, there is neither the Aeschylean vision of eternal justice, nor the Euripidean questioning of justice. It is a play about Oedipus, with the cause of his suffering and the reason for his reward both allowed to remain a mystery.

It is not surprising that the historians should have considered man rather than God. Herodotus, recounting the great story of the wars of Greeks and Persians, certainly shows himself hospitable to the marvelous and particularly interested in the oracles which were so very important an element in the belief of his day. But aside from a conviction that Fortune, good or bad, is impermanent and that too great prosperity invites her envy, he can hardly be said to have any theory of the eternal scheme of things, and the actions and conditions of men so fascinate him that he has little attention left to give to gods. To Thucydides, more strictly an historian of war, the divine economy is still less pertinent, and little is to be learned from his pages about ancient belief. In the same way the orators, while they pay the necessary conventional respect to orthodoxy, have their minds fixed on other things. But it is important to realize that there was an element of choice in this understandable characteristic of fifth-century prose. The great sophist Protagoras coined the phrase "Man is the measure of all things," but he by no means invented the state of mind which the phrase expressed. The sophistic educational movement, whose least noble form was an unprincipled competition for success, was the counterpart of that public worship of power which forced the Greek states into and through the trials and the horrors of the Peloponnesian War. This was consistent enough with the splendid ritual which exalted the glory of the virgin goddess of the Acropolis, but it certainly ignored those difficult aspects of her being which were not satisfied by the conception of glory. The teachers and the statesmen of Athens could certainly not be classed as unthinking men, but they preferred to think of other things than the nature of the gods.

There were, on the other hand, those by whom the question could not be ignored. Full of a desire to find answers which should be eternal and complete, they looked upon the Homeric Pantheon and found it sadly insufficient. Of the thinkers to whom religion was of primary concern, Socrates is the earliest of whom we have a clear picture. The work of his disciple Plato, that great artist through whom chiefly he is known to us, is the most fascinating and uplifting of ancient essays on the riddle of the cosmos. The vital but insoluble problem of disentangling the philosophy of the master from that of the pupil need not be dealt with here. The words are the words of Plato in whatever proportion he drew his wisdom from Socrates, Pythagoras, or from others. His interest centers in ethics and politics, so that his theology is a secondary matter, but his conviction of the absolute reality of the virtues compelled an examination of the divine sanction of those virtues, and so of the nature of the gods themselves. It is of the first necessity for him that the divine should be perfect. With the gods of Homer, therefore, he deals in very summary fashion. Their shortcomings are too notorious to be forgiven or explained away. Since it is impossible to credit vices in divine persons, it follows that these are not real persons at all, but inventions of the poet. The poet's abilities, unfortunately, have given his slanders dangerously persuasive force, and since this is beyond the power of argument to overcome, the only escape is to abolish Homer and all the other poets who have represented the gods as less than they must be. So the Olympians, for their sins, are to be wiped out. It does not follow that the divine persons, whom the poet's fancies have so distorted in man's view, do not exist. Socrates sent Xenophon to consult the oracle at Delphi; in his dying moments he reminded a friend that they owed a cock to Asclepius. Plato's system has place for more gods than one, and he may have felt that there was some residual reality back of the old names. But he never gives sound definitions to replace the abandoned ones, and in his pages the old gods do, in fact, disappear. What appears in their place is just what the Homeric theology most conspicuously lacked, an omnipotent figure, the cause and creator of all. The cosmology of the *Timaeus*, indeed, shows him assisted by lesser gods in the work of creation, but they are merely his agents. The power whom Aeschylus would not name is now portrayed as the vital element in the whole cosmic system.

In getting rid of the vices of the Homeric gods it must be confessed that Plato disposed of their virtues as well. Perfection and omnipotence are not easy things to make real to men, and one wonders how many in the fourth century were able to approach the god of Plato with the assured worship with which the benighted warriors of the heroic age addressed Apollo and Poseidon. Plato's god was so very remote! And the intermediaries whom he supplied were not much help to the human spirit. It was exactly their appropriateness to the system which robbed them of that personality which man perpetually craves in the power he worships. Reaction against a system is an experience which has often occurred in religions including the Christian religion, and, in spite of the nobility of Plato's system, its great advance over its predecessors, and its great fruitfulness for the future, its theology could not possibly be considered as final. For one thing, Plato could not conceivably uproot Homer from the culture of his people; he himself must have been perfectly aware of that. If intelligent men were faced with the alternative of the *Iliad* or the *Republic* the great majority of them, then as now, would certainly choose the former. Homer was a permanency, and his gods had the great advantage of familiarity. To be sure, they were as vulnerable as ever to scrutiny. Those late disciples whom we call the Neoplatonists, following the example of the Stoics in an attempt to rescue the father of literature without betraying their master, subjected Homer to an elaborate allegorical interpretation which is surely one of the great monstrosities in the history of literary criticism. One cannot believe that it ever affected men deeply. In spite of the sentimental associations that cling to the name of Hypatia, in spite of the undoubted power of mind of Plotinus, the real founder of Neoplatonism, its effect on literature, either in creation or interpretation, was trivial. The gods of Homer may never have fully recovered from the assault of the philosophers, but they surely had more vitality in their original form than in the abstractions to which the Neoplatonists would have reduced them. The brilliant success with which they were revived in Latin form by Vergil testifies to a quality in them which lives on in defiance of the power of logic.

Nonetheless, the conception of a supreme and ultimate power, which was no invention of Plato's but which is essential to him, once having been advanced, could never be forgotten. It reappears as Aristotle's Unmoved Mover of all things, and as the Primordial Spirit of the Stoics, from which the world has its origin and to which it inevitably returns. It reappears in the form of the immutable physical laws which Democritus contributed to Epicureanism, that post-Platonic system which definitely endeavored to break the connection between God and man. Unlike the other philosophies of its age, Epicureanism produced a great work of art, the Latin didactic epic of Lucretius. In this the unworthiness of polytheism has produced not merely doubt but the most active hostility. To Lucretius superstition is the source of all evil, superstition being not belief in the gods, but belief that they have any concern for human affairs. The Epicureans by no means denied the existence of the gods, but they held them to be infinitely remote and wholly careless of humanity. They, like men, were products of nature, higher and happier products, and therefore worthy of man's respectful admiration, but to be regarded with neither hope nor fear because they neither could nor would have the least effect on man's destiny. Lucretius' poem is great largely because of the intense moral earnestness with which he urges on the reader the sin and folly of subordinating reason to superstition. For him the crimes committed in the name of religion are unrelieved by any virtues. The path of safety is to abandon all faith in the permanence of personality, human or divine, and adjust one's life to the serene processes of nature, obedience to which is man's happiness. It is a noble doctrine and an austere one, very far removed from the debased caricature which even in antiquity had pre-empted the title of Epicureanism. But its expression is not without its paradoxes. If one reason why the poem is great is that Lucretius is a great moralist, a more important reason is that he is a great poet, and poetry cannot be the wholly consistent servant of any system. He was sensitive to impulses and emotions hardly to be explained by atoms and the void. The very passage in which he decries the fear of death is too expressive of that fear to be a proper example of the calm which is the chief virtue of the Epicureans. The splendid opening address to Venus may indeed be explained since Venus is a mere personification of the force of nature, but in a system devoted to the exaltation of law what need should there be of personification at all except that personality is the hardest of all things to exclude from the human consciousness?

Though Lucretius is quite without parallel in Latin literature, in one sense he is typical enough: all the Latin theological speculation is borrowed from the Greek. There are, to be sure, native elements which appear here and there in writers of the Republic and thereafter, reflections of the old local gods of the Romans, very tenacious of their privileges, and some, such as the gods of the household, very charming, but accepted throughout their long existence with little or no real thought as to their nature. The more important and official gods, such as Jupiter, Juno and Minerva, were early assimilated to their Greek counterparts. They always retained certain thoroughly Roman characteristics, particularly in the ritual of worship, but these were of a kind far removed from the inspired imagination of the Greeks. The Roman's dealing with his god was essentially a contractual matter. Gifts, sacrifices, and temples were for value received or in the lively hope of favors to come. The whole complex of native Roman worship is of great interest to the student of human customs, but has very little to contribute to the experience of the human soul. When a Roman devotes serious attention to the nature of the gods he is certainly indebted to a foreign culture. It is hardly necessary to cite Cicero's essay on that subject, for it is frankly a translation and adaptation of Greek Epicurean and Stoic works to display their lines of reasoning, not to contribute anything essential to theology. But such a phenomenon as the great description of the festival of Isis with which Apuleius closes the *Golden Ass* is Latin only by accident. The power of it is purely oriental.

For the most part we have merely a translation of Greek mythology pressed into the service of the conquerors of the Greeks. The decorative value of the old gods is inexhaustible. It can produce the hymn to Diana of Catullus, who is not a religious poet at all, and the delightful *jeu d'esprit* on Mercury by Horace, whose religion was certainly conventional and unimpassioned. The old gods might be used in new ways for the glory of Rome, as they were by the inclusive genius of Vergil, or they might be combined in a wholly mythological work, as in the remarkable *Metamorphoses* of Ovid. But one who regards that *tour de force* in comparison with the Greek matter from which it is fashioned will see that it is the interest and the beauty of the old gods that has been preserved in this synthesis rather than their reality. If the mode of combination has avoided the difficulties of a strictly logical system which extinguishes personality, it has not cured the evils of divine imperfection, and it has not succeeded in reproducing the vigor and freshness of its ancient sources. It must be confessed that in Roman hands the Olympians shrink away until they become no more than part of the rhetorician's stock in trade, with which a witless flatterer might embellish a panegyric addressed even to so Christian an emperor as Theodosius, in conformity with a convention tolerated because the life was gone from it.

Yet the Romans would have been shocked to be called an irreligious race. For them, religion was not so much the contemplation of gods as the right understanding of the duty of man. They certainly did not invent ethics, and their best ethical writings are pale things beside the profundity of Plato and Aristotle. But the question of duty does pervade Latin literature to a much greater extent than it does Greek. As a late writer remarks, "those are religious who distinguish between what ought to be done and what ought to be avoided." The end of man, so stated, might have been perfectly acceptable to the Epicureans, though they would certainly have rejected the adjective "religious." But the private virtue of the Epicureans was far less admirable to the Romans than the public virtue of the Stoics, whose respect for society perfectly fitted their reverence for the Republic, and whose ethics came as near as anything to expressing the Roman religion in the Roman sense. This theme of the duty of man to man and of man to the community of men fills with its diverse forms the pages of authors otherwise totally unlike: Cicero and Caesar, Livy, Sallust and Tacitus, Horace and Juvenal, Seneca and Quintilian. In the elegiac poets it is reduced or perverted almost beyond recognition, but in Vergil it rises to be the guiding principle of a great epic. Aeneas is pious not from any capacity for adoration, but because he is constantly faithful to his obligation. Of course, duty to the gods generally goes hand in hand with duty to men, but it is the lesser element. A work such as the *Pervigilium Veneris*, in which worship is independent and not the handmaid of ethics, is at once recognizable as foreign to the norm of Latin literature. A conception of religion so restricted would satisfy neither Aeschylus nor St. Paul, but it did give a sound, firm core to the Roman spiritual experience.

But what of the destiny of man? What had he to hope from duty well done or to fear from duty neglected? In most of the ancient mythologies, very little. The underworld in the *Odyssey* is a wan place, inhabited by bloodless spirits. It is not a place of punishment—torment is reserved for a small group of sinners guilty of violence against divinity—but it is a place of bare existence. This kind of continuance, in which the dead are merely ghosts, is common enough in primitive religions, and the conception persists half submerged beneath much more highly developed faiths.

But man's persistent curiosity about an afterlife and his strong hope for the continuity of personality could not leave the question to unimaginative superstition. Early philosophers gave logical or mystical forms to his aspirations, most brilliantly in the myths with which Plato, having exhausted the resources of the language of reason, suggests the final truths which he apprehended beyond reason's horizon. Belief in immortality gave confidence to Socrates' last hours, though he may not have been the author of the logical proofs which Plato puts in his mouth, or have elaborated his faith into the conception of the divine judgment of souls and their courses of relapse, return, and rise which he is made to expound. At all events, it was a courageous faith, fit to enable a man to bear with calmness unmerited death. Moreover, it would seem to have been a faith available to all. The mystery religions had long before introduced the idea of immortality for the elect, and as paganism grew old, more and more mysteries competed for the attention of the believers, but for the uninitiated there was nothing. The Stoics came to preach a very exclusive conception of salvation: salvation for the eminent benefactors of mankind. Hercules and Aesculapius, Romulus and Scipio, might go to heaven as a reward for their labors and their great deeds, but no such prospect was offered to the common man. Socrates claimed no such eminence, nor was his faith based merely on ceremonial purification. Rather, it was that of a man who had loved virtue and tried to practice it, and who faced death without fear, in the belief that the soul was by nature good and could not die. Posterity by no means always shared his hope. The Epicureans rejected it absolutely on principle. It was too simple for some and too high for others. The perpetual night which Catullus faced must have been reality to very many of those who had the courage to find out what they did believe. But now and again the hope appears in later literature, never more beautifully than in Vergil. His picture of the underworld owed much to Plato and to others, but it is a picture which impresses one as essentially the poet's own. Moreover, there is an apocalyptic element in Vergil, which he did not borrow. The Fourth Eclogue, that perpetual enigma, speaks of a new earth in the tones of Isaiah, and explains at once why Christianity took him easily to its heart and why he became the guide of Dante. The Golden Age for which he looked never came to pass, but it has been an inspiration to all since his time who have looked forward to the felicity of the world made anew.

If Vergil slipped easily into the Christian tradition, the same cannot be said of classical writers in general. The complicated and contradictory experiments in spiritual experience embodied in the Greek and Latin writers were an essential part of the world into which Christianity moved when the Gospel had been extended from the Jews to the Gentiles. Much of its character—its inventiveness, its beauty, and its humor—was immaterial to those absorbed in the wonder of a new revelation. As long as the old gods were alive they must be regarded as foes and rivals, and how was classic literature to survive if its gods were rejected? Attempts at compromise were made, but they were poor things. One of the most disappointing of essays is that of St. Basil on the proper use of pagan literature. His doctrine is that the old writers are to be used when they exhort to virtue but to be rejected when they praise false gods. The *Iliad*, of all things, is selected as the great instance of virtue glorified, but how is one to read the *Iliad* and not see Olympus? Much more worthy of respect is the uncompromising vigor of Tertullian, who will not admit the possibility of reconciliation between the old order and the new, or, for that matter, between reason and faith. If he had been as great an artist as he was courageous a spirit a new literature might have begun with him which should have challenged the old on its own ground. But that was not to be, and the two languages, the Christian and pagan, remained in large part incommensurable. Only as the rivalry subsided and the establishment of the new faith enabled it to be indulgent of the old order did the antique grace begin to clothe the thoughts of the Christians and some of the classic writers begin to be received back into the libraries of the devout. Much was laid aside through the Dark Ages and much was lost, but when the great intellectual awakening of the fourteenth and fifteenth centuries burst the bounds of medievalism, a Christianity whose ancient rivals were dead welcomed the literature of those rivals as an essential part of the spiritual as well as the artistic heritage of the Western world.

Yet the religion of the pagan writers can hardly be said to have won from the normal classicist more than the tolerance of inattention. Of course there are those who study ancient religion as a specialty. But I am speaking of the average student or teacher of the classics. He is much more likely to give respectful thought to the syntax, the rhythm, the history, the fallibilities of his author than to his author's estimate of the divine. It is perhaps not surprising that this should be so. No modern teacher feels the need of confuting pagan theology. On the other hand, a healthy mind rejects the vapid, sentimental syncretism which seeks to establish the likeness of alien religious generations by pretending away their differences. Antiquity itself has supplied deterrent examples. The sun worship of the third century after Christ was designed to be all-inclusive, but it was never great, it was only big, and to bigness it sacrificed depth and significance. Nothing was accomplished by trying to identify unlike gods except to obliterate the individuality of them all. If, then, the modern scholar is disinclined to combat Apollo and unable to worship him, he easily solves the dilemma by ignoring him. Thereby much that is useful and illuminating is passed by. The explorations of the human spirit in the realm of theology are as worthy of study as those in the realm of art, and the attentive reader will discover some problems, and some attempted answers whose interest has by no means been exhausted.

There is, for example, the whole body of mysticism. The endeavor to reach the eternal by extrarational means is very ancient; indeed, it may almost be said to antedate the use of reason in religion, and, as already mentioned, it persists through periods of the greatest brilliance in the development of reason. It is an acknowledgment of the limitations of reason, and an affirmation of faith in realities to which there are no limits. It has many forms and many functions. At times it does no more than proffer an escape from a world of actuality which has ceased to make sense. This may result in an otherworldliness as simple as early monasticism, or it may be elaborated into an organism as complex as that of the library of Coptic Gnostic literature just discovered in Egypt, or the intellectual Neoplatonism, both of which attempt to invent a complete new world to take the place of the familiar world of error and frustration. The worshipper at Eleusis could console himself by a faith in mystic reality for the inequities and disappointments of life, and, little as we know directly of the mysteries of Eleusis, they were certainly a powerful influence on some of the finest of ancient minds. To great minds mysticism has again and again afforded not escape but independence of actuality—a very different thing. For though mysticism may tempt a man to abandon his mortal function, it may also strengthen him to transcend that function and to live simultaneously the life temporal and the life eternal. Both extremes may be found in the Greek and Latin authors, as both may be observed in contemporary theology.

Again, there is the attempt, nobly illustrated in Aristotle, to push the use of reason to the very bounds of the universe. To Aristotle, as to many modern scientists, the suggestion of limitations to reason would have been disgraceful. It is interesting to watch Aristotle's cautious and tentative approach to the divine. When he is writing of ethics, where the values are relative, his system can be constructed almost wholly without appeal to divinity. When he is writing of physics and metaphysics, however, where the values are absolute, he cannot dispense with divinity in the end and not only the Unmoved Mover, but the heavenly bodies also are acknowledged to be divine, though the only authority to which he can appeal is ancient wisdom. This closer link between religion and physics than between ethics and religion is a phenomenon on which this generation could meditate with profit.

Such capital questions and very many lesser ones are to be encountered in the pages of the classics, and it is superficial to ignore them. Nothing is more necessary for the classics than to be brought back into the main stream of the humanistic discipline and studied no longer merely as an aristocratic division of learning, but as a brilliant part of the whole history of mankind. For that purpose we must study them anew, entire, and no longer be misled by the false doctrine that what the ancients knew is important but what they believed is negligible. What men believe is always important, and no conception of the relation between a man and his god is without significance for the great question of the true relation between God and man.

6

MUSIC

By JOSEPH S. DALTRY

I. Introduction

The basic assumption of this essay is that music can be, for many, a powerful aid to the life of the spirit. The purpose of the essay is to suggest ways in which the college music teacher can make students aware of this important connection. Two main approaches are suggested, the first through intellectual propositions, the second through worship. The essay falls into the following main divisions:

> Preliminaries and presuppositions, sections I and II.
> Intellectual links between music and religion, sections III, IV, and V.
> Limiting factors, sections VI, VII, and VIII.
> Music and worship, section IX.

In a liberal arts college, where no religious interest on the part of most undergraduates can be presupposed, the explicitly religious slant of the teaching in courses outside the department of religion cannot be great. So far as the subject matter is concerned, the most valuable thing the music teacher can do is to make the music itself as vivid as possible. Since music has spiritual power it will say its own say to those who are sensitive to it, hence the approach of the religiously minded teacher will usually not differ greatly from that of the teacher who makes no effort to recognize religious perspectives.

Even where there is a receptive audience, statements about spiritual value will not, of themselves, have much effect. Although it is a proposition that is familiar to all teachers, it is perhaps worth repeating that actions speak louder than words, and that there have been occasions when students were unable to hear what the teacher said because they were so conscious of what he was. Unless the teacher shows by his daily conduct that he has access to a source of strength and serenity, students are not likely to treat his religious pronouncements with much respect. But if, in addition to professional competence, he displays good humor and kindliness, respect for the undergraduate as an individual and concern for his development, if he is willing to enter into discussions on a footing of mutual respect and is not so concerned with his own importance that he descends to the use of authority to win an argument, he can now and then say something that will arouse in this or that young woman or young man a religious interest that has been dormant.

A great many undergraduates are concerned about religion today, far more than were a generation ago, but comparatively few are willing to discuss religion as religion. Many dislike and distrust what they think of as religion because it stands in their minds for dogma, pretense, hypocrisy, cowardice, intellectual and moral compulsion, stupid repression. Their religious impulse shows itself most commonly in support for such things as the United Nations, the Fair Deal, or movements which oppose racial discrimination, and their effort and enthusiasm are somewhat wasted because they do not understand what is really happening to them. They do not realize that their generous impulses are the Voice of God, and they cut themselves off from the divine power as well as from the comforting and strengthening association of other religiously minded persons. They are likely to intellectualize their impulses, to try to make ethics a substitute for religion, and to seek salvation in the social sciences, never realizing that, in the words of Elton

Trueblood,[1] an ethical code unsupported by religion is a "cut flower," attractive for a very short time but doomed to the early unproductive withering which leaves no seeds. In many cases an emotional push is needed to get such youngsters over the threshold of the House of God, and music can often supply that push.

II. PRESUPPOSITIONS

The first and most fundamental of the assumptions made in this paper is also one of the most controversial. It is, that religion, in the sense of man's attempt to unite himself with a force for good which transcends himself, is the only ultimately important human activity—an activity to which all others whatsoever are either ancillary or opposed. There probably was a time when such a proposition would have received substantial acceptance from all, or almost all, college teachers, but it does not now. Even when it is made plain that we are talking about the aspiration of the individual, not about any special creeds or dogmas or organized churches, there is far from unanimous agreement. There are many members of college faculties who hold that religion is at best an amiable pastime, no more valuable than collecting stamps, and at worst a pernicious form of autosuggestion leading to inability to think straight or tell oneself the truth. Those who hold such antireligious views are often men of conspicuous ability, kindness, and integrity; hence they and their actions cannot be cited as proof that unbelief is inferior to belief. Those who believe that religion is the only ultimately important human activity do so through faith, not because of proof.

From the above it follows that the ultimate justification for the inclusion of music (or any other subject) in the college curriculum or extracurricular activities is its spiritual value. It

[1] D. Elton Trueblood, *The Predicament of Modern Man* (New York: Harper & Bros., 1944).

will be one of the objects of this discussion to indicate the nature of that value.

Though this is by no means a logical necessity, I feel that the first proposition made above implies that, while to attempt to impose an official creed on the student is wrong, the teacher will probably fail to convey much notion of spiritual value unless he has substantially defined his own position, and unless he not only answers serious inquiries about that position frankly, but even goes out of his way at certain times to explain that his attitude toward a particular problem reflects his own spiritual position. This need not prevent him from stating, if it seems desirable to do so, that he may change his mind; that he regards truth (whether spiritual, scientific, aesthetic, or philosophical) as a progressive revelation, to be reapprehended and restated in accordance with the modifications reached as the result of his own arduous search under the guidance of the Holy Spirit, and with every effort to give full consideration to the discoveries of others.

III. HISTORICAL ASSOCIATION

It is quite impossible to avoid religious considerations in any college musical activity that is at all extensive. The football band and some other instrumental groups may do so, but in "appreciation" courses (nobody likes the term but it is a convenient one because we all know what, in general, it means) and most kinds of performance the subject is unavoidable. The greater part of the surviving European music composed before 1400 A.D. is religious, and one can no more discuss it without discussing the Mass than one can discuss sculpture without dealing with the Bible. From 1400 to 1750 the quantity of secular music increases, but the Reformation, the Counter-Reformation, and the multiplication of Protestant sects are all reflected in great music, which cannot be intelligently discussed unless religious questions are dealt with. In at least one case, that of J. S. Bach, the Lutheran background is more important than any other social consideration. From 1750 to 1950 the percentage of secular music increases still further, but who will undertake to deal justly with Mozart, Haydn, Beethoven, Mendelssohn, Brahms, Vaughan Williams, and Stravinsky (the list could be increased) without reference to their religious music and religious beliefs? Throughout the Christian era the music of Western civilization is to a very large extent religious music.

Of pre-Christian music we do not know a great deal, but it is a striking fact that the oldest known example of musical notation is a Sumerian hymn on the creation of man, which probably dates from some time prior to 800 B.C.[2] Sachs has shown that the number of strings on the Babylonian harp was not wholly dictated by musical considerations, but also by the special significance attached to certain numbers. Some harps had five strings, others seven, because the number five was supposed to ward off suffering, the number seven to be holy. In Egypt music was closely associated with the temple, while the many references in the Old Testament to the sacred use of trumpet, harp, psaltery, cymbals, and singing show how largely the Hebrews used music in their worship. Much Greek and Roman music was secular, but of the fifteen pieces of Greek music which survive (some of them mere fragments) the two largest are Delphic Hymns to Apollo and others are hymns to the Muse, to the Sun, and to Nemesis. In Asia music has been extensively used for religious purposes, while among the aboriginal inhabitants of Africa, America, and Australia music was largely an adjunct to the cult. This may have been even more true of prehistoric man, who probably attached a magic-religious significance to music that is preserved in our own

[2] Mentioned by Gustave Reese, *Music in the Middle Ages* (New York: W. W. Norton & Co.) as are also the statements concerning the Babylonian Harp and Greek music. See also Curt Sachs, *The History of Musical Instruments* (New York: W. W. Norton & Co.) for numerous references to magic and ritual significance of various instruments.

language by such words as *enchantress* and *incantation*, both derived from *cantare*, to sing.

IV. THE DOCTRINE OF PERFECTION

In appreciation courses questions of aesthetics are sure to arise. Intelligent undergraduates participating in a vital course inevitably ask such questions as: What is art? How does it function? Has it a moral purpose? Does the aesthetic experience differ from the intellectual? Do the arts overlap? And so on. Many expect quick and final answers. They have made substantial educational progress when they have learned that these are among the most difficult questions that man asks himself—that no answers worthy the name can be reached without much thought and study, and that even those which are reached after such effort may not command wide acceptance. Since the appreciation course must be devoted chiefly to music and only very briefly to philosophy the teacher can only suggest lines of thought and areas of study, but two questions which are apt to arise from purely musical collateral reading are not only of considerable philosophical interest, but also have important religious significance. These questions are discussed in this and the following section.

The English-speaking student who wishes to deal intelligently with musical criticism will read Tovey, in whose *The Integrity of Music* he will find the following: "The perfection of works of art . . . is a quality inherent in the very conception of art, as I have already implied in suggesting that the individual work of art is a microcosm. The conditions of music are specially favorable to the actual attaining of perfection." If the student reads Schweitzer's *J. S. Bach* he will find the following quotation from Martin Luther: "When natural music is heightened and polished by art, there man first beholds and can with great wonder examine . . . the great and perfect wisdom of God. . ." Later in the same book Schweitzer himself says "In no other art does the perfect consign the imperfect to oblivion so thoroughly as it does in music." This notion that perfection is attainable in art appears to be somewhat akin to Croce's proposition that ". . . art remakes ideally, and ideally expresses my momentary situation. Its image, produced by art, becomes separated from time and space, and can be again made and again contemplated in its ideal reality from every point of time and space. It belongs not to the *world* but to the *superworld*; not to the flying moment, but to eternity." [3]

The point of these quotations is that many have felt that imperfect, finite, confused man can, through great art and particularly through great music, catch a glimpse of perfection, eternity and absolute understanding. They have felt that art gives an insight unobtainable through science and philosophy, and that that insight, that assurance of an understanding transcending intellectualism and of a perfection beyond the scope of logic, is an earnest of God's grace. To quote Tovey again "A work of art, in as far as its purpose is unmixed, is a single coherent whole, and as such expresses our faith in the possibility of wholeness and coherence." [4] Many feel that such wholeness and coherence are more possible in music than other arts because the musician has a freer choice of material than other artists and comes nearer to creating his own universe. A musical theme need conform to no outward phenomenon, but is the direct expression of the composer's inner state. (Evidently the recent trend toward abstraction in the pictorial and plastic arts is in part an attempt to obtain a similar freedom.)

This notion that perfection is attainable in art, particularly in music, with its accompanying assumption that perfection is not attainable elsewhere in human experience, is by no means universally accepted. Many maintain that imperfection is as inescapable a part of music as of any other human undertaking

[3] *Aesthetic*, appendix, Ainslie translation, 1909.
[4] Donald F. Tovey, *The Integrity of Music* (Vol. I of *A Musician Talks*, New York: Oxford University Press, 1941), p. 6.

and that perfect art, like perfect truth, is an ideal which man strives for but never attains. It is not my purpose to maintain here that either point of view is correct or is superior to the other. Such matters are not susceptible of proof. It is my purpose to maintain that the doctrine of artistic perfection has inescapable religious connotations. If one accepts the view that perfection is attained in art one is not compelled to agree that this is an evidence of the existence of a perfect divine Being, but one is compelled to examine the proposition that it may be.

Those who reject the doctrine of perfection usually hold that the form is the essence of the music—that the expression *is* the music and that any failure of expression is an imperfection. They show that there is quite wide acceptance of such propositions as that Brahms's orchestration is thick and Beethoven's use of the voice awkward. They point out that many conductors (e.g., Toscanini) change the orchestration of some masterpieces, and that such changes imply not only that the works changed are imperfect, but that the conductors are competent to improve them.

Their opponents feel such matters to be irrelevant, outside the scope of the idea of perfection they cherish, because that perfection resides in the completeness of the spiritual experience enshrined in the great piece of music and the completeness of the music lover's absorption in recreating it as listener or performer. They hold that if the human spirit is deeply moved, nothing else matters. In the moment of transport the enrapt listener is as unconscious of small imperfections as the lover during the ardor of an embrace.

It is this total immersion in music that makes such people resent as strongly the interruptions of those who insist on talking or making other noises while great music is being performed as the devout believer resents similar interruptions of a religious service. The music lover feels the interruption to be a sacrilege, a desecration, by which he is as deeply offended as would be the picture lover who should see a great painting smeared with tar. To him who is thus absorbed the spiritual elevation is everything, the details nothing, and to some the sheer intuitive feeling of rightness and inevitability is a proof of God's prevenient grace.

V. Freedom of Judgment

Russia has carried the theories of Plato,[5] Augustine, and many others to their logical conclusion by imposing penalties on those creative artists who deviate from the official position. Whenever those theories are accepted it is possible that such action may follow; hence it will be well to remind ourselves that the essence of Plato's doctrine is that certain kinds of music are morally superior to others. The following passages from *The Republic* make this clear:

> "Which are the soft and convivial modes?"
> "There are Ionian and Lydian modes which are called slack."
> ". . . shall we use those for men who are warriors?"
> "By no means . . ."

> "Your young men . . . will be chary of incurring any need of law, since they will be trained in that simple music which, we have declared, engenders temperance."

> "In a word, the overseers of the city must devote themselves to this principle, preserving it from secret destruction and guarding it with all care—the principle, namely, that there shall be no innovation of the established order in gymnastics and music . . . [they] must beware of changing to a new kind of music, for the change always involves far-reaching danger. Any alteration in the modes of music is always followed by alteration in the most fundamental laws of the state."[6]

These and similar passages show that Plato believed that music can be rigidly and accurately divided into categories;

[5] See Julius Portnoy, "Platonic Echoes in Soviet Musical Criticism," *Journal of Aesthetics and Art Criticism*, June, 1950.
[6] The quotations are from A. D. Lindsay translation, Everyman's Library.

that the effect of the music of any one category will be the same for all men and can be foretold; and that the categories differ not merely on a basis of preference, but on the fundamentally important basis of morality.

The difficulty with the Platonic doctrine is that it is impossible to obtain general consent as to the effect of particular works of art. Anyone who makes a few inquiries among his friends will find differences as to whether a given piece of music is gay, dignified, satirical, simple, sweet, and so on, and if he makes more extensive inquiries he will find that a number of tests similar to the one made at Columbia University and reported in Douglas Moore's *Listening to Music* show that whenever a large group of persons is asked to write down the effect of each of a series of pieces of music, the areas of agreement are small. Surprisingly small, for, until inquiry is made, each person tends to assume that all others will react to any given music as he does.

And, of course, there is some similarity of experience. For instance, it is true that most people find tunes in the minor mode sadder than those in the major. But compare the gaiety of the Scotch folk song *Charlie Is My Darling*, which is in the minor mode, with the poignant grief and tragedy of the *Dead March*, in Handel's *Saul*, which is in the major mode. The fast tempo and rhythmic piquancy of the folk song effectively remove the sadness of the minor mode, while the slow tempo and rhythmic austerity of the *Dead March* establish sadness, which cannot be counteracted by the major mode. But stop! We have just passed judgment as to the effect of two pieces of music, and we scarcely have the words out of our mouth when somebody says with a mixture of astonishment and indignation, "But I don't find the *Dead March* tragic and sad, I find it merely dull, and there seems to me a haunting sadness about *Charlie Is My Darling*, a feeling of the tragedy implicit in the Jacobite cause, that no sprightliness of rhythm can disguise."

Differences of aesthetic effect are inescapable facts of considerable importance. They are inherent in human diversity. They cannot be dismissed or explained away on grounds of naïveté or sophistication, high or low I.Q., degree of musical training, or on any other grounds. It follows, therefore, that any attempt to establish a canon, to say that this music is morally superior to that, whether the attempt is made by Plato or Stalin, is bound to collide with one of the strongest instincts of free men. If men cannot agree as to whether *Charlie Is My Darling* is gay or sad, it is surely too much to expect them to agree as to whether it is conducive to good or bad action. The kind of pronouncement about music that is made in Russia (as, for instance in the recent condemnations of Shostakovich, Prokofieff, and others) and was made in Germany under Hitler, presupposes a dictator, or somebody who wants to be one, or an oligarchy. It implies that somebody (or some group) is prepared to say, in effect, "I know the truth—it has been wholly and unmistakably revealed to me; therefore it is wrong for you to trust your own judgment. You must accept mine. Whenever we differ I am right and you are wrong, and I will use force if necessary to suppress you if you persist in differing from me."

This, of course, is the position of the dictator in all matters, if his is the enduring kind of dictatorship that rests on ideas (as distinguished from the ephemeral kind which rests merely on personal prowess, arrogance, and appetite). It is this denial of the right of choosing that distinguishes tyranny from freedom. In religious matters the problem has generally been thought of in terms of freedom of the individual conscience, and the whole concept of democracy ultimately rests on it. No one needs to be reminded that it is of such fundamental importance that millions have been ready to die for it. That many will face the scaffold or the firing squad for the sake of aesthetic judgment seems improbable—there is a difference of degree. But, *mutatis mutandis*, the same kind of choice has to be made in both areas.

Fortunately, the problem is not so acute in the democratic countries as it is in Russia and was in Nazi Germany. The victims of the *Kultur Bolschevismus* persecution who escaped to this country are officially subject neither to censure nor approbation, and although Boston continues to censor in accordance with its own brand of bigotry, Bostonians who purchase forbidden works outside their own city can safely have them in their homes.

But though the problem is less acute here than in Russia, it would be a mistake to suppose it to be nonexistent. It does exist and is particularly evident in college circles. There is nearly always, paradoxically, an unofficial official position based on one of those swings of opinion and taste that take place from time to time, which are often described as swings from classicism to romanticism or vice versa. At the present time, for instance, the correct position is that the music of the period 1825–1900 is bad, because it is romantic, sentimental, and too intensely personal. We are in the midst of a violent swing away from romanticism, and those who crave the safety of an official position have exploited it by picking out the composers they consider most romantic and condemning them roundly. They have accordingly established the doctrine that, of all the sinners of the nineteenth century, Schumann and Wagner are the worst, and they pour scorn on those benighted ones who maintain that there may be something in what the composers of the last century wrote after all, and that Kipling really spoke the truth when he said:

> There are nine and sixty ways of constructing tribal lays,
> And every single one of them is right.

Readiness to see good in many different kinds of art is repugnant to those arrogant or frightened persons who establish official positions; so they go on making ex cathedra statements in spite of the obvious fact that official positions are generally reversed, either by the whim of the dictator or by posterity.

Individual choice based on individual judgment is always dangerous. He who insists on liberty in religious matters says, in effect, that the voice of conscience is the voice of God, and that it gives a more reliable command than any human person or group. But, as has so often been pointed out, it is very easy to mistake the voice of appetite or ego for the voice of conscience. To follow one's own line in matters of faith and morals, when it runs counter to that of the majority, is difficult and dangerous, particularly when the line of the majority has been adopted because of the example of the saints. The majority position must be reckoned with, however much it may seem to consist only of lip service to a mechanical code which lacks the spirit of the saints. The reluctance of the timid and uncertain to enter on an original and rigorous examination of the creed of the majority, particularly when they feel themselves unqualified by scholarship and intellectual capacity, is understandable, and without such examination nonconformity seems unjustified.

But spiritual growth ceases unless the effort to examine is constantly made, and for any person or group to condemn this effort seems wrong. Similarly, the individual grows aesthetically only through the exercise of individual judgment, and the sneers of those who cannot tolerate any judgment but their own are a mild form of tyranny. If music has, as is here maintained, a great spiritual power, it follows that there is imposed on those who have spiritual convictions the same kind of obligation to make individual judgments about music that exists in all spiritual matters.

VI. Limitations of Talent and Sensitivity

Just as it is the naïve instinct of every man that all will share his aesthetic judgments, so he who is profoundly moved by music assumes that all men are similarly moved. This leads to the common assertion that music is the best road to religious experience, but the statement is so sweeping as to be false. It must be subjected to limitations and qualifications before it becomes true. It would be better to think of music as a compass by means of which some travellers may find the right road among many, or as a vehicle in which they may travel along that road at a better speed than would otherwise be possible.

We must guard, first of all, against the idea nearly always implicit in such metaphorical use of the word, that music is a one-way road, i.e., that it always leads to the spiritual life. In fact, we find persons of cultivated musical taste whose conduct shows clearly that the cynical materialism they profess is indeed their guiding principle. We must therefore admit, that music does not necessarily or invariably, by its own unaided power, propel man toward the spiritual life. Indeed, there are those who assert that some music can have the opposite effect, and who cite, in support of this proposition, the fact that many of the highly placed Nazis, whose actions we find most horrible, were fond of the music of Wagner. Evidently this argument is far from conclusive. Perhaps the Nazis would have been still worse if they had not loved music, perhaps their taste in music was as irrelevant as their taste in cigarettes, and they would have been just as bad if they had listened to Beethoven instead of Wagner. Be this as it may, we cannot dodge the fact that repeated doses of Wagnerian music appear to have had no ameliorating effect on the Nazi love of cruelty and tyranny.

We also must guard against the idea that, since we are talking about a public road, open to every traveller, all who wish to lead the spiritual life can increase their spiritual capacity through music. This would be true only if musical sensitivity were as nearly universal as the ability to walk. In fact, some people have it to so small a degree that, for all practical purposes, they do not have it at all.

This is a provocative statement which will be challenged by many. It will be said that musical aptitude is the product of environment rather than inheritance and that it will increase wondrously where there is persistency and a good teacher; that, to take the lowest extreme, even the tone-deaf can be trained to sing; and that, since those who are tone-deaf comprise only a small percentage of the total population, it follows that most people can avail themselves of music with comparative ease.

There is just enough truth in this kind of statement to make it dangerous. To be sure, musical ability, like any other ability, can be increased. No matter how small it may be to begin with, it will grow under the right circumstances. But it is equally true that there is a limit to the extent of the possible growth, perhaps not theoretically, but certainly practically, and the older the person the greater the limitation. The training of "tone-deaf" persons illustrates this. Enough have been trained to sing to show that it is probably true that any person of average intelligence (say I.Q. 95 or better) who has no physical defect of hearing or speech can learn to sing if he is sufficiently persistent and has good training. But the process is so lengthy and laborious (it resembles that by which the spastic patient is trained to walk or the deaf-mute to talk) that the rewards are almost never anywhere near great enough to justify the effort. The same is true of all who are noticeably deficient in native musical aptitude, even though they are not actually tone-deaf.

Musical difficulty seems to be analogous to the language difficulty that is now being widely recognized by educators. In the case of spoken language the effort to raise the ceiling is worth making because the whole process of living is severely distorted and cramped by inability to achieve a certain minimum lingual efficiency, but in the case of music the effort is probably not worth making because the cost of failure is not so high and the goal is different. Spoken language is a practical tool as well as the raw material of the literary arts. He who suffers from a language difficulty will probably never learn to derive aesthetic satisfaction from great literature, but he can learn to write social letters and make clear his needs and wishes when buying an insurance policy. But music has no such utilitarian value.

Even if the individual does succeed in raising his musical ceiling it does not follow that he will obtain aesthetic satisfaction from music, for musical aptitude and musical sensitivity are not the same thing and one does not presuppose the other. Musical *aptitude* exists in varying degree and includes various things, but its basic component, without which it cannot be said to exist, is the ability to identify and remember patterns of sound in terms of pitch, rhythm, intensity, tone quality, and so on, whereas musical *sensitivity* is the capacity to be moved by music. Musical aptitude is a matter of memory, and its possession does not imply musical sensitivity any more than the ability to recite the *Second Inaugural* from memory proves the reciter to be sensitive to great literature. Most experienced teachers have known persons whose musical memory was at least average, and in some cases better than average, who, in spite of reasonably extensive exposure to music and discussion of it, found in it so little attraction and satisfaction that they largely excluded it from their lives, listening to it under social compulsion but not from choice. Conversely, some who, in spite of repeated hearings, cannot be sure whether they are listening to the Mozart G *minor* or the Beethoven *Eroica* are nevertheless so attracted and moved that they often go out of their way to hear music, and that under circumstances which make it extremely improbable that they are adopting a pose.

From this it would appear that the statement (commonly made) that music is the art which leads most surely to religious experience is false. There is evidence in support of the proposition that, deeply moving as music is to some, poetry, drama, and other forms of literature are equally moving to others, and the visual arts to still others. Music may dissolve Jones into ecstasies and bring all heaven before his eyes, but he must not, for that reason, distrust Smith's statement that music leaves him largely unmoved, nor jump to the conclusion that Smith is a pachyderm incapable of responding to any art. It is quite likely that Smith is ravished by Milton as Jones is by Mozart. It seems probable that all the statements made in this essay concerning the spiritual power of music apply with equal force to the other arts.

So far as the college music teacher is concerned, the point of all this is that it is an error to urge the musically insensitive student to continue the study of music because of its spiritual value. Probably every student should devote a year to music appreciation, but if the teaching has been at all competent those who are as bored at the end of the year as at the beginning will generally do well to abandon the effort. Perhaps one of the other arts will be more rewarding (though there appear to be some who are not sensitive to art in any form), and the time will not have been entirely wasted because the student can mention Schoenberg, Stravinsky, Bartok, neoclassicism, and expressionism with a suitably light touch in polite conversation, and the information that Haydn was a contemporary of George Washington, or that Machaut's patron fought at the Battle of Crecy, may come in handy in history exams.

VII. LIMITATIONS OF SACRED MUSIC

The college music teacher who wishes to make students aware of the religious significance of music finds the subject easy to introduce when he is dealing with sacred music, because the full significance of the music cannot be grasped unless its spiritual intention is recognized. The teacher is bound to deal as fully with the religious life of the composer as with his social and economic status, and he must deal with the religious implications of the music itself just as he does with its form and texture. The matter comes up naturally and inevitably, and the teacher is free from any suggestion of preaching or hypocrisy.

It would be a mistake, however, to jump to the conclusion that religious music is in general more spiritually valuable than secular, or that the religiously minded teacher should place more emphasis on it. The spiritual value of music derives from its ability to elevate and cleanse man's spirit and thus to help him to that union with a higher power which I have posited as the basic fact of religion. It seems probable that this property inheres in all great music, whatever its label. To be sure, there is some sacred music which seems to most cultivated listeners to achieve a particularly high degree of spirituality. The names of Bach and Palestrina come instantly to mind, and to this writer some of the music of Josquin des Pres has a quality of holiness unmatched elsewhere. But this is such a personal matter that it would be very unwise to generalize about it. Even though most cultivated listeners may agree to the general proposition that some works are more spiritual than others, the area of agreement is considerably reduced when specific works are discussed. Is the *St. Matthew Passion* more elevating than the *Ninth Symphony*? It would be interesting to take a poll, always supposing one could decide who should be polled. Even if the vote went strongly in favor of one work or the other (which seems unlikely), it would be of little importance for the individual who disagreed with it. One might as well tell A, who finds onions indigestible, that he must go on eating them because B, C, and D find them nourishing.

The fact that the composer intended the music for sacred use often has little bearing on its character. Most of the thousands of organ pieces with titles like "Meditation," "Elevation," and "Communion" that have been produced during the past century are as insipid as music can be, and scarcely anything from Tin-Pan Alley can match the triviality and vulgarity of the poorest Gospel hymns. On the other hand, it has often been remarked that there is no essential difference between the style of Bach's religious and secular works, and while it must be admitted that most people find nothing in the secular cantatas that equals the wonderful exaltation of the best of the sacred choral works, it is also true that such secular works as the *Chromatic Fantasy* seem to reach greater heights than some of the choral preludes. Since Bach was above all else a church musician (he defined music as *"eine wohlklingende Harmonie zur Ehre Gottes und zulässiger Ergötzung des Gemuths"*) it is not surprising that whenever he put forth his powers he produced music of such nobility that it can quite properly be called sacred. What *is* at first sight surprising is that the same can be said of Brahms and Beethoven, who were by no means church composers though they made powerful settings of sacred texts, and, to a lesser degree, of Gibbons, Handel, Mendelssohn, and others.

Is there, then, a real distinction between sacred and secular music? We must recognize that there is a difference imposed by certain conventions concerning tempo and rhythm. Most churchgoers would consider the scherzos of Beethoven's *Third* and *Ninth Symphonies* too fast and too strongly rhythmic (too reminiscent of the dance) for church use, and there can be little doubt that most people, whether regular churchgoers or not, would agree; hence it is possible that the matter is not one merely of convention. Yet music which is strongly reminiscent of the dance has very often been widely accepted for church use. Mendelssohn's "How lovely are the messengers" from *St. Paul* has been used in thousands of services, in spite of the fact that it is often performed in such a way that it strongly resembles a Viennese waltz, and such revival hymns as "Whosoever Surely Meaneth Me" could be used in the ballroom without change. Handel's "For He is like a refiner's fire" (*Messiah*) and Bach's "Sind Blitze sind Donner in Wolken verschwunden" (*St. Matthew Passion*) cannot be said to move as fast or with as strong accent as the Beethoven scherzos, but it may not unreasonably be claimed that they approach them in character. Certainly they are a long way from the mythical adoration of Byrd's *Ave Verum Corpus* or the serenity of

Bach's *Jesu, Joy of Man's Desiring,* which are the kind of thing most people think of as typically sacred music.

But if we exclude music which suggests the dance, is there any other basic difference between sacred and secular? Somebody will immediately mention Wagner, somebody else Tschaikowsky. It will be said that Wagner's is the music of eroticism (*Tristan*), Fascism (*The Ring*), and chauvinism (*Die Meistersinger*), and that Tschaikowsky produced music of indecision, defeat, melancholia and tearful sentimentality. Such assertions are undoubtedly made seriously and sincerely, but they appear to be examples of the error already repeatedly referred to, of supposing that all men react to the same stimulus in the same way. Though nine listeners out of ten find the *Tristan Prelude* erotic, the tenth finds it as deeply moving and as free from sexual suggestiveness as Beethoven's overture *Leonore No. 3,* and the same man may find the last movement of Tschaikowsky's *Sixth* equally elevating, in spite of the fact that many consider it neurotic. It would appear, therefore, that this matter of sacred versus secular is but a part of the larger question of individual judgment and its moral implications which was discussed in section V, and that no person or group can pass judgment as to what music is sacred and what secular, any more than he or they can decide what music is moral and what immoral. The only useful generalization that can be made is that those charged with providing music for public worship should avoid, as far as possible, works which are known to give offense. To a given organist the *Tristan Prelude* may be a work of great spiritual power, but he will be wise not to play it as an opening voluntary.

But what shall he play? It is worth noting that, just as there is almost no music which does not have spiritual value for some, so there is none which is not offensive to others. Bach, Des Pres, and Palestrina are the staples of the average college choir nowadays, and the organist chooses his chapel repertoire chiefly from the works of Bach and his predecessors, and from Purcell, Hindemith, and the modern Frenchmen. But many undergraduates and faculty members find these works dull and meaningless, and ask for Batiste, Dubois, Maunder, Stainer, and others like them. The problem of what music to use in public worship is almost never an easy one, but in this respect the position of the college church musician is much better than that of his colleague in the average parish church. Since the college is an educational institution the musical director of the chapel is on firm ground in insisting that his is an educational as well as religious task and that undergraduates shall not hear trivial or vulgar music. He knows, moreover, that at undergraduate age tastes change readily, and familiarity with a new and more exalted idiom will often breed love, whereas the parish church musician knows that at least half the members of his congregation are middle-aged or elderly and therefore take to new things much less readily.

Before we go on to other matters it may be worthwhile to glance for a moment at a proposition that is sometimes advanced in connection with what has just been discussed. It is presently the fashion in certain circles to regard Wagner as a second- or third-rate composer, and Tschaikowsky has always been so ranked by most; hence some feel that no valid comparison can be made between their works and those of composers like Bach and Beethoven, who have long been placed in the first rank by most competent judges. It is argued that it stands to reason that a first-rate composer who sets out to write sacred music will produce something more elevated than a second-rater. This kind of oversimplification is faintly analogous to that of the purveyors of race prejudice. The Negrophobe says, in effect, "The Negro race has, on the whole, achieved less than the white race; hence any Negro is inferior to any Caucasian." However faulty the analogy between them, the two propositions are equally false. In all the arts there are

examples of men who, but for one or two works (often quite
small) of great beauty, would be unknown. Surely nobody
would class Farrant and Purcell with Bach and Beethoven,
yet *Lord, for Thy Tender Mercies' Sake* and *Thou Knowest,
Lord the Secrets of Our Hearts*, though simple and short, are
widely regarded as among the most completely devotional
pieces of church music we possess.

VIII. Limitations of College Choirs

Just as one is tempted at first glance to suppose that sacred
music provides the spiritually minded college music teacher
with the best means of enlisting the spiritual interest of his
students, so the choir which supplies the music for the college
chapel would seem at first sight to be the most promising organization through which to work; but it is probable that the
second proposition is no better than the first.

In the first place there is the difficulty of performance.
While there has been great improvement during the last thirty
years in the technique of performance and in the caliber of
the music performed, it is still true that very few college
chapels can offer a musical experience comparable to that
which is available in the concert halls of most big cities, or
even through the radio and the phonograph record. Most
college students who are interested in music have heard so
many excellent performances that their critical standards of
performance are high, and the earnest and laudable efforts of
the college choir may leave some unmoved, perhaps even a
little irked.

In the second place there is the difficulty of text. In much
sacred music the theology, or the symbolism, or both are offensive to many, even though they are by training and native
bent spiritually minded. Changing taste has removed "There
is a fountain filled with blood" from the repertoire of most

colleges, and so we are spared that gruesome horror and most similar ones, but many stumbling blocks remain. What many feel to be the anthropomorphic symbolism of the Trinity, which persists in the texts of much sacred music, including many of the hymns that are musically of the first rank, e.g., *Nun Danket* and *All Creatures of Our God and King,* is disturbing to those who find it a clumsy and primitive way of suggesting the many-sidedness of God. Texts which contain phrases like "The Lamb of God," which presuppose original sin and the vicarious sacrifice, offend others. Such phrases from the creeds as "He descended into Hell" or "I believe in the resurrection of the body" cause even greater difficulty in some quarters, while the terrified egocentricity of *Libera Me* and other parts of the requiem mass are not only unacceptable theologically, but a source of acute dislike.

It is not my purpose to suggest that those who have these difficulties are necessarily more advanced spiritually than those who do not. The latter are probably to be envied, whether their serenity derives from a kind of fundamentalism which accepts the phrases quoted as exact statements, or from a familiarity with and facility in symbolic expression which allows them instantly and easily to apprehend such language in spiritual terms. My sole purpose is to point out that the difficulties mentioned are real and important, and do much to reduce the spiritual effectiveness of a great deal of sacred music which is otherwise of a high order. It is true that this difficulty may decline where the text is in a foreign language—particularly if it is in Latin. In the first place, most choristers will have little or no idea of what they are singing. In the second place, Latin is, as Stravinsky has pointed out, a language of convention and ritual which can be treated as merely phonetic material.[7] Even those who went far enough with Latin to know that *Agnus Dei qui tollis peccata mundi* does deal with

[7] Igor Stravinsky, *Chronicle of my Life* (London: Victor Gallancz, Ltd., 1936).

the vicarious sacrifice seem to be less troubled by it than by the same phrase in English. The Latin acts as a sort of filter which largely removes the feeling of explicitness that goes with English. But in spite of all this the textual difficulty persists because the text is an integral part of the whole composition and cannot be dodged. The listener in the appreciation class must cope with it to some extent and the chorister is likely to find it even more inescapable. Many choral directors feel (correctly, in my opinion) that the chorister should be aware of the meaning of the words he sings and should try to place himself in the frame of mind of the composer who set the words. Like the actor who plays a part foreign to his own personality, the chorister should try to put himself in the composer's place even though he cannot share the composer's conviction. But this appears to be a faulty basis for religious experience, in which sincerity is surely a necessity. Only those who are able to accept the text, or who can ignore its explicit meaning while concentrating on the elements of faith and reverence it preserves, can cope with it successfully.

One final difficulty with sacred music is that those who perform it are largely debarred from making it an act of worship, if the dictum be accepted that the first requisite for worship is spiritual concentration. The singer or player who takes part in a performance of the *St. Matthew Passion* cannot, during that performance, give his attention primarily to worship, any more than he can do so while driving a car at high speed on a busy highway. In both cases the most engrossing attention is required for the technical task.

In spite of the negative tone of the above it is not my intention to suggest that singing in the college choir is incapable of promoting any spiritual growth; it is only my intention to show that it has its negative as well as positive side. The important advantages of choir membership are that many musically sensitive persons get a better grasp of the true inwardness of a piece of great music by participating in actual

performance than by mere listening,[8] and that such direct
participation is far easier in choral than in instrumental music.
Comparatively few have the ability or the patience to master
the violin or the oboe, hence the orchestra and the chamber
music group are closed to most; but the instrument of the
choralist is the voice which he uses every day in speech. Speech
is not sufficient training for singing, but the experience of great
numbers of undergraduates in many college choirs shows that
a very little group instruction in vocal technique—a tiny fraction of what is required for instrumental facility—is sufficient
to produce results which, while not equal to those of the best
professional choirs, are still valuable—amply good enough to
make the experience meaningful for most participants and
many listeners. In short, my point in this section is that the
spiritual value of the college choir should not be overrated,
and that it is primarily valuable not because it is an instrument
of the college chapel, but because it provides some undergraduates with a good first-hand experience of great music.

IX. Music and Worship

In sections III, IV, and V some ideas were suggested which
arise naturally in many general discussions of music. They
establish a connection between music and religion which is
primarily intellectual. But just as religion involves something
beyond the intellect, so music presents, in addition to its intellectual content, something that is more than intellectual.
It is this supra-intellectual quality that connects music with
religion most intimately. The connection is most apparent in
worship, but that is precisely the area which is hardest to discuss and is most likely to seem irrelevant to many students. It
is also the most dangerous topic because it is the one in which
it is easiest to give offense. In spite of these obstacles the

[8] See Gerald Johnson, A *Little Night Music* (New York: Harper & Bros.,
1937).

teacher can occasionally, with some classes, if he has been able to establish the proper kind of *rapport*, say something—a very little—about worship. If he can do it effectively he will have performed an important service to religion.

The religious significance of music derives from the fact that, like other arts, it has the power to cleanse and elevate. He who is already a believer often uses music as an aid in making the difficult transition from worldly to spiritual thought and mood. He who is not a believer may in course of time become one because music produces in him a mood of combined humility and exaltation in which it seems impossible to do anything mean, dirty, deceitful, or cruel. While he is in that mood belief in the spiritual life seems inescapable. It is this power which has led to the close connection between music and worship. For our present purpose worship may be divided into three categories:

1. Thanksgiving and praise.
2. Prayer.
3. Meditation.

Thanksgiving and praise are essential parts of the worship of many persons. The man or woman who feels that religion is not merely *an* important part of life, but *the* important part, the one activity to which all others are incidental and ancillary; who is conscious that God's love is something as constantly and unfailingly available as the law of gravity—a power which can always be used by those who establish suitable circumstances; who is able to draw, however slightly, on that unfailing source of strength and serenity, so that every disappointment gives place to hope, and every fall to a new rising; he or she who feels all this must find it a source of joy, and many who feel such joy are so strongly impelled to express it that not to do so does violence to their inner natures. They praise and give thanks, not because they wish to flatter the Deity or curry favor, but because there are times when nothing else seems so important as their urge to express their sense of their own joy and gratitude.

Now this is artistic creation, or something very close to it. To be sure, art, if it is to endure, must be a communication as well as an expression, must have an audience to consume as well as a composer to create, but that does not mean that the composer has to be conscious of the audience or direct his thought toward it. Doubtless many composers do try to speak to a particular audience, but most of those who have felt the urge to create know that there are times when sheer expression is everything—when nothing else in life seems so important as to capture, to give shape to, to play or write down, that maddeningly vague something that has welled up out of some mysterious depth and has obliterated every other thought and emotion. Of course the result may not amount to anything as a communication. It may be so narrowly personal that nobody else can apprehend it, or so similar to what has been done before as to be hackneyed, but surely it comes into being through the same kind of urge to express as that which produces great masterpieces. In so far, then, as they are expression (not communication), praise and thanksgiving are sacred art.

This being the case, it is not to be wondered at that praise and thanksgiving are so commonly expressed in music. Although most Quakers and a few others have largely excluded it from their worship, the greater part of mankind expresses religious joy most easily through music. Among civilized men the point is readily illustrated by those exclamations of "Hallelujah," "Amen," "Hosanna," "Praise the Lord," which used to be, and I presume still are, heard at revivals and camp meetings. These words are seldom enunciated as they are in ordinary speech. One does not hear the brief "Hallelujah" of the well-bred curate reading the Sunday morning lesson, one hears "Ha-a-a-le-lu-u-u-jah," the vowels sustained over a substantial period of time on notes of definite pitch. It is a song rather than spoken utterance, and appears to be the same kind of thing as the melismatic jubilation, sometimes textless but often sung to the alleluia, of which Augustine speaks.[9] Such spontaneous and unorganized outbursts of the early Christians developed into the sequences of the medieval church, and, indirectly, into all that wealth of melismatic and contrapuntal utterance which culminates in such things as the *Sanctus* and *Osanna* in Bach's *Mass in B Minor*. The exclamatory utterance of revival and the camp meeting is, therefore, the naïve and primitive form of expression of religious joy, differing from the greatest works of some of the greatest composers in breadth and scope and organization but not in initial impulse. Evidently one of the tasks of the college music teacher is to show how, by organization and extension, the great work becomes vastly more expressive than the primitive utterance.

The position of music in the other main divisions of worship is less simple because prayer and meditation are less simple activities than praise and thanksgiving. Jubilation is a product, not an original activity. The worshipper *becomes* joyful because he has derived assurance, comfort, and serenity from prayer, meditation, or new-found faith. Jubilation is a comparatively effortless *effect*, prayer and meditation are *causes* which must be initiated by the worshipper at the cost of greater or lesser effort. Prayer is easier than meditation, and since it is necessary to distinguish between the two it will be well to deal with prayer first.

Prayer is asking. In its lowest terms it is the routine, mechanical repetition of formulae, involving no more effort than is necessary to put other matters aside for the period of the prayer. Even at some higher levels prayer is asking for things. The worshipper prays for rain, good crops, a better job, a handsome husband, relief from pain, or something of the sort. Such asking is probably less common today in Western civilization than it was fifty years ago, but it is still very wide-

[9] Schaff, *et al.* (eds.), *A Select Library of the Nicene and Post-Nicene Fathers of the Christian Church*, Series I, Vol. VIII, Psalms xcv and c.

spread and is a source of comfort and aspiration to many. Throughout the Christian era and probably in pre-Christian times it has been extensively and closely associated with music. In the Mass, for instance, the *Kyrie, Agnus Dei* and *Dona nobis pacem* are wholly prayers, and the *Gloria* is in part (*... filius patris qui tollis peccata mundi, miserere nobis ...*"). Who will undertake to count the musical settings of the Mass that survive, to say nothing of those that have been lost? And who would deny that some of the settings, from Machaut to Bach, are among the greatest music we have?

Outside the Mass the musical settings of prayers are legion. One thinks at once of the wonderful series of motets stretching from the Latin of the thirteenth century to such vernacular masterpieces as Brahms's setting of parts of Psalm 51, but these, numerous as they are, are again but a part of the literature. There is no form of prayer which has not been set to music, and no kind of singing that has not been used for prayer. Not only in the restrained beauty of plain chant and the magnificent elaboration of the great choral works, not only in the compositions that the musician considers great, but in the gospel hymn and popular music, are prayers found. A recent setting of the Lord's Prayer has achieved great popularity, and while it strikes the person of cultivated taste as trivial and superficial, and has undoubtedly been used by many simply as a means to a somewhat sentimental experience not far removed from that produced by some popular love songs, there is also no doubt that it has been of definite religious value to many. In short, music goes as readily with prayer as with praise. One form of worship leads to music as naturally and instinctively as the other. Conversely, the music associated with prayer can establish a mood of intercession, just as a setting of the *Te Deum* can move the worshipper to praise.

Meditation is prayer raised to a higher power. Many people have abandoned the practice of asking for things, partly because such prayers seem to be seldom "answered" (i.e., the things prayed for appear to be received no more frequently than they would be on a basis of pure chance), partly because the notion of a God who capriciously grants individual and special favors is much less satisfying than that of a God whose love is unfailingly present for all who will avail themselves of it. The worshipper therefore ceases to be concerned chiefly with "Give us this day our daily bread" [10] and begins to fix his attention on the extensions and implications of "Thy Kingdom come, Thy will be done." He begins to realize that the only gift he can pray for with complete sincerity, hope, faith, and humility is the presence of God, and that that is the only thing worth praying for, for if he has that, nothing else matters. He therefore begins to rely much less on words and much more on intellectual and spiritual attitude. Words are essential to the worshipper who asks for things because they are the only means by which he can be specific, but they become less and less important to him who seeks only the presence of God, because the one thing asked for needs no description, and the answer is something felt inwardly, sensed by the spirit and the highest reaches of the mind, not something apprehended by the physical senses and desired for their gratification.

When this stage is reached the worshipper begins to move on from prayer to meditation. He begins to learn to place himself in a state of intense awareness and receptivity, a condition in which the ego is pushed more and more out of the way, no words are needed, but in silent adoration the soul is opened to the Divine Power as the flower opens to the sun. It is a condition which demands a degree of concentration equalled only by that of the scholar who loses himself in a difficult problem, and it surpasses the condition of the scholar because it demands a total denial and surrender of the ego which the

[10] If this term is regarded, as it usually is by the layman, as referring to ordinary physical diet; but see Gerald Heard's *The Creed of Christ* (New York: Harper & Bros., 1941), chap. iv, where are briefly summarized the arguments of many scholars through the centuries in support of the notion that this phrase refers to no ordinary bread.

scholar does indeed approach, but which comes to him intermittently as a by-product, not steadily as a conscious objective. What has music to do with it?

Nothing directly. In the moment of meditation music, however great, is a distraction, something which makes meditation difficult, and therefore, in most cases, impossible. A man meditating is like the mountain climber who hangs on by the tips of his fingers to the edge of the precipice. His whole being is concentrated on hanging on. Drop an extra pound of weight on his shoulder and he will let go, and music, or speech, or anything whatsoever is likely to be that pound weight. This may be one reason why the Quakers often have no music. Their silent worship is, at its best, meditation assisted and heightened by human fellowship, and when the silence is complete the experience can be tremendous.

But music can do much to prepare the worshipper for the effort of meditation. Until a high degree of spiritual development is reached, meditation is often approached with some reluctance. It is itself so difficult, and it demands such a difficult pushing aside of appetites and material preoccupations, that the beginner often shrinks from it. Let him listen to fine music for whatever period seems desirable, however, and the effort is much less forbidding. If he is by nature and training sensitive to it, the splendid power of music can draw him away from the material toward the spiritual. Great music is the permanent expression of the most exalted experiences of some of the most sensitive men who have lived, and it is capable of carrying the listener upward with much less effort on his part than would otherwise be required. It is like the rocket booster that helps a heavy airplane leave the ground. It is one of the stairways that save man from the necessity of making what may otherwise be an agonizing leap. It is one of the most shining and endearing examples of God's love and grace. It is for some the pathway to heaven.

He whose talents particularly fit him to show this path to young men and women can give himself to no better task. As indicated above, he can almost never make more than the briefest reference to it in class and often cannot do even that. But not infrequently the way may be paved by such intellectual exercises as have been suggested—by drawing attention to the age-old association of music and religion and to such areas of speculation as the ideas of perfection and freedom of choice. If the teacher has created an atmosphere of confidence; if his students believe they can trust him to the extent of wearing their hearts on their sleeves and exposing those areas of their being which are most sensitive—which is what any man does who talks about his deepest religious experience and aspirations; if all this has taken place, a few will, with great hesitation, and with the utmost readiness to withdraw at the faintest suggestion of callousness or cynicism or impatience, seek private conversations. There the matter can be carried quite far and the student can be helped to translate what he may have supposed to be the purely humanistic experience of music into an important part of the all-enveloping life of the spirit.

7

PHYSICAL SCIENCES

By HUGH S. TAYLOR

I

In the ancient University of Alexandria the hierarchy of learning, it is said, occupied various levels in the building. Chemistry was assigned to the basement. In our own times, science, by the common consent of the world, has been elevated to a position of exalted stature without parallel in recorded history. The remarkable successes of experimental science are everywhere evident; everyone is conscious of them through the technological applications. Science and the scientists are regarded with a mixture of awe, fear, and an admiration that oftentimes approaches veneration. Whereas formerly it was the exception for the scientist to be consulted with respect to matters concerning the general welfare, today we find him occupying a central position in human affairs, to be consulted in every variety of human endeavor, in peace and in war, his methods employed in every aspect of human relations, his role that of the modern oracle. The success which has attended his efforts in his own domain has led to the adoption of the "scientific method" in many other phases of human effort. We read of the scientific study of history, the scientific approach to problems of economics and politics. Not least, a contemporary discussion of the place of religion in human life and activity may well elicit some such inquiry as "What has Science to say with respect to the doctrine of the Incarnation?"

Concurrently with this obvious exaltation of the role of

science in human affairs it is apparent also in the history of
the last five hundred years that the role of religion has become progressively less central in human conduct, has yielded
place to science with a role as a substitute-religion. It is the
purpose of this essay to deny that science can ever assume the
central position in human affairs to which present tendencies
appear to urge it. It will suggest that these tendencies arise
from a mistaken view with respect to the nature of science and
ignore its limitations. It will set forth, briefly, the essential
nature of science. It will trace, in barest outline, how science
developed from its earliest origins to the position of intellectual hegemony into which it may be elevated. It will record
how religion and science have areas which they share in common and how also they each possess areas distinct and characteristic. The particular focus of the effort is the student, in
college or university, who, dimly conscious of the resource and
power of each approach to the problems of life as he apprehends them, would welcome the point of view of one who
essays to combine both scientific effort and religious practice in
harmonious relation each to the other.

II

The scientist is concerned with the nature of the physical
world as it is apprehended through the senses. His method is
experimental, with planned activities to elucidate particular
areas of observation. It is also theoretical, in that an attempt
is made to correlate observations and provide a unified structure of reasoning which will embrace, ever more successfully,
the sum total of things observed. This theoretical activity
often passes beyond the realm of pure observation, into the
area of coordination or interpretation of the facts or of the experiments. In this activity, whether consciously or unconsciously, the scientist becomes the philosopher. The older
designation of science, natural philosophy, is indicative of this

phase of the scientist's activity. The scientist could never rest content with a meaningless assembly of facts. Sooner or later he will concern himself with their interrelations and interconnections. He will wish to pass from description toward comprehension.

The wise scientist readily grants, however, that, beyond the limits of his scientific observations, there are areas into which, as scientist, he does not venture. He recognizes beauty in art and in literature, in form and expression. He recognizes problems of fundamental import involving values, ends and purposes of life. While such problems are compelling in their urgencies in many aspects of human activity, he can, in his purely scientific pursuits, abstract both observation and correlation from such urgencies and recognize that they lie in the provinces of philosophy, morality, and of religion. The wise scientist recognizes both the power and the limitations of his science.

It was in the sixteenth and seventeenth centuries that the whole pace of scientific activity quickened. The change that took place stemmed from a new attitude, for which Francis Bacon bears a large measure of responsibility, the examination of our universe by observation and experiment instead of through the medium of philosophy and the deductive method. From his vision there resulted in 1662 the Royal Society of London. Similar movements had occurred elsewhere, rather earlier in Italy (1600), whence it had spread to France (1633). Leibnitz established the Akademie der Wissenschaften in Berlin in 1700. In each case a similar pattern was followed with a small group of active-minded and inquiring men meeting together to share their observations of nature, discuss their problems, formulate programs for their solution by the collection of pertinent facts or the devising and performance of appropriate experiments. Bacon in the *New Atlantis* (1627) had stated explicitly his belief that from accurately ascertained facts one could attain "the knowledge of causes and secret notions of things and the enlarging of the bounds of human empire, to the effecting of all things possible." Somewhat earlier, in the *Novum Organum*, he had forecast that "there are still laid up in the womb of Nature many secrets of excellent use having no affinity or parallelism with anything that is now known . . . They too, no doubt, will some time or other . . . come to light of themselves just as the others did; only by the method of which we are now treating they can be speedily and suddenly and simultaneously presented and anticipated." In this faith began, among small groups of "curious men," the organized pursuit of scientific research. Such research-minded men have doubtless existed in every generation since the first awakening of reflective thought in man. It was, however, the seventeenth century which saw the small beginnings of the organization of research scientists. By continuous growth and development there has resulted the modern condition where, by the hundreds of thousands, in many directions of thought and action, men undertake scientific research individually and in organized groups to uncover "secrets of excellent use . . . speedily, suddenly and simultaneously." Scientific research today is in process of becoming a primary function, even a principal function of humanity.

The prestige which science now enjoys, admirably exemplified in the esteem in which, for example, the Royal Society of London is held today, contrasts very significantly with some very general attitudes towards the members of the same Society in its early formative years. Even the Royal Patron, King Charles II, ventured to doubt the wisdom of his action in granting the Society its charter, since, as Pepys records, he "mightily laughed at Gresham College, for spending time only in weighing of ayre, and doing nothing else since they sat." By many the experimental method was equated with intellectual folly. There were, doubtless, as in all new movements, experiments made with lack of discrimination, others which could rightly be held up to ridicule. The minute book of the Royal Society's experiments contains the following example: "A circle was made with powder of unicorn's horn and a spider set in the middle of it, but it immediately ran out. The trial being repeated several times the spider once made some stay on the powder." [1] Miss Syfret, of Girton College, Cambridge, who recently published this extract from the minutes, points out that the purpose of the experiment, to test the belief that a spider was charmed into immobility by powder of unicorn's horn, so intrigued the members that the authenticity of the powder passed unchallenged. Shadwell, Samuel Butler, Addison, and Swift are among those who held up the "Virtuosi" in the Society to ridicule for one or another reason. Addison in the *Spectator* suggested on one occasion that "the first design of those gentlemen who set on foot the Royal Society" was to turn "many of the greatest geniuses of the age to the disquisitions of natural knowledge who, if they had engaged in politics with the same parts and application, might have set their country in a flame." On another occasion, he writes:

> . . . since the world abounds in the noblest fields of speculation, it is methinks, the mark of a little genius to be wholly conversant among insects, animalcules, and those trifling rarities that furnish out the apartment of a Virtuoso . . . Some men . . . are utter strangers to the common way of life, they are able to discover the sex of a cockle, or describe the generation of a mite, in all its circumstances. They are so little versed in the world, that they scarce know a horse from an ox; but at the same time will tell you with a great deal of gravity that a flea is a rhinoceros and a snail an hermaphrodite . . . I would not have a scholar wholly unacquainted with these secrets and curiosities of Nature; but certainly the mind of man, that is capable of higher contemplations, should not be altogether fixed upon such mean and disproportionated objects.[2]

[1] R. H. Syfret, *Some Early Reactions to the Royal Society,* Notes and Records of the Royal Society of London (1950), Vol. VII, pp. 207-58.

[2] R. H. Syfret, *Some Early Critics of the Royal Society,* Notes and Records of the Royal Society of London (1950), Vol. VIII, pp. 20-54.

Addison is here touching upon a sore point, whether such experiments were beneath the dignity of human beings, especially Christians. Others more explicitly found that the aims and pursuits of the Society tended to the subversion of religion. Nothing in the activities of the leading spirits in the organization of the scientific societies in those centuries could justify such a view. On the contrary, much of what they wrote indicates their recognition of the need for both science and religion. Bacon specifically states the threefold limitations of science:

> The first that we do not so place our felicity in knowledge as we forget our mortality. The second, that we make application of our knowledge to give ourselves repose and contentment, and not distaste or repining. The third, that we do not presume by the contemplation of nature to attain to the mysteries of God.
>
> The last or furthest end of knowledge . . . (is that it be) a rich Storehouse, for the glory of the Creator and the relief of man's estate.[3]

Robert Boyle, one of the most illustrious of the early fellows of the Royal Society may be cited in illustration of the temper of his age concerning "divine science" and the science of nature. The twentieth-century initiate in science remembers Boyle for his observation (Boyle's Law) that the product of the pressure and the volume of a gas is constant at constant temperature. He would not know of Boyle's piety and benevolence, his promotion of the circulation of the Bible in the East, his institution of the Boyle lectures, still annually given in defence of Christianity. He would know nothing of Boyle's treatises on *The Christian Virtuoso,* designed to show "that there is no inconsistence between a man's being an industrious virtuoso, and a good Christian." Nor would he recognize Boyle as the author of *Some Physico-Theological Considerations about the Possibility of the Resurrection,* or of *A Disquisition about the Final Causes of Natural Things,* or of a tract on *The*

[3] Francis Bacon, *The Advancement of Learning.* Collected Works.

Excellence of Theology, Compared with Natural Philosophy.
In Boyle's view,

> the vastness, beauty, orderliness of the heavenly bodies; the
> excellent structure of animals and plants; and the other phe-
> nomena of nature justly induce an intelligent and just ob-
> server to conclude a supremely powerful and just author.

Is it wise, he asks,

> to dispute anxiously about the properties of an atom, and be
> careless about the enquiry into the attributes of the Great
> God, who formed all things; to investigate the spontaneous
> generation of such vile creatures as insects than the mysterious
> generation of the admirable Son of God.

Concerning those who labored to deter men from inquiries
into nature as from a study unsafe for a Christian he states:

> For I, that had much rather have men not philosophers than
> not Christians, should be much better content to see you
> ignore the mysteries of nature than deny the author of it.[4]

Of Newton, Louis Trenchard More summarizes his religious beliefs in the following words:

> It is quite impossible to give a clear idea of Newton's
> theism because of his distaste for any public expression of his
> personal beliefs; it is certain, however, that he was a theist; be-
> lieving in a personal and spiritual God, and that he thought
> God was best revealed in the laws of nature. He even doubted
> whether the cosmic system could continue to operate without
> at least divine control and adjustment—a control 'not blind or
> fortuitous, but very well skilled in mechanics and geometry.'

Again and again through the writings of those years one
meets continuously this interaction between science and religion, the interrelations of faith and knowledge. Bacon writes
of the

> two principal duties and services . . . which philosophy and
> human learning do perform to faith and religion. The one

[4] Louis Trenchard More, *The Life and Works of the Honourable Robert
Boyle* (New York: Oxford University Press, 1944), pp. 160–87.

because they are an effectual inducement to the exaltation of
God . . . The other, because they minister a singular help and
preservative against unbelief and error.

Milton defines as the end of learning

> to repair the ruins of our first parents by beginning to know
> God aright, and out of that knowledge to love him, to imitate
> him, to be like him, as we may the nearest by possessing our
> souls of true virtue, which being united to the heavenly grace of
> faith makes up the highest perfection.

Science could also be absorbed into the whole structure of
intellectual life. Newton demanded the Muse, as Marjorie
Hope Nicolson has so delightfully revealed;[5] the scientific
ideas of Newton were woven into the whole fabric of literary,
poetical, and critical effort in the eighteenth century.

> With Newtonian eyes the poets discovered new beauties in
> the most familiar aspects of nature, which had always been the
> stuff of poetry; in individual colors seen through the rainbow, in
> sunrise and sunset, in the succession of colors throughout the
> day . . . They delighted in their own intellectual maturity,
> feeling that they had outgrown the childlike attitude of the
> simple swain who seeks a pot of gold, or of Noah, to whom the
> rainbow was a miracle. They did not believe that Newton had
> taken beauty from poetry; he had added new beauty, because
> he had added new truth.

When the modern phase of science began, it was still possible for the intellectual to look at life and see it whole. Since
that time the dominant trends in Western culture have been
an increasing specialization and fragmentation of knowledge
and a progressive secularization of the total culture. In our
modern society the process has culminated in a fragmentation
of the culture that has proceeded so far that communication
among the several disciplines is progressively more difficult;
and all disciplines are, to different degrees, divorced from their
common, unifying spiritual core.

[5] Marjorie Hope Nicolson, *Newton Demands the Muse* (Princeton:
Princeton University Press, 1946), pp. 20–54.

In the colleges and universities of our times it is possible to perceive how far this fragmentation of subject matter in educational curricula has proceeded. Everyone realizes how readily a student can take a full four-year course in a particular area of science without hearing of any of the limitations of science generally, without any answer to the question: Science for what? Wherever such conditions obtain, it should be realized that what is being provided for the student is actually more nearly a school of technology rather than a college of liberal arts and sciences or a *universitas*; that to teach the power of science without emphasis on the limits of science may well be "practical" education but can never be humane education.

Throughout the span of centuries in which modern science has grown and developed it would seem that the impact of religion on the life of the average man has become progressively less and less. Here, also, the pace of change is autoaccelerative, though in the reverse direction from that of science. Those who began their lives toward the close of the nineteenth century have witnessed both the spectacularly rapid growth of science and technology in human affairs and a progressively more rapid decline in the religious habits of mankind. To the intellectual of the Middle Ages it was normal to expect a descending stream of grace to match the ascending effort of the mind. To the modern that condition is exceptional and, in large measure, it is the spiritual elements in life which have been abandoned or lost. The tendency to ignore these elements can be especially strong among those intellectuals who have immersed themselves in the mental activities of the scientists, since ends and purposes of life can be most readily excluded from the formulation of the abstract scientific problem. When, however, the products of pure scientific thought emerge in the solutions of technological problems it can then immediately arise, sometimes terrifyingly so, that the consequences of abstract scientific thought begin to tie up intricately with problems of ends and purpose. Einstein, working in the area of relativity theory, can elucidate the mass-energy relationship, that energy is equal to mass multiplied by the square of the velocity of light, without particular attention to problems of good and evil. When the theoretical equation is translated, however, into a practical weapon which can destroy hundreds of thousands of lives in a small fraction of a second, it can immediately be sensed that scientific bread alone may not be a sufficient sustenance for an increasingly scientific and technological world.

The experience of the last decade has brought this aspect of the relation of science to human life vividly to the attention of mankind. Toward the close of the Victorian era, at the end of the nineteenth century, there was an implicit faith in progress and in the ability of science to enter the vacuum and fill the void which the loss of religious temper among men was producing. This optimism at the turn of the present century among the intellectuals has spread, in the interval, to the common man, who has acquired a naïve faith in the ability of science and technology ultimately to solve all his woes. But, before the century had reached its mid-point, those scientists most closely concerned with the problem of atomic energy and the atomic bomb were engaging in serious self-questionings as to the ethical and moral aspects of their labors, asking themselves whether, in the realm of pure science and its pursuit, there might be a place for something in the nature of the Hippocratic oath that is regarded as essential in the medical profession.

It ought, however, to be recognized and stressed that the advances in science and technology do not pose any new tests of human character. They merely demand a more intense application of the age-old tests. The advent of the telephone, the airplane, of radio and television, while they have enormously shrunk this world of ours and have facilitated beyond measure intercommunication and transport, have not imposed new standards of human behavior; they do demand a more rigorous observance of the old and unchanging standards. These still remain, as in the days of Bethlehem and Nazareth and the years of Christ's public life, our love both of God and our neighbor. The advances in science involve that our neighbor today is not only the traveller down the nearest road but also millions in far-off lands, India, Iran, China, the islands of the Pacific, the inhabitants of the African continent. The measure of our justice, our charity, and our mercy toward all of these is at once, also, the measure of our desire to walk humbly with God.

If some such sketch of life is generally valid there devolves on the colleges and universities the especial task of seeking a right adjustment of the problems that are before us. These institutions are dedicated to the dissemination of knowledge and to the enlargement of the horizons of that knowledge. In them, society has the right to expect a more perfect ordering of thought and culture than can be attained outside the college and university campus. It recognizes that, down through the centuries, the universities have been the sources of developments that have transformed both human thought and human life. Society can well take the position that, in return for an ever increasing measure of support, it will expect an increasing coordination and correlation of all the varied aspects of human thought; especially so in these times when the consequences of change diffuse so rapidly throughout the world, in spite even of barriers which may temporarily or locally be imposed. So-called security devices may decelerate the flow of knowledge; they cannot prevent entirely the diffusion process.

Within the universities we must look for the integration and the harmonization of all the various factors that have entered into the structure of what we recognize as Western culture; when we have ordered our life within our own communities and trained our pupils to recognize that order, we can, with confidence, expect, in the future as in the past, that from these centers of knowledge and of understanding there will pass out those who can transmit some measure of that order and harmony to the world outside. We shall show to our students how from classical Greece we derived the inspiration for understanding and the intellectual process; for beauty, for truth, for the attributes of the mind; how Rome provided the concept of a society with stability deriving from law and institutional administration; how the Christian revelation concerned itself with man's nature, his dignity, his personality and the rules of behavior and conduct, the ideals on which truth and justice could prevail; how, finally, discovery and the processes of scientific endeavor can enlarge the scope of man's activity, can provide a material environment in which beauty, truth, law, justice, and right conduct can be more completely realized. What we may ask of the colleges and universities is a larger measure of unity in the total effort for cultural education. To this end it is essential that the specialist shall himself be aware of the unity, and shall be able to communicate to the student a confident faith in the values that stream from such unity. Such a unity will include science as the study of the world outside of man, history, in the large sense, including man in all his relations to his fellow men, humane letters, dealing with the problem of the inner man, philosophy, concerned with the first principles of both thought and action, and religion, concerned with all the problems that lie beyond such principles. It will be a unity in which the resultant scholar can reveal both a general competence and a specialized excellence.

III

With such a concept of the educational process and of the several elements which enter into its structure we may now proceed to a more detailed consideration of the specialized area of science instruction and an examination of the manner in which religious perspectives can enter into such an instructional effort without sacrifice of educational integrity.

It will be at once apparent that in many areas of scientific instruction the religious aspect will seldom if ever intrude itself. It would be difficult to formulate a set of conditions in which such a question of ultimates could result from the exposition of a problem in Euclid, a trigonometric identity, the differential or integral calculus, the theory of numbers. A chemist demonstrating to a class of students that hydrogen and oxygen combine to form water in definite and simple ratios both of volume and mass, or discussing the more refined problem of the presence of six hundred and two thousand million million million molecules in two grams of hydrogen or thirty-two grams of oxygen does not normally expect that his exposition will result in a discussion of first causes. Even if the teacher insists that the second decimal place in the number, 6.02×10^{23}, which is the number of molecules in a gram molecule already cited, has significance and that the count is more accurate than can be achieved by the census takers in the U.S.A. during the current year, the student may receive the exposition with skepticism or enthusiasm, dependent on his temperament, but without commitment with respect to first cause. In physics one can cite many parallel instructional themes, Newton's laws of motion, Hooke's measurements of the extension of springs under loads, Millikan's precision measurements of the charge of electricity on oil drops, many such can be communicated, digested, and accepted without arousing questions of purpose or design.

The observant reader will have already noted that the examples just chosen belong in the main to the realm of empirical observations representable, to a certain degree of accuracy and within prescribed limits, by quantitative statements generalizing the observations. They have excluded observations which immediately suggest the query, Why?; nor are they examples which interact with the philosophical, cultural, and historical concepts of the age in which they were discovered. Yet, even in the sciences of physics and of chemistry, many empirical observations do possess implications of design and purpose. The simple observation that the density of ice is less than that of water, in sharp contrast to the normally greater density of the solid forms of most material substances, can readily precipitate discussions as to the significance of this exceptional behaviour. The observation that, by reason of its lighter density, the rivers and lakes freeze on the surface and not from the bottom up, with conservation during freezing weather of the living things which are normally found in such environment, can easily lead to a consciousness on the part of the student that teleology may be involved.

In contrast with much in experimental physics and chemistry, the sciences of astronomy, geology, and biology enter much more directly the provinces where religious problems are at issue. A variety of scientific evidence now points to a universe some two or three thousand million years old. The irreconcilability of this with time scales stemming from some earlier theologians in units of a few thousand years constitutes one example of discordance. The student is all too familiar with the overthrow of the Ptolemaic theory of the earth as the center of the cosmos, of its supersession by the Copernican system and the concern of the Inquisition in Galileo's exposition of the new thought. He will come to know of the remarkable uniformity in composition of many of the heavenly bodies, the earth, the planets, the sun, the stars of the Milky Way, the different spiral galaxies, independent stellar systems, and even the diffuse interstellar material, the cosmic dust. He will learn about the expanding universe in which distant galaxies are interpreted as receding from the observer at velocities reckoned in thousands of kilometers per second. He will be told of the scientists' speculation that space and time began when an "ur-atom" of tremendous density underwent a process of explosion, or of the more modern version that in the "first half-hour of Creation" a mixture of neutrons, protons, and electrons at temperatures of a few billion degrees began the process of expansion, with consequent fall of temperature, to a point at which combination of protons and neutrons to form the nuclei of elements could occur. In this view, the nuclei of heavy hydrogen, deuterium, and tritium were the first steps in Creation, and helium and the heavier elements came later. Against this concept of Creation he will remember the presentation in Genesis: "In the beginning God created heaven and earth." He will learn that the radiation of the sun was approximately the same as it is now several hundred million years ago when the fossil layers of coal were formed; that the energy radiated by the sun is so tremendous that all early efforts to account for it fall far short of practicability; that the same process of nuclear synthesis as is postulated in the processes of the expanding universe is operative today in the sun's atmosphere and is adequate to account for the energies needed, and could continue with radiation at its present rate for forty thousand million years. On the astronomical-geological scale, time stretches both backward and forwards from now, here on earth and for all the universe.

The geological study of the earth's crust, telling the story of geologic ages, with a variety of methods to assess the duration of each of the transformations tends to an estimate of the age of the universe of about 2 billion years. Paleontologists have traced the different stages of vegetable and animal life as it is revealed in the various epochs and can follow in detail the progress of life; they have laid bare processes indicative of slow evolution in which, from elementary stages, living things in greater and greater degrees of perfection have been located in the successive geologic ages. From all such evidence the best paleontologists now consider evolution, the passage of life from one species to another, and, as a consequence, the animal origin of the human body, to be an established fact. This concept of the evolutionary process has dominated, as the young student rapidly learns, the thoughts and activities of the biologists from Darwin's time in the mid-nineteenth century down to the present day.

It is discoveries such as these which present the student, who is a Christian, with serious problems which it is the duty of the Christian teacher to help to resolve. The faith of the Christian and the advance of scientific knowledge must be reconciled. The discoveries of science must be harmonized with the teachings of the Bible. There will be many teachers, in these days, who will counsel the acceptance of science and the rejection of faith. There will be other timid Christians who, in the name of their faith, will feel themselves compelled either to shut their eyes to the discoveries of science, or reject and deny them. They would invoke the authority of the State or of a Church to condemn these discoveries of science.

It is necessary for the Christian teacher to reject both of these alternatives and to convince his students that there is another and better alternative. At the outset, it will be necessary for him to establish the various ways in which man can attain to knowledge and through knowledge to truth. It will be necessary to insist that science is not a single pathway to truth but that all paths if true, starting from different points, covering different areas of investigation, employing essentially different methods, can arrive at truth which is one and indivisible. It will be necessary to distinguish clearly the variety of such activities and their limitations.

The perturbed student can be assured at once that the problem with which he wrestles is no new problem. It can be found back through the Christian record even to the Fathers of the Church. In the fourth century St. Ephrem and St. Basil were defending the interpretation of the days of Genesis as a real succession. Gregory of Nyssa argued against the views of Basil. Toward the end of the fourth century St. Augustine was engaged on a commentary on the book of Genesis and over the next fifteen years dealt with the problem in the *Confes-*

sions (X-XIII), *De Civitate Dei,* and particularly in his work *De Genesi ad litteram (libri duodecim).* Another manuscript with the same title was published as an unfinished work. It is in these later volumes that Augustine is teaching the natural evolution of the world. It can be deduced that, from the last years of the fourth century, Augustine regarded the succession of the six days in Genesis as figurative. In the Middle Ages, St. Thomas Aquinas weighed the problem anew, emphasized that one could accept the succession of works in the six days figuratively, without commitment to other aspects of Augustine's thought.

The mid-nineteenth century saw the argument break out anew with increasing intensity consequent on the formulation of the theory of evolution by Charles Darwin. Again the theologians entered the battle, oftentimes with more ardor than discretion, oftentimes ill-equipped to meet the factual evidence that the sciences were bringing to light.[6] Protestantism, in all shades of thought from extreme liberal to extreme evangelical, argued again as Basil and Gregory and Augustine. The Vatican appointed a Biblical Commission to report on the problem. This Commission formulated principles of guidance in the interpretation of the Sacred Scriptures so far as they appear to deal with matters studied by the natural sciences. One important fundamental principle could well be emphasized by all science teachers counselling students in such matters.

> On those matters which form the proper object of the physical and natural sciences, God taught nothing to men by the intermediary of the sacred writers, since such instruction could not be of any use for their eternal salvation.

This principle, which goes back directly to St. Augustine at the end of the fourth century, is indeed an extract from *De*

[6] H. de Dorlodot, *Darwinism and Catholic Thought,* translated from the French by E. C. Messenger (London: Burns, Oates & Washburne, Ltd., 1922).

Genesi ad litteram, more particularly defined and applied to the physical and natural sciences.

In a recent article on "Science and the Bible," written by a French ecclesiastic, Achille, Cardinal Lienart, amplifies this concept of the relation between the Biblical writings and the findings of modern science:

> Since God's work, even in the order of grace, is put into operation in this world and among men, it happens that the Bible deals with matters that belong also to science and history. But it should be carefully noted that the Bible does this in its own way. There, this kind of data is not presented in the exact form of a scientific or historical document, as happens with us today . . . In expressing these truths the Bible employs a whole gamut of literary forms, from popular tales or poetical compositions, which have no scientific character, to other forms which are more objective but whose scientific and historical character must be interpreted in the light of the ancient Semitic mentality. It would be a mistake therefore to try to interpret them literally and in ignorance of these factors.

Cardinal Lienart goes on to make the further observation that

> the Bible's use of scientific data has this peculiarity: it pre-scinds for the most part from space and time, which science considers so important. Its method of localizing and computing is generally indefinite, more schematic than real, sometimes completely omitted . . . We might well say that God's word coming from a world where time does not exist, quite freely abstracts from it. In any case, we see from all this that the Bible offers us only scanty information in the field of science and therefore *does not dispense us from continuing our researches in that field.*[7]

It is worth emphasizing in respect to the scientific concepts of space and time, as Emil Brunner has recently pointed out, that we must go back to Augustine for a great discovery,

[7] Achille, Cardinal Lienart, "Science and the Bible," *The Commonweal,* June, 1949, pp. 241–43, 265–67. Italics supplied by the present writer.

when he first dared to propose, in the *Confessions*, that the world is neither atemporal and eternal nor created at a certain moment in a sequence of time, but that the world and time have been created together, they have the same beginning in creation . . . The depth and boldness of this idea cannot be adequately admired by us, but if we consider the most recent results of astro-physics we can only be astounded at the genius of the thinker who recognizes intuitively, as a truth of faith, without any scientific basis, an idea which—paradoxical as it may appear—imposes itself today to scientific thought as truth: the result partly of Einstein's theory of relativity and Planck's quantum physics.[8]

It is well to stress such instances of the approach to truth through faith rather than through science in order to dispel a too current illusion that the paths of scientific research are the only reliable avenues to truth, an illusion which increasingly imposes itself on the unthinking. The student of science must be compelled to recognize whole areas of truth to which the approach is never via the scientific textbook or the scientific inquiry. The student can be confronted with a wide variety of facts and especially events which, with a greater or lesser degree of certitude, must be accepted as true, without the possibility of testing their truth by any scientific procedure save in the most accidental circumstances. A group of such events might include, for example, the raising of the dead man to life by Jesus as recorded in the gospel narrative; the invasion of England at Hastings by William the Conqueror in 1066; the recovery from "tubercular peritonitis" of one Marie Bailly within the space of twenty minutes at a grotto in Lourdes, observed in 1903 by Alexis Carrel, a French doctor, later a Nobel Laureate in medicine;[9] or finally—to come down to more recent and more mundane events—the victories obtained on a given Saturday afternoon in October, 1950, when a New

[8] Emil Brunner, "The Christian Sense of Time," translated by Joseph E. Cunneen, *Cross Currents*, No. 1 (Fall, 1950), pp. 25–33.
[9] Alexis Carrel, *The Voyage to Lourdes*, (New York: Harper & Bros., 1950).

York baseball team won, as expected, the World Series and a football team from Notre Dame unexpectedly suffered its first defeat for several seasons. Some or all of these most men will hold to be true. Yet no one of them can be proved to be true by the methods of science. In the final example selected, some 50,000 people in each case can testify, from their own observations, that the events thus recorded are true. The remaining hundreds of millions of Americans who were not present at these events nevertheless accept them as true, and act accordingly, even to the extent of giving and receiving monies bet on the outcome of the game. They are convinced of the truth of testimony, received by them by word of mouth, over the radio or through the printed word in the newspapers. They recognize the validity of conclusions from testimony. Science on the other hand cannot accept testimony unless it can be corroborated by observation through experiment. Scientific literature is largely composed of the testimony of scientists concerning their observations and experiments, but the scientific data therein recorded are susceptible of further test and verification. Indeed, the essential basis of the scientific method consists of experimentation and presentation of the findings from such experiments in scientific literature in such a form that the experiments can be repeated by other scientists and the findings verified, i.e., found continuously by repeated trial. Science derives its validity from the accessibility of its accumulated findings to the check of any scientist without limitations of chronology or (in a free world) of geography.

The major fraction of history is, on the other hand, based on testimony which cannot be corroborated by experiment and observation. As such it has no *scientific* validity. This does not mean that the historical event becomes any the less true. Science can indeed, in certain areas, through the science of archaeology, provide some measure of corroboration. This science seeks out relics of the historic past, uncovers fossil remains to fill out the pages of pre-history. Modern physics is contributing in increasing measure to the verification of testimony. Television is now capable of providing a larger fraction of the population with the spectacle of a Saturday-afternoon football game or an evening of opera at the Metropolitan in New York. But, it is worthwhile to recall, parenthetically, that the truth of an event so recorded involves a *faith* on the part of the observer at the television screen that what he observes is actually occurring at the place announced by the commentator. Records in motion picture and the radio of historical events can enhance the belief of the audience in the validity of the testimony thus supplied; but again it is yet another species of testimony, which is not recognized as science.

Science can supply corroborative evidence for the validity of conclusions from testimony. A notable example of this has recently come to our notice. Radioactive carbon has become a time-clock of history. This carbon owes its time-measuring properties to the fact that it disintegrates at a definite rate, unchanged by external influences such as temperature and pressure, so that after 5580 years just one half of the original radioactivity has disappeared. Since radio-carbon becomes part of the substance of which plants and animals are formed and because it decays at the rate already stated, the date at which the plant or animal lived can be determined by measurement of the amount of the original radio-carbon left. In this way, scientists of the Institute of Nuclear Studies in Chicago have been able to date a wide variety of carbon-containing materials from trees now growing, back through the centuries wherever wooden objects of historically verifiable age could be located. The scientific estimates of the age of wood from coffins from the time of Egyptian dynasties show excellent agreement with the conclusions from historical research. History can accept such corroboration. But, for our present purposes, it is more important to emphasize the other service which science thus performs: *it validates testimony and history as vehicles for the attainment of truth.* It compels us to give due consideration to all forms of such testimony, whether in the gospels or in the observations of a doctor in Lourdes, even though the testimony is of things outside the range of common experience. We can shrug off the Lourdes experience by assessing at a low level the observation made. Would our conclusion as to its truth be the same had the motion-picture camera or the television been available at the time of the event?

An interesting example of the confirmation by modern science of testimony from ancient days was recorded some years ago by F. Sherwood Taylor of the Museum of the History of Science in Oxford.[10] In St. Jerome's "Life of St. Hilarion," which was written about A.D. 392, it is recorded that, from his thirty-first to his thirty-fifth year, Hilarion took for food barley bread and vegetables cooked without oil. But finding that his eyes were growing dim and that his whole body was shrivelled with an eruption and a sort of stony roughness he added oil to his food, and, "up to the sixty-third year of his life followed this temperate course, tasting neither fruit nor pulse, nor anything whatever besides." Similar eye affections and hyperkeratosis have been recorded in 1936 with Chinese patients who received a diet not unlike that of Hilarion. These patients were speedily cured by cod-liver oil or carotene. Modern science confirms the testimony of St. Jerome and suggests that by use of what was probably a crude olive oil Hilarion secured for himself in the later decades of his life a sufficiency of vitamin A to avoid night-blindness and skin eruptions.

Science serves competently many other areas of effort both in the social sciences and the humanities but its service is occasional and not essential to the discipline involved. Thus mathematics, especially in the field of statistics, can be of signal use in both economics and political science. In the area of

[10] F. Sherwood Taylor, "St. Jerome and Vitamin A," *Nature*, CLIV (December, 1944).

the humanities the service of science can be well illustrated by
the science of acoustics in the art of music. But as Roger
Sessions has recently observed:

> A great deal of musical theory has been formulated by at-
> tempting to codify laws governing musical sound and musical
> rhythm, and from these to deduce musical principles. Some-
> times these principles are even deduced from what we know of
> the physical nature of sound, and as a result are given what
> seems to me an essentially specious validity. I say 'essentially
> specious' because while the physical facts are clear enough, there
> are always gaps, incomplete or unconvincing transitions, left
> between the realm of physics and the realm of musical experi-
> ence, even if we leave 'art' out of account.

After detailing some of the "many ingenious and even brilliant attempts" to bridge these gaps, Sessions concludes:

> It seems to me clear that physics and music are different
> spheres, and that, though they certainly touch at moments,
> the connexion between them is an occasional and circumstan-
> tial, not an essential, one . . . Since music is created by human
> beings, we must regard the sources, or raw materials, first of all
> as human facts. For it is not rhythm and sound as such but
> their nature as human facts which concerns us. And if we look
> at them closely we perceive that they are human facts of the
> most intimate kind. We see that these basic facts—the raw ma-
> terials, the primitive sources, of music—are facts of musical ex-
> perience and not the physical facts of sound and rhythm.[11]

Science, indeed, is abstracting from the realm of music
exactly that portion which is susceptible to treatment by the
study of acoustics. This is what science also does in many of
the scientific disciplines. In physiology the scientist is concerned with the manner of action and of interaction of the
organs of human and animal species. In biochemistry he concentrates on the particular chemical processes which are
operative in and determine the functions of living species. In

[11] Roger Sessions, *The Musical Experience* (Princeton: Princeton University Press, 1950), pp. 9–11.

psychology he is concerned with the science of man's thought, the study of the mental processes and reactions of man. In all of these and other sciences related to the human being we, as scientists, are abstracting a particular set of data from the whole complex, studying them with ever greater intensity and success. We must, however, if we are frank with ourselves, confess that our individual sciences are the sciences of a part of man, of that which is found in the material parts of the species; they do not comprise the whole man, who in some way, difficult to define, is greater than its parts, just as music is greater than the acoustics, the harmonies, the rhythm, the structure, and all other aspects of the musical work.

If we can realize the incompleteness of the contribution by science to the apprehension of nature, if, after we have perceived, analyzed, synthesized as scientists, if, after the disciplined perception of the artist, we still find that something is wanting, then perhaps we may be disposed to look at nature from a religious point of view, envision man, nature, the whole universe as a consequence of the presence of God and God's will,

> *Anima Mundi,* World Sustainer
> Sower to whom all seeds returned
> Through earth's dissolving mist of atoms
> The Body of God in splendor burned.[12]

IV

The data of astronomy, biology, chemistry, geology, mathematics, or physics have little to tell us concerning the regulation of human conduct. These sciences provide answers as to observed behavior; but they do not answer the question whether such behavior is right or wrong. The whole area of ethical judgments or conclusions lies outside the province of

[12] Alfred Noyes, *The Torchbearers* (London: Sheed & Ward, Inc., 1937), p. 422.

these sciences. They cannot answer the question: should I do this; ought I to do that? They may record in minutest detail what will happen if you chloroform a cat. They cannot answer whether you are justified or not in performing such an experiment. Justification of a choice is not contained within the limits of these sciences. Choice demands a definition of ends or values. Anyone who surveys the international scene today can soon realize that there are major divergencies in the ends and values on which different groups of men set their hearts or wills. Every variation in shade of opinion from the belief in the dignity of the human person to a dedication to the supremacy of the State is to be found in some section or other of the world. Science is powerless to provide the right answer to the question as to which is the *summum bonum*. A pattern of conduct must come from some area outside of science.

This is not to say that science is sterile in dealing with problems of human conduct. It does provide a sanative influence in behavior problems. Its end is knowledge, *scientia*, and it can testify to the qualities that are conducive to those ends. In the attainment of those ends the scientist will employ a whole spectrum of virtues. Industry, fidelity, detachment, objectivity, patience, perseverance, cooperation, these are among the qualities which he will bring to the solution of a scientific problem—and he learns that by their employment he can the more effectively gain his objective, new scientific knowledge. Science and the works of the scientist call attention to the primacy of truth and reason, can reveal the virtues of a life dedicated to rational values and emphasize the dangers of any attack upon truth. But these virtues and dangers are not exhibited only in the scientific disciplines. Philosophy, history, art, theology, all emphasize the virtues of reason and the pursuit of truth, the dangers that stem from the assault, from whatever quarter, on such activities.

At the best, however, it must be recognized that the truth secured by science is proximate truth and not ultimate truth. Any scientist past his middle age in life who soberly analyzes the concepts of scientific truth with which he has been familiar in his professional lifetime is forced continuously to recognize the proximate nature of the scientific "truths" which he is called upon to communicate to succeeding generations of students. An example drawn from personal experience may serve to point up this aspect of the science teacher's activity. As students, our generation learned that the electrical conductivity of a solution of common salt, sodium chloride, varied with the concentration. Arrhenius proposed in 1887 that this variable conductance was to be attributed to a progressively increasing dissociation of salt into charged ions, sodium and chloride ions, with increasing dilution. The electrolytic dissociation theory was the "true gospel" of physical chemistry from the late years of the nineteenth century to the third decade of the twentieth century. During this period Arrhenius received the Nobel Prize for the enunciation of his theory.

By 1920 it was definitely evident that the concept of progressive dissociation of salt into constituent ions with increasing dilution in solvent water would have to be abandoned, since it had been shown, in other areas of science, that even in solid crystals of sodium chloride the constituent units of the crystal were already completely ionized, electrically charged and separate sodium and chloride ions. Dissolving these in water could not result in recombined ions of sodium chloride. New thoughts led to new formulations. Debye and his associates showed that all the experimental data were consonant with the view that salt is completely, not partially, dissociated into ions in water solutions and that the effects which Arrhenius had attributed to partial and progressive dissociation of salt molecules could be equally well, indeed better, interpreted on the postulate that the variations in electrical conductance were due to interaction between the oppositely charged ions sodium and chloride and that no molecules of sodium chloride were present. Debye, in his turn, received the Nobel Prize for this and other contributions. No one would suggest that the prize received by Arrhenius should be withdrawn since now it was proved that his concepts were inadequate. They were actually "proximate" truths, immensely fertile, stimulative of extraordinary development in the science of physical chemistry, with a residuum of truth with regard to a particular group of substances which the chemist knows as "weak" electrolytes, of which acetic acid (vinegar) is an excellent example. It is incumbent on the science teacher steadily to impress upon his students this aspect of scientific truth.

The science teacher concerned with the limitation under which the pursuit of science continuously operates would also do well frequently to insist on the large measure of faith which enters into all his activities as a scientist. No one can test personally all the facts and factors which are important in the area of operations in which he is participating by his own researches. Much of what he employs daily is in its essentials based on acts of great faith and trust. He trusts, with the aid of his own judgment, the records of other achievements in his field. He relies on the accuracy and objectivity of the records available to him until he has evidence forcing him to abandonment of the trust. He places great faith in principles which cannot from their very nature be *proved*. Thus, the physical chemist and the physicist both affirm their belief in the first and second laws of thermodynamics. Each affirms as an article of his scientific creed that energy (or matter-energy) can neither be created nor destroyed (first law) and that it is impossible continuously to utilize the immeasurably large heat energy of the Atlantic Ocean to drive the Queen Mary or any other vessel across the ocean. He can affirm his belief in these two "laws" with the same conviction that a Christian can assert, "I believe in One God." But the scientist cannot *prove* that his belief is true. The most that he can yet say is that it is a fact of human experience, thus far, that no one has succeeded in creating perpetual motion machines which are respectively denied by the first and second laws of thermodynamics.

He can go further than the affirmation of his belief in their truth. He can show that, having made his affirmation, he can proceed, acting on the assumption of their truth to discover new results stemming from the acceptance, which results can be tested experimentally, and with a high degree of rigor, and can be shown to be valid within the framework in which he is operating. He gains thereby a pragmatic sanction for his creed, fortifies it by continuous use and continued test, and emerges with an ever increasing respect for the scientific creed by which he lives.

It is useful also to insist again on the proximate rather than the ultimate character of these truths. The proximate nature is revealed by the use of the words "energy" (or "matter-energy") in a paragraph just read. Early nineteenth-century science knew nothing of the duality of matter and energy, formulated its conservation principles separately with respect to both. Only with Einstein, at the turn of the present century, was the proximate nature of the two conservation principles of matter and energy revealed and merged in a generalized principle of conservation of mass and energy.

The original atomic hypothesis, the newer concepts of electrons, of protons, of neutrons, of mesons, and of neutrinos are all indices of the proximate nature of the hypotheses which the scientist has developed to formulate what facts his restless experimentation revealed. Atoms which formerly were indivisible are now smashed in modern nuclear machines. Atoms of the same element which in the "early faith" were all alike in mass now are known to exist in isotopic species varying, as is the case with the three hydrogen isotopes, in the mass ratios of 1 to 2 to 3, and in the case of tin existing in no fewer than

10 different masses of the same element. Every amateur radio or television operator knows that the tubes with which he amplifies radio-signals to yield a voice or a view utilize electrons; or so his scientific faith decrees, for no one has yet exhibited electrons. The more we pursue scientific investigation the more we discover that it does not lead to knowledge of the *intrinsic nature* of things. The knowledge it attains is *symbolic* knowledge rather than *intimate* knowledge; behind the symbolism there is a reality which escapes the measuring techniques. As Eddington wrote: "The subjective is to be identified with the physical and the objective with the conscious and spiritual aspects of experience . . . Our observational techniques give us many laws of nature with a small n; but the laws of Nature with a capital N are laws of the objective universe." A poet has expressed the same point of view with a somewhat different emphasis:

> Yet the mind runs back
> Along those dwindling roads, explaining still
> The greater by the less, until they reach
> On every line of thought, that vanishing point
> Where all runs out in absolute mystery.
> There, at the last, seeking for that which *Is*
> In its own right, and needs no other cause,

the dwindling roads, he avers, take an upward turn to reveal, in the ascent,

> a height coequal with the peaks
> Of human thought; and infinitely higher
> Because that world beyond evolved our own;
> And we must find upon the summits there
> A self-subsistent Cause, the eternal Fount
> Of all that flowed into our world with Christ
> And showed us, in His Face, the Face of God.[13]

The science teacher also will sooner or later face the inquiring student who will have learned, somewhere, somehow, that "determinism" is the basic assumption of natural science.

[13] Noyes, *op. cit.*, pp. 408–9.

He will have learned that modern science pushes ahead precisely because it has assumed that all natural phenomena are determined by natural laws. He will wonder whether his deterministic habit of thought tends to undermine religious belief. It will be necessary for the teacher to be equipped to meet the issue.

It can, at once, be asserted that a spurious scientific determinism might well undermine religious belief, but that a right concept of the proper position of determinism in science can decidedly strengthen religious belief. Spurious scientific determinism is merely materialistic fatalism, a version in modern dress of the ancient concept of predestination, but with biological, physical, chemical, psychological, economic, and other factors supposedly hampering the individual in the exercise of free will. Chesterton once meditated on this melancholy attitude towards individual behavior and concluded that, were it shown to be true, he could think of nothing better to do than to proceed to the nearest milestone, sit down, and wait for Destiny to overtake him.

The determinism implicit in the scientific world is the assumption of *order* as opposed to capriciousness; obedience to definite laws, which the natural scientist tries to discover by means of physically observable phenomena. Many of these laws of nature are laws of probability, statistical conclusions, based generally on a large number of participating units or of events. A well-trained chemist can determine what fraction of two volumes of hydrogen and one volume of oxygen will react to form water vapor at room temperature and at the temperature of the sun. Techniques of science permit verification of the results determined. The accuracy of the determination is based, however, on the fact that, in the smallest volume of gas which could be studied by these techniques, there will be more molecules present than there are inhabitants on the earth. What the scientist records is the statistical behavior of the crowd. Actually no scientist can answer the question what will happen when two single reacting molecules (not volumes) come together. Statistical laws break down when applied to individual events.

Insurance companies will insure all who pay a certain fee prior to a railroad or airplane journey anywhere, to an amount determined by the fee paid. They make money in the enterprise because they know that, in the long run, more fees will be paid in than insurance will be paid out to the survivors of those who are killed. No insurance company, however, can tell John Doe whether or no he will survive his next flight to California. Bankers, insurance companies, industrialists, manufacturers have great confidence in such statistical data, pin their faith and their millions on predictions from them. They have given to science much of its present prestige.

Not all the predictions of science conform to this statistical pattern. The student may ask about the prediction of an eclipse in the year 1999, its location and the best areas in which to observe the phenomenon. Clearly this example is more deterministic in type; it excites in the layman a large measure of enthusiasm and respect for the scientist, enhancing still further his prestige. Such determinism is based upon the assumption of order which the scientist has found to have operated in the past and will, he assumes, continue to operate in the future. In this particular case the problem involves the motions of the sun, moon and earth and the laws of gravitation. The prediction involves an extrapolation of a relatively few reasonably accurate and precise scientific rules, through time, to yield a prediction of an event. There is nothing in the techniques and operations of the scientist that are deterministic in the sense of causation. The eclipse does not occur because of any prediction. It will occur in the absence of any prediction. The accuracy of the prediction is a measure of the success with which the scientist has mastered the intricacies and details of the underlying motions and laws. Small errors in the prediction lead him to the refinement of his apprehen-

very elaborately by numerous older authors, most notably, perhaps, by William Paley in his *Natural Theology* (1802) and by Lawrence J. Henderson in the *Fitness of the Environment* (1913). All that I have in mind is to point out that the advent of Darwinism and modern science has not, as is generally supposed, in any way affected the ancient arguments. If the finding of a watch on a remote island convinces you that man has been in that region, then it is quite unaccountable if you do not recognize the handiwork of a greater mind in the indescribably more complex and more wonderful mechanisms of nature. If you *can* find a watch and *not* believe it is the product of an intelligent designer, then you are entitled to dispense with belief in God. But I do not believe you can, no matter how hard you try. If the continued study of nature discloses not only innumerable special mechanisms, but also a *single*, stupendous, over-all mechanism capable of coordinating all of the minor processes and producing not merely watches and computing machines, but the men who make watches and computing machines—so much greater the glory of the designer! And furthermore, it would merely confirm what the church has always claimed—that there is but *one* God who created the heavens and the earth and all that therein is.

For some time it has been the style among many philosophers to say that Kant's arguments in the *Critique of Pure Reason*, and, more extensively, in the *Critique of Judgment*, demolished the teleological argument for the existence of God. He did, of course, show very effectively that this argument leads to no *absolute* proof, or "apodeictic certainty" as he expressed it; but then, absolute proof is not available for anything beyond simple verbalisms. And Kant asserted with equal emphasis that this argument "so strengthens the belief in a supreme Author (of nature) that the belief acquires the force of an irresistible conviction." That is all that I mean to assert. I am content with any argument which leads to "irresistible conviction"—what else might I mean by "irresistible"?

sion and understanding of the phenomenon involved, and a more precise effort in the next prediction. But, nowhere in the process, has the scientist determined or caused anything. He is the observer and as impotent in respect to the event as Canute in front of the waves. Pressed for opinion with respect to cause he must confess that the answer does not lie within the province of his science. Pasteur, at once scientist and Christian, suggested that the answer is to be found in the Infinite, transcending all human science.

Science, knowing little of ultimate causes, cannot determine ends, nor can it direct society to ends which are external to its discipline. That is why in matters concerning ends, peace, justice, liberty, or any other heart's desire, the scientist as scientist cannot be and is in fact not conspicuously superior to other educated men. We do not go to the scientists to seek out the saints or the sanest in modern society. Indeed, it may justly be said that, to the extent that the scientist is ignorant of the social sciences, of history, of philosophy, of art, and of the humanities, he may well be a danger to society precisely because of that ignorance. The success which attends his method of abstraction in the solution of a scientific problem may make him susceptible to solutions of human conduct or national welfare in which important elements in the problem, personal, social, political, have been ignored by him as scientist. A further danger must also be recognized in that the techniques of planned attack by disciplined teams of specialists, while immensely fruitful and profitable in the technological application of science, may result in an atmosphere favorable to regimentation in other areas of life with loss of liberties and freedom. Indeed, the success which has attended "team-work" in the applications of science to technology has led a not inconsiderable group of scientists to defend planned science and derivatively all forms of planned economy. Against this tendency it is necessary to stress continuously the necessity for freedom in science, especially in basic science. It cannot be insisted too often that science also needs four freedoms, of choice, of association, of inquiry, and of speech and publication. In insisting on such freedom the scientist has something to contribute to the general problem of freedom in human society. Professor Michael Polanyi has stressed this aspect of scientific inquiry:

> There is inherent in each new claim to discovery the practical affirmation of a coherent system of truth which is capable of indefinite extension into yet unexplored regions. For the extension of this system scientists rely on methods embodied in the common practice of research. Scientists accept, utilize and transmit certain traditional procedures and standards. They uphold certain traditional ideals . . . The dedication of scientists to the advancement of an intellectual process beyond their control and to the upholding of values transmitted to them by tradition represents the sense in which science does pursue a coherent task. We may express the existence of such a task by saying that scientists form a community believing in a certain spiritual reality and covenanted to the service of this reality . . . By defending the foundations of freedom in science we may help people to recover a clear conception of freedom in general . . . It seems that unless we radically reaffirm the transcendent foundations of our civilization the logical outcome of their present inadequacy will not be delayed for long . . . A consistent vindication of freedom in science may point the way toward the necessary reaffirmation of our whole civilization.[14]

This freedom to roam wherever the scientific spirit moves, to test hunches, to formulate hypotheses, and subject them to the acid-tests of analysis and experiment cannot be subject to certain types of external restraint. The thoughts of Galileo cannot be compelled within the framework of an Inquisition. Lest we be too harsh in our judgment of this incident in the earliest years of the modern phase of science, let us also recollect that twice within our brief lifetime in the twentieth cen-

[14] M. Polanyi, *Physical Science and Human Values* (Princeton: Princeton University Press, 1946), pp. 124-32.

tury two dictatorships have ventured also to restrict the freedom of science. The flower of German and Italian science fled from Nazi- and Fascist-imposed restrictions. Today we witness a restriction on the freedom of scientific inquiry which would compel it to conform to the vague concepts of dialectical materialism, to the dictates of which the findings of biological research must conform; the abstract concepts of relativity in physics and of resonance in physical chemistry must yield to a more materialistic interpretation defined in terms of "brute facts."

Freedom in science can tolerate no such compulsions whether from the middle or the modern ages. The heresy that is inherent in all such attempts to compel is due to the failure to recognize that freedom in science is a freedom to pursue knowledge. It is restricted to knowledge and is distinct from the pursuit of wisdom. The attempts to harness the pursuit of science to a medieval or to a modern philosophy represents an attempt to compel science to enter into the realm of ends and values in which it has no part. "Science sitteth apart attent on her other own Invisibles."

And yet, the briefest recollection will reveal that there are restrictions which are recognized as applicable to scientific inquiry. We are all familiar with, while we do not all recognize the validity of, the efforts of well-meaning citizens who seek to outlaw the employment and vivisection of animals for scientific ends. Such people share, with many in the East, a horror of any form of mutilation or destruction of animal life. Western society, in the main, tolerates such animal experimentation because it is convinced that the benefits accruing to the human race from its employment far outweigh any pain and suffering which the animals endure. Stringent regulations govern such techniques of animal experimentation, always designed to minimize the pain and suffering by the free use of anaesthetics, general or local. Modern biological science and the art of healing in the human race abundantly justify the license to use animals for such purposes. Science in such areas is a unit in Society and has responsibilities towards Society.

Most of the same people who would insist on the necessity for continued animal experimentation would recoil, however, from the proposal to use human beings for similar ends. The horror among the Western peoples that was expressed when it was revealed that such experimentation had been carried out forcibly on helpless inmates of German concentration camps is definite evidence of the general opinion in this matter. Such human experimentation is sanctioned, however, when, in the interests of the objective to be attained, volunteers can be secured for the particular experiment. Doctors have frequently submitted themselves to such tests. Soldiers, conscientious objectors, those interned in prisons, have often similarly volunteered. The voluntary act springs from a desire, through pain, suffering, or danger, to contribute to the general welfare. It belongs among the acts of heroism of which the human race is capable. It is a considered action on behalf of Society.

Scientists cannot define these limitations on human experimentation in terms of their several sciences. Other sanctions outside the areas of the sciences are involved in the differentiation between human and animal experimentation. The concept of human dignity and human inviolability thrusts itself immediately into the problem, and science has little if anything to say concerning these. The Christian scientist recognizes this condition and insists that unless his freedom to experiment is animated, tempered, and restrained by sanctions outside his science, which have their origins in *meta*physics or religious creed, there is no limit to the horrors that might be perpetuated in the name of a purely materialistic science, entirely amoral and aspiritual. Again the Christian scientist insists that science must be supplemented by wisdom.

In the pursuit of wisdom the teacher of science must find the opportunity to convince the student that beyond the areas covered by science and scientific conclusions, beyond the testimony of history, there are areas of truth which supplement those of knowledge to yield *sapientia*. These embrace art, literature, philosophy, and religion. They include emotional and symbolic conclusions, which require discipline and training no less than those activities practised in the laboratories, and which require a critical appreciation that can estimate the ultimate work of an art, of music, of literature, of all forms of effort that can lead to valid emotional reactions. The emotions will need to be fortified by a disciplined capacity for ethical, philosophical, and religious conclusions. The urgent need is not for the science specialist but for the liberally educated man. Such a man will recognize the necessity for a return to unity in place of a supposed dichotomy between scientific techniques on the one hand and moral idealism and religious faith on the other. There is no necessary reason why a scientific world civilization need be sundered from a universal religious faith. The rationalism that is necessary to the ordering of the material world in the minds of men need not be divorced from a religious approach ordering human life toward spiritual ends. Indeed, it may be urged that a fusion of the two into a common unity is the signal need in the world of today to resolve the stresses and strains. Unless we can ennoble the material realities that are available to us with the spiritual realities that are even more fundamental, the outlook is dark indeed. It is the age-long struggle for primacy between the material and the spiritual. Now, when man's capacity for control over the material through science is becoming ever more potent, it is even more essential that he pursue with equal intensity the principles of a spiritual order. Somehow or other the teacher of science must communicate in his teaching, in his work, in his life, the truth that our physical universe can go down into physical death unless we can at the same time make of it a sacramental universe. In the dark days of our time there will be many opportunities for all of us to

8

BIOLOGY

By EDWARD McCRADY

To the average contemporary professional biologist the subject "Religious Perspectives in Biology" may appear to be not only unfamiliar but suspect. It is not only not customary to introduce such digressions as religion into a course of lectures in science, but would it not be a bit shameful, perhaps, and backward, like the transparent moralizing of the medieval *Physiologus* which assumed the guise of a natural history only to provide erudite and edifying similes for use in sermons? [1] So far as religion is artificially injected into science it is obviously inappropriate and even spiritually degrading like any other form of insincerity or indirection in serious matters. But what has been most remarkable in the teaching of science for some decades past is the way in which it has avoided open reference to religious subjects when they were most germane and pressing for attention. Let no one suppose that the subject of biology is so detached from all religious questions that it can be adequately taught without reference to them. As anyone who has taught the subject knows, the students will see connections and ask about them whether the professor wants to discuss them or not. One can hardly broach the subject of evolution, for instance, without stimulating some

[1] See for instance, the account of the lion: "The lioness giveth birth to cubs which remain three days without life. Then cometh the lion, breatheth upon them, and bringeth them to life. . . . Thus it is that Jesus Christ during three days was deprived of life, but God the Father raised him gloriously." Such inaccuracies and incongruities do no good service to religion.

student to ask whether this theory is not incompatible with Christianity.

Within the brief compass allotted to this essay I shall offer a thumbnail sketch of some of the religious implications of evolutionary theory which deserve open discussion in any course intended to give a sophisticated acquaintance with biology. Then I shall add a few comments about the extent to which religious subjects already permeate the curriculum in an unacknowledged form, and the need for bringing them out into the open where they may be dealt with more adequately.

It is probably not necessary to convince most readers of this essay that evolution has occurred, though we should keep clearly separate in our minds questions of historic fact and questions of causes. We know far more about the former than we do about the latter. At an early stage of learning one is likely to get the impression that everything is known about both the actual sequence of events and the causal factors. Then if one's interest persists long enough to lead to a professional acquaintance with the theory, one may become so impressed with the shortcomings of our knowledge of the mechanism as to recover some degree of doubt as to whether evolution actually occurred at all. But the evidences of the fact do not depend in any way upon our knowledge of the means. There are vast gaps in our understanding of how it is possible for a chicken to develop from an egg, but remarkably little uncertainty about whether it actually occurs. Indeed, if it were not such a commonplace matter of everyday observation, it would be clearly recognized as one of the most incredible facts of experience. Similarly, I believe that anyone who submits himself unreservedly to reflection upon the evidences from paleontology, geographic distribution, and comparative morphology will arrive at the conclusion that evolution has happened, despite the fact that it is no easier to believe, or to explain, than embryology.

This conclusion in itself has no religious importance. Innumerable theists and Christians from the days of St. Augustine, when he wrote his *De Genesi Contra Manichaeos,* to the time of Darwin, when he wrote his *Origin of Species,* have believed that God's method of creation was not instantaneous and without process, but was one of creative evolution. Indeed, this was the customary interpretation of Genesis by the fathers of the church from the fourth century until the sixteenth. But in Darwin's later years (when he wrote his *Autobiography*) he came to believe that he had discovered in natural selection a mechanical process which made the postulate of a creator unnecessary; and it is in this connection that the theory of evolution acquires a religious significance.

Now, it would not seem that the discovery of a mechanism of evolution could disprove the existence of a creator any more convincingly than the discovery of the mechanism of an automobile, and the realization that it runs itself, could prove that there had never been a designer and constructor. On the contrary, it is often true that the most effective witness of intelligent design is found in intricate and admirable mechanisms. But further, the extent to which natural selection provides a mechanistic explanation of evolution is often misconceived.

The essential ideas in the theory of natural selection are simply: (1) that all living beings tend to produce more offspring than can survive within the limitations of food and space available on the earth; (2) that the offspring vary among themselves in innumerable ways; (3) that the overpopulation results in competition or a struggle for existence; (4) that the variations result in some individuals being better fit, which thus live longer and have more offspring; (5) that the advantages which lead to survival are transmitted to the offspring. The interactions of these five factors automatically result in progressive improvement or adaptive evolution of each species, so that a remarkable degree of fitness is ultimately possessed by all or most surviving individuals.

For the most part these five propositions are either self-evident or easily demonstrable. It is true that many of the variations which Darwin studied and thought to be heritable turn out to be fortuitous, or environmental (i.e., not transmissible), and hence of no evolutionary significance. But there are plenty of differences between individuals which are transmissible, and it seems obvious that such differences are subject to natural selection whenever they involve any advantage or disadvantage with respect to survival or reproduction. Accordingly, I do not question the actual operation of such a process in nature; but how far may it be said to provide a mechanistic explanation of the evolution of living beings?

Obviously, natural selection as outlined above can only operate among individuals already so constituted as to struggle or compete for survival in some sense (not necessarily volitionally or consciously to begin with), and capable of reproduction or multiplication, and most important of all, capable of *developing appropriate, adaptive, hereditary variations* (including consciousness and will). As initial assumptions for a theory reputed to explain everything so completely as to make a creator unnecessary, this is a rather large order. To realize the full enormity of the assumptions one has merely to propose to construct such a prerequisite specimen in the laboratory from dead chemicals (or from no matter at all, if one really means to be rigorous about dispensing with the notion of a creator altogether). But unless the origin of this prerequisite type of organism can be accounted for mechanistically the claim that a mechanistic explanation of the origin of fitness has been provided is not justified. Such a prerequisite animal or plant already has a type of fitness perhaps more remarkable than any details it might later acquire with the permission of natural selection. The type of improvement with which natural selection is concerned may be likened to the mutual adjustment of the moving parts of a new automobile; but it does not account for the origin of the automobile itself, or explain away the teleological aspects of its structure.

Natural selection *permits* evolution in certain directions, *forbids* it in other directions, but cannot *initiate* it at all. When there is a change of external conditions affecting survival, natural selection destroys those species which do not adjust themselves successfully, and spares those which do, but it cannot cause any species to adjust itself successfully—i.e., to produce appropriate hereditary adaptations. If it is to be described as a cause, one must go beyond the notion of simple causes to something like the Aristotelian system of causes, in which natural selection might be classified as a formal cause, but not an efficient, or material, or final cause. For most people not versed in Greek philosophy, it would be clearer (and just as accurate) to describe natural selection not as a cause, but as a limiting factor, the function of which is to *prevent* evolution in certain directions.

To illustrate this point vividly, let us suppose that the Earth were to explode this afternoon, and I were to meet you on the Moon tomorrow. In reply to a question from you as to how I got there, suppose I should say, "If I hadn't, I should be dead." You might, then, justly accuse me of evading the question. My statement could be perfectly true, but it would not explain how I got there. In the same way, natural selection does not explain evolution. It explains that in many cases species which did not evolve were exterminated, and species which did evolve were not exterminated. It says that if they hadn't evolved, they'd be dead, but it completely evades the questions, What caused them to evolve? and, How were they able to?

And these are very important questions. I do not know how it was possible for animals to develop eyes or ears, though I fully recognize the advantages which they confer when developed. It may very well be that in our time the possession of special senses enabling us to detect high voltage in a wire, or α, β, or γ radiations without the aid of instruments, would be of distinct survival value, but I haven't the faintest idea of how to go about evolving such advantages. How shall we begin? In the past it seems that our remote ancestors developed organs capable of detecting light, heat, sound, pressure, chemical odors, tastes, etc., all of which were common in their environment. If high voltage electricity and nuclear radiations become common enough in our environment to affect survival, will we correspondingly evolve the proper organs for detecting them? Well, if so, it will not be by means of natural selection; because natural selection could only destroy those of us who fail.

To say that the rocks on the mountain side which deflect the downrushing stream and determine to some extent its course are the cause of the stream's motion is not an adequate account of the facts. But it is precisely the same sort of mistake which is made in calling natural selection the cause of evolution. It influences the course of evolution by preventing it in certain directions and allowing it in others, but it does not *cause* it in any direction. The cause of the stream's descent to the sea is the force of gravity (or space curvature, if we prefer that terminology), and, until we discover some analagous force or comparable explanation behind evolution, we have not ascertained the basic cause at all, but merely some of the limiting circumstances.

The conventional reply to such a criticism would be that though natural selection would not cause organisms to produce advantageous mutations, there is no evidence that mutations are other than random; and complete randomness of the mutation process would lead to progressive adaptation under the influence of natural selection, if time enough were allowed. Many paleontologists (with so-called orthogenesis in mind) would question the statement that there is no evidence that mutations are other than random, and might argue that the random mutations caused by ionizing rays are not relevant to the subject of evolution, since it can be shown that ionizing radiations are not abundant enough in nature to account for more than one-tenth of 1 per cent of natural mutations. As long as the cause or causes of the remaining 99.9 per cent is, or are, unknown, we are not in a position to say whether they are random or not.

Even if we could know that mutations are, indeed, quite random, the argument that natural selection, acting upon such random changes, would produce in sufficient time all the marvelous adaptations in the living world would still be equivalent to the suggestion that five monkeys (or one) drumming away at random on five typewriters (or one) might in the fullness of time produce all of the sonnets and plays of Shakespeare without the omission of a comma. Logically this possibility cannot be denied, but mathematically it is so improbable as to paralyze one's imagination, or at least one's credulity. The trouble is that most people do not comprehend the degree of the improbability. As soon as they hear that something is not logically impossible, they are prone to think it likely, which is quite a different thing. Perhaps the way to make the force of the argument clearest would be to publish an article seriously claiming that, since we don't know who *did* write Shakespeare's works, we might as well account for them as suggested above. Given enough time, it is not impossible that they arose by a random process; and this explanation may be easier for some people to believe than that they were planned by a purposive author, though for my part, I see no reason to consider chance the more likely explanation.

But the clinching argument against randomness in the changes which make evolution possible is simply that sufficient time is *not* available. Even for the origin of one protein molecule by chance alone, Professor Charles-Eugene Guye has shown that 10^{243} billions of years would be required if the number of combinations were some 500 billion per second, and if the number of atoms from which its components came were equal to the number in the earth. But protein molecules are known to have arisen on this earth in a span of time less than 2 or 3 billion years. It would take an incredible act of faith to believe in so remote a probability as that this occurred by chance alone. Personally, I find it quite beyond my gullibility.

The next recourse in the conventional argument is to say, "Oh yes, of course; but chance *alone* is not really the explanation. The chemical properties of atoms limit the kinds of combinations possible; and similarly, at the biological level, the molecular structures of genes determine the kinds of mutations possible; and if enough limitations on possible directions of change are imposed, the time required to account for evolution may not be greater than the time which has actually elapsed in the process." Quite so; but keep well in mind that once we abandon the argument for pure chance, we reopen the question of design. If enough limitations on possible directions of change are imposed to accomplish a useful but otherwise improbable result, this is exactly what we recognize as evidence of purposeful planning. This is, for instance, exactly what we see in a steam engine. The motion of the various parts, such as the walls of the cylinder, the piston, the connecting rods, the crankshaft, the flywheel, etc., are not permitted to proceed in just any direction at random; though this is all that the expansion of the hot gas might accomplish on its own, since the random impacts of its molecules are impartially applied in all directions. But what makes an engine out of it, instead of a junk pile, is the fact that the parts are so constructed and assembled as to restrict the motions for the most part to those which lead to a useful result. No one, I dare say, who has ever seen such a mechanism and understood its function has failed to know that it did not just happen—it was obviously planned by an intelligent mind.

Now Neo-Darwinians are, perhaps unwittingly, but nonetheless definitely, abandoning the hypothesis of purely random change for just such limitations on possible directions as provide the evidence for design in any mechanism. Consider, for instance, the puzzles about the progressive reduction which seems to take place in useless organs which are at the same time harmless, like the eyes of cave animals, or the hind legs of whales. The old-fashioned Lamarckian argument that this is due to the inheritance of the effects of disuse is very difficult to support after a century and a half of sterile effort to collect supporting experimental evidence. Professor Weissmann imposed a condition of maximum disuse when he amputated the tails of rats on the day of birth. But though he persisted in this practice for a good many years and through a good many generations, he made no progress at all toward producing a strain of "Manx" rats. Indeed, what he found, instead of supporting Lamarckism, might well be advanced in defense of a much older notion that "there is a divinity which shapes our ends, rough hew them though we may." Furthermore, if one is more interested in human data than in animal experiments, one should note that the Jews have conscientiously performed an amputation experiment for some two thousand years, without, we are told, making any progress whatever against heredity. But what alternative explanation have we for the conspicuous fact that in nature unused organs do generally tend to atrophy and even to disappear altogether? Darwinism has always found the explanation of this a great stumbling block. In an environment of no light at all an eye is certainly useless; but, unless its possession can be shown to impose a real handicap which would shorten life or reduce progeny, natural selection would not seem to be able to account for its gradual reduction and eventual elimination. Recently an explanation purporting to be Darwinian has been proposed. It seems that an actual count of mutations which have been observed to affect the size of any organ whatever discloses that most of them cause reduction rather than enlargement. If this trend is universal among mutations affecting size, then in combination with natural selection it would account for the progressive reduction of all organs not significantly advantageous in the struggle for existence. Where the maintenance of a certain size *is* of survival value, natural selection eliminates the majority of mutations, and permits the preservation and transmission to successive generations of only those few which are favorable. But where no such selective elimination occurs because no advantage or disadvantage is involved, the tendency of the majority of mutations to be reductional automatically assures the progressive reduction of useless organs. This is a very interesting suggestion and possibly correct; but it is not what Darwin thought he had found—a mechanism which requires nothing but random variation. The variations here postulated are not random. The energy which causes mutations may be random, but the structure of the gene molecule is such that it can respond in only certain ways. It is biased in a very clever manner which makes for an efficiency beyond anything which could otherwise be achieved. That is to say, if natural selection can eliminate or reduce only organs or features which are positively detrimental, it can never get rid of any which are useless but also harmless. If one argues that all useless organs are really harmful in that they require nutriment in return for nothing, they would still not be eliminated by natural selection unless the disadvantage involved were so great that, in caves, for example, salamanders with good eyes have fewer offspring which survive to maturity than salamanders with poor eyes. This is certainly hard to believe, but the suggestion offered above does not require any such far-fetched faith. It indicates an ingenious device for obviating this difficulty and providing a most extraordinary refinement of efficiency. Such an arrangement looks far less like a "fortuitous concourse of events" than like a deeply laid plan, and in proposing it the evolutionist should realize that he is abandoning the concept of random variation.

It is not my purpose at this point to start enumerating or multiplying evidences of design in nature. This has been done

But why can't we believe that all the properties of matter and all the laws of nature have existed forever without having been created or inaugurated at all? A few years ago such a position seemed scientifically legitimate, and indeed such beliefs were commonly held; but within the last decade it has become untenable. Evolution has expanded beyond the realm of biology to embrace not only the development of inorganic mechanisms, but the origin of the properties of matter itself. So many evidences have come from so many directions and have converged with such remarkable unanimity upon the conclusion that the material universe came into existence all at once in a great creative act some three to five billion years ago, that it would require either a lot of new evidence or a special prejudice to hold any other opinion. All that we now know about the recession of the spiral nebulae, the dispersion of star clusters, the separation of binary stars, the origin and age of the moon, the salinity of the ocean, the relation of radioactive isotopes to their stable daughters in meteorites and in the crust of the earth, the relative abundance of the different elements throughout the universe, tells the same story. If today we do not believe in creation, it is in spite of, not on account of, the testimony of science. And I mean creation by supernatural means—that is, by processes quite literally outside the laws of nature. For the second law of thermodynamics applies to all physico-chemical processes—that is, to all events involving relations between matter and energy—and it asserts the progressive disorganization of energy. Now it is a mere truism to point out that progressive disorganization is possible only if organization exists first. And it is equally obvious that the prerequisite organization cannot have been achieved by means of progressive disorganization. Therefore the starting point had to be provided by means outside nature.

It is not feasible to preserve scientific naturalism by saying that, if violations of the law of entropy occur, then such violations are a part of nature; on the grounds that whatever occurs is a part of nature. Such an attitude would merely rob the word nature of any useful meaning. It would merely assert that anything whatever may have happened, and whatever else such a statement may be, it cannot be called scientific. The word "nature" must be delimited somehow if distinctions between "natural" and "supernatural" have any meaning. Will any scientist suggest a better definition of natural processes than "those which conform to the law of entropy"?

Perhaps, as a last resort, we might define "natural" not in terms of adherence to any one scientific law, but merely in terms of causality. Whether we now know all or any of the laws of nature accurately or not, by "natural" we may choose to mean "occurring according to laws of cause and effect," not without cause. But surely if this is all that we mean, no theologian will have any objection whatever to calling all events natural, for even what he calls supernatural he has never asserted to be without cause.

When science concludes that the material universe came into existence in a violent event at a definite time in the past, it cannot be content with the idea that this event was uncaused, since the very essence of science is the belief that nothing happens without a cause. But as soon as science postulates a cause behind the creation of the entire physical universe, it has postulated a god of some sort, since "creator of the universe" is one of the meanings of the word "god." Furthermore, it cannot mean that this ultimate cause was a blind impersonal force, for this would contradict the whole principle of conservation, which is that more organization cannot proceed from less. It is only this principle that distinguishes science from magic. When a magician takes rabbits from a hat we are astonished only because he seems to have obtained something from nothing, or more from less. But scientists, of course, do not believe that he really accomplishes such a miracle. They believe that if a thorough investigation of the performance were permitted, it could be shown that he does not get rabbits from nothing; or, indeed, from anything less than rabbits. In other words, scientists believe that results cannot exceed their causes. The opposite belief is what is called superstition, or voodoo, or magic. Now, no matter how much or how little we know about the means or method, it is certain that the cosmic process has produced minds; and therefore we must conclude that the cause of the process cannot be less than a mind. He might be more, as the man who makes a watch is more than a watch; but he could not be less. Man is more than a watch both in the sense that he is a more complex mechanism, and also and more importantly in the sense that there exists in man's mind each feature and property of the watch before it becomes manifest in the watch itself, and every function which the mechanism serves is first conceived in man's mind, and his mind generally includes more than is incorporated into any one contrivance he constructs, and in any case not less. To believe that the universe and man's mind were caused by anything less than man's mind is simply to abandon science for magic, and is more preposterous and incredible than the belief that a watch or a gaseous diffusion plant has come into existence as a result of factors incapable of making a plan or having an intention. The fact that many men who cannot believe the latter feel quite confident that they can believe the former is one of those foibles of human nature which I shall not attempt to explain.

According to the latest findings of nuclear physics all of the kinds of atoms in the universe came into existence very suddenly some 3 to 5 billion years ago. It all happened in about half an hour after a flash of light such as no man ever saw. Then a period of some thirty million years elapsed before galaxies and suns and planets (including our Earth) differentiated out of the expanding gas. Even this was a very short interval on the scale of cosmic history, representing not more than 1 per cent of the time since the beginning of everything, so that it is quite proper to say that scientific evidence now suggests that the Earth is almost as old as the universe itself. The moon cannot have been circling around this Earth for as long as four billion years. Radioactivity of the rocks gives evidence that the solid surface of the Earth is probably not more than about three billion years old. The ocean is younger than that. Life first arose in the sea in the form of one-celled organisms, which were plants in the sense that they could obtain their nourishment directly from inorganic materials, which animals proper cannot do. From them all the higher plants and animals evolved by a process of colony formation and individuation which was repeated several times at different levels of complexity. The plant kingdom was the first to invade dry land. This happened during the Silurian epoch some 400 million years ago. At that time all of the phyla of animals were represented in the ocean, but none had adapted themselves to living on the land. The conquest of the land by animals began with the appearance of the first centipedes in Devonian times (some 300 million years ago) and the amphibia and reptiles during the Carboniferous (250 to 220 million years ago). The mammals and birds arose from the reptiles in the late Triassic and Jurassic, respectively (150 to 100 million years ago). And finally, the most recent of all major types, man, appeared about one million years ago near the beginning of the Pleistocene.

It is perhaps worth mentioning that this is not a very different story from that found in the first chapter of Genesis. It would certainly be hard to devise a more realistic account of the opening event than the statement that before the origin of matter (i.e., when "The Earth was without form and void," which is to say, without shape or content—empty), God created light. The ancient author could have had very little appreciation, compared with that of a modern cosmogenist, of how profound a truth he was uttering. Proceeding promptly from an account of this most primordial of all events to details about our planet might have seemed out of order a few years ago when unthinkably long periods of time were supposed to have intervened during the evolution of the galaxies, but now that the cosmogenists tell us that the age of the Earth is probably 99 per cent of the age of the universe the ancient author seems surprisingly modern. The account of the period when there was a universal cloud layer (the waters which were above the firmament) and a universal sea (the waters which were below the firmament), before shrinkage and wrinkling led to the gathering of the waters into the hollows and the emergence of the dry land, is not disproved by any modern evidence of which I know. The next statement, that the earth brought forth plants of various kinds, could mean either that the first form of life on the Earth as a whole was plant life; or it might mean that the earth, in the restricted sense of dry land, was populated by plants before it was by animals. Either interpretation is satisfactory as far as the text is concerned, and both are true scientifically. If there was a universal cloud layer at one time (as there is, for instance, on Venus), then there must have been a time, as the Earth cooled, when a sufficient proportion of the water could remain as a liquid upon the surface to allow the cloud layer to break, and the sun, moon, and stars to appear in the firmament for the first time. This, at any rate, is the next event noted in Genesis. Then comes the story of animal life, at first in the waters and then on the land. Reptiles (creeping things), birds (the fowl that fly in the open firmament), and mammals (the beasts of the earth) are all mentioned as appearing before man. On the whole, this is an excellent account—far and away the best of all ancient ones, and in some details remarkably modern. Probably no one would ever have thought of it as conflicting with science if it weren't for the word "Yom," meaning day, which fundamentalists take to mean a period of twenty-four hours. The great theologians of the fifth to the fifteenth centuries believed that it meant an era, or epoch, or indefinite period of time, as it does in English when we speak of what happened in Julius Caesar's day, etc. That the author of Genesis so meant it seems fairly obvious from internal evidence, for after describing in detail what occurred on each of *six* days, the author refers to the *one* day in which it all happened—"These are the generations of the heavens and of the earth when they were created, in *the day* that the Lord God made the earth and the heavens" (Gen. 2:4).

If there is a difficulty for the modern reader in connection with the biblical account of creation, it is not the problem of reconciling it with science, but that of accounting for its remarkable adequacy. But it seems to me that there are much more important connections between the theory of evolution and Christianity than questions concerning the degree of scientific accuracy in Genesis. I am confident that the Bible was not intended to be a textbook of science, and whoever reads it for that purpose wastes his time, or, at any rate, misses his opportunity. By way of illustration of more important connections between evolution and Christianity, I want to mention a great teaching of the Church, the meaning and value of which to me have been immeasurably enhanced by evolutionary evidences.

Individuality among living beings is a fascinating and astonishing phenomenon. You and I, perhaps, apprehend the meaning of the term most vividly in connection with our own individual selves. Each of us experiences his own unique consciousness, setting him apart from other living beings and from inanimate objects. Each of us knows that amidst all the complexity of this variegated universe somehow I am I, not anybody else, not any other thing—apart from and distinct from, though not independent of, all else.

But in the process of living our own lives, we each encounter innumerable other selves of various sizes and degrees of complexity, which seem in a similar way to be living their own individual lives and experiencing their own trains of consciousness. Some of the other individuals are so small as to be invisible to us without the aid of a microscope. And yet when they are studied carefully they are seen to give the same evidences of consciousness and will, which we recognize in the larger and more familiar individuals which we encounter in everyday life. Whether they are as large as elephants or as small as amoebae, these individuals seem each as unique and separate as you and I, and it would seem almost inconceivable that any two or more of them could unite to form another individual with the same degree and kind of unity which each of us experiences in himself. Yet that is exactly what is taught by the science of biology. Was any more mysterious, more incredible, more astounding doctrine ever promulgated by any other group? Can you conceive of any organization ever becoming an organism in the same sense in which you are? Do you believe that a community can become a person, not just an analogy to a person, but a real and complete one with a private conscious will just like yours? Well, that is what evolutionists believe, and on very substantial grounds. After you have fully realized that, you should never again be deceived by the common opinion that, whereas religion deals with incomprehensible mysteries, science confines itself to simple, demonstrable, understandable truth. Such an attitude reflects only a superficial acquaintance with science. The truth about the universe is not simple, or easily discernible, or fully comprehensible, from any approach. If we pursue any field of thought conscientiously, we soon encounter mysteries which no man understands; but if we are honest, we must try to surrender ourselves to the evidence no matter where it leads.

The evidence that evolution has occurred is, as far as I can see, irresistible; and it indicates that all of the higher animals, for instance, have evolved from microscopic single-celled animals by a process of colony formation, with progressive division of labor and coordination of functions until the colony achieved a unity and individuality of its own, which even includes a separate consciousness of the whole assembly, not the sum of the consciousness of the parts. I, for instance, certainly have a stream of consciousness which I, as a whole, experience; and yet I include within myself millions of white blood cells, which give impressive evidence of experiencing their own individual streams of consciousness, of which I am not directly aware. It is both entertaining and instructive to watch living leucocytes crawling about within the transparent tissues of a living tadpole's tail. They give every indication of choosing their paths, experiencing uncertainty, making decisions, changing their minds, feeling contacts, etc., that we observe in larger individuals. If their dimensions were in feet rather than in micra, and if they carried on identical activities in such a familiar environment as one's back yard, no one would hesitate to attribute consciousness to them on the same grounds that one does to a dog or to another person. Indeed, unless one can disprove consciousness in all living beings (including people) other than oneself, denying it to leucocytes is arbitrary and indefensible. So I feel compelled to accept the conclusion that I am a community of individuals who have somehow become integrated into a higher order of individuality, endowed with a higher order of mind, which somehow coordinates and harmonizes the activities of the lesser individuals within me.

Moreover, this miracle of transformation of colonies into individuals seems to have occurred not once, but repeatedly in the evolutionary process. Not only did protozoa become incorporated into multicellular individuals, but these in turn became compounded into individuals of a third order. Polyps, for instance, form colonies, which show all stages of transition between temporary associations of autonomous individuals and permanent associations with different degrees of division of labor and coordination of parts, until in such genera as *Physalia* we find true individuals of a third order, including within their bodies multicellular individuals, the polyps, composed in turn of still lower individuals, the cells. And, again, in the flat-worms and annelids we find every stage of transition from un-segmented genera like *Planaria*, through temporary linear colonies like *Microstomum*, to permanent linear colonies like *Taenia*, and segmented individuals like *Polygordius*, *Peripatus*, *Lumbricus*, etc. In the Arthropoda we find even a fourth order of individuals in all stages of evolution, from solitary forms through the primitive social groups in which all members are alike, to the complex societies of termites and ants, in which there has not only been an elaborate division of labor but in the highest forms apparently the achievement of complete in-dividuation of the colony as a whole. According to W. M. Wheeler and others, the highest ant societies are individuals, not merely in semblance, but in reality. The little six-legged creatures which we see running about are parts of a higher organism (not merely organization), in just the same sense in which the cells of our bodies are parts of ourselves.

Doubtless, on first hearing, most people would reject this theory as incredible in view of the visible discontinuity of the parts of the alleged higher individual. But this objection is really illusory. All of what we ordinarily describe as physical continuity is an illusion due to the limited resolving power of our means of observation. A neutron can pass through your body without ever touching you, because there is plenty of space between your parts. But even at much higher orders of magnitude we are less solid than we appear. The cells in our blood streams are no more in physical continuity than are the fish in the sea, but they are parts of us nonetheless. The leucocytes not only wander about within our bodies like ants within a nest, but they also crawl outside through wounds, or through the alveoli of the lungs, and back inside. In pelecypod mollusks the corresponding cells even swim out into the water of the mantle cavity entirely out of contact with the rest of the body, and back into it again; but they are parts of the higher individual all the while.

The progressive development of individuals of higher and higher orders which incorporate within their bodies individuals of lower orders thus turns out to be not an isolated phenomenon, but one of the main themes of evolution. It has been going on for at least half a billion years, and there is no reason to think it has stopped today. The evolution of human society shows very remarkable parallels to the evolution of hymenopteran societies, though I do not mean to suggest that it is likely to follow the arthropod model in every detail. The vertebrate phylum as a whole has diverged from the arthropods so greatly in the structure and function of the nervous and endocrine systems, that it is probably impossible for human society to conform to the arthropod pattern in certain important respects. A group is not integrated into an individual until all of the functions of the members are harmonious with the good of the whole. Harmonious coordination in all of the insect societies is achieved by means of instincts—a behavioral mechanism in which human beings are conspicuously deficient. No anarchy can ever occur in an ant society because no ant has imagination enough to think of it, or adaptability enough to learn to perform functions other than those of the caste into which he was born. The difference between ant minds and human minds is vast. Ants inherit nervous systems into which are built the mechanisms for automatic useful reactions to innumerable situations, which result in efficient performance of the group as a whole without the delay and awkwardness of learning. The kind of nervous tissue associated with what is called intelligent or plastic behavior, the ability to change response in the light of experience, is reduced in them to a minimum. Just the opposite is the case among men. The cerebral cortex is enlarged and the basal ganglia reduced. We are born with almost no instincts, and have to learn almost everything that we need to know. In a previous publication [2] I have summarized the difference as follows. The Hymenopteran society founded

[2] *Journal*, Tennessee Academy of Science, XX, pp. 315–20.

upon instinct instead of intelligence, leads to predestination or slavery for the members, associated with peace, but not happiness—a sort of Nirvana, or Buddhistic conception of the perfect goal; whereas human society, founded upon plastic behavior instead of inflexible instinct, leads to freedom instead of slavery, entailing struggle instead of automatic peace, but with the possibility of happiness, instead of oblivion; in other words, the possibility of the Kingdom of God on Earth, instead of Nirvana. The advocates of slavery and of totalitarianism fail to realize the full significance of the difference between ant minds and human minds. Totalitarianism can succeed in one, but not in the other.

But if human society embraces free agents, it can be truly unified only by voluntary cooperation, not by coercion. Coordination must be won, not compelled. The only possible basis of permanent harmony among free men is love. And this is closely associated with a second distinction between ant societies and ours. Only a mind capable of abstractions can develop a conscience and a system of ethics, and this is the same type of mind which develops science and commerce, both of which lead inevitably to expanding horizons. Whereas an insect society may achieve complete integration on a local scale, if men are ever to have a completely harmonious society it can only be on a global scale. It is no accident that the last two wars have been world wars. It is characteristic of this stage of our evolution. All future wars will tend to involve the globe. Isolationism is not possible for men, even though quite natural for insects. The type of nervous system on which our society is based is not the type upon which theirs is based. Ours leads inevitably to world-wide communication, world-wide transportation, world-wide trade. From now on whatever happens anywhere is your concern and mine, whether we like it or not. If we are to have security, it must be predicated upon security for the world. If we want a high standard of living, we must seek it only by means which promote a high standard for the world.

Artificial barriers intended to guarantee us a high standard at the expense of the rest of the world will only mean more wars and worse ones. This is not sentimental twaddle, but stark realism.

Having come to the conclusion that a survey of biological facts leads to the conviction that mankind, as part of a process which we can trace back through hundreds of millions of years, is evolving toward a superorganism of planetary dimensions in which we shall be constituents comparable to the cells in our own bodies, retaining our individual consciousness, but co-ordinated by a single spirit of altruism, it is interesting to note that the church has been teaching this for two thousand years. The doctrine of the church as the Mystical Body of Christ teaches that the Spirit of Christ, or the Holy Spirit, which is love instead of hate, altruism instead of selfishness, can bring the Kingdom of God on Earth; that it must not be local or tribal, but must be taught to all men in all the world; that all races of men must be brought into the Church, which it describes not as an organization, but an organism—the body of Christ, in the sense and to the extent that it is governed and made one by the Spirit of Christ. Even the language is strikingly scientific. This idea that men can achieve the perfect life only by incorporation into a single great Person is just what the evidences from evolution should have prepared us for. If it seems mysterious and fanciful, remember that it is just as mystical as the unity of your teeming body under your own spirit, and just as literally realistic. Never were the meaning and force of this doctrine so vividly impressed upon me as they have been by this biological approach.

But recognition of the developing Kingdom of God on Earth, the process of unification of the faithful by the Holy Spirit as the proper culmination of the evolutionary process, does not mean conceiving it as inevitable. Innumerable species, innumerable nations, innumerable individuals, have gone downward rather than upward in the past. We can, if we will, lead ourselves and our species straight to perdition; and we are very prone to. No shallow optimism is justified by this scientific approach.

Now it would be possible to extend such discussion of religious implications of biological theory through a great many more pages than are available here, and I intend to do so in another publication, but for the purposes of this essay it is more important to make two general points about all such treatment of religious subjects in science classrooms.

The first point is that I do not mean in any case to suggest that religion is dependent upon scientific support as its foundation. It may be, as it has been for me, enhanced by scientific illumination. It may be deepened and enriched by knowledge, and what is true in it cannot be incompatible with what is true in science; but its real foundation is in experience, not logic. This is true of all important truth. Science itself had to revolt from the sterility of formal logic, and resort to experiment before it made progress. Doubtless, it has gone too far in this direction, and would profit now by re-examining the laws of reason, but reason alone is not sufficient for the solution of really weighty questions. Christ himself recognized the need for an experimental basis for deep convictions when He said (John 7: 16–17), "My doctrine is not mine, but His that sent me. If any man will do His will, he will know of the doctrine, whether it be of God, or whether I speak of myself." In other words, in defense of His doctrine, He did not suggest that we think it through before we believe it. He suggested that we perform an experiment, and that by this means we can find the answer which is too deep for us to ferret out by our unaided reason. This is the real basis for both religion and science. Experience is the source of all new learning, and reason is primarily the means of understanding what we have already learned.

The second point is that the religious perspectives of all parts of the curriculum deserve serious attention and deliberate

emphasis today because of a widespread antireligious development in our educational system, which, I believe, has already
had a profound effect upon our civilization. Sometimes it
takes the form of a studious evasion of the subject in certain
places where its discussion is obviously appropriate. But religion and education are no more properly separable than
geography and education are. Education which omits religion
is incomplete. Whether religion is good or bad, it is a subject
which has occupied the minds of men of all races in all ages,
and has influenced their behavior immeasurably, and still does
today. So, learning about it is certainly at least as important
as learning about any other subject.

But even worse than overt omission of religious teaching is
an insidious counter-indoctrination which actually pervades
most teaching at the college level and is hard to combat because it is so often not recognized for what it is. Even if all
formal instruction in religious subjects were forbidden in tax-
supported institutions, this could only shield people from an
open and honest presentation of the case for Christianity or
any other religion. It would not prevent the teaching of religion. Inevitably this does and will go on—covertly, perhaps
unwittingly, but nonetheless effectively. It may be very bad religion, but religion is taught indirectly in almost every course
in the curriculum.

Make no mistake about it! When the English professor
teaches that moral issues should not be considered in judging a
poem or a novel, he is taking a positive stand on a religious
subject. It was Henry James, I believe, who said that to ignore
all moral issues in judging a novel is as arbitrary and indefensible as to ignore all four-syllable words or all portions
written by candlelight. When an Economics professor teaches
that all the problems of society are due to monetary factors
and can be corrected by economic reform, he is denying the
effectiveness of spiritual factors in promoting the Kingdom of
God on Earth. When a professor of History or Politics tells

you that statesmen use moral arguments only to conceal their real motives, which are dictated by the selfish struggle for existence, he means to assert the futility and irrelevance of moral consideration, though he inadvertently contradicts himself, since if moral considerations were really without influence in history, they could be of no use as a cover. When a professor of Sociology tells you that moral systems have no absolute basis, are not really good or bad, or better or worse, but merely conventional styles, or habits, which vary from race to race and from time to time, he is saying that they should not be taken seriously. A delightful exhibition of rather pompous naïveté in this connection was published a few years ago in a study of the Zuñi and Dobu Indians. After much fanfare in the first part of the book concerning our new knowledge of the relativity of morals and the absence of any absolute foundation for them, the author points out an advantage which we now enjoy over our fettered forefathers. Being liberated by our new learning we are now free to discard any portion of our own code which we find unattractive, and by shopping about among all the morals of other races and other times we should be able to assemble a new eclectic system superior to any of the old ones. Having paid appropriate lip service to the new sophistication, she suddenly acts as if she really knew better all the while; or is it possible that she just failed to notice the inconsistency? Well, she doesn't tell us; and, as in the case of Hamlet's "madness," we may never know. At any rate, it did not require much penetration on the part of a critic to reply, "But what do you mean by a *better* system? I thought you said that your purpose was to show that there is really no such thing as better or worse." Such obviously muddled arguments would not mislead any attentive reader, but I fear there may be a fairly large proportion of college students who could read the book without noticing or remembering much beyond the fact that they were encouraged to feel liberated from their inhibitions. And any such impulse to irresponsibility would be confirmed and fortified by those professors of Psychology or Philosophy who teach that man is only an automaton responding mechanically to his environment, so that moral responsibility is necessarily an illusion.

The sciences very often join in the same chorus. When the professor of Physics or Chemistry tells you that physico-chemical laws are responsible for everything which happens in the Universe, he asserts that spiritual factors either do not exist, or are mere by-products. And finally, when a biologist tells you that the mechanism of evolution removes all need for postulating a Creator, he can hardly be described as avoiding a religious subject.

If religion really is genuinely related to nearly every course in the curriculum, let us bring this fact right out into the open and discuss it whenever it is appropriate. It will not be wholly bad to have religion thus woven into the entire fabric of education instead of isolated in little fragments delivered to a relatively small clientele.

9

EXPERIMENTAL PSYCHOLOGY

By ROBERT B. MacLEOD

THE PROBLEM—RELIGION AND THE SCIENTIFIC ATTITUDE

Can a person be both religious and a psychologist? The
answer obviously hinges upon the interpretation of the two
crucial terms. A psychologist is a person who is curious in a
disciplined way about human experience and human behavior.
He tries to understand people and in doing so he marshals the
best resources of science to aid him in his task. If religion were
only what to many nonreligious people it probably appears to
be, that is, a set of assumptions about life which may not be
challenged, or a framework of thought within which facts are
evaluated before they are scrutinized, or a readiness to be
shocked by behavior that differs from ours, or a smug feeling
of superiority over people who do not belong within our particular circle—the answer would clearly be "No." The psychologist is a scientist, and such attitudes are the antithesis of
the scientific attitude. We cannot be scientific about human
experience and behavior if we have passed judgment on it before we have even looked at it. If, however, to be religious is
to be sincerely, humbly, and persistently searching for the
truth, to see the truth of the moment as merely a part of the
truth yet to be discovered, to accept discovered truth as an imperative for conduct, then the conflict disappears. For, from
this point of view, to be truly scientific is in no sense incompatible with being religious. This essay will have a dual thesis:
(1) that psychology ought by now to be sufficiently grown-up

to be able to accept the phenomena of religion as a worthy
object of scientific curiosity; (2) that religion ought by now
to be sufficiently grown-up to face the scrutiny of the psychologist. Since it is being written by a psychologist, and
primarily for people with a psychological interest, it is the
first of these theses that will be stressed.

Psychology's Threat to Religion

There is at present no hot war between psychologists and
religion; but it is an uneasy peace. Relatively few psychologists
now are actively opposed to religion; but neither are there
many who would care to be openly identified with a religious
organization. Interest in religion among academic psychologists is not high. Few departments of psychology have courses
in the psychology of religion, few psychologists publish on the
subject, and at psychological meetings one seldom if ever finds
a session devoted to the psychology of religion. In the absence
of reliable evidence, one is inclined to judge the prevailing attitude of psychologists toward religion as one of wary detachment or mild hostility. The psychologist in this country does
not apprehend religion as a threat to his freedom, as he might
in some other countries; but he knows that to be labelled as
"religious" is to risk the loss of status among his professional
colleagues.

Religion, on the other hand, is definitely threatened by
psychology. One important clue to the understanding of a
person is found in the list of things he feels as threats to himself, and in the ways in which he protects himself against
those threats. The same holds true for religion. At one time or
another religion has felt itself threatened by many scientific
developments; for example, by astronomy's discovery that the
earth is not the center of the universe, by the completely materialistic philosophy promised by the Newtonian physics, by
the biologist's suggestion that man is merely one member of

an evolving animal series. But religion has conquered or assimilated each challenger in turn. The theologian now welcomes every extension of the universe as further evidence of God's greatness. He delights to draw analogies between the physical and the spiritual; and many a distinguished physicist has, in turn, openly confessed the limitations of a merely physical view of the universe. Evolutionary biology continues to be somewhat upsetting, but the thundering denunciations of even twenty-five years ago have for the most part subsided. It is no longer shocking to think of ourselves as animals, as long as we reserve for ourselves the topmost rung of the evolutionary ladder.

Where religion continues to feel the threat, however, is in the realm of the psychological and the social sciences. By attempting to bring the phenomena of human behavior under the scrutiny of the scientific microscope, by suggesting that values are in the last analysis facts, and human decisions events in the natural world, the social sciences are attacking the inner ramparts of religion's citadel. If human conduct proves eventually to be as measurable, as predictable, and as controllable as any other event in nature, if psychological science can finally define the conditions responsible for human well-being, the priest will have been deprived of the last vestige of his authority. In the quest for peace of mind or peace of soul the people will turn from the priest to the psychologist, just as they have turned from the medicine man to the scientifically trained physician.

That this threat is being felt is clear. We have, on the one hand, the recent example of an eminent Roman Catholic vigorously denouncing the psychoanalysts. One does not attack unless one feels that something precious is in jeopardy. On the other hand—and this is more characteristic of the Protestant reaction—we find the proponents of religion scrambling, sometimes with undignified eagerness, to incorporate the "new psychology" into their doctrine and their practices.

The very haste with which dubious psychological theories have been proclaimed as Christian truth from the pulpit, and allowed to dictate the procedures of religious education, is in itself an evidence of insecurity. A religion that is sure of itself would be less ready to adapt its doctrine to the psychological jargon of the moment.

Psychology's current threat to religion does not spring from the discovery of new arguments; all the psychological arguments against religion are hoary with age. It is rather that new evidence is being presented, evidence that is now clothed with the aura of science, that can no longer be so readily dismissed by mere argument. To mention but a few examples, we have had centuries of argument and counter-argument over such questions as: Is man free to make his own decisions? Can man on the basis of his own resources arrive at secure knowledge? Is man anything more than a machine? Are there any moral absolutes? Psychology has not provided answers, but the evidence from the experimental study of motivation, cognition, and the biological and social basis of behavior revives our uncertainty. The psychology of motivation has in recent years focussed a great deal of attention on the analysis of animal behavior. What looks at first glance like rational goal-directness begins to break down as we learn more about the role of organismic deficiencies in the initiation of behavior, about chemical regulators, and about the ways in which cleverly applied rewards and punishments can apparently change the direction of behavior. Even the much heralded purposiveness of the instincts seems to become merely the resultant of interaction among controllable field forces. Similarly, the psychologist has begun to study intensively the motivation of the twisted personality. Observations of the neurotic, the psychotic, the psychopathic personality, and even of the person with mild psychosomatic disorders, lead us toward the conclusion that the "real" directors of conduct are never found on the level of simple awareness; they are to be sought deep down in the biological constitution of the individual, and in that vast unknown realm that has been called the unconscious. The manipulation of mass behavior by suggestion, the experimental use of hypnotic techniques, even the rigorously controlled observations of the laboratory, seem to support a theory of motivation in which there is no place for the concept of freedom. This is not a new idea, but today's new evidence makes it a more potent threat to a religious doctrine of man.

In the psychology of cognition we have a similar revival of an old threat. Ever since the beginning of organized religion the religious authorities have held that they are the sole purveyors of true knowledge, that man has not within himself the basis for determining what is right and what is wrong. Modern science rebelled against the doctrine of revelation. Its only alternative, however, was to demonstrate scientifically that man's own resources provide a sufficient basis for secure knowledge. Modern Protestantism has come to lean heavily on this kind of scientific faith, although with frequent returns to a doctrine of revelation. The belief that we can gain true knowledge through the normal processes of perception and reasoning is seldom challenged by the physicist. It is the psychologist who, every now and again, gives us a push in the direction of a skeptical epistemology. When the psychologist brings the processes of perceiving and thinking into the laboratory, or when he traces the development of social attitudes, the evidence he finds is more suggestive of fallibility than of reliability. It is his evidence rather than that of the physicist with which religion must cope if it is not to revert to a blind authoritarianism.

The theory that man is a machine has cropped up from time to time ever since the days of Democritus. Descartes, in spite of his careful reservations, gave it its modern scientific formulation. Successive discoveries in physiology and neurology—sensory thresholds, the integrative action of the nervous system, the localization of function in the brain, the synaptic theory, the effects of hormone secretions, and so forth—have modified the simple machine model, but have served merely to support the essential doctrine. The opponents of mechanism have always taken consolation from the thought that in the inaccessible recesses of the brain there must be lodged processes that can never be encompassed by the mechanical model. The phenomena of experience seem to demand more than a merely mechanical explanation. But now the mathematicians and electronic engineers are designing calculating machines, capable of performing mathematical operations far beyond the capacity of any single individual; and, together with physiologists and psychologists, they are working out theoretical brain models capable, they hope, of eventually representing even the most complex of psychological operations. Is it possible that the machine theory in some form will win the day after all?

And, finally, psychology along with the other social sciences is striking further blows at the props that support any notion of absolutes in the realm of moral conduct. Not a new threat, of course, but the findings of the anthropologists are being steadily buttressed by researches in the experimental psychology of learning. It is an old doctrine that man is highly plastic. Now we have concrete evidence to show in detail how behavior can be modified almost without limit. The concept of conditioning, for instance, applied to everything from the modification of a knee-jerk to the acquisition of a scale of values, has been hailed as final scientific support for a completely relativistic doctrine of moral conduct. How can we be sure that our beliefs are right when we have always the disturbing thought that perhaps we believe these simply because this is the way in which we have been conditioned? Threats such as these are not likely to disturb the nimble philosopher or the firmly indoctrinated theologian. For them science is not a sacred cow. For the student, however, whose courses include much more science than philosophy, and no theology at all, the evidence of science is convincing. If the student is to develop a respect for religion, he must have more than the friendly chaplain's assurance that there is no essential conflict between science and religion, or that "obviously science is not enough." He must have evidence, as tough and challenging as anything he meets in the laboratory, that in religion there is something to be discovered, and that its discovery is worth the effort.

RELIGION'S CHALLENGE TO PSYCHOLOGY

Our interest as psychologists is, however, less in the threat of psychology to religion than in the challenge that religion presents to psychology. Here is an area of experience and behavior which is still relatively unexplored. Since psychology became an empirical science there has been little interest in the psychological analysis of religious phenomena. One can count almost on the fingers of one hand the really significant studies that have appeared. For the most part the psychology of religion has been concerned either with peripheral aspects of religion, the peculiarities or curiosities of religious behavior, or with a more or less moralistic evaluation of the variables in character development. Chapters on religion are likely to be found in the books on the psychology of the abnormal, social psychology, mental hygiene, psychological development, or educational psychology. One looks in vain for such discussions in the standard works on the experimental psychology of the normal human adult. Why this neglect of such an obviously important field of research?

Possibly we can understand it in the light of the recent history of experimental psychology. The "new" psychology of the late nineteenth century embodied both a protest and the expression of a scientific ideal. It was a protest against the parent, philosophy. Psychologists were trying to demonstrate that they could stand on their own feet as scientists. It was the embodiment of a scientific ideal, too, the ideal to be found in all nineteenth-century science. Nineteenth-century science gave us in its clearest form the promise of an ultimate explanation of all natural processes in terms of their elements. It believed that if we could find the characteristics of the elements of reality we would find revealed in them the laws that govern the universe. In other words, by reducing to the lowest possible terms we come closer to the truth. Nineteenth-century atomism represented a rejection of the Aristotelian teleology that had come down to us by way of the church. Instead of vague purposes, final causes, the scientist wanted brute facts, efficient causes. And the psychologist naturally accepted the physicist as his hero. If the physical world was to be explained in terms of atoms, so the world of mind would have to be explained in terms of atoms. Nineteenth-century associationism gives us the classic example of a thoroughly reductive analysis of mental phenomena. Whether this reductive atomism took the form of introspective analysis or behavioral analysis the effect was the same so far as religion was concerned. If you reduce religious experiences to elementary sensations, feelings, and images, the content of religion is lost; if you reduce religious behavior to elementary reflexes, emotional reactions, and acquired dispositions, its meaning likewise disappears.

Another significant nineteenth-century development was the rapid and enthusiastic acceptance of the evolutionary point of view in biology. With the doctrine of evolution extended to include human behavior, the most plausible explanation of behavior lay in its origins in animal instinct or in early childhood experience. If we are to understand behavior we must spot the primitive tendencies which underlie it. This kind of analysis leads us to see religion as a second-order phenomenon, which the psychologist must trace back to elementary dispositions to fight, to love, to hate, to run away. Religion becomes a derived sentiment or an escape mechanism, with no explanatory value of its own. Our modern genetic psychologies have, for the most part, rejected psychological atomism; but they have maintained the reductive principle. They "explain away" by reducing to origins rather than to elements.

The relegation of religion to the category of things to be "explained away" received support from a third nineteenth-century development. The rapidly increasing interest in psychological deviations, ranging from the fascinating examples of multiple personality to the humdrum individual differences in reaction-time, coupled with the sharpening of statistical tools, led to a prejudging of psychological phenomena in terms of their position on a normal probability curve. Curiously enough, two opposite prejudices developed. For one group normality, in the statistical sense, became the criterion of psychological validity. For the other group, notably the clinicians, the glamorous extremes provided the principles for the explanation of the normals. For neither group has religious behavior proved particularly interesting. It is a deviation from the normal, to be dismissed by one group because it is a deviation, to be "explained away" by the other as merely one more example of abnormal behavior. In neither case is it accepted as a kind of behavior to be studied on its own merits.

Finally, there is the practical emphasis that has become so strong in the psychology of the past fifty years. Putting it in the language of instrumentalism, we have come to think of psychological processes primarily in the context of what they can do. Religion is accordingly to be evaluated in terms of its contribution to the adjustment of the organism. In this practical context religion is interesting in so far as it may help to ward off psychological conflict, to guide the child toward the development of proper habits, to cushion life's blows. But it does not encourage the study of religious phenomena as something to be curious about.

Thus we find that, in contemporary psychology, religion tends to be something secondary to be reduced, something peculiar to be explained away, or something of practical value to be exploited. In no case have we the invitation to a real scientific inquiry into the nature of the psychological phenomena of religion.

It may be that the time is now ripe for a fresh approach on the part of experimental psychology. Part of the thesis of the present essay is that such a study might contribute significantly to the development of psychological theory. Assuming that we recognize the legitimacy of the problem, however, will not the question be raised as to the availability of adequate methods? Have we in psychology any techniques subtle and sensitive enough to enable us to probe to the essence of religious experience or religious motivation? The answer is obviously that we have not, but equally obviously that we shall never develop such techniques until we attack the problem. In every science we have those who select their problems for investigation in terms of available techniques and those who select the problems first because of their importance and then try to develop the appropriate methods. Both types of scientist are undoubtedly valuable. What the psychology of religion needs now, however, is the scientist of the second type. The techniques of traditional psychology have so far failed to give us a good psychology of religion. If we are to design new and more adequate techniques, we must begin by attempting to suspend our traditional biases and take a fresh look at the phenomena. The task is not easy, but it is certainly much easier than it was fifty years ago.

What, then, are the psychological phenomena of religion that invite scrutiny? How can they be related to the more familiar concepts of psychology? In what respects do they demand reformulation of existing psychological theory? All one can do in a brief essay is indicate a line of attack.

Let us begin with a simpler question. What are the characteristics of the religious man that invite our curiosity? In what
ways do religious people differ from other people? One thinks
immediately of the peculiarities of religious behavior. The religious man sometimes has utterly irrational beliefs, and he is
so sure of these that he may be quite intolerant of any contradiction. If challenged to defend them he may take final
refuge in mysticism, or he may condemn his challenger as perverted and lost. Some religious men have a kind of crazy devotion that may lead them to extremes of self-sacrifice, even
to martyrdom. The hermits, the flagellants, the ascetics, even
the modern conscientious objectors, behave in ways that are
often difficult to understand. The religious man may hit both
extremes of emotional disturbance. He may be irrationally
happy or irrationally depressed, reaching at one moment the
peaks of ecstasy, at the next the depths of grovelling guilt. Religious people of this sort would seem to belong properly in
the psychiatric case-book.

If, however, we neglect the extremes and look at the ordinary everyday people who seem to be religious, we get a different perspective. What impresses us now about the religious
man is his serenity, his courage, his loyalty, the firmness of his
faith, his conviction that life has a deep meaning and that
whatever happens to him as an individual is relatively unimportant compared with that which is greater than himself.
Far from giving the impression of being a twisted person, this
kind of religious man seems to have achieved something great
in life, something that the rest of us would surely like to understand. Putting it in a formal and somewhat traditional way,
we have in the psychological study of religion problems of
cognitive structure, problems of feeling and emotion, and problems of motivation. In each of these categories we find challenges to further psychological inquiry.

Let us consider the cognitive problem first. The modern
psychology of cognition has had much to say about perception,

but has tended to leave the problem of belief to the philosophers. Yet how can we discuss the processes whereby things,
events, and relationships become present to the individual without asking why they are accepted as real? This is in essence the
psychological problem of belief. What is it about the phenomenal tree or house, for instance, which makes me accept
it as real? In the traditional psychology of perception we have
had two kinds of theory, a representational theory and a projection theory. According to the representational theory there
is to begin with a real world, to be described in terms of physics.
Some characteristics of this real world are conveyed by means
of sensory processes to the organism. What is apprehended as
real, then, is simply that which is a direct reaction to what is
physically there. From this point of view, what is real is determined according to the criterion of correspondence. Most
of our percepts are correct, but occasionally we make mistakes;
and then we have illusions. The task of the psychologist is to
distinguish between what is illusory and what is a true representation.

At the opposite extreme is the currently popular projection
theory. From this point of view we apprehend as real what we
wish to apprehend as real. There is no question of correspondence to physical fact. On the contrary, the correspondence is
to the preparatory sets of the observer. The key to the understanding of perception is to be found in the motivation of the
perceiver. The apparently objective world is a mere projection
of our expectations and desires.

Needless to say, both extreme positions are vulnerable.
Even the beginner in the psychology of perception realizes
that it is impossible to draw a clear line between what is correctly and what is incorrectly represented. He is forced to the
conclusion either that all perception is illusion or that the
concept of illusion has no meaning. At the same time the
projection theorist runs into insuperable obstacles. He can
demonstrate easily that our wishes, or what he pleases to call

our values, may have an influence on what we perceive. But then he runs into some brute facts. What he sees in the ink-blot may vary from mood to mood, but no amount of projective effort will turn a square into a circle, a table into a chair, a person into an insect. Perceptual theory is thus faced with two alternatives. It may, on the one hand, accept a lame compromise between the two extreme positions, and regard each percept as a product of two sets of determinants, one internal, the other external to the organism. Such a compromise, however, leaves the essential problem unsolved, for it provides no way of assessing the relative contributions of the two determinants. On the other hand, it may temporarily suspend the question of determinants and attempt a restatement of the essential phenomena of perception in more purely psychological language. The latter approach, that of psychological phenomenology, is what is here recommended.

One of our main sources of confusion in perceptual theory is our frequent failure to distinguish between what is properly a psychological and what is properly an epistomological problem. It is the philosopher's duty to worry about the nature of ultimate reality. It is the psychologist's privilege to worry about it, too; but as psychologist he has a different duty. The psychologist's duty, in this context, is to discover, to describe and if possible to measure the processes that underlie the experience of reality, or, if a different language is preferred, that underlie reality-oriented behavior. For the psychologist, reality must be considered initially as phenomenon, i.e., as a dimension or property of the phenomenal world, analogous to the phenomena of redness or sweetness or roundness. Only after we have wrestled with the phenomenological problem can we profitably attempt a psychophysics or a psychophysiology of reality.

Since our interest is in the psychological basis of belief, let us limit ourselves to one dimension of the reality—phenomenon. Basic to the distinction between the real and the irreal is the phenomenological distinction between objectivity and subjectivity. On the level of the simpler perceptual processes the distinction is easy to make. What I see is objective; what I feel is subjective. In my visual percepts there is seldom any phenomenal dependence on my desires or on my states of feeling. I don't feel the greenness of the leaf. The greenness is there as a property of the leaf. But I feel the pain of my headache as a property of me, not as something outside of or independent of me. I can feel warmth and coldness either as a property of me or as a property of the object; and the two are not the same kind of experience. On the purely phenomenological level this distinction between objective and subjective need have no epistemological connotation whatsoever. It does not imply any varying degree of dependence on the organism. In the context of physical causation all experiences are in the last analysis dependent on the organism.

To believe something, whether it be an object or a proposition, is to apprehend it as having an existence and a validity that is independent of me. The tree and the house are there for me when my eyes are open, and I say that I am seeing them. But my world is so structured that they are there for me when I am not seeing them. They are part and parcel of a world which I believe to exist, whether or not I happen to be in direct perceptual contact with it. Similarly the propositions of mathematics, the location of Paris in Northern France, the current tension between East and West, are there for me as objective facts. Believing is, psychologically speaking, not an act of me; it is my accommodation to facts that are there and inescapable.

Now, how about the obvious fact that people differ in what they can believe? A mother, whose son has been reported missing, continues to believe that he is alive; a child believes firmly that he is really the son of a nobleman; a paranoid schizophrenic believes that he is Napoleon. Do not examples like these support the thesis of the projection theorist? The answer is that this is an epistemological, not a psychological, question.

Take the opposite kind of example. Under opium narcosi everything may appear irreal; after rapid rotation the object of the perceptual world lack their customary constancy and stability, and to a significant extent their reality-character; a we awake from a vivid dream the boundaries of reality are quite blurred. Yet experiences such as these do not shake ou belief in the reality of the external world. We apprehend the irreality as due to a temporary condition of ourselves, not to a change in the world. There are some conditions, however under which the reality-dimension of experience seems to have disappeared, under which we have lost our identity and the world has lost its anchorage points. When the phenomena world no longer contains any stable and dependable structure we have the antithesis of behavior governed by belief.

From the psychological point of view the problem of belie thus becomes that of determining under what conditions a world develops which is clearly, strongly, and stably structured We may, if we like, call this the problem of cognitive structure as long as we recognize that the self is to be considered as one of the structures in such a psychological world. Our debt to the projection theorists is that they have shown, not that sta bility of objective structure is a projection of the needs of the self, but rather that the self is to be considered as one signifi cant structure in a total psychological field, the various part of which are mutually interdependent. The relation between stability and instability of the self, on the one hand, and reality or irreality of objective structure, on the other, becomes the a key problem in the experimental psychology of belief. One conclusion to which we are forced is that the psychology of cognition is not complete without a psychology of the self. Jus as the integrity of the self is a condition of a clear, stable per cept of a tree, so a stably structured self is a condition of well organized beliefs. The fact that a person accepts the tree as real is no proof that the tree exists in the physical world. The fact that a person believes in God is no proof that God exists

But God as an object of belief and the tree as an object of perception are coordinate problems for the psychology of cognition.

Just as the beliefs of the religious man raise problems for the psychology of cognition, so do the goals of the religious man raise problems for the psychology of motivation. In the psychology of motivation we are concerned with the initiation, regulation, and direction of behavior. In everyday language we are trying to find out why people do what they do. Here psychology has rightly reacted against some of the dogmas of traditional theology. It may be true in one sense that "Man's chief end is to glorify God and enjoy Him forever," but certainly no ordinary human being accepts this literally as his sole purpose in life. The multitude of little things we do are not obviously done for the glory of God. An account of man's motivation in terms of an implied final cause is understandably repugnant to the scientific mind, since final causes are not directly observable. In its extreme form a teleological theory would explain the direction of behavior in terms of goals that transcend the experience of the individual. Such a theory would make impossible any empirical science of motivation.

In reacting against teleology psychologists have tended to move toward the opposite extreme, toward an explanation of behavior which holds no place whatsoever for goals. Goals are merely secondary outcomes of behavior driven by needs. The conventional kind of statement involves the assumption that the biological organism is endowed with certain primary physiological needs which when activated drive its behavior. Such needs are hunger, thirst, the need for rest, the need for elimination, and so forth. Through a process of learning there develop secondary or derived needs, the product of an interaction between the primary needs and the stable structures of the environment. Such derived needs are the need for prestige, the need for social support, the need for attention, etc. In some theories the derived needs are always mere substitutes for the elemental needs of the organism; in others they are conceived to develop a status and power of their own. But the derived needs are usually considered to be somehow or other less genuine than the physiological needs. The goals of the individual are products of need, determined by need, defined by need, and disappear when the need disappears.

A need-oriented doctrine of motivation is simple and appealing. If we postulate a list of fundamental needs, plus a process of learning, we can easily explain all the more complicated forms of goal-directed behavior. Part of its appeal is that it enables us to dismiss as secondary, and therefore as of no scientific interest, all the complex purposes, ideals, and values of life. And when we look at the behavior of animals we are indeed tempted to accept such a theory. The rat, the cat, and even our favorite dog seem to live close to the level of biological need. They don't seem to plan, they don't appear to worry, their fears seem to disappear with the disappearance of the threatening object. It is tempting to believe that any goals we think we see in their behavior are imputed by us, not apprehended by them. Animals have no religious motivation; therefore, one might say there is nothing to be learned about motivation from the study of religion.

There are two fatal weaknesses in an exclusively need-oriented theory of motivation. One lies in the genetic bias, referred to above. There is no scientific reason why we should accept phylogenetic or ontogenetic priority as a criterion of what is fundamental. Once we suspend this bias, we become aware of the second weakness. A need-oriented theory does not do justice to all the facts of observation. Even on the animal level, behavior is not merely driven; it is also lured by the object. As McDougall kept insisting, there is ample evidence to indicate that the animal may search for the object as well as respond to it, that, when obstructed, he may make wide detours without losing his essential directedness. The goal may be vaguely defined, and there may be a wide range of possible substitutions; but the behavior is never merely random. The essential fact about motivated behavior, even on the most primitive level, is its directedness. The paradigm of motivation is an organism not merely in a state of need, but in a state of need-goal tension. At different times and on different levels of organization the relative dominance of need and goal may vary. In general, as we proceed from the animal to the human, from the child to the adult, we find behavior directed and regulated more and more by goals and less and less by needs. When the mathematician solves a problem, it is not the need that directs the solution. The need may generate the energy, but need alone will not account for the appropriateness of the solution.

To recognize goal-directedness as a characteristic of behavior is not necessarily to return to an Aristotelian teleology, for here we are concerned with the goals that are psychologically present in behavior, not with goals logically implied by behavior. Thus, from a psychological point of view, pleasure is not likely to be a goal of behavior. Neither is happiness, nor physiological quiescence, nor equilibrium. These may be predictable outcomes, but they are not end-states toward which the individual is literally directed. Goals are concrete cognitive structures, shaped and limited by man's cognitive capacities. Individuals will consequently differ in the elaborateness, the strength, the stability of their goal structures. For some individuals goals will change with every momentary change of need. For other individuals need will be coordinated to and dominated by enduring goals. If we are to have an adequate understanding of human motivation our study of needs must be supplemented by a study of behavior in the context of goals.

No theory of motivation can avoid the problem of value, least of all a goal-oriented theory. For the present argument a simple distinction between goal and value must suffice. Values are not goals of conduct. Value is, psychologically, a framework within which conduct is regulated and judged. We define value when we try to explain why a particular goal is desirable or worth attaining. I want to become a doctor, because . . . and the "because" indicates some of the things that to me seem good. We tend carelessly to speak of "my" values or "his" values; but this is actually a violation of the phenomena. I do not apprehend values as "mine," as possessions of me or parts of me. Value in the phenomenal world is a property of objective structure, just as space, time, and similar relationships are properties of objective structure. The philosopher may finally decide that space and time are "real," but value imputed; but, so far as the experiencing individual is concerned, value is there as a regulator of conduct. To pursue the analogy, we can think of individuals who are well or poorly oriented in space or time, and we can think of individuals who have a clear or confused value-orientation. The latter constitute just as valid, and fully as interesting, a psychological problem as do the former.

Religious behavior presents a challenge, too, to the psychology of feeling and emotion. We are familiar with the pathological extremes of religious elation and depression, so frequently quoted in the textbooks of abnormal psychology. These are interesting, and we know a good deal about them. What is really challenging, however, is not the cases of imbalance, but rather those cases in which the religious man seems to show heightened rather than weakened emotional control. After a near disaster in a storm, Jesus is reported to have said to his disciples, "Why are ye fearful? Have ye not yet faith?" The word "faith," in its richest meaning, includes more than the stable cognitive structure discussed above as the basis of belief. Faith is something that renders one invulnerable to fear. What is it? In our psychology of emotion we have had innumerable studies of fear and anxiety. We know in detail the physiological concomitants of these emotional states. We have studied case histories of anxiety neurotics, and we know how to condition animals to produce anxiety reactions. But what gives men courage? What is the basis of a life that is not crippled by anxiety? Here are problems that are really worthy of investigation. We experience fear when we are threatened, when the supports on which we have depended have been swept away from under us. This may happen when our chair collapses, when an enemy bomber appears on the horizon, when an inflation wipes away our financial security. Any normal person will give a fear reaction to the collapsing chair, but people will differ in their reaction to the financial collapse. Some will respond in a neurotic way; others will remain serene. Why the difference? We cannot give the answer until we have found out what has been threatened and how important the thing is that has been threatened. This leads us back to the psychology of goals and values. Vulnerability to threat, and, by the same token, susceptibility to any other kind of emotional arousal, are in a significant way functions of the sturdiness of the structures that direct and regulate the life of the individual. No psychology of emotion is complete without an account of these structures.

In the wards of any mental hospital can be found individuals for whom a threat to personal prestige, personal popularity, conventional success, is a shattering blow. But far more instructive would be the study of those who have survived such blows and become stronger as a result. Acute stress may make or break a man. The main emphasis in our psychology of emotion has hitherto been on the processes of disruption. The chapter yet to be written must deal with processes that underlie invulnerability to disruption.

Such an emphasis in the psychology of emotion clearly leads us far beyond traditional psychophysiology. Emotion is not merely a state of the individual; it is a state of his psychological world. It can be fully understood only after we have developed methods of describing and plotting the essential structures and relationships, both subjective and objective, of which that world is composed.

If we accept the phenomena of religion as a worthy subject for experimental psychology, what effect will this have on our basic doctrine of man? Broadly speaking, modern psychology conceives of man as a part of nature, to be investigated according to the accepted methods of science. This observer sees in religion no threat to the scientific study of man as a natural phenomenon. He shares the hope that the application of the scientific method to the study of man will lead ultimately to a full understanding of human behavior. He believes, however, that the concept of "nature" must include more than the constructs of physics and biology, and that "scientific method" cannot be restricted to the method of reductive analysis.

Modern science has been biased in favor of the tangible, the visible, and the measurable. It has been biased in favor of a concept of causation that is bound to rigid, one-way time sequences. In keeping with this view, it has represented man to us as a biological organism, reacting to antecedent causes. This is essentially a materialistic doctrine in the tradition of Democritus. It is probably safe to say that there are almost no modern psychologists who hold to a Platonic doctrine of man; and it is interesting to note that even those psychologists who adhere to the scholastic tradition manage to keep their experimental psychology fairly well protected against teleological concepts. The Aristotelian framework is still there, but the detailed causal accounts of behavior and experience are thoroughly in accord with the modern scientific tradition. At the risk of oversimplification, one can say that a materialistic functionalism has conquered the field. The act psychology of Brentano has virtually disappeared. The structural analysis of consciousness represented by Wundt and Titchener has been given a modest place in physiological psychology. The configurationist protest against atomism has for the most part been approved, but it, too, has been absorbed into the prevailing biological functionalism. Just as the key concept of evolutionary biology was adaptation, so the key concept of a functional psychology has become adjustment to environment. If one's thinking about man were a faithful reflection of the psychology of today, one might easily come to the conclusion that no alternative doctrine of man is now possible.

But there are, in fact, alternatives. Man may be understood in many contexts, of which the biological is merely one; and all may be equally compatible with the ideal of science. If we are prepared to accept all phenomena of experience as facts, and if we try to observe these, so far as possible, without allowing our observation to be dictated by a particular set of constructs, we may conclude that the biological-functional frame of reference is not fully adequate. Some of the phenomena may demand a different set of constructs. In this writer's opinion, the study of religious and aesthetic experience may yield just such phenomena. The psychologist has, in some contexts, been stubborn in his resistance to dictation. He was right, for instance, in his refusal to admit a transcendent teleology into his system of explanatory constructs. Where he was wrong, however, was in his failure as a psychologist to look at the phenomena that invite a teleological explanation. Values, goals, purposes, intentions, the self, are facts. It is a fact that behavior is directive. These are facts on the human level, and as such are part of the essential subject-matter of psychology. To deny these facts because an interest in them might make one look like a teleologist is to fail in one's duty as a scientist. If man is a part of nature, the facts of experience are also facts of nature, and our theory of nature must be extended to include these psychological facts. Similarly, our doctrine of causality, and ultimately our criteria of a scientific explanation, must be flexible enough to take into account the phenomena of experienced causation. If we find in experience a kind of causation that does not resemble the simple billiard-ball paradigm, we are not therefore required to deny the experience. What we must do is to broaden the concept of causality, and ultimately our notion of science. The psychologist may derive some comfort from the realization that the simpler mechanical models are gradually being discarded by physics and biology. But the psychologist need not wait until his elder brothers take the lead. Psychology should now be sufficiently mature to look at its own facts with an unbiased eye and to let those facts speak for themselves.

RELIGION AND THE TEACHING OF PSYCHOLOGY

What will be the effect on the teaching of psychology of an interest in the psychological study of religion? Our answer to this depends in part on our answer to the more fundamental question: Why should we teach psychology anyway? If our objective in the teaching of psychology is to load the student with a good sampling of the best established facts of psychology, or if our purpose is to drill him in the use of well-tested techniques, then the effect will be bad; for the psychological facts of religion are still unclear, and we have no adequate methodology. If, on the other hand, we are trying to inculcate in our student an attitude of disciplined curiosity, if we are trying to present science to him as a quest rather than an achievement, if we are trying to open up to him the whole realm of human experience and human behavior as something worthy of understanding, then our teaching will be enlivened and enriched. Psychology in this writer's view is the best medium for the cultivation of the scientific attitude, not because of the facts and techniques we possess, but for the very reason that we have so few. Psychology is close to the frontier of research, its subject matter is available to everyone, it is a crossroads at which the traffic from all the other sciences meets. If we awaken a psychological interest in our student, we have opened up to him a world that will continue to grow in scope and in interest.

The purpose of the psychological study of religion is not to make the student pious. It is not to indoctrinate him with a particular set of beliefs or allegiances. As teachers we are all, of course, inveterate indoctrinators, in the sense that we try to convince our students that truth can be discovered and that its discovery is worth the effort. We try to whet his appetite and to sharpen his vision. But, if we are good teachers, we realize that the only truth he can really absorb is the truth that he discovers himself. If there is truth in religion, we can rest assured that it will stand the test of psychological scrutiny, and, if we have indoctrinated him with a truly scientific attitude, we can be sure that he will accept what he finds as an imperative for conduct.

10

SOCIOLOGY AND SOCIAL PSYCHOLOGY

By TALCOTT PARSONS

The following topics are briefly considered in this essay: (1) introductory definition of terms, (2) motivation of religious beliefs and behavior, (3) complications of religious and secular motivations, (4) religion as a source of creative innovation, (5) some features of the religious situation in America, (6) the sociologist as teacher.

The present essay is written from the point of view of the social scientist, not that of the representative of any religious denomination. The social scientist, like any scientist, is not, however, only an investigator; though specialization in that direction is inherent in the development of a science it must be balanced by other functions which derive from the fact that science is an integral part of the culture of a society, and the profession which specializes in a science is part of that society. It is universally recognized that imparting its findings not only to colleagues but to nonspecialists through publication and teaching is one of the major functions of the professional group which specializes in any science. This function derives above all from the fact that science contributes to human life in two directions, first in giving men knowledge about the world in which they live so that they may orient themselves more intelligently to it, and second in making it possible, through technological applications of the findings of science, to satisfy human needs and wants more effectively.

These characteristics of science in general are eminently important in the case of the social sciences, because for every man his place in his society and culture, his relations to his fellows, and their significance to him constitute the most important part of the empirical world in which he lives. But the function of the teaching of science, if that term may be understood to include both publication and communication by the spoken word, is not merely a matter of imparting information in which others may happen to be interested, it is a responsibility in a larger sense, and pre-eminently so in the case of the social sciences. For though it must be part of the credo of the scientist that to know is good in general, if not the only or the supreme good, he must also become aware that, in human social affairs particularly, specific changes in the state of knowledge in a field may often have seriously disturbing consequences, because our interests and sentiments have come to be bound up in particular systems of beliefs about ourselves, our fellows, and the place of all of us in the world. Hence the responsible social scientist does not teach without regard for the consequence of what he is doing to human individuals and to social groups any more than the responsible physician, let us say, blurts out disturbing diagnostic findings without regard to their effect on the emotional state of his patient. This is not in either case a justification for suppressing truth or what we believe to be truth, but it is very much a caution as to our responsibilities with respect to the *ways in which* we handle the dissemination of truth.

These considerations, of course, apply pre-eminently to the field of religion, since religion is so greatly a field of strong sentiments and "touchiness"—indeed, it is proverbially a field about which responsible and considerate people refrain from arguing indiscriminately. Nevertheless, the social scientist has an obligation to set forth what he feels to be some of the most relevant facts and generalizations about the relations of religion and society, and particularly to the college student, because the latter is in process of assuming the role of a mature, intelligent, and responsible person, who must be aware of the "facts of life" if he is to live up to his responsibilities. But he must also be made aware that the facts are seldom equally congenial to all people, and perhaps some of them are difficult for virtually all to face. Some of the facts we will cite will be highly congenial to the "religionist," though many of them will be more congenial to those of one denomination than of another—and therefore highly disconcerting to the "positivist." Some of the facts, on the other hand, will be disconcerting to the religionist for it is often hard to believe that a force with which one feels himself to be deeply identified can be seriously involved in responsibility for events which are contemplated with horror.

Part of the problem is concerned with the meanings of words; therefore, before going further, we had best define our terms. First, the sciences which here concern us in their perspective toward religion. Sociology we will define as the science interested in the institutional structure of social systems and the motivational processes in human beings which are involved in the maintenance and change of institutions. Social psychology is an interstitial science between psychology and sociology, much like biochemistry in the natural sciences. It is concerned with the study of motivational processes of behavior and the structure of personalities, in the context of their relevance to social systems and their problems, notably their institutional structure.[1]

A religion we will define as a set of beliefs, practices, and institutions which men have evolved in various societies, so far as they can be understood, as responses to those aspects of their life and situation which are believed not in the empirical-instrumental sense to be rationally understandable and/or controllable, and to which they attach a significance which includes some kind of reference to the relevant actions and events to

[1] For elucidation of the meaning and implications of these definitions see especially Talcott Parsons, *The Social System* (Glencoe, Ill.: The Free Press, 1951), particularly chap. xii.

man's conception of the existence of a "supernatural" order which is conceived and felt to have a fundamental bearing on man's position in the universe and the values which give meaning to his fate as an individual and his relations to his fellows.

Defined in this way a religion or religious system will include at a minimum: (1) a more or less integrated set of beliefs concerning entities which are "supernatural," sacred, or, as Durkheim said, "set apart" from the ordinary objects and events of utilitarian or instrumental significance for human affairs and interests, on his relation to which the meaning of man's life is fundamentally dependent; (2) a system of symbols, objects, acts, persons, empirical and nonempirical, which have the quality of sacredness and in relation to which men express the emotional states relevant to the religious sphere, in short, a system of expressive symbols; (3) a set of more or less definitely prescribed activities which are interpreted as important and often obligatory in the light of the beliefs involved, but which from the point of view of the instrumental interests of daily life are "useless" in that they do not "accomplish anything." These activities will usually be prescribed for different types of occasions, forbidden on others and may be differentiated for different statuses in the social group; (4) to some degree a sense that "we" who share common beliefs of this character, and participate in what is felt to be an integrated system of such activities, constitute a "collectivity"—a group which by virtue of that fact is bound together in what Durkheim called a "moral community"; finally, (5) a sense that man's relation to the supernatural world is in some way intimately connected with his moral values, with the nature of the goals he is called upon to live for, and the rules of conduct he is expected to comply with. The sharing of these common moral values as well as more specifically "religious" beliefs and practices will be constitutive of the moral community spoken of above.

In addition to these five minimum features of what the sociologist would call a religion or religious system, certain others may be expected to appear in different types of religious systems. These are all aspects of the differentiation and corresponding modes of organization of the social relationship systems which religious beliefs and practices involve. The most important aspect of differentiation is the differentiation of the roles of individuals and of classes of them relative to those of others participating in the same religious system. There are in turn two main aspects of this differentiation. The first is the differentiation of types of individuals and groups relative to their relations to the sacred and supernatural sphere independent of functions on behalf of the religious collectivity, while the second is differentiation of roles with such specialized functions. In the first direction we find such types as the individual ascetic or monastic order. In the second falls the minister or priest who functions on behalf of his congregation. The prophet can be regarded in both contexts, as having established a *new* relation to the supernatural and as the leader of a *movement* to implement its implications in the life of society.

Closely related to the differentiation of roles is the development of the character of the religious collectivity itself. There are several important aspects of this, but two may be singled out for mention here. One is the mode of integration—or lack of it—of the religious collectivity itself with the rest of the group structure of the society. Thus it may be an aspect of a single over-all collective organization, as in the case of the most nonliterate societies, or there may be a distinctive religious grouping as with the Christian Church or denominational organization. The other aspect is that of the internal organization of the religious collectivity, above all, the ways and extent of the development of formal organization of explicit canons formally interpreted and enforced, and the like.

The analysis of the conditions determining the specific type of belief or symbol system, of activities or moral roles, of differentiation of roles, of modes of collectivity organization, constitutes one main aspect of the sociology of religion in a more detailed sense. The other main aspect concerns the way in which differences of religious systems in these respects are interdependent with other aspects of the social systems of which they are a part. Unfortunately, limitations of space preclude entering into the fascinating analysis of these problems here. The reader should, however, keep in mind that solid grounding of many of the empirical generalizations stated in later sections of this essay would require carrying through the relevant analysis on this level in full detail. It is only space limitation which makes this impossible.

Motivation of Religious Belief and Behavior

With the above sketch of some of the principal components of religious systems on the social level in mind, we may now turn to some aspects of the "social psychology" of religion, of the characteristics of man as an "actor" in a situation, and of that situation, which help us to understand his need for and relations to religious institutions. We will develop this theme in two sections; in the present one we will attempt to sketch some of the main sources of the motivation to religious belief and behavior, and in that following to indicate some of the complicated interrelations between religious and secular motivations on this level.

Man is distinguished from the other animals, from the point of view of the social scientist, above all by the fact that he is a creator and bearer of culture. He creates and lives by systems of symbols and of artifacts; he not only modifies his environment, but his orientation to it is generalized in terms of systems of symbolic meaning; he communicates with his fellow men through language and other symbols; he perpetuates and develops his knowledge, and he expresses his feelings, not directly and crudely, but in elaborately symbolic form.

A "culture" is not and cannot be just a discrete collection of disconnected artifacts and symbols, but to a greater or lesser degree must constitute a *system*. It must, that is, have coherence as a set of orientations which tie together the many particular aspects of men's experience and needs. Above all it has three types of functions. In the cognitive aspects, as a system of beliefs, it attempts to answer man's questions about himself and the world he lives in, and we all know that we cannot consciously hold contradictory beliefs without strain. Secondly, it provides "forms" or expressive symbols for expressing and communicating his feelings, forms which conform to standards of "taste." Finally, and from the sociological point of view perhaps most important, it provides standards for evaluation, above all, the moral standards which regulate man's conduct, particularly in his relations with his fellows. It can be proved quite definitely that, once the step from regulation by "instinct" to the plastic dependence on learned patterns of behavior has been taken by man as organism, a society of men cannot subsist without what sociologists call the institutionalization of a relatively consistent system of patterns of culture, above all of moral values.

The role of culture in human life implies that men must be concerned, in a sense somewhat different from the animals, with the *meaning* of their experience, that is, not merely with whether a given experience gratifies a wish or fills a need or, contrariwise, involves pain or deprivation, but also with the *fit* between the *expectations* of experience which have been defined for him in his culture, and the *actuality* which he himself experiences.

There is in every system of human action, in every society, a smooth, "normal" pattern of everyday functioning, of ways in which people go "about their business" without particular strain, where the means available to them are adequate to attain the goals they have been taught to strive for, and where the all-important other people fulfill their expectations. But if all human life were like that, religion would certainly not have the significance that it does. We would be much more likely to think of the "problems" of life as mainly of a practical "utilitarian" kind, to be solved by good "horse sense."

There are certain fundamental respects in which this is an inadequate picture of the human life situation. In whatever kind of society *some* human expectations, in the fulfillment of which people have acquired a deep emotional investment, are doomed to frustration. These frustrations are of two main types. One of them consists in the fact that men are "hit" by events which they either cannot foresee and prepare for, or control, or both; to which, however, they must make major adjustments, sometimes practical but always emotional. The type case of this kind of frustration is the occurrence of premature death. Certainly, the fact that though we all know we have to die almost no man knows when he will die is one of the cardinal facts of the human situation. But not only for the person facing death himself, if he has time to think about it, but quite clearly for the survivors, there is a major problem of adjustment, for the simple reason that the human individual as an object of emotional attachment is of such fundamental importance. Even the loss of a "beloved enemy" can, we know, be very upsetting. Though religious orientations to death, which are universal and fundamental to religion, contain many shadings of belief about the "life after death," the fundamental feature of this orientation is not "wishful thinking." As one historian of religion has put it, "No major religion has ever claimed to be able to 'beat death.' " [2] The dead are dead, and cannot be brought back to life; but the living must still adjust themselves to that fact. From the point of view of the social scientist, what they believe and do in this situation has significance as a set of "mechanisms" which in some ways facilitate this adjustment. From the secular social point of view, to hold funeral ceremonies does not "accomplish anything"; the functions of such ceremonies are "latent," but they may none the less be highly important.

[2] A. D. Nock, in unpublished lectures.

In general, it is extremely conspicuous that ceremonialism not only concerns the directly bereaved, but directly symbolizes the belongingness of the deceased and of the bereaved in larger social groupings. On the one hand these larger groups which are not so directly affected give their "support" to the bereaved, but on the other they set a "tone" for the occasion which in general says, "The traditional values of the society must be upheld." Death must be only a temporary interruption; the important thing on one level is to "get over it" and to go on living. Though it is by no means obvious, there are many features of funeral ceremonies which are closely similar to those of psychotherapy.

There are other types of uncontrollable events besides death which have what in certain respects is a similar bearing on human interests, natural catastrophes being one of them. Furthermore, it should be noted that not only frustration in the usual sense, but unexpected and therefore "unearned" good fortune may also have an upsetting effect and require processes of adjustment. Perhaps our own Thanksgiving fits in that category. The Pilgrim Fathers may well have felt that they were extremely "lucky," or as they said, favored by God, to have survived their first terrible year in the wilderness at all.

A second type of frustrating experience is connected with what has come to be called in a special sense "uncertainty." By this is meant the very common type of situation where there is a strong emotional investment in the success of certain human endeavors, where energy and skill undoubtedly count for much, but where unknown and/or uncontrollable factors may and often do intervene to upset any "reasonable" balance between action and success. The exposure of agriculture the world over, with few exceptions, to the vagaries of uncontrollable and unpredictable weather is one of the most important examples. No matter how industrious and capable a farmer may be, his crops may be ruined by drought or flood. The field of health is another classical example, and there are a variety of others. The unpredictable character of human conduct in many fields, from love to war, is also prominent.

In all these situations rational techniques must of course loom large; no farmer ever grew good crops by magic alone. But these are the classical situations in which what anthropologists call magic flourishes. Whatever the distinction made, magic is always continuous with religion; it always involves some relation to the strains occasioned by uncertainty, and to human emotional adjustment to such situations. Magical beliefs and practices constitute, from the point of view of social psychology, mechanisms of adjustment to these situations of strain. They give an opportunity to "act out" some of the psychological products of that strain, thus to "place the blame" for the frustration—most conspicuous in the cases of belief in witchcraft. They give people the sense of "doing something about it" in areas where their rational techniques are powerless or untrustworthy. Above all, they act as a tonic to self-confidence; they are a protection against allowing the risk of failure to lead to a fatalistic discouragement, the attitude that since success cannot be assured, it is no use trying at all. At the same time, magic may act as a stereotyping agency in situations where empirical knowledge and technique are applicable, and thus block technological advance—this in spite of the fact, which Malinowski makes so clear, that magic cannot take the place of rational technique. The Trobriand Islander does not believe that he can make up for failing to cultivate his garden properly by more and better magic; it is a supplement, not a substitute.

The frustrations of established expectations of which we have been speaking pose "problems of meaning" in a double sense. On the one hand, man, being a culture-bearing animal, does not merely "take it" when things go as he does not expect. He has to give these things a meaning, in the first instance emotionally, so that his adjustments to such experiences can become integrated in the *system* of experience, which means among other things that his reactions are coordinated and organized with those of his fellows; he can communicate his feelings and receive adequate responses to his communications.

But beyond this, as we have noted at the beginning of this section, the culture in which a social group lives constitutes a more or less integrated system. As such it must have a certain level of consistency; it must "cover" the principal ranges of men's experience in such a way that all of them to some degree "make sense," together as a whole.

Besides the direct problem of emotional adjustment to the frustration of particular experiences, the "generalization" which is involved in the integration of a cultural system brings up two further particularly crucial "problem" areas. The culture links the experience and expectations of any particular individual or subgroups with those of others in a society. There is not only the question of why must this happen *to me*, or to those close to me, but why must it happen at all to anyone? Above all, since men universally seek gratification of their wishes and needs, there is the generalized problem of suffering, of why men must endure deprivation and pain and so unequally and haphazardly, or, indeed, at all, and, since all societies must live by moral standards, there is equally the problem of "evil," of why men violate the moral standards of their society and why the "economy" of rewards and punishments fails, as it *always* does to some extent, to balance out. Good fortune and suffering must always, to cultural man, be endowed with meaning. They cannot, except in limiting cases, be accepted as something that "just happens." Similarly it is impossible to live by moral standards and yet be wholly indifferent either to the extent of conformity with them or to the fate of conformists and violators respectively. It is necessarily disconcerting that to some degree "the good die young while the wicked flourish as the green bay tree."

The sociologist is in a position to state that some significant degree of discrepancy between expectations in both these respects and the actual state of affairs in a society is inevitable, though it varies greatly in degree and in incidence. Both expectations of gratification and moral standards vary from society to society, but this fundamental fact of discrepancy seems to be a constant, grounded in the nature of human personality, society, and culture and their relations to each other.

This complex of circumstances constitutes from a certain sociological point of view [3] the primary focus of the differential significance of religion in human life. It is made up of aspects of the life situation to which, men being what they are, they cannot remain emotionally indifferent, and which at the same time in the long run they cannot evade. But adequate adjustment on either the emotional or the cognitive level to these situations cannot be worked out through the "ordinary" techniques and attitudes of practical utilitarian life. The content and incidence of the problems vary, but their presence is a constant. Almost another way of putting the essential point is to say that tragedy is of the essence of the human situation.

In one sense, all religious ideas involve what may be called a "transcendental reference"; this, indeed, is what has been meant here by saying that they concern the "supernatural." But this need not imply that the "locus of values" is put primarily in the "other" world. Indeed "naturalism" in the sense of sanctioning the interests of this life in health, wealth, happiness, long life, is more common than not in religious traditions. But the existence of the transcendental reference plus the tension which necessarily to some degree obtains between "ordinary" expectations and the discrepancies of experience with reference to them may be related to a development by which the primary locus of value is placed in the transcen-

[3] More positive aspects of religion, independent of the strains inherent in the human situation, may be equally important, but are more difficult to get at in the context of the intellectual traditions of modern social science.

dental sphere itself, in a life after death, or in some other form of "salvation" from the involvements of ordinary human social life. Indeed, the problem of balancing the books of the human economy makes this very likely, though the "displacement" may not be into a transcendental world, but may emphasize a future state of human society, as in Western "progressivism" or "revolutionary" utopianism. Furthermore, the degree of radicality of repudiation of the things of "this world" may vary greatly, from a desire to "reform" some secondary unsatisfactory features of it, to the view that ordinary secular human life is intrinsically evil, that man is sunk in utterly hopeless degradation and sin, and that *only* in transcendental terms is any positive value whatever to be found.

Whatever the situation in these respects, the religious problem par excellence in the more generalized sense is the "justification of the ways of God to man," is "making sense" out of the totality of the human situation, both in the cognitive sense of a "theory" in which the discrepancies and the established order can be brought within a single view, and in emotional adequacy so that man can adjust to his own fate and that of the societies with which he is identified. Thus, though religious ideas on the sophisticated levels are "philosophical" in content, we will not speak of their being religious so long as the basis of interest is merely intellectual, the solution of baffling cognitive problems. They become religious only so far as a commitment in emotion and action to their implications becomes involved, as, in that sense, to quote Durkheim, they are "taken seriously."

From the psychological point of view, then, religion has its greatest relevance to the points of maximum strain and tension in human life as well as to positive affirmations of faith in life, often in the face of these strains. It is most deeply and intimately involved with the "emotional" problems of men, precisely as these are related to the higher levels of culture, to the problems to which in the widest sense man finds it most difficult to adjust. We will attempt to follow the implication of these facts in two main directions. First, in the next section, we will go somewhat more in detail into some of the psychological complexities which appear in the religious field, then, in that following, into some of the larger-scale social phenomena which are related to the same context.

Our immediate concern is the association of religion with some of the major situations of strain in human life, strain in which the "emotions" are deeply involved. Psychologically we are in a position to say something about certain typical phenomena which appear in reaction to such situations. We will assume that strain consists in the actual or anticipated frustration of established expectations relative to the needs of the personality. In the first place experience of such frustration in a situation, especially if it has been repeated, will tend to produce anxiety, an expectation of the likelihood of being "hurt," which operates in advance of the actual event and motivates behavior oriented to avoiding the dangerous situation or to coping with it in such a way as to prevent or minimize the damage. Anxiety may come to be more or less generalized from the original sources of frustrating experience, to apply to objects and situations which are felt, often irrationally, to be sufficiently similar, also to be dangerous. There may thus, as in certain phobias, be displacement of anxiety on a symbolic representative of the original object, because the motivation is ambivalent and the object is both feared and a source of attraction at the same time.

This ambivalence of motivational reactions to strain is a fundamental feature of it. One is not subjected to emotional strain in this sense unless the object or situation "means" something, is emotionally important. There is, therefore, always a motivation to retain the meaningful, gratifying relation to the object and continue to receive satisfaction in relation to it. But at the same time there is the fact that a fully satisfactory relation is blocked, and therefore there are reactions of resentment and hostility directed against what is *felt* to be the source of the frustration. Strain therefore tends, in addition to anxiety about the future development of the situation, and in the presence of objects and situations felt to be dangerous, to be accompanied on the one hand by feelings of need for the desired relation to objects and by phantasies of the fulfillment of these needs, and on the other hand by feelings of resentment and hostility and phantasies of aggressive action against the source of injury. Finally, one other feature of human psychology is so important that it needs to be mentioned here. The human child is more deeply dependent on adults than is any other young animal, and we know that this dependency is an essential condition of the process of socialization. "Maturity" is in one sense a state of having "outgrown" childhood dependency needs, but they are never completely eradicated, and situations of strain certainly tend to reactivate them. Hence it may be presumed that on the positive side of reaction to strain there will be disposition to find objects on which to be dependent, or to intensify dependence already present to a greater than normal degree.

A person under strain is thus inevitably a person in conflict in a psychological sense. He has impulses which cannot all be carried out in action and must resort to what are called "mechanisms of defense," like repression, displacement, projection, reaction-formation, and phantasy-gratification, if the pressure cannot be sufficiently eased so that the impulses themselves subside. There are of course enormous variations in degree of the intensity of such conflicts, and of how far they have affected the structure of personality itself; in the latter case "neurotic" phenomena appear, whether they are culturally defined as such or not.

We have said that strain, and hence emotional conflict, must be defined as relative to expectations. It is clear that the most important expectations men have are those relative to human beings and their action, not only others but themselves.

Any individual has grown up in a particular circle of human associations and relative to a particular set of institutionalized patterns of culture. Therefore, the negative component of his reactions to strain is largely constituted by what may be called "alienation" from the persons and the normative patterns in relation to whom and which he has lived. Alienation is always *relative* to the social situation in which it arises, it is always hostility to some persons and some patterns, more or less generalized to others.

This excursion into the psychology of reaction to strain has been necessary as a basis for understanding the social psychology of what is involved in many of the concrete phenomena of religion. Most emphatically, religion in general is not a "pathological" phenomenon in any psychological sense. It is an essential part, in the broad sense in which we have defined it here, of the institutional organization of a normal society. But because of its peculiarly close relation to situations of strain the same components of human motivation which are prominent in the phenomena of psychopathology are also often to be found in the religious sphere. In some cases religious institutions constitute effective "mechanisms of social control" in that they serve to "cope with" the products of strain in such a way as to protect the normality of the personality and the orderly functioning of the society. But sometimes the "deviant" aspects of the motivational complex may get the upper hand, and behavior in the name of religion can be highly disruptive both of personality and of social order. When this is said it must, however, be remembered that "deviance" is defined as relative to a particular pattern of social order. Therefore, there is the inherent problem of discriminating creative innovation, which from the sociological point of view is very often founded in religion, from merely destructive disturbance of the social system. This essay in no way wishes to disparage the enormous significance of the role of religion in the former context, but at the same time must insist that the record shows

a substantial element of the latter. The two cannot, empiri
cally, appear in complete dissociation from each other.

We may develop this point in terms of a few concrete
examples. It has been noted that a component of alienative
motivation is inherent in reactions to strains. But the condi
tions under which alienative, hostile, impulses have been
aroused are not by themselves sufficient to account for the
form in which they are expressed.

Some of this hostility is generated by the impact of genuine
abuses judged by the moral standards of the society—abuses
rightly met with indignation. More of it may often be gener
ated in less obvious ways, by elements of conflict and strain not
directly intended by anyone, and for which no one can reason
ably be held responsible. In any case, expression directed
against the immediate sources of strain is only one of the pos
sible channels of expression—it is often possible for a variety
of reasons that hostility should be "displaced" on other objects.

The very fact that religion involves an inherent transcen
dental reference is an important element of this situation. Be
cause there is a "higher" authority which cannot directly hold
its adherents responsible, action which is dubiously legitimate
in more human terms may be carried out in the name of this
higher authority as one form of displacement, and hence dis
tortion of the more genuine values of the society.

It is by some such process as this that religious actions can
often become the vehicle for expressing feelings of resentment
which are humanly understandable but often difficult to justify
in terms of any moral or religious values. The numerous occa
sions on which the adherents of various branches of Christian
ity, which itself glorifies universal love, have treated others with
violent and bitter hostility, if for example they refused to con
form with the tenets of the particular denomination in ques
tion, may serve to illustrate this fact. Such considerations may
help one attempt to understand how, in the seventeenth cen

tury, the religion of love came to be the focus of a whole series of religious wars which nearly destroyed European society. The "religionist" cannot treat such facts so simply as to say that what happened was merely that religion was "corrupted" by evil political or economic influences. Its very corruptibility would not be understandable unless hostility were very intimately involved with the system of religious sentiments itself.

The other side of the motivational complex which produces hostility under strain is the production of unrealistic phantasy gratifications and "utopian" ideas. Some of this element is undoubtedly "projected" into the transcendental sphere and helps account for such phenomena as the persistent strains of "goody-goody" wish-fulfillment phantasies about the blissful existence in heaven after death. Such a strain, though present in Christianity is by no means universal, but is balanced by the theory of transmigration in Hinduism, with its belief that one will have to live through an endless series of terrestrial lives with all the attendant grief, and that, except for mystical techniques, there is no escape from the "wheel of Karma." Furthermore, in Christianity itself, the wish-fulfillment element is balanced by equal extremes in the other direction, by conceptions of terrible divine punishment which border on the pathological in their attribution of vindictiveness and inhumanity to God, and thus are exceedingly difficult to reconcile with the conception of love. They indicate an extreme degree of what psychologists call "intra-punitiveness," the turning of hostility against the self.

But the positive, utopian side is sometimes, in religious contexts as elsewhere, directed to the ordering of life in this world, and hence a utopian strain is prominent in many religious movements. The effect may be to subject the adherents of such movements to much practically unnecessary torture and grief because their religious beliefs, often with regard to many matters of legitimately secular concern, interfere with a sensible handling of the situation. It is difficult in this field to discriminate genuine differences of value from distortions of reality, but the latter certainly are not absent.[4]

Cases of this kind are more frequent than is generally realized. It is not meant to single out any particular group as an example. Furthermore, cases involving natural science can certainly be matched by cases with respect to the practicability of social arrangements. Thus the tendency of some Christian sects to repudiate the use of force or coercion in any form as radically evil can be shown sociologically to have had two types of effects. On the one hand, since there are reasons to believe that *some* coercion is inseparable from the minimum conditions of social life in a high culture, it has relegated the adherents of such beliefs to a position of minimum influence on the higher cultures. A group which insists on the acceptance of conditions which realistically it is impossible to grant, *must* be rebuffed by precisely the most responsible, and therefore morally serious, elements of the society in which they attempt to proselyte. But, secondly, in cases where the adherents of such a doctrine have in fact come to assume positions of responsibility in the organization of social relationships, they have been directly faced with the problem of the *control* of coercion and the use of force. Wherever a religious movement has survived over any considerable period, it has had to accept *some* use of coercive means on its own part in order to cope with the situation. There are limits to social utopianism as there are to the control of the body. Beyond a certain point mortification of the flesh, however high the level of spirituality, becomes suicide. Similarly, beyond certain points, which are admittedly difficult to identify, neglect to provide the mini-

---

[4] One type of case is illustrated by the beliefs about health which have been prominently institutionalized in Christian Science. There seems to be no doubt that much very real suffering and many premature deaths of persons whose lives could have been saved have been occasioned by the religiously motivated refusal of Christian Scientists to avail themselves of the services of the medical profession.

mum conditions for an orderly society is social suicide; a religion which pushes certain doctrines regardless of such limits is, from the the social point of view, inevitably a disruptive influence.

This is of course in no way to say that any particular current state of affairs with respect to the control of the use of force is to be considered ideal. Particularly in a time when we live under the shadow of the possibility of extremely destructive war, it would be criminal folly to minimize the seriousness of the problem. But a sociologist may venture the opinion that learning to *control* force more effectively is more likely to minimize the risk of war and limit its destructiveness than is turning one's back on that responsibility by refusing to be implicated in the moral evil of the use of force in any way.

One final point. We have noted that alienative motivation often leads to the venting of hostility not only against the abuses of the secular world, but more generally. This type of reaction may very well be combined with the disposition to withdraw from a secular world defined as more or less radically evil. It is by some such path that the religious doctrines of the need for radical salvation seem to have evolved. The conception of the supernatural provides the opportunity to transfer what we have called the locus of values completely to the transcendental world. This world, then, in the extreme case, becomes only something to escape from, not something to live in. It is seldom that doctrines have been pushed to such a radical extreme. But when they are, if the religion is to survive as a movement, certain things will have to happen. Religion is, in important respects, a reaction to the inevitable strains of ordinary human life. But in certain respects it may sometimes create an order of strain to which it in turn must react by modification of the movement itself.

COMPLICATIONS OF RELIGIOUS AND SECULAR MOTIVATIONS

Human society differs from the phenomena of "nature" precisely in the sense and to the extent to which it is itself a product of human action, of human ideas, aspirations and values, and not of the "conditions" to which men are subjected. There is a very important sense in which to a degree man *is* what he wants to be, or what he believes he should be. But at the same time this "voluntaristic" aspect of human society is intermeshed with subjection to a whole set of given conditions, which are not creatures of man's will but must be adapted to. This does not in the least mean that such conditions cannot be creatively used, for obviously they can. But man does not succeed in controlling or using them solely on his own terms as it were. He has to learn how they work and take advantage of those ways in which they can be made to work which fit his needs and desires.

The familiar examples of physical technology will illustrate the point. Man is sometimes said to have "annihilated space." Taken literally this is sheer nonsense. Man does not simply, godlike, say that spatial limitations are a nuisance, let them cease to exist. He comes laboriously to understand how movement in space works in the physical world, and on the basis of that understanding is able to devise means of transportation and communication which are able to transport men and goods farther, quicker, and cheaper than before, or to transmit communications across spatial distances. He adapts himself more effectively to the *conditions* governing relations in space; he does not annihilate space. Above all, though he changes many concrete things in the physical environment, for example, by building railroads which did not exist before, he does not change the *laws* by which physical phenomena and processes operate; he understands them and uses them, which is a very different thing.

There is no reason whatever to believe that things are in these respects essentially different with the "human material" out of which organisms, personalities, and social systems are composed. Man can create his own society within limits to his own desire because he can control and manipulate this "human material." But he cannot control it in contravention of the laws of its own "nature," but only by conforming with the possibilities and opportunities presented by those laws. He may well hit on some methods of control by "chance," that is, by processes other than a rational understanding of the situation and how to take advantage of it. But none the less his successes and failures are a function of the "conformity" of his action with the processes which govern the material he tries to influence.

The above position is stated, not primarily as a philosophical position, but in accord with the whole of this essay from a scientific standpoint. Many religious adherents will interpret both the laws governing the physical world and those governing "human nature" as ordained by God for His own good reasons, and similarly the values which men attempt to realize in this world as prescribed by God. Whether this philosophical view or some other is taken does not affect the task of the scientist, or the methods by which he comes to understand these laws. Newton was a devoutly religious man, but his formulation of the laws of gravitation was not a deduction from his religious beliefs. There is conflict only when a religious claim is advanced that *specific* knowledge of how "nature" (human or otherwise) works has been divinely revealed; therefore empirical investigation, the results of which do not agree with this revelation, is superfluous. On this point, in relation to society as well as other fields the scientist has a definite position. He fully recognizes many limitations both on his current knowledge and on what scientific methods can produce. But he cannot admit a priori and without scientific investigation that, within the specific field of his competence, *in principle* any other source of specific knowledge must be held to supersede his own. To do so would be tantamount to the abjuring of his profession. To this extent and only to this extent does he take a philosophical position. It is of course freely admitted that he does not know the limits of his science in detail; but he holds that the *only* way to find them is to try; that it is not legitimate to say on a priori grounds that a whole range of problems is scientifically insoluble, unless actual and competent attempts have been made to demonstrate it. Such assertions have been repeatedly made in the intellectual history of the Western world, and repeatedly proved by the event to be false. Even today certain humanists and even natural scientists are saying that social science in principle is impossible, at the very same time that social scientists themselves are proving them wrong by actually doing the allegedly impossible, that is, creating a science.

Consideration of the above points has a bearing on a discussion of the process of adaptation of a religious movement to the exigencies of continuing life in human society. The essential point is one of relativity of points of reference. *Some* of the empirical features of human society are particular to the specific society in which the movement itself originates, and such a movement will, in the nature of the case, attempt to change many of these and will be likely to be partially successful in doing so; religion is, in this sense, a creative source of social innovation and change. But *some* of the features of every society are necessary conditions of the long-term existence of society itself, or of societies of particular kinds and where, as has frequently been the case, the religious movement attempts to abolish these it will not succeed, but on the contrary will have to accommodate itself to them.

As we have noted, a religious movement, particularly one with a strongly transcendental emphasis, usually starts in a position of alienation against many of the features of the current society, which will include both religious and secular institutions. In the case of early Christianity, it was on the one hand "paganism," and on the other the structure of the Roman Empire, particularly as symbolized by "Caesar." Such a group is, in the nature of the case, a "minority group." The most it can expect immediately is a certain tolerance from the rest of the society which enables it to exist at all, and perhaps to spread. The evidence is that Roman society and its government were unusually tolerant, that this fact had much to do with Christianity's getting its chance to survive, and that its first adherents were on the whole inconspicuous "little people," who did not come to the attention of the authorities.

Throughout the earlier phases, of course, the movement was dominated by the expectation of the imminent Second Coming and had no thought of the long-run problems of its relations to a going society. This was the background of the famous phrase, "Render unto Caesar the things which are Caesar's," in that "Caesar" was responsible for the secular world as it was, and Christianity had no thought of attempting to "take over." The minimal organization of the little community of Christians themselves was the extent of Christian concern with secular society, along with the concern for preventing contamination from the evil world and for spreading the Gospel.

The process which led to the acceptance of Christianity as the official religion of the Roman state by Constantine was long and complex, but from that time on the movement was certainly faced by the necessity of a quite fundamental change, one which was in some ways obscured by the process of decline in Roman society itself, a process which was by that time far advanced and was probably to some degree helped along, though certainly not fundamentally "caused," by the spread of Christianity itself.

In a very broad way, ever since that time there have been two great trends in Christianity with respect to these problems. One has been the main trend, the development of the idea of the institutional church as an integral part of the Christian society, the other the conception symbolized by the phrase "my Kingdom is not of this world" when used to motivate an attitude ranging from aloofness to active hostility to *all* things worldly, *including* the institutionalized church and the regimes of "Christian" monarchs and governments. There have been innumerable shadings and accommodations, as in the integration of the religious orders in the Catholic Church itself, but the two fundamental trends have remained.

From certain religious points of view it is difficult to see how the proponents of the anti-institutional trend have been wholly wrong, for it is quite clear to the sociologist that it is impossible to be the institutionalized religion *of* a concrete society without being implicated up to the hilt *in* that society. We may illustrate this fact by the problems of power and of wealth, which have continually disturbed Christianity. It is in the nature of a proselytizing religion that it wishes as many converts as possible and that it wishes these converts to guide their lives as completely as possible by the tenets of the religion. But history will certainly bear out the generalization that large-scale mastery or influence over the minds and spirits of men seldom if ever occurs without organization and leadership. Further, ascendancy over the spiritual life is not fully separable from ascendancy over conduct in many spheres of life. But in the nature of the case an organization which has "control" over the conduct in important respects of large numbers of people has "power." A church may or may not define power over men as intrinsically evil. But, precisely because and as a result of success in its religious mission, it itself becomes a "great power" in the society. There is no escape from this dilemma. The only question is *how* the power is to be used, not whether the church shall or shall not have power. This is a dilemma as deep as the great dilemma of the "knowledge of good and evil." It is not possible to have knowledge of the good, without also knowledge of the evil. It is not possible to choose the good, without having the possibility of choosing the evil. It is not possible to influence the lives of men, without all the implications of having taken the responsibility for influencing them, that is, without being involved in the moral dilemmas of power.

In proportion as the society became a Christian society, in just that proportion the church became the most important power in the society. The medieval church eased part of the burden by sharing power with the secular authority. But when the church convicted a man of heresy in an ecclesiastical court and "the state" proceeded to burn him at the stake, the church was necessarily responsible for the burning even though all physical punishment was formally in the hands of the "secular power," since heresy was equally a religious offense and a civil crime in a Christian society. Certainly in the medieval view it was the *religious duty* of the secular authority to burn heretics; they were just as much an agency of the divine mandate as was the church itself. The Catholic Church has of course faced this problem squarely and accepted the responsibility, but this is only one of many illustrations of the fact that the church in Western history has been deeply involved in the problems of power. Furthermore, since power is the capacity to influence men as such, there can be no neat division between religious and secular power.

The case of wealth is parallel. Wealth is essentially a class of means of exercising power. It is control over the facilities necessary to meet human wants, whatever they may be. Certain trends within Christianity early developed the view that poverty was in itself a virtue, and that the truly religious should take vows of poverty. But poverty even for monasticism came to mean only that the control of wealth was transferred from the individual to the ecclesiastical corporation, not that "religion" was relieved of the temptations of wealth. So eventually the Christian church in its various capacities became the "owner" of something like a third of all the land of

Europe. There is nothing surprising about this; a cathedral is
inevitably a form of wealth; you cannot glorify God in stone
and stained glass without creating something of value in the
economic as well as the religious sense. The "treasures of the
church" in land and buildings, in vestments and works of art,
are, proverbially, "priceless"; they constitute wealth in the
most literal sense. There is no escape from this fact. Again,
the alternative is not *whether* or not the adherents of a religious movement are to acquire wealth, but *how* their wealth
shall be used and controlled. And the more successful a religious movement is, in the purely religious sense, the more,
necessarily, will it come to control a large proportion of the
wealth of the society of which it is a part.

These examples will suffice to make the main point. But
it may be added that there is a still deeper sense in which the
institutionalization of religion, as the sociologist calls it, must
involve it in the structure of a secular society in a twofold
way. We called attention to the fact that alienation against
the institutionalized values of the going society is a prominent
feature of religious movements in their early phases. To
spread, a religious movement must almost in the nature of
the case exploit people's dissatisfactions with their lives in
"the world." The movement tends to appeal to people who
are disposed to nonconformity, to disagree with their fellows,
with the current moral practices, and with the expectations
of those in authority. But, as a direct result of gaining ascendancy in a society, the "shoe is on the other foot" for a religious
as well as for a radical political movement. If the movement
is to consolidate its position of ascendancy, and stabilize its
position in the society, it must create motivation to conformity with the expectations of an *established* order and of the
authorities which are duly constituted in it. The mainstay of
an established religion, therefore, cannot in the nature of the
case be the *type of personality* which must be the spearhead
of the rise of such a movement in a necessarily hostile environ-

ment. The question sometimes asked, What sort of treatment would Jesus receive in an established Christian community? is not without its point. Jesus was not a social revolutionary, but he was certainly a rebel. He said, "It is written, but I say unto you"—something in conflict with essential parts of the established tradition. He stood in self-conscious opposition to the duly constituted religious authorities of his day, to the "Scribes and Pharisees." Though, of course, there was much continuity in the tradition he founded, the function of Jesus was necessarily different from that of an ideal bishop of an established church; it is more than possible that one of his temperament would have stood in opposition to the bishops of a later age. But, whatever the personalities, certain aspects of this dilemma, like those of power and wealth, are inevitable. If a religion succeeds in its mission, it must establish what is in *some* sense an orthodoxy, and it must oppose those who attempt to destroy orthodoxy no matter how high their motives may be, to themselves and to their followers.

Indeed, the ultimate paradox is that a religion which starts out to save men *from* the world, because of the very fact that it succeeds on this earth *as a religion*, that is, in influencing human society, *itself becomes the world*, at least one of the most important parts of it. Then those to whom, like the founders, the world itself is evil, must often, if they are contemporaries, be turned against by the very religion which institutionalized the point of view they represent. The successors of the *founders* must often turn against, thus in a sense betray, these founders, because their attitude toward the world, if it includes repudiation of all worldliness, is incompatible with taking responsibility, in exalted or humble station, for the welfare of a religious organization, just as much as of any other kind of organization. Thus there is a deep sense in which the tragic side of human life, which religion itself so profoundly expresses and depends on, is not only something to which religion helps men to adjust, but is part of the fate of religion itself; for religion, whatever the supernatural element of it, is inevitably a part of the way of life of human beings, and is caught up in dilemmas of the human situation just as much as any other part.

Perhaps the most important note on which to end the discussion of this particular problem is to point out that it is the teaching of sociology that religion, like every other phase of human society, can be *only relatively* stable. Men, in turning to religion, are sometimes motivated by a search for an ultimate security, for something which stands fast in the endless flux of human affairs. Many have felt they found it in the ultimate objects of their faith, in their relation to God. But religion *as human institution* cannot provide that ultimate security, for it too is subject to the flux. We will find many prophets in the future as in the past who purport to set up *the* religious institution which can never fail. The sociologists' view is that *all* such promises are illusory. The Roman Catholic Church is one of the most successful attempts in human history to provide this unbreakable stability of institutional structure for religion. This is one aspect of the symbol of Rome as the "Eternal City." But even the Catholic Church is a human institution, subject to the vagaries of social change. It has undergone many transformations in its long history and certainly will undergo many more.

Religion as a Source of Creative Innovation

The last two sections have stressed some of the ways in which religion can be, and sometimes is, not only a way of helping men to adjust themselves satisfactorily to the elements of strain in their life situations, in both a personal and a social sense, but also in one sense a source of otherwise "unnecessary" strains. Stress on these facts should not, however, be allowed to upset a balanced view of the complex relations of religion and society. One reason they have been introduced is that there is a tendency for the American Protestant groups, among which many of the readers of this essay will be found, to take, in common with American culture generally, a somewhat overoptimistic view, to understress the element of tragedy in which religion itself is deeply implicated. Religion is, quite correctly of course, held to be a "good thing," and hence there is a certain reluctance to believe that many things which, from the point of view of our social and religious values are not good, are also associated with religion. But this fact does not obscure the massive impression of the overwhelming positive place of religion.

In order to balance the impression, we may speak briefly of another main aspect of the significance of religion, namely, its place in the process of creative innovation in cultural development. From the sociologist's point of view the moral patterns of value which are institutionalized in a society are at the very core of his theoretical interests, and these patterns in turn are heavily dependent on the ideas which give them cognitive meaning. In the nature of the case, as we have several times remarked, these values and these ideas are either directly of religious origin or most intimately connected with religion.

In most "primitive" societies, and in highly stabilized and traditionalized higher cultures, religion tends to be mainly a conservative force; it is as it were the balance wheel of the society which prevents it from departing from the established ways. So much is this the case that it is highly probable, for instance, that, as Max Weber put forward cogently, the fact that a traditional priestly class did not have great social power in classical Greece was an essential condition of the great cultural creativity of the Greeks. Conversely, the social ascendancy of the Brahman priestly caste in India is inseparable from the fact that Indian caste society is perhaps the most conservative large-scale society the world has ever seen.

But this relationship by no means holds without exception. The very fact of the association of religion with the areas of strain and tension in human life on the deepest emotional levels means that it is likely to be one of the main areas in which responses to such situations are creative rather than traditional. But for the same reasons this creativeness is very likely to be inextricably intermingled with turmoil and many of the types of "irrational" reaction of which we have spoken above. Furthermore, the most creative periods of religious development tend also to be times of social turmoil rather than settled peace.

It is a remarkable fact that roughly the same period saw the development of Confucianism in China, philosophical Brahmanism and the beginnings of Buddhism in India, and the prophetic movement in Judea, to say nothing of the beginnings of the great development of the classical culture in Greece of the seventh and sixth centuries B.C., which certainly had a most important religious component as well as later religious consequences. In each of these countries, furthermore, it was a period of rapid social change and considerable unsettlement. The warring feudal principalities of China were beginning the process by which eventually a great unified empire arose. India likewise was involved in many internal conflicts, in the difficult relations between the Aryans and the indigenous populations, in feudal wars, and in rivalry for social supremacy between the Brahmans and the Kshatriyas. In Judea the Israelitic Kingdom had already seen its heyday and was gravely threatened by the rising power of Mesopotamia, while, finally, in Greece the little city-states were maintaining a precarious existence in relation both to each other and to the terrifying power of Persia to the east. It was an age of turmoil in some respects comparable to our own across the whole civilized world.

It was in this age that, largely from religious sources, the great cultural systems of values which have guided civilization ever since took their shape. Confucianism, Hinduism, and Buddhism have provided the main frameworks of the way of life of the great civilizations of the Orient, with the one major exception of Islam, which came later but was in many ways intimately related to Prophetic Judaism. The Hebrew Prophets were the authors of the world's first universalistic ethical monotheism, who dared to say, contrary to *all* previous religious tradition, that all mankind is subject to the will of a single God and that their history has meaning in terms of His great plan for the development of the world He created. Greek society created the analytical and speculative intellect of Western civilization. Christianity came some centuries later, but in many respects may be treated as a great synthesis of the Hebrew and the Greek traditions. Without the background of Prophetic Judaism there would have been no universalistic ethical monotheism. But without Greek philosophy there almost certainly would have been no rational theology in the Christian sense. Indeed, some of the most distinctive features of our Western culture undoubtedly stem from these sources.

Christianity itself arose in a similar situation, in which society and human values were in flux. The Jewish people were undergoing, after many experiences in foreign rule, the difficult adjustment of absorption in the Roman Empire. That the adjustment was not easy is attested by the outbreak of the Jewish wars only a generation after the crucifixion of Jesus. The prevention of the absorption of the Christian movement in the community of the Jewish people, which was only settled by St. Paul, was one of the most decisive events of the history of civilization. But this could hardly have happened without the peculiar character of Roman imperial society, with its extraordinary range of individualism and tolerance.

It was thus the great religious movements of the creative age of the seventh to fifth centuries B.C. which laid the foundation for the fundamental differentiations of the great civilizations for the next two thousand years, as Max Weber so clearly demonstrated in his remarkable comparative studies in the sociology of religion. Without taking the space to delineate the features of Confucianism, Hinduism, and Buddhism which differentiate them and the civilizations they have influenced from Christianity and the West, perhaps a few of the distinctive features of the latter may be noted.

The pre-eminent place should, in these terms, undoubtedly go to two fundamental patterns which run through the whole history of Christianity, namely what may be called "universalism" and "activism." Both are deeply involved in the special way in which Christianity conceived the transcendental character of its God, as Creator and Ruler of the world, standing outside and above it, not as an immanent principle of order in the universe, a conception which, with variations, underlies all the great oriental religions.

Activism means essentially that man's goals and values are conceived not primarily as concerned with adaptation to or escape from a given set of physical and social conditions, but with mastery over them. The prototype of the first attitude is found in Confucianism, with its orientation of the organization of a stable social order, sanctioned by a completely stable religion; that of the second is the great mystical religious orientation, the mystical absorption in "nature" of the Taoist, the escape from the Wheel of Karma of the Hindu mystic, or the Nirvana of the Buddhist.

In Christianity, on the other hand, the keynote through all its various forms is doing the will of God in spite of the obstacles presented in the situation, by *overcoming* the obstacles. This may mean, as in early Christian asceticism and of course later, mastery over the flesh without further reference to life on this earth. But this drastic individualism soon gave way to the conception of a more extensive Christian ideal. The medieval conception still retained the view that the Christian society existed to prepare souls for the afterlife; but with what Weber called the "ascetic" branches of Protestantism, notably Calvinism and its derivatives, there emerged the direct conception of the Kingdom of God on Earth, which it was the duty of man to create by divine ordinance. This whole idea of mastery, then, has oriented man to the control of the world in which he lives as distinct from a fatalistic "acceptance" of things as they are. Such acceptance has of course appeared from time to time in Christian societies and groups, but has never been the dominant keynote to anything like the extent it has been in the Orient. Furthermore, though we have undergone a high degree of secularization, even our secularism is active rather than passive. It is not "floating along on the stream of life," but is an attempt to make over the world by active intervention, in the service of human goals; it is an attempt to create the "good society."

Universalism, as the second dominant strain, is closely connected with activism. Its roots lie in the conception of the universal and only true God of the Prophets and the intelligible world as conceived by the Greek intellect. Neither ideas nor morality can be relative to the particular time and place and social group. There must be universal truths, which are as true for the "heathen Chinee" as they are for any Christian group. And the moral good cannot be defined in terms only of what is good for others, as distinguished from good for me, but the same principles must apply impartially to all men, with allowance for difference of circumstance of course, but nevertheless in principle to all. The enormous significance of this universalistic strain in Western civilization is one of the principal themes of the modern social sciences. And there can be little doubt that without Christianity it could scarcely have developed.

Three fields of application of these two major strains of the Christian tradition may be mentioned. First is the very notable fact that, in spite of the prominence of the "warfare of science and religion," it is only in the Western world that science itself has developed to a really high degree. Beginnings there are elsewhere, but in no case, except for a few specialties, beyond the level attained by the classical Greeks. Many Christians certainly have grave misgivings about where the development of science is leading us. But science is most assuredly a fully legitimate child of Christianity (which, however, is only *one* of its "parents"). It is the *active* and not merely the receptive search for truth. Nature is not merely observed, it is *investigated*, nature is "forced to give up her secrets," not merely contemplated. Man, precisely because he is conceived to be made "in the image of God," is endowed with reason, which he is meant to use actively to understand. In Puritanism this strain reached a high culmination in giving direct religious sanction to the great development of physical science of the seventeenth century. The keynote was that the scientist could come to know God through His Works.[5] The place of universalism in science is too fundamental and obvious to need special comment.

A second fundamental direction of Christian influence is in the field of the universalism of law. This of course was foreshadowed by the great development of Roman law, in part a child of Greek thought, notably that of the Stoics. But after the decline of Rome law in the Western world had sunk to the level of a completely tribal pluralism; there was one law for Goth and another for Frank and so on. It is no matter of chance that it was in the Canon law of the church that Roman law was preserved, and that the great development of medieval civilization as a whole soon came to include the revival of Roman civil law and the gradual creation of universalistic systems of law. Had a particularistic rather than a universalistic religion dominated medieval Europe, there is little doubt that Roman law would never have been revived and English common law never created.

Finally, we are all aware that there is a fundamental strain of universalistic individualism in Christianity. Each human being has an immortal soul, all of the same religious worth. Though many branches of Christianity have made drastic con-

[5] Cf. R. K. Merton, *Science and Society in 17th Century England.*

cessions to social inequality reaching far beyond the minimum needs of a functioning society, generally on the plea that equality applied only to the spiritual realm, there is little doubt of the fundamental character of the contribution of Christianity to the egalitarian strain of modern Western civilization; the most dramatic contrast of course is the religious sanction of caste in Hinduism, the most radical conception of human inequality to be found anywhere. The relation to the conception of the dignity of the human individual, and his right to a fair chance to make his contribution to the life of society and to live his own life independently, is patent.

It should not be assumed that the above argument about the very great influence of religious traditions constitutes a theory of "religious determinism" set over against some version of "economic determinism." There seems to us to be no justification for any simple "single dominant factor" theory of social change. The religious movements we have spoken of were not "immaculately conceived" without roots in all the complex social and psychological forces which influence human action. *Of course* the emergence of Christianity was *in part* economically determined; for example, it is well known that most of its early adherents were the "little men" of the urban communities. That it appealed neither to the rural populations (the "pagans") nor to the upper classes is partly a function of the economic interests of those groups. It was also dependent for peace and order, and for its opportunity to spread, on the political and legal structure of the Roman Empire, which was in no sense predominantly a "religious factor." But demonstration of the importance of these things in no way refutes the claim of the importance of creative innovation in the sphere of religious orientation itself. Economic and other "conditions" limit the incidence of a religious movement; for example, they favor or hinder it, but that is a very different matter from "creating" it. Similarly, in the course of its very complex history the various developments within

Christianity have been intimately dependent on non-religious features of the situation of the time. It seems to be well attested that Luther's success could not have occurred without support from the secular interests of the German Princes on whom he relied. And could the branches of Protestantism which have flourished in America have had their enormous influence if the little colonies had not had a continent over which to spread? Suppose the French has wrested the control of the seas from Britain a hundred and fifty years ago? With North America under French control from the Alleghanies west, what would the religious complexion of this continent have been? A glance at the Province of Quebec is of some significance to the answer.

SOME FEATURES OF THE RELIGIOUS SITUATION IN AMERICA

The college teachers and college students who will be the principal readers of this essay are for the most part citizens of the United States of America. It may therefore be appropriate to call attention to a few of the features of the religious situation in this country which are of particular interest from the point of view of the sociologist and social psychologist.

First, it is a society with such strong religious components in its history, that it seems quite justified to call it a "Christian Society" even though it is rather far advanced in what is sometimes called a "process of secularization." Second, the overwhelmingly predominant influence in that background is "nonconformist" Protestantism. That is, its Protestantism is only secondarily derived from the Anglican Episcopal Church, but it is strongly Anglo-Saxon in its flavor because of the ethnic origin of the overwhelming majority of the earlier settlers.

Though in New England the European conception of church and state as correlative was the original pattern, the seeds of religious toleration which were present in the nonconformist churches of the English and Dutch Reformations

combined with the secularism derived from the French Enlightenment to establish not only religious toleration in the
British form, but also the separation of church and state as
the fundamental religious policy of the new Republic, the first
case of its occurrence in the Christian world. This in turn
meant, far earlier than elsewhere, full toleration in a Protestant community for Catholics and also for Jews. However,
though there is official toleration for other religions altogether
outside the Judeo-Christian tradition, they have remained
negligible, so it is still correct to speak of this as at widest a
Judeo-Christian society with a considerable degree of secularization.

The separation of church and state, related as it was to the
diverse denominational complexions of the thirteen colonies,
crystallized the system of "denominational pluralism" as the
characteristic religious constitution of American society. This
fact has undoubtedly had a most important influence on
American social development generally and is one of the cardinal features of contemporary America. Its positive influence
on growth and stability respectively may be traced above all in
two directions. First, in relation to growth, denominational
pluralism has had much to do with the fact that this has been
to such pre-eminent degree an "open society." When it is
conservative, religion can be, as we have noted, very conservative indeed. But in American conditions no single united religious organization could acquire the position of influence in
the community which would enable it to set the tone for the
community as a whole. Though admittedly the contrast is
very sharp, the position of the Catholic Church in the Province of Quebec will illustrate what has happened under other
conditions. There are of course differing value judgments on
such matters. Some feel sincerely that the extent to which
French Canada has at least until recently been able to retain
a social situation so amazingly close to that of rural France in
the seventeenth century is its chief glory. But, clearly, the

United States as a world power, as the scene of the greatest industrial development the world has ever seen, as the pioneer in the democratic extension of education and the applications of science, and as the seat of one of the great experiments in political democracy, would be incompatible with such a situation in the field of religion.

There are certain respects in which the American situation is comparable to that of classical Greece, though it is extremely different in others. There the fact that priesthood, so far as it survived at all, became essentially a function of the ordinary citizen, and that there was a pluralism of city-states as religious units effectively prevented well-integrated religious groups from influencing the society in the direction of traditionalized crystallization of the culture. Similarly, America could be the land of individualism, of enterprise, of technological innovation, and of political experiment to a considerable degree because its religious organization made religious interference with these activities impossible or, where it has sporadically occurred, ineffective.

Second, there is one extremely important respect in which denominational pluralism has served to protect social stability. The larger European countries have of course all been deeply involved in the great social changes of the political and industrial revolutions from the eighteenth century on. In all of them, substantially modified only in England, the basic religious tradition has been that of the established church. In Continental Europe everywhere, the development of "modern" attitudes in the context of great economic and social changes has tended to polarize the population in such a way that the "right" tended to combine the defense of the vested interests of the old upper classes and their political regimes with the defense of religion in the sense of the established church, whereas the "left" tended to attack both the vested interests of the old upper classes and religion as such. This fateful polarization first appeared on a grand scale in the

French Revolution and ever since then France has been torn between the "clericals" and the "anticlericals" as an integral part of the political problems of the society. The identification of the Lutheran Church with the state in Protestant Germany and of the Orthodox Church with the Czarist state in Russia presented similar problems. It is in the light of this situation that the Marxian aphorism "religion is opium for the people" is to be understood. The Anglo-Saxon world has fortunately very largely escaped this accentuation of the instabilities inherent in the recent social changes of Western society. The French "radical," the Marxist, and the Nazi versions of bitter hostility to religion as such, have none of them taken root in this country. To be sure we have had our Robert Ingersolls, and our coteries of Marxist intellectuals, but that is a very different matter.

Though the pattern of denominational pluralism has not been congenial to all religious groups, there is little doubt that it has been so to most of the branches of American Protestantism. But there has been a price, and from the religious point of view probably the most important part of that price has been exposure to secularizing influences to a much greater degree than in many other societies. There is no doubt that the degree of direct concern with religious matters which was so characteristic of colonial, and even of later, New England has passed out of American life except for a few "fundamentalist" islands. The churches have come to a position where they have to struggle to keep a hold on their people, and some feel it is a losing battle.

Apart from the general tendency to secularization, there are from a religious point of view perhaps three areas of difficulty and strain which will repay a word of comment here, though it is not possible to go into them thoroughly. Each of these is particularly distressing to the liberal wing of Protestantism, which takes its integration with liberal democracy so very seriously.

1. The first of these is the position of the Catholic Church, a subject so delicate that it is often tactfully passed over in silence. From a sociological point of view there can be little doubt that the rise of the Catholic Church to its present position has introduced what we sociologists call a "structural strain" of considerable proportions into the American society, that there is no easy solution for the problems involved, and that, perhaps above all, simple tolerant "good will" and avoidance of prejudice are not enough.

There are three main sources of the strain. The first is that the structure of the Church itself, and the kind of relation to secular society which is best adapted to it, are in certain respects out of harmony with the main structure of American society. If rightly understood, the formula that the difficulty centers about, the "authoritarian" structure of the Church, is on the whole correct. In the religious sphere itself the conception of the priest as the vicar of God, who holds absolute power over religious matters, is strongly antithetical to the Protestant conception of the direct relation of the individual to his God, and correspondingly to the Protestant conception of the minister as a leader and teacher, not as wielding religious authority directly. Furthermore, through the claim to control all matters of faith and morals, the Church as an organization has a certain tendency to encroach on the freedom of the individual as that is conceived in relation to our basic doctrine of the separation of church and state. The church itself seems to be clear on the issue; it does not believe and never has believed in principle in religious toleration in the specific American sense; it accepts it, because being in a minority status it has no alternative. But there is little question that if the Catholic Church were clearly the dominant religious group, it would tend to work toward the restoration of its old ideal of a society in which all members are Christian in a Catholic sense. This could hardly fail fundamentally to alter the traditional American pattern.

This attitude toward religious authority, particularly as extended into the sphere of "morals" as well as faith, is connected with a variety of other points. Just to single out one, the United States has, at least since de Toqueville observed it more than a century ago, been notable among Western countries for the freedom of women. In general, not only does the Catholic Church forbid divorce and birth control, taking a view not shared by most Protestant denominations, but it puts strong pressure on its adherents to maintain a conservative pattern with respect to the position and interests of women and of the family generally, which is in strong contrast to some of the most prominent general American trends. Certain elements in these trends may be interpreted to be symptoms of disorganization; but others are probably essential features of the adaptation of family life to the conditions of a highly urbanized and industrialized society. It is at least legitimately doubtful whether the official Catholic view of the family and the proper position of women is in the long run compatible with the needs of the type of society which, for better or worse, has developed in the United States.

Second, American Catholicism has been in a special position, which differentiates it from its European counterparts, because it has mainly been brought in with the great masses of immigrant population. It has thus tended to be associated in special ways with class, ethnic, and other social divisions within the population, as shown by the fact that the Catholic population is overwhelmingly urban and concentrated in the northeast sections of the country. There is some coloring derived from the fact that the Irish group has had such a prominent place in the church, and it has tended to identify religion with a sometimes rather militant nationalism relative to things Protestant and of English origin. In general, the Catholic groups have been more recent comers and of lower status than the dominant Protestant groups—hence have become involved in the kinds of status-tensions which commonly develop between established elites and lower status elements.

The third point concerns the way in which the Catholic Church has tended to modify the competitive relations of denominations with each other in the American scene. There is no doubt that the very features of the Church which Protestants tend to find disturbing give it a certain superior effectiveness as an organization. By using authority in an outspoken way, by strong centralization, by refusing to compromise at many points where most Protestant denominations would compromise, it tends on the whole to keep a more effective control of its people than do most Protestant denominations. Furthermore, and because it is such a large, powerful, and well-organized unit, it tends to be able to exercise a greater influence on community affairs, which can moreover be a consistent influence over time and in different places. Though this aspect is, of course, by no means predominant in the religious sphere, it is none the less true that there exists a struggle for power among religious denominations. Precisely *because* of the sincerity of their religious convictions, the members of each denomination naturally seek to extend its influence, and much extension of the influence of *any* one *must* be at the expense of some others. The system of denominational pluralism in this respect is necessarily delicately balanced. The emergence of a large and well-organized unit to such a prominent position, which is not as well integrated with most of the others as they are with each other, is necessarily a disturbing factor in such a delicately balanced situation.

2. The second major problem field, that of racial and religious prejudice, is closely related to the problem of the Catholic Church. It is precisely one of the most important points at which the values of liberal Protestantism and of American democracy fuse, that there should be sympathetic toleration for all views and practices within the limits compatible with effective order in the community, and lack of interference with

the rights of others as individuals or groups. Much in Protestant history, however, and many of the strains in the contemporary situation, both those just discussed and others which are more indirectly manifested, make it difficult for non-Catholics to tolerate Catholicism with full objectivity. Indeed, to a sociologist it is not at all surprising that there should be a great deal of anti-Catholic prejudice in non-Catholic circles and vice versa. The basis of this expectation has already been discussed in general terms. It is most important to distinguish this aspect of strain in the relations of the two groups from that of structural strain in fitting elements together into a system which has just been discussed. Even if there were no prejudice at all there would still be some conflict. This is a fact of which some religious liberals do not seem to be adequately aware. But at the same time, conflict between groups provides a focus for the phenomena of prejudice to operate on. Attitudes generated in the particular conflict situation are likely to be more extreme than otherwise because of the elements of strain and these attitudes tend to exaggerate the differences making them seem more radical than they really are. Thus, over such issues as public support for parochial schools or legislation affecting birth control, tempers are very apt to flare up on both sides.

In addition to this there is the well-known "scapegoat" mechanism, which social psychologists have greatly illuminated in recent years. The essence of it is very simple. We have spoken of the generation of hostile feelings in all sorts of situations of strain. There is often such strain associated with the relations within groups to which their own solidarity is essential, like families, local communities, or indeed church congregations. Since it would be dangerous and wrong to freely express overt antagonism toward the members of the in-group, it is often psychologically easier to "displace" the affect onto an out-group in relation to which there already exists some basis of antagonism. "Scapegoating" thus rarely appears without *some* "reasonable" basis of antagonism in that there is a real conflict of ideals or interests. But it is recognized by the fact of "overreaction." People become excited and agitated out of proportion to the significance of the real occasion for it. Thus, though there is a real conflict of interest, some people see a "Papal plot" to conquer the United States, not by legitimate proselytization of the Catholic Faith, but by Machiavellian political machinations.

Unfortunately, prejudice is not only directed by *individuals* against scapegoat groups, but can readily become a phenomenon of *group* attitude, that is, become partly institutionalized. Then, instead of being disapproved by members of one's own group for being prejudiced against the out-group, one is punished for not being prejudiced.

Among other problems of prejudice, the one of greatest interest to religion is that between Christians and Jews in our society. The tragic story of Hitler's Germany is sufficient evidence that anti-Semitism is much more than a superficial phenomenon in the Western world. Anti-Semitism fortunately has not been nearly so serious in this country, but we all know it exists. The nature of the problem is, however, particularly from the Protestant point of view, very different from that of the Protestant-Catholic situation. In fact, neither in doctrine nor in religious organization is there a comparably serious source of division between Judaism and the more liberal branches of Protestantism. Indeed, Unitarianism is in a strictly religious sense almost indistinguishable from liberal Judaism. The Jews, however, are an ethnically distinct community, with a history of religious distinctness from Christianity and of antagonism symbolized in the extreme case by the epithet of "Christ-killers." But the Jews also happen to be an ethnic group which, for a variety of reasons, has been extraordinarily successful in occupational competition with the native American, on the whole very fairly, and precisely according to American values of enterprise, intelligence, and so on. Fundamentally, it may be suggested that American anti-Semitism is a version of the "sour-grapes" attitude. There are two main subtypes. One, which may be called "snobbish" anti-Semitism, centers in the groups which are or want to be considered socially elite; its primary manifestation is exclusion of Jews from "select" residential districts, clubs, resorts, and the like. Essentially, these people are expressing through the scapegoat mechanism their own sense of guilt that no longer are they basing their claims to status on the achievements of the individual, in which they are tacitly forced to admit that the Jew is fully their equal, but rather on social class and its symbols. It is not a matter of *what* you do, but of *who* you are. The second variety centers perhaps in the lower middle class, it is "envious" anti-Semitism. Essentially, it is a rationalization of failure or of fear of it. The keynote is always that the Jew wins because he fights unfairly. The "honest man" never has a chance because a "slippery" Jew will always outsmart him. Of the two, the latter is by far the more dangerous; it is deeply involved in the protofascist movements which are never wholly absent in this country or anywhere else in the Western world.

3. Finally, the third problem for brief mention is that of the more general relation of religious denominationalism to the class structure. It is well known that in any American community the churches have a rough rank order of social prestige. In New England the Unitarian and Episcopal churches are those of the "best people," perhaps the Congregationalists next, then the Methodists, then the Baptists, etc. In the South the Presbyterian, because of the Scotch influence, takes the place of the Unitarian. In the Middle West the Methodists rank, relatively, considerably higher. Connected with this is the further fact that people who rise in social status are very likely to change their religion in the process.

Especially to those Protestants who consider any human inequality to be religiously suspect, this is a most distressing situation. Of course, a still more distressing set of facts concerns racial segregation, as when Negroes are either not admitted at all or are not very welcome in white churches.

In broad lines, something of this sort may be said to have certain positive functions in American society. The essential point is that some differentiation of class status is inevitable in a society which values personal achievement so highly, which must be dependent on large-scale organization, and which at the same time attempts to maintain a workable family system. Wives and children must to some degree share the status of adult men, hence their *differences* of status. But by its very nature the Protestant congregation is a rather loosely organized voluntary group. It depends heavily on spontaneous consensus. This is much easier if its members are all the "kind of people" who readily understand each other. It seems very likely that a religious organization which could effectively cross all class lines on a big scale would have to approach the established churches of Europe in its organizational structure. The stratification of religious denominations is essentially a result of the looseness of religious organization in general, combined with the fact that America has a very real, if also loose, class hierarchy. It would not be easy to abolish.

The Sociologist as Teacher

Before concluding we may attempt to speak very briefly of the problems of the teaching of the contributions of sociology and social psychology to the understanding of religion. As we suggested at the beginning of this essay, we consider it central to the values of our society that soundly established knowledge should be *valued*, equally that it should be responsibly disseminated and used. The educated citizen of a free commonwealth cannot be one from whom essential knowledge is deliberately withheld or who himself refuses to face essential facts.

But to face facts is not to cultivate the smart "debunking," "know-it-all" attitude. The social scientist above all should know how great a difference is made by the attitude and the context in which things are taught. True sophistication for him and for his students must include a deep humility concerning the limitations of his own knowledge and an equally deep respect for the opinions *and feelings* of others.

The diversity of religious beliefs even within our own society is such that it is obviously impossible for the teacher to agree with them all. He should certainly seek to avoid a shallow eclecticism, which is almost as bad as outright bigotry. He should not parade his personal convictions, but at the same time in no way seek to evade their relevance or refuse to state them. He should perhaps seek particularly to convey a sense both of the complexity of the intellectual problems and of the depth of the human emotions involved, at the same time that he gives genuine enlightenment and not, again, merely a sense of complication.

It is this writer's strong personal conviction that in the field of religion as elsewhere these requirements for good teaching are at bottom simple applications of the fundamental ethics of science itself. These are essentially two. The first is the *moral* obligation to maximize technical competence. To the scientist, and thus to the teacher of science, there is a positive moral obligation to *know what he is talking about.* This tenet alone enjoins a humility which would eliminate most of earlier positivistic "antireligious" attitudes in the social sciences. The second is that of the scientist's obligation of responsible integrity in his role as trustee for society of the knowledge he possesses and hence in certain respects of responsibility for its uses. The very basis on which society allows the scientist to do his work at all presupposes that *as teacher* he will act in the full light of his social responsibilities.

As scientist, then, the sociologist or social psychologist must maintain the fundamental integrity of his high calling; he must be competent, objective, balanced, and tentative. He must take responsibility for teaching in such a way as to promote the welfare of his fellows as he sees it. He must be aware that what he does and says may have serious repercussions on others. As scientist he cannot be a partisan of any particular religious faith, but as an individual he must have a set of personal convictions of his own. He must not attempt to conceal these from his students, but equally must not attempt to use his position as expert and as teacher in order to convert his students to his own views.

The interdependence of the different parts of our culture is such that persons whose primary role is not that of scientist will inevitably make use of the findings of social science in this field in teaching as well as otherwise. We feel that they, also, as good citizens of a liberal society, should feel bound by the ethic of science so far as they use its results. But the highest order of discipline in maintaining a precarious and difficult balance is required of him who has accepted the vocation of the rational understanding of man as his personal vocation.

The scientist, by virtue of his calling, thus cannot, we feel, *directly* give the student a set of convictions to live by—to attempt to do so would be incompatible with his special role. But by giving him an understanding of what many men have lived by in a spirit of humility and respect he can, we feel, help the student to clarify and deepen his own convictions, to reach a position of his own which is more than an "emotional reaction" to the experiences of his life situation, which, in line with the great tradition of Christianity, is a rationally thought-through and grounded position. As we noted above, in spite of the elements of conflict which have appeared from time to time, Christianity and science have a very deep foundation in common—it is not by chance that Christian civilization has been the mother of science. The rise of social science, and with it of the scientific study of religion itself, is a development which is a logical and inevitable outcome of the evolution of Christianity itself. There can, in this writer's view, be no inherent and inevitable conflict.

In Conclusion

This essay has covered, in a most fragmentary and inadequate fashion, a few of the highlights of the relations between
religion and society as they appear important to, and capable
of illumination by, the social sciences of sociology and social
psychology.

There are perhaps two outstanding impressions I would
hope the reader will take away with him after reading this.
The first is that, in a society where the academic disciplines
are perhaps more secularized than the rest of the society, there
has, as a result of scientific study of religion and society in these
disciplines and in history and anthropology, emerged an overwhelming impression of the fundamental importance of religion in human affairs. Like the historian, the sociologist can
now say unequivocally that the fairly recent popular positivistic
view that religion was essentially grounded in the ignorance
and superstition of a prescientific age, and could be expected
rapidly to disappear in our era, is definitely in error. The pro-
ponent of this view is the victim of his own ignorance and
counter-superstition. True, *many specific features* of historic
religions are related to a low level of scientific development and
could not persist in a scientific age. But this is not true of the
fundamental significance of religion. What purports to be the
abolition of religion is really only a new form of it, in exactly
the same sense in which it has been rightly said that the philosopher who purports to abolish metaphysics is only indulging
in a naïve and uncritical brand of metaphysics. By implication
he is making assumptions about the nature of ultimate reality
which will not stand up to sophisticated philosophical criticism. So it is with religion.

The second crucial fact is that religion is involved in all the
deepest complexities of the human lot. While inevitable, and
certainly in the broadest sense good since human life is good,
religion is not good in the "polyanna-ish" sense. It registers,

in the human record, man's faith and love, but also his moments of deepest despair, his hatred of life, and of his fellow men. Religion, in short, to whatever degree it may or may not be divinely inspired, is human in the fullest sense, as tragedy and sin are human.

The reader may feel that in the foregoing discussion the "seamy side" of religion has been unduly stressed. If there is a bias in this direction a word of exoneration may be permitted. As we noted above, American temper leans in the overoptimistic direction, and the temper of its dominant religion is on the whole no exception. If we Americans are to be not only a prosperous and a powerful people, but a great people in the deeper sense of historical greatness, we must achieve a high level of "maturity." Maturity in this sense is never aided by refusing to face the truth about ourselves or the world. To know the truth to its fullest and not to be dismayed is one of the marks of genuine maturity. Surely the deeper interests of religion as well as of secular society can only be served by helping, in any little way that is possible, those of a generation on whom the burden of great responsibility will soon fall to see with clarity and understanding and humility what the world they live in is like.

BIBLIOGRAPHY

Both in order to record my indebtedness for many of the ideas put forward in this essay, and to guide the reader who might wish to go farther, it seems well to append a brief bibliographical note.

In terms of fundamental theory, what may be called the "modern" sociology of religion rests overwhelmingly on the work of two men, Emile Durkheim and Max Weber. Durkheim's most important direct contributions to the field are published in his last book, *Les formes élémentaires de la vie réligieuse*, available in English translation as *The Elementary Forms of the Religious Life*, published by the Free Press. Several of his other works, however, are relevant. For Max Weber the most important contributions are in the three volumes entitled in German *Gesammelte Aufsätze zur Religionssoziologie*. Perhaps the best-known part of this was translated by the present author, *The Protestant Ethic and the Spirit of Capitalism*. The remainder of the first volume, the study of Confucianism and Taoism, has just appeared in translation by Hans Gerth as *The Religion of China* (The Free Press). The other two volumes, on Hinduism and Buddhism and on Ancient Judaism, are in process of translation by Professor Gerth. Some excerpts from them are included in the collection *From Max Weber, Essays in Sociology*, edited by Gerth and Mills.

Perhaps some of the most important "sociological" studies besides those of Durkheim and Weber are by historians of religion and civilization. Among these may be mentioned especially W. Robertson Smith, *The Religion of the Semites*, Marcel Granet, *La pensée chinoise* (greatly influenced by Durkheim), and above all Ernst Troeltsch, *The Social Teachings of the Christian Churches* (a contemporary and close friend of Weber).

Another most important source is from anthropological studies of the religion of nonliterate peoples. There is a very voluminous literature in this field. We will mention only, first the classical starting point, E. B. Tylor, *Primitive Culture*, and most especially B. Malinowski, *Magic, Science and Religion*, and *Coral Gardens and their Magic*. On more special points such as witchcraft see Clyde Kluckhohn, *Navaho Witchcraft*, and E. E. Evans-Pritchard, *Azande Witchcraft*. A recent general work is William J. Goode, *The Religion of the Primitives*.

On the psychological side two works stand out as pre-eminent. The first is the classic of William James, *The Varieties of Religious Experience*. The second, with all the reservations which must be attached to them, the works of Freud on religion, *Totem and Taboo*, *The Future of an Illusion*, and *Moses and Monotheism*. These works should, however, be read very much in relation to Freud's psychological theories, and not just as monographs on religion.

Finally, an author inevitably draws on his own previous work, so attention may be called to the principal treatments of religion in that work. First is *The Structure of Social Action*, especially chaps. xi, xiv, xv, and xvii. This book contains a careful general analysis of the theories of Durkheim and Weber, on religion as well as other subjects. Then there is an essay, republished in *Essays in Sociological Theory*, on "The Theoretical Development of the Sociology of Religion" (chap. iv). Finally a new work, *The Social System* (1951), contains considerable discussion of religion, particularly in chaps. viii and ix.

11

ANTHROPOLOGY

By DOROTHY D. LEE

This essay is concerned with the most widely taught branch of anthropology, that which deals with culture. Culture has been described recently by Clyde Kluckhohn as "a way of thinking, feeling, believing."[1] The late Edward Sapir regarded it as defining "for every society, the world in which it lives."[2] In both these statements, we find the implication that religion is of the very fabric of culture. To teach about culture as a totality, then, as a unit with inner consistency and integrity, anthropologists must include religion in their teaching as a matter of course.

I

In the pages below, we shall speak of various conceptions of man's relatedness to human and nonhuman nature, to reality and circumstance, and of his view of his own place within the universe. Since his universe includes the divine, or is itself divine, his world view is pervaded by religion. We shall speak about deities, but more often, we shall speak of the religious dimension of experience and behavior, since these permeate all living. It is this religious dimension of experience which should be included by the teacher in the description of the different

[1] Clyde Kluckhohn, *Mirror for Man* (New York: McGraw-Hill Book Co., 1949), p. 23.
[2] Edward Sapir, *Selected Writings in Language, Culture, and Personality*, ed. David G. Mandelbaum (Berkeley: University of California Press, 1949), p. 347.

ANTHROPOLOGY   339

areas of culture, when he speaks of agricultural practices, or
about health measures, or about hunting, or what we call art.
To include religion in the teaching of anthropology, it is not
necessary to teach a course in Primitive Religion; and, to my
mind, it is misleading to isolate religion in a separate course,
since it occurs usually as an ingredient of daily life.

We do not always find deities in primitive cultures, or not
always deities who have reference to the daily living of men.
We do find societies where a Supreme Being is recognized; but
this Being is frequently so far removed from mundane affairs
that it is not present in the consciousness of the people, except
on the specific occasions of ceremonial or prayer. But in these
same societies, we find communion with the unperceivable
and unknowable in nature, with an ultimate reality, whether
spirit or power, or intensified being, or personal worth, which
evokes humility, respect, courtesy, or sometimes fear, on man's
part. This relationship to the ultimate reality is so pervasive
that it may determine, for example, which hand a man will use
in adjusting his loin cloth, or how much water he will drink
at a time, or which way his head will point when he sleeps, or
how he will butcher and utilize the carcass of a caribou.

Material culture, therefore, should be taught with full recognition of the religious aspect of the operations involved. The
background of the activity, man's relationship to his own
work and to that upon which he is operating, is usually per-
meated with religion. All economic activities, such as hunting,
gathering fuel, cultivating the land, storing food, assume a relatedness to the encompassing universe, and, with many cultures, this is a religious relationship. In such cultures, men
recognize a certain spiritual worth and dignity in the universe.
They do not set out to control, or master, or exploit. Their
ceremonials are periods of intensified communion, even social
affairs, in a broad sense, if the term may be extended to include
the forces of the universe. They are not placating or bribing
or even thanking; they are rather a formal period of concen-

trated, enjoyable association. In their relationships with nature, the people may see themselves as the offspring of a cherishing mother, or the guests of a generous hostess, or as members of a democratic society which proceeds on the principle of consent. So, when the Baiga in India were urged to change over to the use of an iron plow, they replied with horror that they could not tear the flesh of their mother. And American Indians have hunted many animals with the consent of the particularized essence of these animals, after establishing a relationship of reciprocity, with man furnishing the ceremonial, and Buffalo or Salmon or Caribou making a gift of his flesh. The great care with which so many of the Indian groups utilized every portion of the carcass of a hunted animal was an expression, not of economic thrift, but of courtesy and respect; in fact, an aspect of the religious relationship to the slain. The Wintu Indians of California, who lived on land so wooded that it was difficult to find clear land for putting up a group of houses, nevertheless used only dead wood for fuel, out of respect for nature. An old Wintu woman, speaking in prophetic vein, said the following: "The White people never cared for land or deer or bear. When we Indians kill meat, we eat it all up. When we dig roots we make little holes. When we build houses, we make little holes. When we burn grass for grasshoppers, we don't ruin things. We shake down acorns and pinenuts. We don't chop down the trees. We only use dead wood. But the White people plow up the ground, pull up the trees, kill everything. The tree says, 'Don't. I am sore. Don't hurt me.' But they chop it down and cut it up. The spirit of the land hates them. They blast out trees and stir it up to its depths. They saw up the trees. That hurts them. The Indians never hurt anything, but the White people destroy all. They blast rocks and scatter them on the ground. The rock says 'Don't! You are hurting me.' But the White people pay no attention. When the Indians use rocks, they take little round ones for their cooking . . . How can the spirit of the earth like the White man? . . . Everywhere the White man has touched it, it is sore." [3]

The anthropologist then has to deal with people who do not so much *seek* communion with environing nature, as *find themselves in* communion with it. So when he teaches even a subject as apparently mundane as economics, he cannot fail to include religion, unless he makes an artificial exclusion. In many of the cultures to which he refers, or which he describes, or from which he takes illustrative material, not even mysticism is to be found, in our sense of the word. For us, mysticism presupposes a prior separation of man from nature; and communion is achieved through loss of self and subsequent merging with that which is beyond; but for many other cultures there is no such distinct separation between self and other, which must be overcome. Here, man is *in* nature already, and we cannot speak properly of man *and* nature. Take the Kaingang, for example, who chops out a wild beehive. He explains his act to the bees, as he would to a person whom he considered his coordinate. "Bee, produce! I chopped you out to make beer of you! Yukui's wife died, and I am making beer of you so that I can cut his hair." Or he may go up to a hive and say simply, "Bee, it is I." [4] And the Arapesh of New Guinea, going to his yam garden, will first introduce to the spirit of the land the brother-in law whom he has brought along to help him with the gardening. This is not achieved communication, brought about for definite ends. It implies an already present relatedness with the ultimate reality, with that which is accepted in faith, and which exists irrespective of man's cognition or perception or logic. If the teacher were to abstract, out of this situation, merely the food-getting or the operational techniques, he would be misrepresenting the reality.

The same present relatedness is to be found in some societies where the deity is more specifically defined. The Tikopia,

[3] Cora Dubois, *Wintu Ethnography* (Berkeley, 1935), p. 75.
[4] Jules Henry, *Jungle People* (Richmond, 1941), p. 87.

in the Solomon Islands Protectorate, sit and eat their meals
with their dead under the floor, and hand food and drink to
them; the dead are all somewhat divine, progressively so as they
come nearer to the original, fully divine ancestor of the clan.
Whatever their degree of divinity, the Tikopia is at home with
them; he is aware of their vague presence, though he requires
the services of a medium whenever he wants to make this
presence definite. Firth describes an occasion when a chief,
having instructed a medium to invite his dead nephew to come
and chew betel with him, found himself occupied with something else when the dead arrived, and so asked the medium to
tell the spirit—a minor deity—to chew betel by himself. At
another time, during an important ceremonial, when this chief
was receiving on his forehead the vertical stripe which was the
symbol that he was now the incarnation of the highest god, he
jokingly jerked his head aside, so that the stripe, the insignium
of the presence of the god, went crooked. These are the acts
of a man who feels accepted by his gods, and is at one with
them. And, in fact, the Tikopia appear to live in a continuum
which includes nature and the divine without defining bounds;
where communion is present, not achieved; where merging is
a matter of being, not of becoming.

In these cultures, where religion is an ever present dimension of experience, it is doubtful that religion as such is given
a name; Kluckhohn reports that the Navaho have no such
word, but most ethnographers never thought to inquire. Many
of these cultures, however, recognized and named the spiritual
ingredient or attribute, the special quality of the wonderful,
the very, the beyondness, in nature. This was sometimes considered personal, sometimes not. We have from the American
Indians terms such as *manitou*, or *wakan*, or *yapaitu*, often
translated as power; and we have the well-known Melanesian
term *mana*. But this is what they reach through faith, the
other end of the relationship; the relationship itself is un-
named. Apparently, to behave and think religiously is to be-

have and think. Certainly, the teacher of culture finds that to describe a way of life in its totality is to describe a religious way of life.

II

In past years, when anthropology was predominantly atomistic, the ethnographer analysed activity, or even one act alone, into its secular and religious components, and presented one group of elements under the heading of agriculture or manufacture, and the other in a separate section of the book, under the heading of magic or ritual or religion. It was natural, then, that technology should be taught as completely secular "material culture," that courses in "social organization" or "primitive society" should include only positivistically defined structure, and religion should be taught only as a separate course in the curriculum, containing along with the discussion of cosmology and the pantheon, those taboos and ritual acts which were included in the daily activity of the people in the various societies covered.

This compartmentalization was often completely foreign to the culture under consideration. For example, when preparing seed for planting, one of the several things a Navaho does is to mix ground "mirage stone" with the seed. And in the process of storing corn, a double-eared stalk is laid at the bottom of the storage pit. In actual life, these acts are a continuous part of a total activity; should they be divorced from this in presentation, and presented discretely? The distinction between the religious and the secular elements may even separate an act from the manner of performance, a verb from its adverb. The direction in which a man is facing when performing a secular act, or the number of times he shakes his hand when spattering water, often have their religious implications. When the Navaho planted his corn sunwise, his act reflected a total world view, and it would be nonsense to separate the planting itself from the direction of the planting in presentation. Yet such separations have often been made by students who had been trained to see religion as a thing apart, or at best as something additive.

Those anthropologists who present religion as separate from "everyday" living, reflect, moreover, the distinctions of a culture which will identify six days with the secular in life and only the seventh with religion. In many primitive societies, religion is rarely absent from the details of everyday living, and the ceremonials represent a formalization and intensification of an ever present attitude. We have societies such as that of the Hopi of Arizona, where ceremonials, and the preparation for them, cover most of the year. Some years ago, Crow-wing, a Hopi, kept a journal for the period of a year, putting down all events of interest or importance. By far the largest number of the entries contain some casual reference to a religious activity; sometimes the sole subject is a ritual, or the preparation for a ceremonial. After a few weeks of such entries, we come to a sequence of four days' entries which are devoted to a description of a ball game played by two opposing groups of children and enjoyed by a large number of spectators. But, in the end, this also turns out to have been ceremonial in nature, helping the corn to grow. Crow-wing was a layman, reporting those events of interest to the layman; but, like every Hopi, he was not completely secular, since he had a responsible role in maintaining the universal order; and this was a role which he filled every day, all the time; not one assumed on special days or special occasions.

III

Today, some anthropologists continue to deal with culture atomistically, considering that only through prior analysis and, at most, subsequent artificially created synthesis, can a scientific approach be maintained. Other anthropologists speak of the basic configuration of culture, the patterning of activities, the totality of beliefs and attitudes, the design for living. But even these often present the totality analytically, separating each act from its context, voiding it of its meaning. Faced with the need to present their material clearly, and in a form which is readily comprehensible to young members of our own culture, they choose to analyse, to isolate, to arrange, and organize in ways which make sense to their hearers, instead of presenting the material situationally, as they find it. Observed acts taken out of the confusion of meaningful reality can be presented "objectively," they can be measured and counted. Quantification endows the material with a semblance of the scientific, but it often violates the reality. When a subsequent synthesis is made, there is danger that the teacher will read his own interpretation, his own motivations, ends and values, his own meaning, into the practices which he has described. To avoid this danger, the teacher would have to study each culture in its completeness, its whole system of attitudes, of values, of concepts, its social structure, from which the individual practice derives meaning. But it is arduous and time-consuming to do this, when all one wants is an example to illustrate the cultivation of yams.

The choice seems to lie between covering a wide range of illustrative material and presenting only a few instances in their totality. The teacher who believes that there is integrity or totality or design in culture, who believes in interrelatedness of traits, will have to choose the latter course if he is to act on his belief. He will make no arbitrary separations and exclusions; and, as a consequence, he will present his cultural facts with their religious dimension.

In teaching about the economic life of the present-day Maya, for example, such a teacher will be speaking of religion when he describes the cultivation of corn. As Robert Redfield and W. Lloyd Warner write:

"The agriculture of the Maya Indians of southeastern Yucatan is not simply a way of securing food. It is also a way of worshipping the gods. Before a man plants, he builds an altar in the field and prays there. He must not speak boisterously in the cornfield; it is a sort of temple. The cornfield is planted as an incident in a perpetual sacred contract between supernatural beings and men. By this agreement, the supernaturals yield part of what is theirs—the riches of the natural environment—to men. In exchange, men are pious and perform the traditional ceremonies in which offerings are made to the supernaturals. . . . The world is seen as inhabited by the supernaturals; each has his appropriate place in the woods, the sky, or the wells from which the water is drawn. The village is seen as a reflection of the quadrilateral pattern of the cosmos; the cornfield too is oriented, laid out east, west, north, and south, with reference to the supernaturals that watch over the cardinal points; and the table altars erected for the ceremonies again remind the individual of this pattern. The stories that are told at the time when men wait to perform the ceremony before the planting of the corn or that children hear as they grow up are largely stories which explain and further sanction the traditional way of life." [5]

When the teacher sets out to present Navaho art, he has to explain first the Navaho concept of harmony between man and the universe as basic to health and well-being; the concept of continuity, the religious significance of the groups of four, the door of contact opened through the fifth repetition, the need to have no completely enclosing frame around any of their works so that continuity can be maintained and the evil inside can have an opening through which to leave. When he speaks of the so-called sand-paintings the teacher will be speaking of religion; because these are no more art than they are ritual, myth, medical practice, or religious belief. They are created as an integral aspect of a ceremonial which brings into harmony with the universal order one who finds himself in discord with it; or which intensifies and ensures the continuation of a

[5] 1940 Yearbook of Agriculture, *Farmers in a Changing World* (Washington, D. C.), pp. 989–90.

harmony which is already present. Every line and shape and color, every interrelationship of form, is the visible manifestation of myth, ritual, and religious belief. The making of the painting is accompanied with a series of sacred songs sung over a sick person, or over someone who, though healed of sickness by emergency measures, has yet to be brought back into gear with the universal harmony; or in enhancing and giving emphasis to the present harmony. What we would call purely medical practices may or may not be part of all this. When the ceremonial is over, the painting is over too; it is destroyed; it has fulfilled its function.

This is true also of the art of the neighboring Hopi, where the outstanding form of art is the drama. In this we find wonderfully humorous clowning, involving careful planning and preparation, erection of magnificent masks and costumes, rehearsals, organization. Everyone comes to see and responds with uproarious hilarity. But this is not mere art. It is an important way of helping nature in her work of growing the corn. Even the laughter of the audience helps in this. More than dramatic rehearsal and creation of costumes has gone into the preparation. The actors have prepared themselves as whole persons. They have refrained from sexual activity, and from anything involving conflict. They have had good thoughts only. They have refrained from anger, worry, and grief. Their preparation as well as their performance has had a religious dimension. Their drama is one act in the great process of the cyclical growing of corn, a divinity indispensable to man's well-being, and to whose well-being man is indispensable. Corn wants to grow, but cannot do so without the cooperation of the rest of nature and of man's acts and thoughts and will. And, to be happy, corn must be danced by man and participate in his ceremonials. To leave the religious dimension out of all this, and to speak of Hopi drama as merely a form of art, would be to present a fallacious picture. Art and agriculture and religion are part of the same totality for the Hopi.

If the teacher, in describing the Hopi takes the economic life as his starting point, he is again bound to include the religious aspect if he is to give a true picture. In our own culture, an activity is considered to be economic when it deals with effective utilization or exploitation of resources. But this definition cannot be used when Hopi economics is taught. To begin with, it assumes an aggressive attitude toward the environment. It describes the situation of the homesteader in Alaska, for example, who works against tremendous odds clearing land for a dairy farm, against the inexorable pressure of time, against hostile elements. By his sweat, and through ingenuity and education and the use of brutally effective tools, he tames nature; he subjugates the land and exploits its resources to the utmost. The Hopi, however, working on the land, does not see himself in opposition to it. He works *with* the elements, not *against* them. He helps the corn to grow; he cooperates with the thunderstorm and the pollen and the sun. He is in harmony with the elements, not in conflict; and he does not set out to conquer an opponent. He depends on the corn, but this is part of a mutual interdependence; it is not exploitation. The corn depends on him, too. It cannot grow without his help; it finds life dull and lonely without his company and his ceremonials. So it gives its body for his food gladly, and enjoys living with him in his granary. The Hopi has a personal relationship with it. He treats it with respect, and houses it with the care and courtesy accorded to an honored guest. Is this economics?

In a work on Hopi economics we are given an account of the Hopi Salt Journey, under the heading, "Secondary Economic Activities." This expedition is also described in a Hopi autobiography, and here we discover that only those men who have achieved a certain degree of experience in the Hopi way can go on this journey; and then, only if their minds are pure and they are in a state of harmony with the universe. There is a period of religious preparation, followed by the long and perilous journey which is attended by a number of rituals along the way. Old men, lowering themselves from the overhanging ledge onto the salt deposits, tremble with fear, knowing that they may be unable to make the ascent. The occasion is solemnly religious. This is no utilization of resources in the eyes of the Hopi. They go to help the growing corn; the Salt Journey brings needed rain. Twelve adult men will spend days and court dangers to procure salt which they can buy for two dollars from an itinerant peddler. By the standards of the students' culture this is not an efficient use of human resources. But when the teacher presents the situation in all its aspects, including the religious aspect, the students see that the Hopi has achieved his ends with efficiency.

Matters which the student has been taught to regard as purely economic are often couched in religious terms; and it is the task of the teacher to guide the student in understanding them as they occur in different cultures. Land tenure, or the transference of land, operations involved in hunting and agriculture, are often a part of a religious way of life. In our own culture, man conceives of his relationship to his physical environment, and even sometimes his human environment, as mechanistic and manipulative; but the student must be taught not to assume that this attitude is present in other cultures. Any presentation in the field of economics, must take into account the religious conception of nature, what Ruth Benedict has called the animistic attitude toward nature and man. Here the teacher finds a place for practices which are often classified miscellaneously together in ethnographies, under the heading of superstitions or taboos. The courteous speech to the bear about to be killed, the offering to the deer world before the hunter sets out, the introduction of the brother-in-law to the garden spirit, or the sacrifice to the rice field about to be sold, the refraining from intercourse, or from the eating of meat or from touching food with the hand are some of these. They are the practices we find in a democratic society, which considers the right of others, as opposed to the brutal efficiency of the dictator. They reflect the attitude of people who believe in conference and consent, not in coercion; of people who generally find personality or *mana* in nature and man, sometimes more, sometimes less. In this framework, taboo and superstitious act mean that man acts and refrains from acting in the name of a wider democracy which includes nature and the divine.

With such a conception of man's place in nature, what is for us land tenure, or ownership, or rights of use and disposal is for other societies an intimate belongingness. So the Arapesh conceive of themselves as belonging to the land, in the way that flora and fauna belong to it. They cultivate the land by the grace of the immanent spirits, but they cannot dispose of it and cannot conceive of doing so. This feeling of affinity between society and land is widespread and appears in various forms and varying degrees of intensity, and it is not found only among sedentary peoples. We have Australian tribes where the very spirit of the men is believed to reside in the land, where a bush or a rock or a peculiar formation is the present incarnation of myth, and means security and religious value; where a social class, a structured group of relatives, will contain in addition to human beings, an animal and a feature of the landscape. Here, when a man moves away from the land of his group, he leaves the vital part of himself behind. When a magistrate put people from such societies in jail in a distant city, he had no idea of the terrifying severity of the punishment he was meting; he was cutting the tribesman off from the very source of his life and of his personality, from the past, and the future, which were incorporated and present in his land.

In presenting the technology of such societies, the teacher again is dealing with material where the religious and secular are not distinct from each other. We have, for example, the description which Raymond Firth gives of the replacing of a worn-out wash strake on a canoe, among the Tikopia. This operation is expertly and coherently carried out, with secular and religious acts performed in continuous succession or even concurrently. A tree is cut down for the new wash strake, a libation is poured out to the deities of the canoe to announce this new timber, and a kava rite is performed to persuade the deities to step out of the canoe and on to a piece of bark cloth, where they can live undisturbed, while the canoe is being tampered with. Then comes the unlashing of the old wash strake, the expert examination of the body of the canoe in search of lurking defects, the discovery of signs indicating the work of a borer, the cutting of the body of the canoe with a swift stroke to discover whether the borer is there, accompanied by an appeal to the deities of the canoe by the expert, to witness what he is doing, and the necessity for doing it. Now a kinsman of the original builder of the canoe, who is one of the tutelary deities, spontaneously drops his head on to the side of the canoe and wails over the wounding of the body of the canoe. The borer is discovered, in the meantime, to be still there; but only a specially consecrated adze can deal with him successfully. The adze is sent for, dedicated anew to the deity invoked, and finally wielded with success by the expert. All this is performed with remarkable expedition and economy of motion. So, even when the teacher is discussing such supposedly purely economic matters such as time-saving procedures and efficiency of operation, he will be speaking of religion; because the Tikopia are not concerned with time-limits, with speed; but in this case their concern for the dispossessed deities whose home must be made ready for their return makes for speed and time-saving procedures. The end result is efficiency; but unlike our own efficiency, this is not rooted in the effort to utilize and exploit material and time resources to the utmost; it is rooted in that profound religious feeling which also gives rise to the time-consuming rites and the wailing procedures which, from the purely economic point of view, are wasteful and interfering.

IV

Courses dealing with systems of thought in primitive cultures, as a rule, cannot but include religion. The world view of a particular society includes that society's conception of man's own relation to the universe, human and nonhuman, organic and inorganic, secular and divine, to use our own dualisms. It expresses his view of his own role in the maintenance of life, and even of the forces of nature. His attitude toward responsibility and initiative is inextricable from his conception of nature as deity-controlled, man-controlled, regulated through a balanced cooperation between god and man, or perhaps maintained through some eternal homeostasis, independent of man and perhaps of any deity. The way a man acts, his feeling of guilt and of achievement, and his very personality are affected by the way he envisions his place within the universe. In presenting a world view, the teacher has only to point out and emphasize the religious element which is so much a part of the picture as to be in danger of being taken for granted and overlooked.

If the teacher, for example, takes up conceptions of man's effectiveness in the universe, he has to discuss them in terms of the religious system, beliefs, and attitudes of each society under consideration. For example, there are the Tiv of Southern Nigeria, who people the universe with potentially hostile and harmful deities and powers, the *akombo*. Man's function in the maintenance of his own life and the well-being of the land and of his social unit, is to defeat the evil intent of the *akombo*, to render safe through preventive rites, to purify through rites of expulsion and purging. His own role is preventive, negative, saving the normal course from interference.

Vis-à-vis the universe, his acts arise out of negative motives. For example, what corresponds to a gift of first-fruits to a deity in other cultures is phrased as a rite for preventing the deities from making a man's food go bad or diminish too quickly; fertility rites for a field are actually rites preventing the evil-intentioned from robbing the fields of their normal fertility.

To cite another example, the way the Ifugao and neighboring tribes in Luzon conceive of their own effectiveness patterns their activities in every field; and here, again, the teacher will be dealing mainly with religion when he speaks of man's effectiveness. These people either accept what comes as deity-given, or act without being themselves the agents; they believe that no act can come to a conclusive end without the agency of a specific deity. The Ifugao have a specific deity often for every step within an operation and for every part of the implement to be used. R. F. Barton recorded the names of 1,240 deities and believed that even so he had not exhausted the list. The Ifugao associate a deity with every structured performance and at least a large number of their deliberate acts. They cannot go hunting, for example, without enlisting the aid of the deity of each step of the chase, to render each effective, or to nullify any lurking dangers. There is a deity for the level spot where "the hunter stands watching and listening to the dogs"; one for when the dogs "are sicked on the game"; one for when "the hunter leans on his spear transfixing the quarry"; twelve are listed as the deities of specific ways of rendering harmless to the hunter's feet the snags and fangs of snakes which he encounters. If he is to be successful in the hunt, a man does not ask the blessing of a deity. He pays all the particular deities of every specific spot and act, getting them to transitivize each act individually. Even so, in most cases a man remains non-agentive, since the function of many of the deities is to save man from encounter, rather than to give him success in his dealing with it. For example, in the area of interpersonal relations, we have Tupya, who is invoked so that "the creditor comes for dun for what is owed, but on the way he forgets and goes about other business"; and Dulaiya, who is invoked so that "the enemies just don't think about us, so they don't attack." His tools, also, are ineffective of themselves; so that, when setting a deadfall, he invokes and bribes such deities as that for the Flat Stone of the Deadfall, the Main Posts of the Deadfall, the Fall of the Deadfall, the Trigger of the Deadfall. Most of the Ifugao economy is involved in providing sacrifices to the deities, big or little according to the magnitude of the operation and the importance of the deities. There is no warmth in the sacrifices; no expression of gratitude or appeal or belongingness. As the Ifugaos see it, the sacrifice is a bribe. With such bribes, they buy the miraculous intervention and transitivization which are essential for achievement, health, and good personal relations.

The Ifugao show no humility in the face of this ineffective role in the universe; they merely accept it as the state of things. They accept their own failures, the frequent deaths, the sudden and disastrous flaring up of tempers, as things that are bound to happen irrespective of their own desires and efforts. But they are neither passive nor helpless. They carry on great undertakings, and, even now, they go on forbidden head-hunts. They know when and how and whom to bribe so as to perfect their defective acts. When, however, a deity states a decision, they accept it as immutable. A Catholic priest tells a story about the neighboring Iloko which illustrates this acceptance. A Christian Iloko was on his deathbed, and the priest, trying to persuade him to repent of his sin, painted to him vividly the horrors of hell; but the dying man merely answered, "If God wants me to go to hell, I am perfectly willing."

In making a study of the conception of man's own effectiveness among the Wintu Indians of California, through an analysis of linguistic categories, the present writer found that a study of the religion was necessary for adequate understanding. The students, asked to analyze the cosmological myths of the tribe, discovered that man had a limited agentive role, shaping, using, intervening, but never creating. They found that man needed skill for his operations, but that specific skill was useless without "luck," which a man received through communion and pleading with some universal power. This circumscribed agentive role was found to be implicit in the linguistic categories also. The language was found to have a verbal category for referring to subjective experience, to the area where man is an agent, where he perceives, feels, knows, thinks, desires, intends. A derivative stem refers to this area, and a large number of suffixes are used with this stem, documenting the experience in great detail, giving specific source of information, state of the perceived, etc. Another category, using the primary form of the stems, refers to that reality which is irrespective of man and the agency of man; here, concepts such as that of futurity, potentiality, necessity, probability, and succession are covered by one suffix. And in this category, the only personal suffixes are those expressing unalterable promise and those implying the possibility of interception or avoidance. So, even within the area where man has no agency, he can at least intercept or avoid the inevitable. Language, as well as mythology, was found to express man's relation to the universe.

It is to this limited role of man, geared to the working of the universe, that the teacher was referring when he spoke of Hopi drama and agriculture. Without an understanding of this role, no Hopi activity or attitude or relationship can be understood. The Hopi have developed the idea of man's limited effectiveness in their own fashion and have elaborated it systematically in what they call the "Hopi Way." Laura Thompson says of the Hopi:

> "All phenomena relevant to the life of the tribe—including man, the animals, and plants, the earth, sun, moon, clouds, the ancestors, and the spirits—are believed to be interdependent through one Law which may be thought of as a 'Law of Universal Reciprocity' . . . In this system each individual—human

and non-human—is believed to have its proper place in relation to all the other phenomena, and each has a definite role
in the universal order. The scheme does not operate immutably,
however, on account of the special role played by man. Whereas
the non-human world is controlled automatically by the rhythmic reciprocity principle, man is a responsible agent who may or
may not completely fulfill his function in it . . . To the traditional Hopi, the movements of the sun, the coming of rain, the
growth of crops, the reproduction of animals and of human
beings depend (to a certain extent at least) on man's correct
and active participation in the fulfillment of the natural Law
. . . The universe is not conceived as a sort of machine at the
mercy of mechanical law. Nor is it viewed as a sum total of
hostile, competitive forces struggling for existence. It is by
nature a harmonious integrated system operating rhythmically
according to the principles of immanent justice, and in it the
key role is played by man's will . . . The Hopi believes that
each individual is a responsible social agent through the creative development of his will, and hence Hopi interest in the
whole man centers in the development of the will through both
mind and body . . . Man has definite responsibilities which
should be carried out according to a rather complicated set of
rules. These rules embody cosmic Law reduced to the level of
human thought, feeling, and behavior. They form an informal
and unwritten ethical canon known as the Hopi way." [6]

The Hopi Way is mainly religious in nature, and is expressed
in its greatest intensity in the ceremonial cycle throughout
the year.

The Indians of the Plains, such as the Crow and the Sioux,
have given a somewhat different form to this conception of
man's circumscribed agency. The aggressive behavior for which
they have been known, their great independence, their self-
assurance and assertiveness, and, in later years, their great dependence and apathy, have been explained as an expression of
this conception. These societies envisioned the universe as
pervaded by an undifferentiated religious force on which they
were dependent for success in their undertakings and in life

[6] Laura Thompson, "*The Hopi Crisis*" (Mimeo.), pp. 42-45.

generally. The specific formulation differs in the different tribes; but, essentially, in all it was believed that each individual, and particularly each man, must tap this universal force if his undertakings were to be successful. Without this "power" a man could not achieve success in any of the valued activities, whether warfare or the hunt; no leadership was possible without this power; and when the government put a stop to the activities through which the universal force was tapped, these Indians became dependent and apathetic. This was a force enhancing and intensifying the being of the man who acted; it was not, as with the Ifugao, an effectiveness applied to specific details of activities. The individual himself prepared himself in the hardihood, self-control, skills, and areas of knowledge necessary. Little boys of five or seven took pride in their ability to withstand pain, physical hardship, and the terrors of running errands alone in the night. The Sioux did not appeal for divine intervention; he did not want the enemy to forget to come. Neither was he fearless. He appealed for divine strength to overcome his own fears as well as the external enemy.

The relationship with the divine, in this case, is personal and intense. The Plains Indian Sioux did not, like the Hopi, inherit a specific relatedness when he was born in a specific clan. Each man, each pre-adolescent boy, had to achieve the relationship for himself. He had to go out into the wilderness and spend days and nights without food or drink, in the cold, among wild beasts, afraid and hungry and anxious, humbling himself and supplicating, sometimes inflicting excruciating pain upon himself, until some particular manifestation of the universal force took pity upon him and came to him to become his life-long guardian and power. The appeals to the universal force were made sometimes in a group, through the institution of the Sun Dance. But here also they were individual in nature. The relationship with the divine was an inner experience; and when the Sioux Black Elk recounted his autobiography, he spoke mainly of these intense, personal religious experiences. The Hopi Crow-wing made very frequent reference to religion, also, in his journal; but his reference was not to individual experience, but to group activity; the first person singular *I* is of very rare occurrence in the journal.

V

At present, many courses are taught on the application of anthropological knowledge to present-day world problems, such as the problems and issues involved in the introduction of technological change in many areas of the world. We know that, in attempting to introduce measures which make for improvement in living, workers have discovered that a knowledge of the religion of the particular group is imperative. Without this, the attempted changes are often ineffective; and, worse than this, they run the danger of disrupting or destroying the values of the people, that which gives meaning to their lives. It is essential that the students in these courses do not learn merely effective techniques for inducing change; they must be impressed with the need to understand, respect, and take into account the religion of the people in question.

Attempts to introduce change in areas such as agriculture, health, nutrition, land-ownership, have come up against profound religious attitudes. Workers could not persuade Mexican farmers to save their best seed for planting, since these people believed that God alone—not the quality of the seed—was responsible for a good yield, so long as man performed his share of the work well. In the Middle East, workers found that villagers were not prepared even to recognize that they had ill-health, or polluted or foul-tasting water, since they considered these to represent the workings of God's will, and God's will could not be anything but good. The workers found villagers worrying over the success of a DDT campaign, because the mosquitoes and other bugs had been God-given, and

God might now decide to give worse afflictions in their place. Yet Mohammedan workers in this region were able to introduce changes both effectively and reassuringly, since they worked in harmony with the people's religion. In this way, also, Ibn Saud introduced mechanization and agricultural measures without disturbing the faith of his people.

The teaching of religion must be included in courses on this subject; without it, courses may teach the unreflective student to be merely manipulative. And if culture is to be understood in all its aspects, the teaching of religion must form a part of all courses dealing with culture.

12

ECONOMICS

By KENNETH E. BOULDING

I

The economist—or any other specialist—differs from his fellow teachers mainly by reason of the subject matter which he teaches. It may be, of course, that there is some relation between the nature of a subject and the nature of its practitioners: the social sciences are perhaps more likely to attract those of a reforming temperament, the experimental sciences those of a mechanical temperament, and the humanities those of an artistic temperament. But by and large these differences are small, and there is not much reason to suppose that economists are either more or less religious than biologists or musicians. Religion is a matter for the whole man and the full man, not for the specialized part of him. It is for this reason perhaps that specialization is in itself somewhat inimical to religion; the man who throws his whole being into the narrow channel of a single specialty, be it chemistry or economics, is quite apt to be hostile, or at least indifferent, to the great generalities of the spiritual and moral life. The Love of God escapes both the test tube and the formula. In this matter the economist is not much different from other men: and such differences as there are arise from the peculiarities of the subject which he teaches and investigates. I shall begin my argument, therefore, by considering religion and economics as subject matter, that is, as two great fields of human experience and study; and ask, To what extent are they adjoining, overlapping, or quite independent; to what extent are they enemies or friends, do they compete with or complete each other in the vast ecology of ideas?

We shall consider first the impact of religion on economic life and history. The impact on economic life seems to have been much greater than the impact on economic thought. From its very beginning religion has strongly affected not only the nature of the commodities which form the main subject matter of economic life, but also the economic institutions and practices which so largely determine the course of economic development. Religion built the pyramids, the temples, the cathedrals. It draws resources into the manufacture of vestments, incense, images, prayer rugs, and prayers. More important than this, however, from the point of view of the economist, is its impact upon the minds of men, its shaping of their beliefs, customs, and practices. It is not the physical resources so much as the human resources of a society which determine the course of its economic development, if any, whether toward riches or toward poverty. Men have languished in utter poverty in the midst of great natural resources and have wrung comfort and even luxury from stern and unfriendly physical environments. It is what lies in the minds of men that determines, for the most part, whether a society shall grow in productive power; it is only this growth that has carried man from a pitiful, half-starved savagery to the splendor, comfort, and dangers of civilization, and this growth is closely connected with the nature of his dominant religion.

The exact conditions of economic progress are very complex and imperfectly understood. Certain physical conditions seem to be necessary—e.g., the absence of extreme pressure of population. Given these conditions, however, the most apparent determining factor seems to be the character of the religion of the period—particularly whether it is "prophetic" or "priestly." This distinction corresponds roughly to the "early" or "late" stages of any particular religion or any phase within the history of a particular religion. In its early or prophetic phase religion acts as a revolutionary force, stirring the minds and hearts of men out of their routines, changing them and making them receptive to change. It is in this stage that economic progress is most likely to be rapid, for progress cannot take place without change, and the willingness to change, to try new methods of production, new commodities, and new techniques, and the willingness to tolerate others who are making such changes is likely to be greater in an age of "conversion," when there is also a willingness to try new ideas, new faiths, and new patterns of life. When, on the other hand, religion settles down into its "priestly" stage, it becomes a conservative force making for the persistence of established routines and the satisfaction of creative energies through repetitive ritual rather than through innovation. In this stage religion is likely to be inimical to economic progress simply because it creates a general disapproval of change of any kind. [1]

Besides its influence in affecting attitudes toward change, religion, through its theology and its ethical systems, also influences the attitudes of men toward various forms of economic behavior. Thus a very "otherworldly" religion is likely to lead to a low social status for merchants, shopkeepers, artisans, business men, and other "money-changers" whose activities seem to be centered on "this world," and a correspondingly high status for fakirs, contemplatives, and mendicants, whose contribution to the economic order is that of consumption rather than of production, however great their contributions to spiritual welfare. Such a religion is also likely to discourage accumulation of capital—not so much because of its encouragement of consumption—there is great frugality among the otherworldly—but because of its discouragement of the production

[1] I do not mean to imply, of course, that there is any rigid separation between the prophetic and the priestly stages, nor that each is necessarily embodied in a particular form of organization. Thus the Catholic Church, while priestly in its general organization, has produced a number of "prophetic" movements, such as that of the Franciscans; and the Protestant churches, while generally ostensibly "prophetic" in their form of organization, have passed through many periods of "priestliness."

of tangible objects of desire. On the other hand, a more "this-worldly" type of religion, stressing, for instance, some concept such as the "Kingdom of God on Earth" and emphasizing the attainment of some degree of perfection and satisfaction in this world, is likely to place a higher value on those engaged in the more humdrum tasks of life, and consequently to be favorable to economic progress. A this-worldly religion is also likely to encourage capital accumulation, by its emphasis on productive work, and when this is combined with ideals of frugality and simplicity in living, the favorable effect on accumulation is thereby reinforced.

We cannot, in an essay of this length, do more than illustrate these propositions. The most famous illustration is Max Weber's thesis regarding the influence of the Protestant Reformation on the development of capitalism. The Protestant Reformation (not only in itself, but also in the Counter-Reformation, which it induced) represents a great upsurge of religion of a more prophetic, and also more this-worldly type, than the medieval Catholicism which preceded it. New ideas, ferment and change in the realm of faith and morals, paved the way for new adventures in trade, agriculture, and industry. The puritan morality, with its emphasis on work, "vocation," and activity on the side of production, and its emphasis on simplicity of life, temperance, and frugality on the side of consumption, greatly favored that rise of production above consumption which is necessary for capital accumulation. In a sense also the simplification of religion itself which Protestantism represented enabled men to satisfy their religious requirements with a smaller expenditure of time and energy than before, and hence left more for other pursuits. Instead of the great apparatus of masses, feasts, fasts, confessions, penances, retreats, novenas, and so on of Catholicism, we now have a stripped sabbatarianism fed by once-a-week calls to action from the pulpit rather than by constant daily meditation in the cloister. I shall not debate in these pages whether the spiritual product of the new religious technique was as good as the old; but there can be no doubt that it was obtained much more cheaply in terms of time and effort, and that therefore human energy, which in the Middle Ages was channeled into vast ritual or religious practices and "works," was now available for trade, industry, and economic development. These "worldly" activities, moreover, were themselves sanctified by the idea of "vocation," according to which all things could be done to God's glory and in obedience to His will.

Just as the Lutheran,[2] Reformed, and Episcopal church movements of the sixteenth and seventeenth centuries influenced the so-called Commercial Revolution of this time in England, Holland, and, to a less extent, Germany and Scandinavia, so the even more "prophetic" Protestantism of the Quakers and Methodists influenced the Industrial Revolution of the eighteenth and nineteenth centuries. It is astonishing how many of the basic technical discoveries of the early Industrial Revolution in England are associated with the members of nonconformist sects. This can hardly be an accident. These groups emphasized a "lay," non-priestly religion, stressing conversion and change in the individual, and emphasizing the this-worldly aspects of the Christian gospel in terms of disciplined daily living. They were, moreover, barred from higher education and hence delivered both from intellectual conformity and from easy professional ways of life. They had a deserved reputation for honesty and integrity. It is not surprising, therefore, that they developed iron-smelting, textiles, railroads, insurance, banking, retailing, and were deeply involved in all the technological changes of the period. Nor were these involvements merely of a material nature. The "social inventions" which are equally part of the same revolution in human affairs were also inspired in no small measure by nonconform-

---

[2] It is significant that Lutheranism—by far the most "priestly" of the Protestant movements—exercised a much smaller effect on economic life than did the other Protestant movements.

ists and evangelicals. Social legislation, beginning with the abolition of slavery and the development of the factory acts, was in its beginnings largely the work of nonconformists or evangelicals like Wilberforce, Clarkson, and Lord Shaftesbury and their coteries. Even more important is the influence of nonconformity on the growth of science: a wholly disproportionate number of members of the Royal Society, for instance, were nonconformists; it was men like Priestley, the Unitarian, and Dalton, the Quaker, who were most active in scientific inquiry. It was British nonconformity which set the moral and intellectual tone of American society, and the progressive nature of American economic life is closely connected with the prophetic, evangelical, individualistic, and this-worldly character of American religion. In the United States we are all Methodists now!

These two examples are sufficient to illustrate the intimate connection between religious and economic history; the historically minded reader will think of many others. The great economic development in Europe of the tenth and eleventh centuries—embodied in the Romanesque cathedrals and castles —is closely connected with the earlier conversion of the barbarian tribes to Christianity. The flowering of Arab civilization after the rise of Mohammed is another striking example of the impact of a "prophetic" religion, as its rapid withering is an example of the corrupting effects of a rigid orthodoxy.

II

So far we have looked at the relationship mainly from the point of view of the impact of religion on economic life: we do not have to be a Marxist to admit that this connection is reciprocal, and that in their turn economic institutions and conditions affect the form and content of religion. The economic interpretation of history is little help in explaining the *genesis* of religions, which arise as a result of certain *mutations*

—to borrow a word from genetics—in human personality and experience. Where the economic interpretation is useful is in explaining the survival of such mutations as occur. There are many prophets, but few of them are founders of living religions. A religion cannot survive unless it is accepted among men, and its acceptance depends largely on its ability to satisfy human wants and needs. This is not to say that only those religions survive which enhance material prosperity. To a considerable degree the Bread of Life is a substitute, if not for the bread at least for the cake of this world, and the fire of Charity may warm as effectively as fine clothes and central heating. Indeed, one may say with some confidence that when the tide of religion runs strongly in the minds of men it draws them away from worldly power, wealth, and security, and offers them in return a power, a wealth, and a security which are not of this world, not dependent on the favor of other men, but are secured by a secret inward covenant between the soul and its heavenly Lord. Taking no thought for the morrow, carrying neither scrip nor staff, the heaven-intoxicated pilgrim "walks cheerfully over the world, answering that of God in every man," unencumbered by worldly cares or worldly goods. There have been many such golden dawns of Gospel purity, and, one and all, they fade into the plain light of a workaday world. As the early enthusiasm recedes substitute satisfactions must be found, and when manna no longer falls we must devote ourselves to husbandry. But a religion cannot survive unless it increases men's satisfactions, however compounded these may be of earth and heaven: this is the "economic test." A religion which makes men miserable will scarcely survive its first generation.

The nature of the dominant religion, therefore, is determined in an appreciable degree by the economic opportunities which are open. In some societies, for instance, the pressure of population makes any economic progress almost impossible, and Malthus' "dismal science" is operating at its most dismal.

Any improvement in techniques is immediately swallowed up by the flood of population, and the final result of such improvements is not to improve the lot of individuals, but to enable more people to live in the old misery! In such a situation religion is likely to be otherworldly, ritualistic, and mystical, offering to man hopes of the hereafter and the present consolations of inward experience. On the other hand, in a situation where a rapid increase in the economic welfare of a society is possible through the improvement of techniques and the accumulation of capital, a religion which is this-worldly, economical of resources, and practical in its application is more likely to meet human needs. Thus the religions of the overcrowded East have laid great stress on salvation by withdrawal from the world: in such a society the monk, the contemplative, and the fakir flourish, and the appeal of religion to the mass of men is either that of propitiation of fortune or of hope for a better life elsewhere, whether in a reincarnation or in a heaven. In bustling America, on the other hand, the world has seemed too good to withdraw from, and economic opportunity too great to be spurned: religion has adapted itself accordingly and has become more secular, more "lay," more "practical."

If wealth consists in the satisfaction of wants there are two roads to riches: one is the diminution of wants, the other is the increase in the means of satisfaction. Which road we take depends on their relative roughness. If the increase in the means of satisfaction is denied us by the rigor of economic circumstance, we are more likely to take the *via negativa* toward a nirvana of wantlessness. This is the way we associate with the congested and hopeless East. The West, on the other hand, came later to civilization and had opportunities for geographical expansion northward and westward which the East did not have. Here the increase in the means of satisfaction has always seemed more possible, and the *via negativa* has been less attractive, except in periods of recession and collapse. It is not surprising, therefore, that it was Macedonia (that

America of ancient Greece!) that gave the call to the apostle Paul, and that Christianity became the religion of the West, for Jesus gave Christianity a stamp of this-worldliness which it can never quite escape. At the heart of Eastern religions is a Way from Man to God; at the heart of Christianity is an incarnation of God in Man and a dream of a Kingdom of Heaven on Earth.

It is clear that the causative relationship between religious and secular life in the stream of history is a complex mutual one of a hen-and-egg nature, and that attempts to interpret history solely in terms of one or the other, as in the Marxian economic interpretation, is like trying to develop an egg theory of hens or a hen theory of eggs. A satisfactory theory of history must consist of two elements: an understanding of the principles of ecological equilibrium and succession, and an ability to recognize mutations when they occur. History is the record of the growth and decline of populations, whether of the flora and fauna of a forest or of the characteristics, ideas, and institutions of men. The rise and fall of states, empires, churches, religions, and philosophies is a similar process to the rise and decline of species in the world of nature, and is determined mainly by the competitive or complementary relationships of the various forms of life or organization. The succession of cultures in human history is not unlike the succession of complexes of plant and animal life in the pond or the forest: each culture provides the breeding ground for ideas, institutions, and patterns of behavior which will eventually supplant it. This ecological succession, however, is not confined to any one aspect of life, but covers the whole of it: material and spiritual species interact upon each other ceaselessly and with endless complexity; religions breed civilizations, and civilizations breed and spread religions in a continuous pattern.

Every "ecosystem" (as the biologists call a complete system of mutually interacting populations of different species) is subject from time to time to incursions from without. These may be invasions of new species from other ecosystems, as when Japanese beetles invade the United States or Marxist ideology invades the labor movement. Or they may be "mutations"—changes in the genetic constitution, coming from we know not where or whom. Were it not for these invasions and mutations every society would soon settle down to a position of equilibrium; it is these which keep history perpetually on the move. Both the economic and the religious aspects of society are subject to invasions and mutations. The invention of a new technique in production, or of a new commodity, represents a "mutation" in economic life. The founders of religions likewise represent mutations in the spiritual life. The spread of new techniques, or of new religions, is a process analogous to "invasion." It must not be thought, of course, that mutations are arbitrary. They can take place only within narrow limits set by the existing state of affairs. A mutation from a mouse never turns out to be an elephant. The automobile could not have been invented in the seventeenth century; it could hardly help being invented at the end of the nineteenth. Given the invention of the rudder the discovery of America was almost inevitable—as someone has well said, how could Columbus miss it! It is easy to find these connections in history; they are never, however, as certain or as definite as they look after the event. It is not always easy to recognize true mutations, but it can hardly be doubted that they occur, and that they occur as much, if not more, in the world of belief and ideas [3] as they do in the world of techniques and commodities. We cannot, therefore, understand economic processes in time without reference to the whole universe of social phenomenon, of which religion is a vital and significant part.

[3] To Christians, of course, Jesus represents the most significant "mutation" in history: with him a new spiritual species—the "new man in Christ Jesus" enters the world of time.

III

I have sketched very briefly some of the interactions of religious and economic life in history, and while the details of the interconnectedness may be open to some question, the fact of interconnectedness is abundantly evident. Nevertheless, the student of economics in our universities can easily get through his course, and can be turned out as a full-fledged teacher of the subject, without any awareness of this interconnectedness penetrating his consciousness. It is no exaggeration to say that unless a student happens to come into contact with a teacher whose specialized interests lie, say, toward Max Weber's type of interpretation of history, he can pass through his whole formal instruction without any sense of contact between economics and religion as realms of discourse. Religion, like liquor, is something which he can take or not, according to taste, but unless indulged in to excess it will in no way affect the world of ideas which he inhabits as an economist. The conceptual framework of economics and the practical questions on which it impinges—whether new or old—supply and demand, prices, savings, investment, trade, tariffs, taxes, output, employment—are concepts which inhabit a self-sufficient realm of their own, and seem to have nothing whatever to do with the realm of discourse in which we discuss God, prayer, worship, grace, salvation, communion, justification, and the like.

This is quite understandable, and even up to a point, proper. Although in life and history religion and economics are inseparably intertwined in the great web of reality, in thought and theory they are quite distinct, and have very little contact. Both theology and economics along with all other theoretical frameworks—represent *abstractions* from reality, and hence we should not expect them to cover much of the same material. It is as if economic theory looks only at the black threads, and religious theory (i.e., theology, in its broad sense) only at the gold threads of a great and complex tapestry; the picture that each presents will be very different, yet each may be part of a single reality. Moreover, to him that concentrates on the black, the gold may appear to be simply a meaningless irruption of unnecessary splendor in the chaste material of reality, while to the specialist on gold the black may appear as completely beneath his notice, just an insignificant background to the real splendors of the creation. Other specialists similarly may concentrate only on other threads, to their similar gain and loss.

The economist, by reason of the peculiar history of economic thought, is especially in danger of being *indifferent* to religion. It is difficult for a student of history, or literature, or ethics, or art, to be *unaware* of the intimate connection in life and history of his own speciality and religious life. Some of the natural sciences, perhaps even medicine, have a certain history of hostility on the part of the Church which may lead to a conflict with religion. Economics, however, sprang at least half-grown from the head of Adam Smith, who may very properly be regarded as the founder of economics as a *unified* abstract realm of discourse, and it still, almost without knowing it, breathes a good deal of the air of eighteenth-century rationalism and Deism. Adam Smith, it will be remembered, was an intimate friend of David Hume; between them they almost personify the eighteenth century at its most urbane, like the elegant New Town of Edinburgh that was building around them. They both led blameless lives in a quiet way; they both express the amused tolerance and sweet reasonableness of an age whose fires are banked. Both regarded religious enthusiasm as a serious breach of good taste, yet both are saved from dullness by a good touch of Scottish wit and moral indignation.

Adam Smith's observations on religion are worth mention at this point, even at the cost of some digression, not only because of their intrinsic interest, but because they represent almost everything that economists, *qua* economists, have said on this subject. It is indeed curious that no economist since Adam Smith seems to have dealt at any length with the economics of religion [4]—perhaps it was felt that Adam Smith had said the last word on the subject! His observations are found, oddly enough, in that chapter of Book 5 of the *Wealth of Nations* headed "Of the Expenses of the Sovereign or Commonwealth," under Article III, "Of the Expense of Institutions for the Instruction of People of All Ages." In the previous section ("Of the Expense of Institutions for the Education of Youth") he has applied his principle of the free market to education, denounced educational monopolies and endowed professors, and pointed out that the best teaching is usually done by those whose rewards are related in some manner to the success of their efforts—hence he advocates what is essentially the "elective system." He then goes on to apply the same principles to the church and to point out how the endowment and establishment of a monopolistic state church leads to a diminution of religious zeal, which flourishes most among those whose support depends upon it. "The advantage in point of learning and good writing may sometimes be on the side of the established church. But the arts of popularity, all the arts of gaining proselytes, are constantly on the side of its adversaries. In England those arts have long been neglected by the well-endowed clergy of the established church and are at present chiefly cultivated by the Dissenters and by the Methodists. The independent provisions, however, which in many places have been made for dissenting teachers by means of voluntary subscriptions, of trust right, and other evasions of the law, seem very much to have abated the zeal and activ-

---

[4] A possible exception is found in the writings of a group of American economists in the generation before the first World War, especially T. N. Carver, S. N. Patten, and Richard T. Ely. None of them, however, made particularly significant contributions to economic theory; their works are little read nowadays, and the American Economic Association, which they helped to found, today exhibits practically no marks of their influence.

ity of those teachers. They have many of them become very learned, ingenious, and respectable men; but they have in general ceased to be very popular preachers. The Methodists, without half the learning of the Dissenters, are very much more in vogue." One is tempted to continue the quotation, but the *Wealth of Nations* is easily available, and the reader can continue for himself.

In spite of the fact that he agrees with Hume that an excess of religious enthusiasm, when it manifests itself in violent factionalism, is a grave danger to society, Smith does not follow Hume in what would seem to be the obvious conclusion, that the remedy is to moderate religion by the establishment of a monopolistic state church. Monopoly in religion as in everything else is distasteful to him, and consequently he comes out in favor of free competition in religion, the separation of church and state, and the consequent multiplication of sects, for, he says, "the concessions which they would mutually find it both convenient and agreeable to make to one another, might in time reduce the doctrine of the greater part of them to that pure and rational religion, free from every mixture of absurdity, imposture, or fanaticism, such as wise men have in all ages of the world wished to see established; but such as positive law has perhaps never yet established—because, with regard to religion, positive law always has been, and probably always will be, more or less influenced by popular superstition and enthusiasm." If the enthusiasm of competing sects leads society into too "unsocial or disagreeably rigorous" a moral code, this can easily be remedied by the state's promoting first the study of science and philosophy and secondly frequent and gay public diversions. Then, as a good Scot should, he comes out in favor of the equality, but not the democracy, of the Presbyterian form of government and urges that the clergy should not be too well paid, because "nothing but the most exemplary of morals can give dignity to a man of small fortune."

I doubt if anything so witty and penetrating has ever been written on the economic sociology of religion. Yet nowhere do we find any deep understanding of the *content* of religion. Neither the transports nor the dark night of the soul has any place in this pellucid eighteenth-century air. Adam Smith could never have had any real knowledge of the mind of the Wesleys. Mystical experience of any kind he would have dismissed as "fanaticism and enthusiasm." He is in some sense almost the ideal of the "good" intellectual; a very good, very moral, admirable, almost, one might say, an intellectually pious man. Yet there is clearly a realm of experience into which he does not penetrate. He can tell us a great deal about the forces that make for decay in religion as it becomes entangled with the world; he can tell us very little about the ultimate sources of its life and power. The world and its corruption are much easier to observe and describe than heaven and its purity; the cooling of zeal takes place in public, but it is kindled inwardly. Only those who have in some measure walked the road to Emmaus know how far it stretches through history, and how the heart that is "strangely warmed," whether of a Paul, a Francis, a Fox, a Wesley, or a Booth, can set great movements in motion and change the whole temper of an age. The followers of these movements, it is true, become in their turn "learned, ingenious, and respectable"; but instead of competition reducing all to the stationary equilibrium of a "pure and rational religion" the status quo is perpetually disturbed by the invasion of new enthusiasts and a fresh outpouring of the Holy Spirit—a Spirit neither learned, nor ingenious, nor respectable, but bearing unmistakable marks of heavenly origin.

IV

It is evident that the economist, and especially the teacher of economics, who is at the same time a man of religion—

more specifically, let us say, a practicing Christian—will be exposed to certain rather special temptations and dangers because of the craft which he follows, and it may be well to examine these in further detail. We may note first, briefly, some problems which arise because the economist is of necessity an intellectual by profession, and therefore in common with other intellectuals may be particularly subject to those "higher vices, that have to be paid for at higher prices." Pride, envy, self-love, self-deceit, self-righteousness, cynicism, frivolousness, and cowardice are common diseases in intellectual circles, and of these the most to be feared is pride, a disease utterly devastating in its ultimate effects, yet so subtle that there seems to be no remedy for it save a simple-hearted daily dependence upon God. The teacher also, in general, has certain problems which arise from the nature of his occupation—the temptation to a misuse of authority, or to gain authority over his students by a mere display of wit or erudition rather than by devotion to truth—how much easier it is to say a clever thing than a true one! These problems, however, are not peculiar to the economist, and I merely mention them here. One problem which is especially likely to trouble the social scientist is that of preventing his moral and religious concerns from undermining the scientific integrity of his specialized discipline. Many people are attracted into the social sciences, and especially perhaps to economics, because they feel a concern for the ills of society or wish to learn how to reform them. This is a most proper motivation, yet it needs to be disciplined by a strong sense of scientific integrity and by a willingness to acquire real skill in the abstract disciplines before venturing to make applications. Our notions of what *ought to be* must not be allowed to prejudice our painstaking inquiry into what *is*, and good will is in no sense a substitute for scientific competence—nor, of course, is scientific competence a substitute for good will.

On the whole, however, the atmosphere of our institutions of higher learning is so overwhelmingly favorable to scientific competence that the professional—as opposed perhaps to the amateur—economist is not in much danger of sacrificing his scientific integrity to moral fervor. It is the opposite danger which threatens him—that of becoming so engrossed in the refinements of scientific abstraction—and in the substantial rewards, which in these days often accompany proficiency in such abstractions—that he forgets the ills of society and becomes deaf to the cry of the hungry and blind to the misery of the oppressed. It may be true that a man does not understand the laws of demand and supply any better for being a member of the Communion of Saints. It may be, even, that the clamorous realities of the Communion of Saints actually unfit a man for performing the delicate and beautiful abstractions of economic theory. It is also true, however, that it is possible to retreat into abstraction from the demands which the real world is making upon us, and to take refuge from the demands of the moral law behind a screen of scientific indifference. The prolonged contemplation of abstract systems may also lead to a certain cynicism and weariness: a paralysis of the will-to-good sets in because of a sense of the immense complexity of social life and the ill effects of a rash do-good-ism. It was not the economists who liberated the slaves or who passed the Factory Acts, but the rash and ignorant Christians! Those who have knowledge have a peculiar responsibility to be sensitive to the ills of the world, for if they are not, then it will be the ignorant who will be the movers of events, and the value of knowledge will be lost.

V

I turn now to the problems which are likely to be encountered in the actual teaching of economics. There are perhaps four main divisions of the subject matter: (1) pure theory, (2) the description of present-day economic institutions, (3) the study of economic history and (4) the study of economic policy. This division does not correspond to any division of courses—indeed, the courses given are likely to include something of all four aspects. A course in Money and Banking, for instance, is likely to include some theory of money, some description of financial institutions, some history, and some policy discussion. Pure theory is essentially a branch of mathematics or logic: religion may therefore be expected to make very little impact on it. There is no more reason to suppose a "Christian" economic theory, for instance, than there is to suppose a "Christian" mathematics. Theory is essentially a tool, and should not be even a highly specialized tool. Tools or instruments can only be given moral or religious attributes as they are specialized. There is no such thing as a Christian screwdriver, for screwdrivers may be used either for good or for evil ends quite indiscriminately. It is true, of course, that, historically, economic theory developed as a rather specialized instrument for the interpretation of early industrial capitalism. This limitation, however, has been steadily relaxed, and the progress of theory is toward greater and greater generality; the most significant techniques of economic theory, for instance, are as applicable to socialist or to primitive economies as they are to capitalism. This is particularly true of what may be called "equilibrium economics"; it is less true of the theory of economic change and development, where purely economic abstractions are less useful and a broad interpretation of history is necessary.

Similarly, in the description of economic institutions there is not much contact with religion, though it may be relevant to point out how certain institutions, such as commercial or bank credit, depend on the existence of standards of individual honesty and integrity, which are themselves in part a product of religion. It is when we come to the study and interpretation of economic history, however, that the contact between religious and economic life becomes clear and significant, as we have shown earlier. In considerations of economic policy, also, the *ends* of society cannot be left out of the picture, and the abstractions of pure economics can only carry us a small part of the way. We may say, in fact, that in any field which involves the *application* of economic principles there is great danger among specialists of confounding abstraction with reality, and of drawing unwarranted conclusions from abstract logic.

The nature—and dangers—of the economic abstraction are so little understood, even among economists, that a brief digression on this topic may be in order. The focus of interest of economics is the *commodity*—that is, something which can be exchanged, produced, and consumed. Exchange, production, consumption, and accumulation are the main human activities on which economics concentrates. Economics is not, however, primarily interested in human behavior as such; it is interested in the "behavior of commodities." The world of commodities is something which is regarded as following its own laws of motion, like the planets of the solar system; the men who move them are not the focus of interest, any more than the angels, if any, who move the planets are a focus of interest of the astronomer. We know, of course, that in reality it is not commodities that behave, but men, and that commodity prices, outputs, accumulations, exchanges, and so on are ultimately the result of human behavior. But if human behavior is regular enough, it can be neglected, just as astronomers can neglect angels. And *in the mass* human behavior is fairly regular—which explains, incidentally, why so much of economics assumes the mass-interactions of perfect competition and why indeterminacy appears in the theory of oligopoly —i.e., in the interaction of *few* exchangers. It may be noticed incidentally that the same difficulty crops up in physics, where the law of behavior of gases, being a statistical law involving enormous numbers of molecules ("perfect competition"), is nicely determinate, but where much less is known about the behavior of individual molecules, and where the strangest indeterminacies crop up in the oligopolistic interactions of the few in the atom. This remoteness from human behavior is seen most clearly perhaps in the Keynesian economics, which consists of "models" (solar systems!) whose component variables (national income, consumption, investment) are vast statistical aggregates which enjoy cozy relationships among themselves but which are only distantly related to the millions of flesh-and-blood people of whose experiences these aggregate variables are in some sense a sum.

The economist is quite falsely accused of creating an "economic man"—that revolting creature of popular imagination who knows, in the words of Oscar Wilde, the price of everything and the value of nothing. If ever there was an economic man (which I doubt), he certainly died at the hands of Philip Wicksteed, a Unitarian minister, and perhaps the greatest economist of the late nineteenth century. In his *Common Sense of Political Economy* Wicksteed established economics firmly as a general theory of choice under conditions of limited resources, and the student who has read his illustrations of the theory of value in terms of how much one should shorten family prayers in order to speed a parting guest to the train, or how high a cliff one should jump off to save a mother-in-law will have little doubt of the generality of economic principles. It is evident from the above also that economics cannot be accused of being materialistic. Economics clearly recognizes that all material objects are intermediate goods, mere means which serve the end of increasing that ultimate spiritual product known technically as "Utility." The economist does not know what utility is, any more than the physicist knows what electricity is, but he certainly could not do without it.

The danger in the economic abstraction lies in its very success. I am not attacking abstraction as such—it is absolutely necessary if the huge complexity of human life-experience is to be reduced to manageable terms. Moreover, the economic abstraction is reasonably coherent and is very illuminating in the interpretation of history, both in the large and in the small. But because of its coherence, its beauty and its success, its practitioners—especially those skilled in mathematics—are apt to forget that it is an abstraction, and that it is men and not commodities that are the ultimate social reality. A good example of both the necessity and the danger of economic abstraction is found in the study of labor: unless we understand clearly that labor *is* a commodity, in spite of all pious pronouncements to the contrary, we shall never understand the phenomena of industrial relations. But we shall also not understand industrial relations unless we realize that labor is much *more* than a commodity, and that the labor-bargain involves a complex set of psychological, sociological, even theological relationships out of which the commodity aspect is abstracted.

It is at this point, I think, that the teacher whose acquaintance with religion is something more than secondhand can be of great help to his students, not only as persons but also as economists. To seek God is to find man. To live deeply with the life of Jesus, as revealed in the Gospels, is to know the glory, wonder, folly, and depravity of man in his fullness. Unless the economist has something of this sense of the fullness of man he will be in constant danger of misusing his abstraction, particularly as applied to the interpretation of history and in developing an appraisal of economic policy. It is not, of course, the business of a teacher to interlard his teaching with sermons, and there are, of course, the familiar dangers: the danger of using a position of authority in one field to give weight to opinions or indoctrinations in another; the danger of insensitivity to the religious susceptibilities of students of differing faiths on the the one hand, or of tampering with truth to avoid giving offense on the other. A teacher who makes clear, however, when he is speaking as a specialist and when as a whole person, and who approaches his task with a proper humility, can avoid these dangers and give his students a sense of the significance and setting of his specialized knowledge in a way that is impossible for one who never transgressed the narrow limits of his own discipline.

VI

It remains to consider some of the responsibilities of the economist toward the church—not so much toward the religious organization of which he is a member, as toward the "Church Invisible," of which the visible churches are manifestations. It is none the less true for being almost a cliché that the crisis of our age is at bottom a religious crisis. Religion, we feel, should be the Center of Town, the integrating factor in the welter of life, experience, and knowledge. There is sting in the remark of a Roman Catholic friend of mine that a State University is a "City of God that is all suburbs"; our innumerable specialties spread around the intellectual map in formless clusters, with only the most congested trickles of communication between them, and there seems to be no center which can relate one to the other. Because of this the increase of knowledge actually threatens to destroy us, and we are faced with the nightmare of infinite power in the hands of unregenerate man. The trouble is, of course, that the town has grown so big! The little medieval center, with its quaint narrow streets and lovely cathedral, is quite inadequate to handle the traffic of the vast suburbs that have grown up in the past three centuries. The highways that could handle the traffic from Ptolemy and Aristotle with comfort have hardly adjusted themselves to Copernicus and Darwin, and are hopelessly congested by Freud, Keynes, and Einstein! Consequently, the true center is by-passed, rival centers of nationalism, Fascism, Communism, and so on are set up, and the whole vast city threatens to disintegrate. And so we long for a new and greater Aquinas, to bring together once again Grace and Truth, Wisdom and Power, Faith and Knowledge, in blessed union.

In any such synthesis the social sciences must find a place. We are apt today to think of the natural sciences, with their ominous threat of atomic or bacteriological destruction, as the greatest danger to mankind. It may well be, however, that the social sciences, all of which seem to be on the threshold of a vast expansion of knowledge, ultimately constitute an even greater threat to human dignity, welfare, or even existence. In the sciences knowledge inevitably leads to power, and power is of itself neutral—it can be power for evil just as for good. Indeed, it may not even be neutral, for the existence of power may even predispose to evil. But whereas the natural sciences lead mainly to power over nature, the social sciences lead directly to power over man. The horrors of psychological and sociological warfare may exceed those of atomic warfare, for the physicist can merely kill and maim men's bodies, whereas the social psychologist may be able to kill and maim their souls. A greater nightmare than that of atomic destruction is that of a world tyranny resting on the unshakable foundation of social-scientific knowledge of the manipulation of men—the "Brave New Worlds" of Aldous Huxley or George Orwell. Between us and this triumph of learning, ingenuity, and respectability there stands that strange force in history which can only be called the Holy Spirit: the foolishness of God, the naïveté of children, and the disreputability of saints, this spirit of Christ, of divine love. Unless men—including scientists, social or natural—can be brought under the gentle domination of this spirit, all science is dismal, and leads to the damnation of man and not to his salvation, for knowledge leads to power, and power without holiness—i.e., the right will—is damnation.

To say that there is danger in knowledge and power does not mean, however, that there is virtue in ignorance and impotence. And even if there were, there seems to be no way short of catastrophe by which knowledge and power can be lost, any more than innocence can be regained. There is no way of uneating the Apple, no way back to the Garden of

Eden, and the only way out of the City of Destruction leads to the City of God, to the redemption and not the suppression of knowledge.

The economist, along with others who are gifted with specialized knowledge, has a responsibility here to bring his knowledge to the service of the church and to keep the channels of communication open between his own specialty and the "center of town." This task has its own special dangers. In a subject like economics which deals with the commonplaces of life and which for the most part uses the language of ordinary life, the specialist finds it difficult to be patient with the amateur, and is apt to pretend to a greater degree of certainty of knowledge than he possesses in order to impress the unspecialized. The professional economist is apt to be impatient with the "easy answers" of the preachers, such as prohibition, "sentimental unionism," and the "cooperative commonwealth." He faces on the one hand the naïve conservatism of fundamentalist Protestantism, with its limitation of interest to the grossly identifiable sins and its narrow concept of regeneration, and on the other hand the almost equally naïve liberalism of the "social gospel," with its emphasis on social sins which are not identifiable enough to trouble the individual conscience and its undue optimism in regard to regeneration by legislation. He is apt to be equally impatient with the millennialist crudities of Marxism, with its subtle substitution of moral judgments for intellectual analysis. On the other hand, his knowledge of the infinite complexities of social life is apt to paralyze his will-to-action and to breed a kind of sophisticated conservatism of hopelessness. For the sake of his own spiritual and intellectual health, the economist must face the challenge of prophetic indignation: on the other hand, the prophet also must be prepared to submit his moral insights to the rigorous discipline of intellectual analysis when it comes to translating these insights into policies.

13

POLITICAL SCIENCE

By JOHN H. HALLOWELL

I

It is probably a healthy sign of vitality that political scientists in recent years have been giving more and more attention to the problem of methodology. For there is much confusion among us as to what political science is and little agreement concerning its exact nature and scope. Yet, in concentrating our attention upon problems of method, it seems to me that we are approaching the problem backwards. We are all very much concerned about the research methods and teaching techniques which we ought to employ as political scientists, but we give little or no attention to the *kind* of knowledge of which we are in search. What *kind* of knowledge is it that we want to find and disseminate among our colleagues and students? We must first answer that question, it seems to me, before we can possibly decide whether the research techniques we are using will reveal the kind of information of which we are in search.

I do not mean, of course, that we can know in advance of our search exactly what we shall find, but I do mean that we have to know in advance of our search the *kind* of thing for which we are looking. Are we looking, for example, for causal laws of political behavior, or are we looking for principles that can guide us in making wise political decisions and means of implementing them in actual situations that confront us here and now? Is it ability to predict future political events, as some political scientists contend, that is or ought to be the distinguishing characteristic of political science? Or is the future only the record of decisions which we make here and now in the present? Should we look for "trends" in an effort to answer the question "What is likely to happen in the future?" or should we look for principles that will enable us better to answer the question "What ought we to do in this particular situation?" The kinds of questions we ask will determine in large part the kind of information we seek. And the way in which we frame our questions will influence the kind of knowledge we obtain.

Whether a method is a good one or not depends upon whether it will yield the kind of information we are looking for, whether it is appropriate to the object of our search. The physicist does not ask the kinds of questions which the philosopher asks and we do not expect the methods he employs to yield answers, therefore, to the questions which the philosopher asks. Neither do we expect the philosophical method to yield information about the physical laws of the universe or the structure of atoms. Should we use the method of the physicist or the method of the philosopher? Framed in this way the question is unanswerable. It all depends upon what *kind* of information we are looking for.

To many political scientists this does not appear as a problem because for them political science is simply concerned with the discovery and dissemination of the *facts* about politics. I think we can all agree upon that. Differences of opinion among us, however, immediately occur when we ask further: What *are* the facts? and, given the facts, What do they mean?

The facts about politics, or about anything else, are by no means self-evident and none of us, moreover, ever succeeds in knowing or imparting all of them. Facts do not present themselves to us already labeled but we attach labels to them. Facts do not seek us out but we seek them out. And the kind of facts we find depends upon the conceptual presuppositions from which we begin our search for them. The facts we find depend in large measure upon the kinds of *questions* we ask, and the kinds of questions we ask depend upon what we think it is both possible and appropriate to know.

None of us, moreover, ever succeeds in finding or in imparting all the facts about anything. Of necessity, and in order to be intelligible, we emphasize some facts and ignore others. When we undertake a research project or endeavor to describe the organization and function of some political institution to our students we have, of necessity, to employ some principle of selection in our choice of facts. We do not regard all facts as being equally significant but, consciously or subconsciously, focus our attention upon some facts and ignore others. If we do not consciously employ some principle of selection, if we do not employ some principle of evaluation in terms of which we decide that some facts are significant and others insignificant, we shall not succeed in being intelligible. The facts we find and present will be relevant to nothing and hence meaningless. Without an underlying principle of selection we shall have but a conglomeration of assorted facts without meaning or value. And no science was ever established upon a conglomeration of unrelated facts. It is not a distinguishing characteristic of the scientific method that it proceeds without some principle of selection. On the contrary, it is by adopting one principle of selection in preference to another that the various sciences are made possible and one is distinguished from another. Every science is interested in facts but each is interested in a different kind of fact. The object of knowledge is different in each case. And each science employs a method most appropriate to the discovery of that object.

Before we can decide what method is most appropriate for the study of politics we must first decide what the object of our search is. How do the kind of facts we want to find differ, for example, from those which the physicist wants to find? What kind of knowledge is peculiar to political science?

II

Whatever else political science may be concerned with it is certainly concerned first and foremost with the behavior of human beings. It is not concerned with the behavior of atoms. And while the methods of physics are entirely appropriate to the study of the behavior of atoms they are not appropriate to the study of human behavior unless, as some may declare— if only for the sake of argument—that man is nothing but a complex, physical apparatus. The very fact that we can entertain such a notion about ourselves, for the sake of argument, seems to me to be itself sufficient refutation of the fact which that argument seeks to uphold. Atoms don't argue. Human beings do. Atoms don't entertain conceptions about themselves but human beings do.

Atoms cannot deliberate over alternative ways of behaving but men can. A man can *think* about the situation in which he finds himself, he can entertain conceptions about the end or ends which he would like to achieve, and he can deliberate upon the means best calculated to achieve his purpose. Human behavior can never be completely explained in terms of the external forces acting upon it—we must always reckon with the human agent himself and with his freedom to choose between alternative ways of acting. While there are situations in which human behavior appears to be coerced or compelled by forces outside the control of the human agent, there are many more situations in which the individual is able to choose between alternative modes of action. Indeed, it is one of the distinguishing characteristics of humanity that man is able both to choose between alternative ways of acting and to deliberate upon that choice. This fact is both the source of man's greatness and the source of his degradation.

Now physics is a science which deals with things which cannot possibly be otherwise than they are. It is concerned with relations which are entirely independent of human volition.

It is a search for *necessary* relations. But because political science deals with the behavior of human beings it is not a science of that kind. The behavior of human beings is never completely predictable but only probable. Political science is concerned not with that which is absolutely necessary but with that which is contingent. It deals with things which may be other than they are. And for that reason it is not a speculative science but a practical one.

Because it is a practical science, political science is more like engineering than it is like physics. The physicist is interested in discovering the physical laws of the universe for their own sake. Whether his discoveries have any practical significance or application is not his concern. But the practical application of the principles discovered by physics is the peculiar concern of the engineer. The engineer is not interested in the principles of physics for their own sake but in order that he may design and construct bridges, and not bridges in the abstract but particular bridges at particular places. Obviously, he must know something about the principles of physics if the bridges he builds are not to collapse but he does not need to know as much about these principles as the physicist does, nor to know them in exactly the same way.

Similarly, political science is a practical science. It is concerned with speculation, not for the sake of speculation, but for the sake of *action*. It is not concerned with the abstract "will" to achieve an abstract "power" but with the particular wills of particular individuals in specific places. An abstract "will" is a nonexistent will and a "power" divorced from the strivings of particular individuals is a nonexistent "power." Power describes a two-way relationship between individuals and in every power relationship there is an element of consent, be it small or large. Since power is not a substantive thing but a relational concept, since it exists only in purposeful action, it can never be a self-sufficient end but only a means toward the attainment of purposes or ends more ultimate than power itself. One of the inadequacies of the definition of politics as a struggle for power is that it obscures, if it does not obliterate, the *purposes* in terms of which power is sought and used and the conflict of purposes out of which politics emerges.

For it is the conflict of purposes that characterizes politics —not the struggle for a "power" divorced from all purposeful motivation. Politics emerges out of the conflict among the wills and interests of particular individuals living in particular societies. And politics is successful when it succeeds in reconciling these individual wills and interests in terms of an interest or good which is common to all. The end of politics is policy—the integration of conflicting interests in terms of certain interests and values which are held in common. The statesman differs from the ordinary politician in that he is able to envisage and inspire support for policies that are in the *ultimate*, best interest of the most people, and however rare the statesman may be, we think of him rightly as the politician par excellence. To the extent that the ordinary politician's vision is limited to that which is immediately expedient, to the extent that he is motivated by narrow, sectional, group or personal interests, we think of him as a failure and the more narrow his vision and selfish his aim the greater the failure.

Although politics comes into being as the result of the conflict between individual wills and interests it presupposes the existence of an interest or good which is common to all, for without this basis for reconciliation there could be no politics. There is a sense in which politics may accurately be described as the art of compromise. But compromise can never be the end of politics because no one likes compromise for its own sake. We are willing to make compromises, when we do make them, because we value some things more than we do the things which we are compromising. Compromise presupposes some agreement upon principles in terms of which compromise may take place. Without some conception of a common good, of a good which is the same for all of us as human beings, there would be no possibility of reconciling our differences in terms of a common purpose or policy, and, hence, no politics.

As a practical science political science is interested in knowledge not for the sake of knowledge alone but for the sake of action. And the action at which politics aims is policy, and, more specifically, legislation. For it is through legislation that policy takes shape and form and the coercive power of the state is put behind it. But the policy at which politics aims is not just any policy but a policy designed to promote the good or well-being of the persons for whom it is designed. The legislation which embodies policy, if it is to command the allegiance and respect of those for whom it is framed, must conform in intention and in content to that which is just. For although men can be compelled, at least outwardly, to obey a bad or unjust law their interests and wills will not be truly reconciled and integrated unless that law is a just one and politics, as we have said, aims at reconciliation and integration. A strong, stable, and genuine political order depends upon the freely given consent of the governed and although a spurious kind of consent can be manufactured to a degree through the techniques of propaganda, a genuine, freely given consent can never be coerced into existence. Despite its outward appearance of strength a tyranny is actually the most unstable form of government. It is the political manifestation not of order but of anarchy. Compulsion replaces consent in every sphere of life because there is no common agreement obliging consent in any sphere.

I have suggested earlier that there is a similarity between political science and engineering, for both, I have argued, are practical rather than theoretical sciences. But there is also a significant difference between them. For the one is concerned with *doing* and the other with *making*. The objects with which engineering deals are inanimate, material things and the engineer is concerned with shaping or making those things into useful objects, such as buildings, bridges, highways, etc. The materials are transformed by the engineer in conformity with some useful purpose which he has in mind. The purpose does not inhere in the things themselves but in the mind of the engineer. Engineering is a science of making things, a productive science or technology. The products of technology may be used for good purposes or bad, but once made the technician's task is completed.

The objects with which engineering deals are inanimate, material things but the objects with which political science is concerned are human beings—human beings who are not things but souls, or, if you like, personalities. Human beings cannot be manipulated like material objects and any attempt to do so will be destructive of their very essence. They are not like so many bricks or pieces of steel that have only to be laid in the right place according to a blueprint. They can cooperate or rebel. Moreover "we do not build a state to live *in* (as we live in a house)—we live the state. Our living state is an integral part of our lives. Here the builders are what they build." [1]

Political science is unlike engineering in that it is not technology, it is concerned with *doing* rather than with making. In order for political science to accomplish its purpose the knowledge it provides must be translated into human action. And political science comes into being in order to assist men in doing that which they are naturally predisposed to do. Man is by nature a social being. He requires the fellowship and services of other men. He does not create society but is born into it. Steel doesn't have to be made into bridges, it has no inherent predisposition to be anything—it can be manipulated and used in any fashion the engineer decides is appropriate to his purpose. But human beings are predisposed to live in society and embody ends in themselves. Men are not content

[1] Helmut Kuhn, "Thought and Action," *Journal of Politics*, Vol. VIII, No. 4, p. 457.

to exist, it is not life alone they want but a good life. And political science comes into being in order to assist men in finding the means that will foster a good life among men.

For these reasons political science is more like the physician's art than it is like the science of engineering. The normal body of the human organism naturally tends towards health. When the body becomes diseased or disordered medical therapy consists in trying to help the organism to cure itself, to assist nature in doing what nature is already predisposed to do. The physician ministers to ends which nature itself pursues. So political science ministers to an end which is not of its own devising but which is inherent in life itself. It comes into being in order to help men to live a good life in society. It does not invent that end but finds that end inherent in all human striving. The task of the statesman is more like the task of the physician than it is like the task of the engineer. It is practical wisdom rather than productive knowledge that is required both of the statesman and of the physician. The statesman is not concerned with making anything but rather with inspiring right action, and right action cannot be divorced from right reason for "to divorce action from thought in politics means to sever the conscience of mankind from its deeds." [2]

If all this be true what then can be said about the kind of knowledge at which political science aims? It seems to me that the kind of knowledge at which political science aims, or ought to aim, is practical knowledge of the best means of promoting justice among men. I say justice because justice is the name we use to describe a good life in society. The best political order will be a just one—when each member of that order fulfills those social tasks for which he is best fitted by virtue and capacity and each is rewarded in proportion to his contribution. No actual political order is ever completely just and each falls short in some way or another of perfection, but by having a standard of justice we are enabled to recognize these short-

[2] *Ibid.* p. 476.

comings and to know in what particulars actual political systems fall short of the ideal. Not only must the political scientist know what ideally is the best constitution for the state but he must investigate the various types of existing constitutions in order to discover how they fall short of the ideal, in what particulars, and how they can can be improved. He must try to discover what kind of constitution or system of government is best suited to particular peoples at particular times and places. He must investigate the causes of revolution, how constitutions in general and particular constitutions have been and are liable to be destroyed. He must investigate how government can be operated most efficiently in order to realize the ends for which it exists. He must consider how much or how little regulation of this or that activity will best promote justice among the members of the particular society. He must consider the foreign policy which a particular state ought to pursue in order to promote justice among the nations and peoples of the world and the best means of defending the integrity of the state from those who would destroy it, whether through internal rebellion or external aggression. In short, the function of political science, as I see it, is not simply the description of existing policy and governmental organization but the analysis of that policy and organization in terms of the end for which the state exists. Perhaps the task of politics has never been more succinctly expressed than in the words of Pascal, when he said: "It is right that what is just should be obeyed; it is necessary that what is strongest should be obeyed. Justice without power is impotent and power without justice is tyrannical. We must then combine justice and power, and for this end make what is just strong or what is strong just." The reconciliation of power and justice through law is the never-ending task of politics. A political science that concentrates upon problems of power to the neglect of considerations of justice is concerned, at best, with but one-half of the political problem.

The way in which we conceive of the end of the state depends upon what we conceive to be the end of man. Before we can decide whether a policy is a good one, whether it will promote the best interests of human beings, we must first ask ourselves: What *is* man? What is his essential nature and ultimate destiny? And in seeking answers to these questions we may very well be led to ask an additional question, namely, Whose is man? It is not, indeed, the function of political science to answer these questions, but political science cannot adequately fulfill the tasks peculiar to it until it has sought answers to these questions and sought them from the disciplines most competent to answer them. The political scientist cannot know whether the means he prescribes are appropriate, adequate, and possible unless he knows the nature of man and the end for which he is destined. For knowledge concerning the nature of man and that which is good for him as a human being, political science must, of necessity, look outside itself to other disciplines. It must look to psychology, to philosophy, especially to ethics and religion.

What difference does it make to politics and to political science what conception of man we accept? It makes, it seems to me, just this difference—that our political philosophies and systems of government will be based upon conceptions of man's nature and destiny that are more or less true. If our conception of man's essential nature and ultimate destiny is false, i.e. unreal, we may be led to seek and apply political solutions to human and social problems that at best are useless and at worst harmful. For the way in which we conceive of the proper functions of the state, the limitations which ought to be imposed upon its activities or the lack of limitations will depend upon what we think about the capacities and predispositions of men and the purpose of human existence.

It is my conviction, shared by many others and based upon a study of the historical evidence, that the present-day crisis in which we find ourselves is in large part the product of the unsuccessful attempt of modern times to found our political philosophies and systems of government upon a conception of man that ignores or minimizes his capacity for evil and hence has no adequate means of dealing with it. It is impossible within the scope of this essay to do more than suggest what I mean but I have tried in another place to explain what I mean in more detail and with considerable more evidence than can be brought forth here.[3] As a consequence I shall simply summarize a few of my conclusions.

III

Ever since the seventeenth century we have been experimenting with the possibility of "freeing" ourselves from the Christian revelation. Divorcing reason from faith, rejecting the belief that man is the dependent creature of God, we have progressively put our faith in the autonomy of human reason and human will. For a time we sought to preserve the Christian ethics while at the same time we rejected the Christian religion. This experiment has borne fruit in the twentieth century in the repudiation of reason, in the deterioration of the Christian conscience, and in the enslavement of men's bodies and souls under the yoke of totalitarian tyranny.

For a long time the dominant climate of opinion politically was that of liberalism. As originally conceived by men like John Locke, for example, liberalism embodied an uneasy compromise between the Christian beliefs of the Middle Ages and the secular philosophy of the Renaissance. Incompatible ideas were merged. It accepted, for example, the Christian conception of the absolute value of human personality and the spiritual equality of individuals. But it radically departed from the Christian tradition in asserting its belief in the autonomy of individual will and in the essential goodness of man. It posited

[3] See J. H. Hallowell, *Main Currents in Modern Political Thought* (New York: Henry Holt & Co., 1950).

the existence of a transcendental order of truth which was accessible to man's natural reason and capable of evoking a moral response and it sought to reconcile the autonomous will of the individual with the demands of this transcendental order through appeals to individual conscience. Thus individual conscience is the keystone of the whole liberal structure, for it is upon individual conscience that the choice between order and anarchy ultimately devolves. In the seventeenth century that conscience was still a Christian conscience but it could not and did not long survive the attempt to separate the Christian ethic from the Christian religion. What appeared "self-evidently" true to the seventeenth-century mind that was still close to the medieval Christian tradition was destined to appear less self-evident as the mind of men progressively "freed" itself from the Christian revelation and the authority of the church.

With the progressive deterioration of the Christian conscience and the substitution in the nineteenth century, through the influence of positivism, of an immanent conception of order, freedom rapidly degenerated into license and the will of men was left without any substantive restraints. Formal procedure alone imposed limitations and since these were but formal limitations they proved to be no real limitations at all. It was no longer a question of "what" one did that was important but "how" one did it. For the early liberal freedom under the law meant freedom from unjust compulsion but to the positivistically minded liberal of the nineteenth century it came to mean simply freedom from illegal compulsion. When the conception of legality was divorced from the conception of justice and positive law was declared to be the only true law, freedom came to mean that the individual was free to do whatever the state had not yet forbidden him to do. Under the influence of positivism the rights of individuals were conceived more and more simply to be concessions to individual claims which the state might or might not choose to make. Although liberalism originally arose in opposition to tyranny it gradually degenerated under the impact of positivism into a theory that was entirely congenial with the rise of tyranny.

Lulled into complacent self-satisfaction by the liberal positivistic doctrine of the nineteenth century, modern man became a blind devotee of the goddess Progress, who, he believed, bestowed her blessings upon man in the form of increased knowledge and control over nature through an automatic and impersonal process, in which man, at best, was but a passive tool of Nature or of History. Where in former times men had looked to God for the salvation of their souls, they now looked to science and technology for the gratification of their desires. Paradise on earth was substituted for eternal spiritual salvation as an inspiration worthy of men's efforts. And this paradise on earth waited only upon the proper execution of a plan to be discovered in the truths and with the methods of the natural sciences. It required no sacrifice on the part of man, no change in his way of life, no moderation of his appetites—it required simply the application of intelligence, directed by science, to social problems. Progress was conceived as automatic, irreversible, and inevitable. Time alone would heal all wounds, cure all evils, and solve all problems. This, at least, was man's fervent hope and his faith.

But the optimism that characterized the nineteenth century has given way in the twentieth to a deep-rooted despair. Most men today no longer believe that progress is automatic, irreversible, or inevitable, though many still cling, if with much less assurance than formerly, to a belief in science and technology as the way out of our difficulties. With the invention of the atom bomb and work begun upon a bomb of even greater destructive power modern man realizes, if he has not realized it before, that the blessings of science are not unmixed, that science can be used for evil purposes as well as good and that science itself is silent as to the use which shall and should be made of its products. Evil has manifested itself so unmistakably in the twentieth century that modern man finds it increasingly difficult to deny its existence.

The liberals of the last century denied the reality of evil and ascribed the appearance of evil in the world to faulty political institutions and to lack of "enlightenment." They proposed to eliminate this "evil" by education and political reform. The Marxians ascribed the appearance of evil in the world to the prevailing capitalistic mode of production, to the private ownership of the means of production, and to the class conflict engendered by that institution. Evil would disappear inevitably and automatically, they predicted, with the establishment of a classless society through the medium of revolution and the dictatorship of the proletariat. With the distribution of material goods in accordance with men's needs, men would no longer be frustrated in their search for material satisfaction and all evil would disappear. Both liberals and Marxians ascribed whatever evil there is in the world to bad or faulty institutions. But why these institutions, political and economic, should be so bad, and so much in need of reform, if men are essentially good is a question to which neither liberalism nor Marxism has a very satisfactory answer.

In recent years one of America's most astute thinkers, Reinhold Niebuhr, has recalled to our consciousness a fact which both liberalism and Marxism have ignored with almost fatal consequences to our civilization. Evil, he points out, is something real, not an appearance only, and the proper name for it is sin. Its locus is not in institutions, which are but a reflection of human purposes, but in human nature itself. It is pride, self-righteousness, greed, envy, hatred, and sloth that are the real evils and the ones from which social evils spring. When man is thwarted in his attempts to realize justice it is because he is thwarted by his own sinful predisposition. The recognition of this inherent predisposition to sin helps to explain why the best laid plans of men never quite succeed.

The deficiency of both liberal and Marxist social theory "is derived from their common effort to understand man without considering the final dimension of his spirit: his transcendent freedom over both the natural and historical process in which he is involved. This freedom accounts for both the creative and destructive possibilities in human history." [4] It is the transcendence of man's spirit over the physical and historical processes which distinguishes man from the beast. It is for this reason that man can never be completely comprehended or explained in physical terms alone. The sex impulse which man shares with the animal is never as purely biological in man as it is in the beast. Sex in man is bound up with love and when man endeavors to make the sexual act a purely biological experience it is only by an act of perversion that he is able to do so. Only man is capable of perverting his natural impulses, animals are not. The same thing is true of economic desires. They are never purely biological but they, too, have a spiritual dimension. Professor Niebuhr has explained this very well when he says:

> Economic desires are never merely the expression of the hunger or the survival impulse in human life. The desires for 'power and glory' are subtly compounded with the more primeval impulse. The lion's desire for food is satisfied when his maw is crammed. Man's desire for food is more easily limited than other human desires; yet the hunger impulse is subject to the endless refinements and perversions of the gourmand. Shelter and raiment have much more extensible limits than food. Man's coat is never merely a cloak for his nakedness but the badge of his vocation, or the expression of an artistic impulse, or a method of attracting the other sex, or a proof of social position. Man's house is not merely his shelter but, even more than his raiment, the expression of his personality and the symbol of his power, position and prestige.[5]

[4] Reinhold Niebuhr, *The Children of Light and the Children of Darkness* (New York: Charles Scribner's Sons, 1944), pp. 59-60.
[5] *Ibid.*, pp. 61-62.

Marx believed that with the coming of Communism it would be possible to satisfy men's wants, that no one would want more than "enough," and that when these material wants were satisfied all crime would disappear and everyone would live forever after in peace and harmony with his neighbor. But his hope is a delusion, for it is based upon a conception of human nature that is false. It ignores the spiritual dimensions of men's wants which are never purely biological or material, but are always compounded with a desire for power and for glory.

The crisis of our times manifests itself most vividly in the rise of the totalitarian dictatorship and in the contempt for human personality that grows everywhere more ominous. Because men have lost sight of the image of God in man, man has become progressively dehumanized. The inhumanity of man to man has manifested itself in varying degrees throughout the ages man has lived but not until modern times has man's inhumanity to man been pursued as a matter of principle. As one writer points out:

> We are entering an inhuman world, a world of inhumanness, inhuman not merely in fact, but in principle as well. Inhumanity has begun to be presented as something noble, surrounded with an aureole of heroism. Over against man there rises a class or a race, a deified collective or state . . . No longer is every man held to be a man, a value, the image and likeness of God . . . The old bestialism, naïve, barbarian, instinctive, was not self-conscious; it was pre-conscious. But modern bestialism is conscious, deliberate, the product of reflection and civilization, self-justified . . .
>
> The new world which is taking form is moved by other values than the value of man or of human personality, or the value of truth: it is moved by such values as power, technics, race-purity, nationality, the state, the collective. The will to justice is overcome by the will to power. The dialectic of this process is very delicate. Man desires power, power for himself, but this leads him to put power above self, above man; it leads him to readiness to sacrifice his own humanity for the sake of power. Power is objectified and drawn away from human ex-

istence. Such values as those of technics, the state, the race or the class bestialize man: for the sake of these sorts of power, any desired treatment of the individual is permitted.[6]

Having alienated himself from God, having discredited the reason with which he was endowed by God, unable or unwilling to identify the evil in the world for what it is—modern man oscillates between extravagant optimism and hopeless despair. As his optimism is shattered more and more by the force of events he sinks lower and lower into the slough of despond. In his despondency he is tempted to strike out against the enemy he cannot identify, whose name he does not know, in desperate action. In his anxiety to escape from utter futility and a meaningless existence, he is tempted to give up his most priceless heritage—his freedom—to any man or movement which even promises deliverance from insecurity and futility. He is tempted to put his faith in the most absurd doctrine, to submit his will to the most brutal dictator, if only he can find that for which he longs with all the passion of his being—a meaningful existence, a life worth living, a way of life worth dying to preserve. Men have turned away from God only to worship false gods and have demonstrated that men's religious aspirations cannot be denied, though they may be perverted.

Today we are confronted with just such a perverted religion, namely, Communism. And we have underestimated its power because we have underestimated the passion which informs it. It is not simply an economic doctrine, a political theory, a different social system but a gospel of salvation through revolution. It promises men deliverance from exploitation and oppression through the medium of revolution and the dictatorship of the proletariat and it embodies a faith for which men are willing to die. The answer to it does not lie ultimately in the atom bomb or in superior military strength but in a faith that is stronger because it is based upon a conception of man

[6] Nicholas Berdyaev, *The Fate of Man in the Modern World* (London: Student Christian Movement Press, Ltd., 1935), pp. 28 ff.

and his destiny that is truer. Our civilization hangs on the brink of the abyss not simply because of the external threats that confront it but because of the internal disintegration of the faith upon which that civilization was established. That faith has its roots in Greek philosophy, in Hebrew prophecy, in Roman law, and, especially, in the Christian religion.

For Christianity has taught us to respect every individual as a soul created in the image and likeness of God, to recognize that (irrespective of our color, our race or our creed) we are all children of the same God. It has taught us that, because we have a destiny that transcends time and, as a consequence, responsibilities that transcend the demands of the particular time and society in which we live, we must have the freedom proportionate to those responsibilities and the rights that are derived from those obligations. It has taught us that there is a law greater than the law of any state, that there is a will greater than the will of any individual or majority of individuals, and that no state can claim our total allegiance. It has taught us that the state exists to promote the good of human persons, that the state exists for men, not men for the state. It has taught us to establish just relations among men but to administer justice with the compassionate knowledge that other men's sins are our own sins and that in their sinning we sin as well. It has taught us, where possible with God's help, to go beyond the demands of justice and to love one another as God loves us. It has taught us that the redemption of the world and of ourselves is not an undertaking for which we are alone responsible, that God is merciful and stands ready to forgive and help those who ask his forgiveness and help. It has taught us that only by aiming above the world can we hope to transform and master the world.[7]

[7] For an introduction to the Christian faith see A. E. Taylor, *Does God Exist?* (New York: The Macmillan Co., 1947); C. S. Lewis, *The Case for Christianity* (New York: The Macmillan Co., 1944), *The Problem of Pain* (New York: The Macmillan Co., 1944), *Miracles* (New York: The Macmillan Co., 1947).

Christianity is not a political philosophy nor an economic program and it provides no short cuts to economic prosperity, social stability, or political order. It does not lessen the need to study our political, social, and economic institutions and to institute reforms or formulate programs which may improve our political and social structure. But it does give us a perspective and provide us with principles in terms of which we may accomplish these tasks better than we would without them. It saves us, moreover, from the illusion that we can establish a system which is perfect or make a reform which is final. Christianity provides us with a realistic conception of man which neither overrates man's motives nor underestimates his potentialities. If man is a sinner, he is also, potentially, a saint. The Christian understanding of man helps us to avoid the extremes both of illusive optimism and of hopeless despair. Christianity enables us to place our political, social, and economic aspirations in proper perspective, subordinating them to an aspiration which should include but transcend them. For no political, social, or economic system is an end in itself, all systems are but means to a more ultimate end and they are good only to the extent that they assist individuals to realize their potentialities as human beings who belong ultimately to God. Christ taught us not to seek peace, or security, or happiness but to seek *first* the Kingdom of God and His righteousness and promised us that if we did so we should then attain the only lasting peace, security, and happiness there is.

There is a truth in liberalism, according to one writer, which modern liberal thought has tried to preserve without its foundations.

> The truth of the liberal idea is that man cannot be confined to his political relationships. He is more than a brick in the social edifice. 'The Christian Revolution' in the ancient world was an affirmation of this truth based upon the positive doctrine of man as a creature of God, with his life reaching out to an eternal world and thereby affecting his life in this . . .

Modern liberal thought tried to preserve the truth without its foundations. It affirmed the dignity of the human person, not in the name of something larger than his social relationships would warrant, but of something smaller. It claimed liberty for the individual man, not on the ground that man is a creature with one part of his being in the eternal world, but on the ground that as a political atom he has a right to exist in himself . . . Instead of claiming liberties *for* the pursuit of positive social purposes directed by man's spiritual relationships, it encouraged demands for liberty *from* this or that encroachment.

In consequence of liberalism's emancipation from the religious basis of freedom for positive ends, the modern world has earned, not a secular freedom, but a drift towards social disintegration that is sending men in self-protection into the arms of oppressive collectivisms.

Our task is therefore to recover, in the conditions of the present world, that positively religious conception of human life that will alone save us from the consequence of the assumption that the State is the source of community instead of an instrument of it . . . It has been for want of an organic relation between man's secular and spiritual life that the natural social functions of industry, commerce, education, family and regional politics have lost a sense of purpose . . .

The *'primacy of the spiritual'* must be upheld, not as a retreat from the secular tasks of life, but as a condition of handling them aright.[8]

Freedom is not an end in itself but a means only, and only when it is directed by the love of God to do His will here on earth do we genuinely experience it. Only in "perfect service" to God is there "perfect freedom."

To the Christian, therefore, man is made for community not only through his membership in a particular human group but also by virtue of his membership in the family of God. Nature and history have bound him to his fellows in the group by ties of sex, blood, division of labor, language, and tradition. But over and above these ties there is a spiritual bond which unites

[8] V. A. Demant, *Theology of Society* (London: Faber & Faber, Ltd., 1947), pp. 64–65, 66. (Italics added.)

him to the universal community of those who seek to do God's will through love of their neighbors. This community is actual in the Church which is its first-fruits, but ideally it should include all humanity. It will, of course, never be realized fully among the kingdoms of this world, for the forces of egoism and pride are arrayed against it. But those whose first loyalty is to it must seek, wherever they are, a form of society which will provide an order of justice and good will and thus approximate in some measure the more perfect love of the Kingdom.[9]

The Christian insists that the only genuine and solid basis of community is love and justice. Such a conception of the community provides us not only with a standard of judgment upon every society but suggests a way in which we may work for that for which all of us long, namely a world community. To a world plunged into despair, anxious and frantic in its search for some measure of security, the Christian hope shines like a star in the heavens, a beacon to all men of good will.

But until we have brought order out of the riot of our desires, until we have ordered our own souls, we cannot expect to create order in the world. The disorder in the world is but a reflection of the disorder in our own lives. The matter has been put succinctly in the epistle of James when he says: "From whence come wars and fightings among you? come they not hence even of your lusts that war in your members? Ye lust and have not; ye kill, and desire to have, and cannot obtain: ye fight and war, yet ye have not, because ye ask not. Ye ask, and receive not, because ye ask amiss, that ye may consume it upon your lusts." (4:1–3) A modern writer has expressed it in this way:

We express no hyperbole in asserting that what is, humanly speaking, the greatest of all achievements, the rebuilding of a civilization, must yet, in the language of ultimate seriousness, be described as a by-work. It is true, as organizers of the peace of the world we must strain every nerve to push on in the direc-

[9] George F. Thomas, "Christianity and Democracy," *The Vitality of the Christian Tradition* (New York: Harper & Bros., 1944), p. 353.

tion in which the Charter of the United Nations points. As organizers of justice at home we must strive with might and main to discard the social evils created by the capitalist system. But in so doing we shall remember that except the Lord build the house, they labor in vain that build it. The very devotion which we give to the labor of construction must flow from a greater devotion, and all the self-giving love which we put into our handiwork must be a sacrifice and thank-offering. Organizing peace on earth is a gigantic task. To be successful in it, in a measure, we shall have to conceive of it not in the spirit of a giant world-builder (the giant might soon discover that he is a pygmy) but of a copyist, with the peace of God before us as a model.[10]

IV

Something remains to be said about the obligations of the teacher of political science. Whether the teacher be a teacher of political science or of any other subject the obligations will be very much the same. Certainly it is the paramount obligation of every teacher to find and disseminate the truth to the best of his ability. If he is loyal to this objective we can tolerate every divergence of opinion, expect that there will be wide divergences, and we can hope that out of the arguments and counterarguments generated by these differences of opinion that we shall come closer to the absolute truth which eludes us all. What is not tolerable is the belief, often feigned, that there is no truth about anything. For if there is no truth about anything the whole learning and teaching process is meaningless. Education degenerates into sophistry and learning becomes propaganda. To say that it is the obligation of every teacher to pursue the truth is not the same thing as to say that he has the truth. None of us ever knows the whole truth about anything and everyone's grasp of the truth he does know will be mixed with error. But only if we are in *search* of the truth

[10] Helmut Kuhn, "The Classical Christian Tradition and the Emerging World," *Theology Today*, January 1946, p. 449.

will we be enabled to correct one another's errors and arrive at a truth that is more complete.

It is only in terms of a truth which is absolute, universal, and eternal that we can say that individual judgments concerning that truth are relative, partial, and particular. To assert, as is common today, that "all truth is relative" is to speak a contradiction, for we cannot even assert this as truth without denying what we have just said. From the fact that individual conceptions of the truth are always incomplete and partially in error, it does not logically follow that all truth is relative but rather that all individuals are fallible. This does not mean that all individual judgments are equally fallible, for there are degrees of truth and degrees of fallibility. It seems to me that the contention which we frequently encounter today, that there is no truth because all individual judgments are fallible, is a confession not of humility but of despair, not of contrition but of loss of faith. Although genuine humility is a virtue, and one that ought to be cultivated by teachers especially, we should not mistake despair of finding the truth for humility. G. K. Chesterton has pointed out that

> . . . what we suffer from today is humility in the wrong place. Modesty has moved from the organ of ambition. Modesty has settled upon the organ of conviction; where it was never meant to be. A man was meant to be doubtful about himself, but undoubting about the truth; this has been exactly reversed. Nowadays the part of a man that a man does assert is exactly the part he ought not to assert—himself. The part he doubts is exactly the part he ought not to doubt—the Divine Reason. Huxley preached a humility content to learn from Nature. But the new sceptic is so humble that he doubts if he can learn . . . The old humility made a man doubtful about his efforts, which might make him work harder. But the new humility makes a man doubtful about his aims, which will make him stop working altogether . . . We are on the road to producing a race of men too modest to believe in the multiplication table. We are in danger of seeing philosophers who doubt the law of gravity as being a mere fancy of their own. Scoffers of old times were

> too proud to be convinced; but these are too humble to be con-
> vinced. The meek do inherit the earth; but the modern sceptics
> are too meek even to claim their inheritance.[11]

Despair disguised as humility and indifference parading as
tolerance are manifestations of the sickness of the modern
world. It is not our reason that we should distrust but ourselves and only if our love of truth is greater than our fear of
error can we learn anything. The most humbling experience
of all is the search for truth and if we would cultivate humility
there is no better way than trying to find the truth. It is not
the scholar and teacher who is in search of the truth that men-
aces the educational process but the teacher who contends
that there is no such thing as truth but only opinion. For such
a belief leads to a dogmatism that is impervious to argument
and inaccessible to rational scrutiny. You can argue with a
man who believes in the truth but you can't argue with a man
who says everything is a matter of opinion.

The teacher has not only the obligation to present the truth
of any matter as he conceives it to be but also to explain how
he arrived at it. He will not insist, of course, that his students
agree with everything he has said but he will let the argument
and the evidence speak for itself. He will himself be receptive
to counterargument and counterevidence and will encourage
his students to take issue with him when they feel so inclined.
The atmosphere of the classroom should be one of tolerance
but not one of anarchy. To the extent that it is humanly possible, reason and not personality should dominate the pro-
ceedings.

One of the most common complaints among students today
is that their professors are reluctant to tell them "what they
believe." And I think the students are often justified in their
complaint. For if the teacher who has been trained as a specialist in some particular field of inquiry refuses to venture any

[11] G. K. Chesterton, *Orthodoxy* (New York: Dodd, Mead & Co., 1947),
pp. 55–56.

opinion of his own, to whom is the student to turn for counsel? If the student knows as much as the teacher does, if his judgment is just as good as the teacher's, why is the teacher teaching and the student learning? Of course no teacher is infallible, but one need not be infallible in order to venture an opinion. The students are impatient, and rightly so, with an "objectivity" which refrains from decisions, for objectivity does not mean that we should avoid making evaluations but rather that our judgments should be based upon reason and objective evidence. The practical consequences of an "objectivity" which refrains from decisions have been amply documented by Julien Benda in his *Treason of the Intellectuals* and we saw in the rise of Nazism in Germany how the "objectivity" of German university professors contributed to that end. If professors of political science have nothing important or significant to say about political policies and decisions, they cannot very well complain when their students turn to demagogues for more specific instruction.

Some teachers may reply that the function of the teacher, as they conceive it, is to teach students to think but not to think anything in particular. This, I believe, is an impossibility, for you can only learn to think by thinking *about* something. There is no such thing as "thinking" in the abstract. A person can no more think and yet think nothing than he can see and yet see nothing. To think means to think about something and arrive at some conclusion, however tentative. One of the tests of sound thinking is the ability to discriminate, the ability to distinguish the significant from the insignificant. Training in thinking, if it is to accomplish its purpose, must certainly include training in evaluation. To avoid evaluation is to avoid thinking.

The teacher has an obligation not only to explain how he arrives at his conclusions, by what process of reasoning and in the light of what evidence, but also to share with his students the presuppositions in the light of which he examines the evi-

dence and follows his reason. For underlying all of our thinking there are certain presuppositions in the light of which
thought is made possible. Very often we are unaware of the
existence of these presuppositions but they are there nevertheless and one of our tasks is to uncover them. Not all of us,
of course, have the same presuppositions but all of us do begin
our thinking, of necessity, from certain principles which we
regard as true and in the light of which we interpret what we
observe. The presuppositions in terms of which we identify
facts are as important as are the facts themselves. We have
an obligation as teachers, therefore, not only to present the
facts but also the presuppositions, so far as we know what they
are, in terms of which we recognize certain things as facts.

There is a rather large group among us which contends that
it has no presuppositions. These are the positivists. They
reject all metaphysical speculation and ethical evaluation as
irrelevant, yet in rejecting it as irrelevant they, too, begin their
thinking from a premise which they accept as self-evidently
true. And, as a matter of fact, the positivist can achieve *meaning* for the facts which he describes only by engaging in the
kind of metaphysical speculation he denounces as improper.
When he insists that we should confine ourselves to the description of those "positive facts" which can be observed without transcending our immediate sensory experience, he is
insisting upon the impossible, for it is only in terms of categories that precede our experience that we are able to experience anything at all. Far from abandoning metaphysical
speculation and ethical evaluation the positivist, of necessity,
indulges in it unconsciously and uncritically. By claiming that
his conclusions are "scientifically" rather than metaphysically
derived he removes his metaphysical presuppositions from the
scrutiny and criticism of reason. The very causal principle in
terms of which he seeks to explain things is not itself provable
by the methods of science but is a metaphysical principle
which science must accept in order to do its work. Science

itself rests upon a faith in a kind of universe the existence of which it cannot prove by scientific methods but the existence of which it must assume if science is to do its work.

The positivist who claims that his conclusions are true, and, of course, all positivists make this claim, must necessarily transcend the empirical observation of successive events. The positivist starts, as the late Professor Alfred N. Whitehead has pointed out, from "an instinctive faith that there is an Order of Nature which can be traced in every detailed occurrence," and tends to believe that the reason for his faith is "the apprehension of its truth." But, as Whitehead cautions, "the formation of a general idea—such as the idea of the Order of Nature—and the grasp of its importance and the observation of its exemplification in a variety of occasions are by no means the necessary consequences of the truth of the idea in question." [12] The world as the positivist sees it "exhibits . . . an involution of paths and a concatenation of circumstances which have arisen entirely by chance. We can describe what has happened but with that description all possibility of knowledge ends." [13] But to claim *truth* for this description the positivist must transcend the methods of science. As one writer has put it:

> To retain . . . the distinction of truth and falsity *even for science alone* we have to enlarge the scientific world and in enlarging it to modify it deeply, for what is added is not something of the same order but something different in kind, not having even an analogy with the rest. Knowing, the process that has to other events the unique relation of apprehending them, is above the causal order, in the sense that, although in it, it also knows it. Science as knowing transcends the scientific world; its claim to be true lifts it above the type of order its content depicts. Deny the claim and the content is worthless; admit the claim and the content is set in a larger context.

[12] A. N. Whitehead, *Science and the Modern World* (New York: The Macmillan Co., 1925).

[13] Whitehead, *Adventures of Ideas* (New York: The Macmillan Co., 1933), p. 157.

Science can explain things naturally, but never itself. It cannot be true in a purely scientific world.[14]

The only rational motive for seeking to understand political institutions and behavior is the human benefit that may be derived from such a study. If our interest in politics is unrelated to human welfare and to such concepts as justice and freedom, there is, of course, no reason why we should seek to describe political behavior in ethical terms. But if our interest in politics is motivated by an interest in human well-being, it becomes not only our right, but our responsibility, to detect corruption, to identify injustice and tyranny, to unmask sophistry, and to guide men along the paths most likely to yield happiness and freedom. With Plato and Aristotle, I believe that the social sciences can be most useful to our society when they are deliberately, consciously, and rationally directed toward helping men to be better human beings—when they seek to discover the principles that make for a free and just society and encourage men by the best means at their disposal to put those principles into practice. If it were true that "good government" is simply a matter of each man's private definition, there could be no government at all.

Research, however dispassionate and detached in its methods, achieves meaning and can lay claim to truth only by transcending itself, only by relating itself to something of significance beyond its immediate concern. Political science achieves meaning only by presupposing that the fruits of its research are of value to human beings who have a capacity to reason, to choose between alternative modes of behavior, to differentiate good from bad, and who have a destiny that transcends the demands of time and place. If we deny these attributes of humanity, we deny at the same time any possibility of understanding political behavior rationally, i.e., the possibil-

[14] T. E. Jessop, "The Scientific Account of Man," in T. E. Jessop *et al.*, *The Christian Understanding of Man* (London: George Allen & Unwin, Ltd., 1938), p. 40.

ity of political science. It would, indeed, simplify the task of political science if man were an automaton controlled by forces completely outside his own control—except that there would then be no political scientists to understand the mechanism.

Finally, what place does religion, and more especially Christianity, have in the classroom? There are a great many who will contend that it has no place at all. Others will say that the only legitimate place for it is in a department of religion. Those who contend that religion has no place at all in the classroom, if pressed for reasons, will generally argue (1) that religion is a subjective, personal matter and that there is no place in the classroom for subjective, personal feelings, (2) that it is based on faith and authority and has nothing, therefore, to do with that which is rational, (3) that since all students are not Christians it will offend those who are not. Let us examine these arguments in more detail.

1. There is a sense, of course, in which religion is a subjective and personal matter but there is also a sense in which it is an objective fact and can be dealt with as such. It is a fact that there is such a thing as Christianity and that it has exerted a profound influence upon our thinking and institutions. To understand this influence is essential whether one is himself a Christian or not. To understand the origins of constitutional government it is necessary to understand the common distinction that was made in the Middle Ages between a true prince and a tyrant and the medieval conception of law out of which modern constitutionalism emerged. And in order to understand the political theory of the Middle Ages it is essential to know something about the doctrinal and theological basis upon which that political theory rested. Even if we confine our attention to "modern times" as some political scientists think we should, we will find it necessary to know something about Christianity. If we would understand what liberalism is, for example, and how it arose we must understand the Deism which was intimately connected with it. But in order to under-

414 JOHN H. HALLOWELL

stand Deism we would have to know how it modified the
orthodox Christian doctrines. Locke's essay on *The Reasonableness of Christianity* is as essential to the understanding of
his thought as is his *Treatise on Civil Government*. Almost
a half of Hobbes's *Leviathan* is devoted to a discussion "of a
Christian Commonwealth," and it will make little or no sense
to us unless we know what the doctrines of orthodox Christianity are and mean. And although a great deal of modern
political thought rejects Christianity it retains a great deal of
it in a secularized and distorted form. To adequately understand the secularized form, even though we may approve of it,
it is essential to know just how it differs from the Christian
belief which it rejects. The modern doctrine of progress, for
example, is understandable only as a secularized version of the
Christian doctrine of Providence. We may personally prefer
the doctrine of progress to the doctrine of Providence, but if
we would understand the idea of progress we would have to
know something about the doctrine of Providence from which
it is derived. To understand Marx it is essential to know the
religious presuppositions which he derived, in part, from
Feuerbach.

If we would understand the role of the Christian Democratic Party in Germany today and of similar parties in other
European countries, it would certainly be of help to know what
the Christian basis for these parties is. If we would understand
American institutions, it would be of help to know something
about the Puritan tradition and beliefs out of which many of
these institutions grew. Ralph Barton Perry has suggested
some of the connections in a book entitled *Puritanism and
Democracy*. A knowledge of the religious beliefs and institutions of the Far and Near East will certainly be essential to
an understanding of the political and social institutions
peculiar to these regions.

Religion certainly has a legitimate place in the classroom as
one of the important factors which has exerted and continues

to exert a profound influence upon our political thinking and institutions. And as such a factor we certainly should be able to treat it with the same kind of objectivity that we employ to discuss other factors. The word "objective," however, does have curious connotations in our modern vocabulary. As a student I have heard Christianity disparaged and ridiculed in the classroom more often than I have heard it praised, but rarely, if ever, have I heard this practice condemned as an injection of personal bias. The attitude of disparagement is often labeled "objective" while the attitude of praise is condemned as "subjective." Genuine objectivity would demand, it seems to me, that we attempt, subject to the human limitations which bind us all, to describe the doctrines of Christianity as accurately as we can and to explain the influence of Christianity and the role of the church as accurately as we would describe the influence and activity of any other doctrine or institution. This may well involve both criticism and praise where each is justified and the reasons for each are clearly stated. Criticism and praise alike become subjective when the reasons for these attitudes are never explained and when they spring from personal bias rather than from objective evidence.

2. Another reason that is sometimes advanced for excluding religion from the classroom is the argument that since it is based on faith and authority it is intellectually disreputable. If we were to exclude from consideration in the classroom everything that is based on faith and authority we would have to exclude probably 90 per cent of what is taught there. All the historical facts which we accept as true we accept not on the evidence of our own experience but on the authority of the historian. I am told by the historian that a man by the name of George Washington was born in 1732 and died in 1799, that he served as Commander-in-Chief of the Revolutionary Army, and was the first president of the United States. All this, and a great deal more besides, I accept on the authority of the historian and I accept it on the same basis that I

accept the fact that Jesus Christ was born in Palestine. I have never been in India but I am certain there is such a place and I accept its existence on authority. When the physicist tells me that the hard surface on which I write is, in reality, a moving mass of molecules I accept his statement on authority. When the physician prescribes penicillin for my children I administer it to them on his authority and with faith in his judgment.

The difference between science and religion is not, as some erroneously suppose, that one is based ultimately on reason and the other on faith, for as a matter of fact both are based on faith. As I have said earlier, and as A. N. Whitehead has demonstrated in considerable detail, science assumes the existence of a kind of universe the existence of which it can never prove by its own methods. Its ultimate basis is not something which rests upon empirical evidence but upon faith. This in no way discredits its methods or findings and no one suggests that we should exclude it from the classroom.

That Christianity excludes all rational considerations is palpably false, as anyone who has read the great works of Christian thought can readily testify. As a matter of fact one of the greatest of Christian thinkers, St. Thomas Aquinas, is sometimes criticized on the grounds that he was too rigorously rational. No thinker before or since has had a greater respect for logic. Indeed, it is one of the claims of Christianity, and one to which many Christians can testify, that rather than shackling reason the Christian faith provides insights and understanding which increase rather than diminish the role of reason in life. It is faith that sustains our reason and gives it direction. It is true that Christianity rejects the Cartesian conception of man as a "thinking thing" but only to insist that man is a creature of passion as well as an intellect and that passion plays a role in the search for truth that is at least as important as reason. Man, it insists, is not a disembodied mind but a creature capable of loving, hating, and willing.

The acquisition of truth is an activity not only of the intellect but of the will and it is the direction of our will that directs our reason. We learn and know only what we want to learn and know and where there is no will to learn, nothing can be taught. The conversion of our will is equally as important as the use of our reason. This truth is expressed in the oft-repeated maxim that "a man convinced against his will is of the same opinion still."

At any rate it seems clear enough to me that if it is legitimate to present arguments in the classroom which disparage man's rationality, and there are many such arguments presented today, it is equally as legitimate to present arguments which uphold his rationality. If it is legitimate, for example, to study the writings of Pareto, it is equally as legitimate to study the writings of St. Thomas Aquinas and let the students decide which is the more rigorous thinker. Professor Hoxie N. Fairchild put the matter aptly in his essay in this book when he said: "Those who hold that it has become desirable or necessary to do without religion must at least be prepared to describe what it is they are abandoning and what they propose to substitute for it. At present there is a marked revival of religion among members of the intellectual class. Whether this is a retreat from reason or a reassertion of the possibility of reason is a debatable question. By all means, then, let it be debated." [15]

3. An additional argument that would exclude religion from the classroom is that since all students are not Christians it will offend those who are not. But there is no reason why a discussion of the meaning and influence of Christianity should offend anyone. It would be offensive if the teacher insisted that students agree with everything that he said but such an attitude on the part of the teacher would be offensive whether he was talking about religion or anything else. If the presentation is offensive it will not be because the subject discussed is

[15] See page 41.

religion but because of the manner in which it is discussed. My own experience has been that rather than resenting the discussion of religion students have welcomed it. Indeed, they often want to go much further with the discussion than time and the subject matter permit and this holds true not only of Christians among the students but also of non-Christians and skeptics.

Another group argues that the only legitimate place for religion in the classroom is in a department of religion. Members of this group think of religion as a subject separate and distinct from all other subjects and while they think it has its place in a university curriculum they want to make sure that it keeps its place and doesn't intrude upon other subjects. This attitude arises from a false conception of the nature and meaning of religion. Religion, as we have been told many times, is not just a subject for Sunday meditation but it has a bearing upon everything we do and think seven days a week. It is an attempt, moreover, to see things whole, to bring, in the words of one writer, all our "fragmentary truths and values into unity by relating them to an infinite Reality and Goodness which transcends them all." [16] In its search for organic unity religion is somewhat like philosophy and while we have separate departments of philosophy we do not think it illegitimate, I hope, for historians, economists, students of literature, or political scientists to bring philosophical considerations into the discussion of the problem of their respective disciplines. I can see no essential difference between discussing philosophy in the classroom and discussing religion. The department of philosophy has no monopoly on philosophy and neither does the department of religion have a monopoly on religion.

There is a great deal of talk among college and university teachers today about the importance of "integrating" our teaching, breaking across arbitrary departmental barriers and

[16] George F. Thomas, *Religion in an Age of Secularism.* An inaugural lecture published by Princeton University, p. 16.

promoting interdisciplinary projects. But if we are to relate one subject to another it must be in terms of something which transcends them both. In religion, which is concerned with the whole of a man's life, with the totality of his experience, we have a body of thought and of experience that sheds light on all aspects of human experience and, as a consequence, can integrate subjects, particularly among the humanities and the social sciences, as nothing else can. Indeed, the origin of universities lay in just such a conviction. And to the extent that universities have lost the faith that originally inspired them they have progressively lost the unity of purpose that made one out of many. The first college in America, Harvard College, was founded *"in Christi Gloriam,"* in the conviction that there could be no true knowledge or wisdom without Christ. And it was this same conviction that inspired the founding of many other American colleges and universities. Many still reflect that conviction in their mottoes although they have departed from it in varying degrees in practice. Those today who are urging the colleges and universities to put religion back into higher education are not urging something upon them that is alien to their nature but are suggesting only that they revive the faith that originally inspired their founding.

VI

What are the special responsibilities of the teacher of political science who is also a practicing Christian? Upon him, it seems to me, falls the special responsibility of relating his Christian beliefs to political science in general and to the particular area within political science that is his specialty. Many do so but there are many who do not. Many endeavor, and apparently with some success, to keep their personal commitments and their academic activities in watertight compartments. How they manage it I am not sure. Some, perhaps, would argue that the practicing of Christianity is a matter of personal conduct and not an intellectual activity. But what one does with one's mind is certainly as important as what one does with one's body and soul. Certainly a Christian life is the best witness to Christianity that anyone can make and it is much to be preferred to an intellectual commitment that is not reflected in personal living. But personal conduct and intellectual activity are not mutually exclusive activities and we need not, I think, choose between them. In actuality the one will reinforce the other. It is something like the relationship between faith and good works; each is essential to the other and each is reflected by the other. The psychologists talk a great deal today about the importance of "integrating" one's personality and if they are right it would seem that a Christian who is a Christian in his intellectual activities as well as in the affairs of personal conduct would be apt to achieve a more "integrated" personality than the one who kept his intellectual activities and his personal life in separate compartments.

The Christian has an opportunity through his writings and in the classroom to bear witness to Christianity intellectually and it is an opportunity, I think, that he is not only justified in using but that he would be remiss to neglect. When the opportunity legitimately arises he is certainly justified in explaining the light which Christianity sheds on the problem under consideration, explaining any misconceptions of Christianity that he may discover among his students and answering any questions that are directed to him about the nature or teachings of the Christian religion. If asked why he holds the beliefs that he does he is certainly justified in explaining.

The teacher who interprets his subject matter in the light of Christian doctrines and philosophy is no less scholarly or less worthy of intellectual respect than the teacher who interprets his subject matter in the light of Hegelian idealism or logical positivism. We do not think it strange that many different varieties of philosophy are represented in most departments of philosophy, that some teach as pragmatists, others as idealists, and still others as logical positivists. If this is legitimate and I think we would agree that it is, it is equally legitimate to have the Christian philosophy represented. All political scientists, whether they know it or not, teach from some point of view and if they contend that all points of view are equally valid, that is a point of view. The important thing is not to have no point of view, which is an impossibility, but to make our point of view explicit. If we think we do not have a philosophical point of view we are deluding ourselves and our students. It is impossible even to observe anything and describe it except from some perspective. If a student knows what our philosophical perspective is, he can discount it if he likes but if we give him the impression that we have no perspective we are not being honest with ourselves or with him. Moreover, the student has the same right to know what Christianity is and to choose it if he desires as he has to know what pragmatism is or idealism or any of the other varieties of religious or philosophical thought.

The Christian who is also a teacher may feel reluctant to bring his Christianity into the classroom because he knows that many of his colleagues will think it an illegitimate injection of a personal bias. Certainly, there is no place in the classroom for personal bias or prejudices but Christianity is not a personal bias. It includes a systematic body of thought about the most significant human problems, a body of thought that has existed for several centuries and attracted the allegiance, intellectual and personal, of countless millions of individuals. Such a body of thought deserves a hearing and there is no one better able to give it a hearing than one who is himself a Christian. If a person is to be able to judge wisely between opposing doctrines or opinions, "he must," in the words of John Stuart Mill, "be able to hear them from persons who actually believe them; who defend them in earnest, and do their very utmost

14

THE PREPARATION OF TEACHERS

By ROBERT ULICH

Any adequate preparation of teachers includes both general or liberal education and specialized training. Consequently the religious dimension in the educational experience of prospective teachers is dealt with in large part in other essays in this series. But it is equally important to understand the religious perspectives in the ideals and motivation of *democracy* of which teachers are trustees in a special sense. It is this theme with which the present essay is primarily concerned. The argument is presented in four parts: (1) the current cultural and educational situation; (2) the religious attitude; (3) the meaning and the teaching of democracy; (4) the responsibilities of those who prepare teachers for their vocation.

THE CURRENT EDUCATIONAL SITUATION

Three aspects of the present cultural situation as it relates to education may be illustrated by reports of three recent conversations.

1. *The Absence of Imagination and Insight.* There came to the office of one of my philosophically minded colleagues a publisher's agent to report that his company was planning a new series of educational textbooks. My friend replied that we already have too many textbooks in education and related fields, though few really good ones.

"What would you recommend instead?" asked the agent.

My colleague's answer was, "I would recommend a series of monographs on the great educational pioneers who through a life of sacrifice and profound thought have given expression and motivation to the cultural aspirations of mankind and prepared our minds for the idea that every human person has the right to develop his productive qualities to the best of his ability. We have many books on great statesmen, artists, and philosophers, but in the Anglo-Saxon countries we have no penetrating monographs of men such as Comenius, Pestalozzi, and Froebel. Could not our students derive lasting inspiration from communication with these leaders of mankind?"

"But," so the agent responded, "who would buy such books? They would not fit into the typical course work. Nor would the public read them. Ask around among the professors of your university whether they would buy a book on Comenius. Most of them would hardly know the name."

My friend had to admit it, though—according to his opinion —the memory of a great man, forgotten by the public, had often been revived by a well-written book. While they were talking I, though listening with enthusiasm, became doubtful about the suggestion. Whom, despite the large number of our universities, could one recommend for such treatises in the interpretation of our educational history? Only a few, already too busy to assume new obligations. The younger men and women might be little interested, and still less prepared for carrying through this kind of study. In our high schools and colleges they have not been trained in the necessary contemplative attitude, the enduring patience, and the knowledge of languages. When they grow older and realize what they have missed, it is usually too late.

Actually, we move in a vicious circle. Especially in our education departments, we have been busy for decades with technical and methodological questions, the importance of which has often been exaggerated to the degree of boredom.

But the sources from which a teacher could receive stimulation that would repay him for his hard work have rarely been opened up.

This is not the fault of education alone. Something similar is going on everywhere, as if imagination and inspiration were forgotten values. Is it because we think they might destroy our scholarly objectivity? Are we perhaps assuming that objectivity is something other than a constant desire for depth and truth, or that this desire can be maintained without enthusiasm? Or does the reason lie still deeper, namely that in our academic world we have lost the courage of conviction from which alone inspiration can come? Have liberalism and democracy of which we and our students hear every day become just a "way" without a goal? Is an enemy or a cold war necessary to remind us of something besides the priority of politics, something that we need to renew and defend constantly? Or are there still sources which feed our souls from within, even as they nourished the souls of all great men who have built the structure of human civilization?

2. *Inadequacy of the Concept "Social Engineering."* At a luncheon I happened to be seated beside the representative of one of our important educational agencies. He shared with me his hope that the social sciences would soon initiate a new historical epoch by applying the same effective techniques in relation to man that the natural sciences apply in relation to nature. I hesitated to disagree, for in a time of general disillusion one likes to hear a hopeful voice. Furthermore, to a degree I share the expectation that the extension of the experimental method into the field of human relations may help us understand ourselves and our society better. Yet, I could not refrain from expressing my regret that there had come about an almost complete separation between the new social sciences and the older humanities, especially history and philosophy.

"Do you mean to say," he asked, "that education, the social sciences, and the humanities belong together, with history and philosophy representing the 'older,' and education and the social sciences the 'new' humanities?"

This was about my answer. "There are now just as deep, and perhaps deeper, revolutions going on in the 'older' field of philosophy as in the 'new' sciences about man and his society. But in that they all have to do with man, or *homo*, they could be placed under the category of the humanities and learn from each other."

"I doubt it," the academic statesman gave me to understand. "We need exact scientific methods. There is no need for educating historians, who look into the past, and philosophers, who look into the transcendental. We have to train scientists in human relations, or, if I may use a more accurate term, we have to educate leaders and engineers in the field of human conditioning. After all, social values are nothing but the results of conditioning. In older times this conditioning was done amateurishly, perhaps even unconsciously. Today, we have to do it scientifically."

"To 'leaders' and 'engineers' in human 'conditioning' I am apparently allergic," I answered my neighbor. "I bumped into such people in Europe, or more accurately, they bumped into me; otherwise I would not be here in the U. S. A. I personally refuse to be 'engineered' and to be treated like a piece of iron or a machine in a plant. In normal civilian life I even refuse to be treated like a soldier in a fighting army. I still have certain convictions about human freedom and its final goals. The vocabulary of the German Nazis was borrowed largely from the field of engineering—*gleichschalten*. Even in peace Hitler called every citizen a soldier, and that was the end of Germany. Are you so certain that in our country the apparently inevitable progress in planning will always stop before it challenges the natural rights of man as proclaimed in the Constitution?"

My neighbor smiled. "Don't you see the difference? The Nazis conditioned people for the Hitler State, but we condition them for the Constitution."

But in "conditioning" men for the Constitution, will we not lose its spirit?

3. *The Fading of an Interest in Reality.* The other day I spoke with two research fellows who view mankind with the trained eyes of the psychologist and psychiatrist. We talked about education, which for them was largely related to such concepts as "id, ego, and superego," "identification," "latency period," "aggression," "frustration," and "learning as tension release."

I listened with interest to their conversation, especially since one of the men was a Freudian, and the other a strictly experimental psychologist. There was much in their conversation with which I agreed, though they mostly disagreed. After a while I asked:

"Are these conceptual schemes, which you use to describe certain functions in man's behavior, adequate representations of man's driving motives, of the world that he enjoys and that he hates, that moves him to act, and that he would like to transmit to his children? I do not mean to blame you, for all of us who are engaged in scholarly rationalization, perhaps most of all the theologians, do the same thing. Theoretical concepts and their relationships are the means by which the scholar must try to order and understand the world. His quantitative and qualitative abstractions are wonderful instruments to deal with the regularities and laws of matter, but when applied to the overwhelming wealth of human reality, do they not miss its essence? Indeed, they are more apt to do so the further they progress on the road of analysis. Is there not something tragic in any scholar's endeavor, as in any life that moves primarily on the level of abstraction? Thought is reflection of reality, but reflection is not reality itself. This is an antinomy we cannot change and under the shadow of which we have to live. But should we not be aware of it?"

The answer I received was as follows:

"Of course, we use only symbols and do not know in what relation they may stand to reality, whatever reality may be. But does anybody 'truly experience' the Copernican theory? If he did, he would go insane. Yet, it explains our cosmos better than the older geocentric theory which sprang from man's naïve and immediate experience. Why should not the same hold true with the theories concerning the human mind, however abstract they may seem to the naïve listener?"

"But there is a difference," I objected. "Scientific theories about matter say something measurable about a world which we suppose to be causally determined, about a world in which there is no freedom, no moral decision, no delight, and no despair in the human sense of the word. Man does not live in this world alone, and the more he is man, the more he frees himself from it. Of course, science has changed our external life. In this respect, the scientific revolution of the seventeenth century has done more than the whole Renaissance with its art and its religious and political revolutions. Yet, whereas modern science has displaced Aristotle's theories about physics, it has not displaced his *Ethics*, or Plato's *Symposium*, or the Sermon on the Mount. In other words, in spite of all its technical power and all the wonderful revelations about man's physical conditions, natural science has not essentially modified man's picture of his moral self.

"Apparently, man has always known that he is in a certain *immediate* relation to the ground of life which reaches deeper than all science. Perhaps, if the objects of nature from the sun down to the smallest leaf of grass could speak to us in intellectual language, they also would tell us that the laws of Newton and Einstein are admirable descriptions of nature's behavior, but just descriptions rather than complete explanations of the creative power of the universe.

"Nearest to this power comes the intuitive insight of the religious prophet, of the great artist, perhaps also of the philosopher, if he dares to be a kind of rational poet such as Plato recording Socrates' conversation with Diotima about the nature of Love.

"Thus, whenever we academic people speak *of* man and *to* man in the derivative language of the scientific investigator, we must know that we move only on the periphery of human existence. We may be further away from its center than the genius with his profound intuition or the so-called common man. For, in spite of all contrasts, both of these men rely on their immediate experience in the great adventure of an active and striving life; and if they need some explanation and contemplation, they rely on the great intuitive revelations of human wisdom and experience more than on analytical discourse. But when decade after decade an increasing number of erudite men with the self-assumed authority of 'exact' investigators tell the common man that the great religious and humane tradition would be better *replaced*, rather than *enriched*, by science, then this common man—to whom we all belong—may finally believe it. He may come to feel very learned and enlightened, but at the same time he may lose contact with that part of life and thought which he needs for sympathetic and courageous living: faith, hope, charity. For all these values do not come from description and analysis. And—naturally enough—the greater the loss in basic and directive beliefs, which spring from our own creativeness, the more we become ripe for control from outside, for control by government, propaganda, and 'social engineers.'

"This, then, will be the end of human freedom. For freedom and its political derivative, liberty, represent aspects of experience which do not belong in the exact scientist's dictionary. How could they? Yet, on them is built our civilization. Even the Communists tell their people that a new freedom is waiting for all men. But in the U. S. A., in the land of 'democracy,' some of our scientists, philosophers, and psychologists tell their disciples that the word 'freedom' has no real 'meaning.' Furthermore, that freedom cannot be 'measured.' "

My two friends looked at me with suspicion. "In other words, you do not talk science, but you talk religion. Do you want us to become preachers of sin, salvation, the Holy Trinity, and eternal hell-fire? Whence do all the psychopathic guilt feelings of our patients come but from so-called religious education?"

"I might ask you," I replied, "how many people get stranded, not because they have been harmed by religion, but because they have never lived in it. But you have misunderstood me, which was probably my fault. I am not against scholarly inquiry into the nature of man and his society, even if it may destroy cherished beliefs. The true and the good life, I am convinced, must be one and the same. And like you I loathe the confusion between religion, superstition, sentimentality, and the fear of new discoveries which makes thinking men suspicious of our churches. Since true religion does not live by science, it cannot be afraid of it. Rather it will be appreciative of its results. But man has the right to protest against partiality which claims totality, as is often the case with modern science.

"Are not most of us who are engaged in scholarly pursuits in such a phobia of anything not describable in scientific terms or deferrable to sensory experience that we may even misjudge the ultimate character of the physical world? For all that exists exists not on itself alone, but reaches into a uniting dimension which we have not the right to deny merely because we are unable to explain it. Thus, if we take our incomplete thinking for the whole of life, we may not even be good scientists; but certainly we are not good humanists, or good guides of our youth. Frankly, I am sometimes afraid we are misleaders of mankind."

"In other words," my psychological colleagues concluded, "you recommend that we go home and commit suicide."

"No, but I recommend that we stop allowing our students, who later may have educational responsibilities as teachers, administrators, psychologists, and counsellors, to go out into the world with a heap of scholarly knowledge, and with less than a minimum of insight into the great spiritual wisdom of the human race. If the young men and women who enter these careers had lived a life full of activity, had reached into the depths of human gladness and human misery, perhaps they could be exposed to a merely scientific training without damage to themselves and other people. They would take it *cum grano salis*. But most of them have not. They have gone through school and college, and perhaps worked for a master's or doctor's degree. Thus they are learned, but they may be far from educated. Should we entrust to them our youth, our society, the people who need courage and guidance with regard to the aims of life and not only with respect to its techniques?"

THE RELIGIOUS ATTITUDE

Now, in one respect my two interlocutors were right. In a sense, I was really talking about the "religious" as different from the "scientific" or even the "scholarly" attitude toward life, though I consider true science and true religion not as enemies but friends trying to climb the same summit from different starting points.

No attempt will be made here to define "religion" or "religious." Every sect and denomination will give a different answer, and we are not concerned here with the historical phenomena of the splitting of the perennial religious experience of a man in its different historical forms, however important they may be. Rather we are referring to certain features which, so we suppose, are somewhat similar in highly developed religious attitudes, though we admit that these attitudes cannot be neatly separated from their historical and sociological settings, their cults, and their expressed beliefs. There always exists an interaction between basic human desires, the attitudes they create, and the forms and institutions within and through which they express themselves.

By its very nature, such a description of basic attitudes under the title of religion exposes one to the reproach of vagueness. Orthodox theologians of all creeds, when speaking to and for their faithful, would even consider it heretical; an expression of opinion in which most men with a sense for a deeper dimension of life could somehow agree and which, for this very reason, would be worthless before their God. This agreement among men of sincere conviction is highly desirable, even though it bears no immediate reference to Catholicism, Protestantism, Judaism, or any other special creed.

The religious attitude of man presupposes a pervading sentiment of highly complex character. From a strictly logical point of view it seems to be paradoxical. For the human mind, so far as it is discriminating and analytical, conceptual and syntactic, can always refer only to a limited and definable number of objects. In distinction, the religious sentiment— though being within man's span of experience, otherwise it would not exist—points at the same time beyond immediate sense perception. It is immanent in sense experience, but it moves out of the limited range of sensuousness. Though constantly appearing in the concreteness of life and nature it is metaphysical. It envisages an embracing and enveloping power, one which opens the soul for the entering of the Infinite.

The religious sentiment provides us with a sense of an abiding and lawful Order; at the same time this Order realizes itself to the human mind only in continual change and motion. It is felt with the might of utter reality, yet it can be expressed only in symbols. It can be apprehended in its strength and depth by the simple and humble, yet the most educated mind breaks down in the attempt to explain it in its completeness. Nor will we receive much help from the usual distinction between the "natural" as the secular sphere, and the "supernatural" as the abode of the Spirit. One deprives nature of its lawfulness, beauty, and dignity if one considers it mere "matter," separate from spirit. And one deprives spirit of its vitality, form, and fullness if one tries to lift it away from cosmic life into a de-substantiated a priori. If nature were without some inner order—which is within, but at the same time something different from, mere matter—it would be chaos. If spirit were without, or outside nature, it could not operate. What we call nature, and what we call spirit, are perhaps but two aspects by which one and the same wonder reflects upon the human mind, the wonder of continual creation. Therefore, all such terms as dualism, monism, pantheism, etc., may be useful for clarifying standpoints and contrasts of opinion, but the moment they are taken as explanations of Reality, they become misleading concepts of presumptuous minds. The dualist encounters difficulty in explaining the relationship between mind and body, while the monist may arrive at a pantheism without a hierarchy of good and evil. Before the grandiose dialectic of the universe human language and its abstractions can never give the final answer. Whatever name we give to this Essence, whether we call it Knowing, Love, Creation, whether we conceive of it as Mind, Power, or Person, how unsatisfactory are all such appellations!

But though, at the first glance, religion seems to be paradoxical from the logical point of view, it is, nevertheless, not at all illogical if we understand that it always tries to relate the individual phenomenon to the whole. Perhaps it can best be described as the attitude that drives man from the single toward that which is total. Religion is the longing for wholeness, for union of the isolated with the universality of being. Is it not significant that etymologically the words whole, holy, wholesome, all can be traced back to the old Anglo-Saxon root "hale," meaning both whole and healthy? Isolation, so people apparently have always felt, makes man sick; wholeness makes him sound.

But though we live in, or with, or on, the whole, it is always greater than we are able to comprehend, for it surpasses the analytical power of the intellect. Though not illogical, one cannot penetrate it by the processes of deduction or induction. It can be apprehended only by the kind of intuition by virtue of which man can become the prophet, the artist, the creative inventor, but it has little to do with the concerns of a pedestrian mind.

These basic characteristics apply to all great world religions. Yet it does not therefore follow that the specific sacraments and cults which distinguish the great religions from each other are all together mere superstructure and unnecessary cargo, which, if dispensed with, would give us the international world religion in which all the specific creeds could and should be absorbed. Though the symbolisms and sacred rituals are not of the essence—many of them are even obsolete superstitutions and should go overboard—they are nevertheless the vehicles by which man approaches the Eternal. As a Christian, I can —perhaps—understand the ideas of Brahmanism, Buddhism, Taoism, Parsiism, and especially of Judaism; I can even worship in their temples and holy places. But with the best of intentions, I cannot really become a Buddhist or whatever I may feel inclined to become. The language in which we have been taught to pray and worship is part of our personality; somehow it goes with us just as does not having been taught to pray and worship. Of course there are profound conversions, but they are often connected with grave inner crises.

On the other hand, if we have been brought up in such a way that we believe it is only *our* language and only *our* prayer the Lord may listen to, then we become incapable of seeing the community of all men who sense the divine in their individual lives. Religious education sailing under such wind is regionalism, nationalism, and imperialism, surreptitiously raised from the secular level, where it is bad enough, to the level of the transcendent, where it is worse. It is the divider, not the unifier of mankind. Such education is not religious, but irreligious, however big and pompous may be the external organization, the ritual, and the phraseology. In our period, when humanity must either come together or perish, we cannot afford such division.

To repeat, if the religious faith expressed in this essay is such that, despite differences of cult, all men can agree upon it, we would then be one step further on the path toward civilization. But they will not agree. For there are too many who never having sensed the language of faith refuse to listen, or who having heard it from dogmatic parents and preachers either go around with closed minds until they die or, once the eyes have been opened to wider horizons, are unable to free themselves from intellectual protest against all that has to do with religion. For these indifferent, or dogmatic, or suspiciously hostile persons this article contains nonsense, or heresy, or both. In them the mental organ is damaged which renders a person capable of relating himself reverentially to the universe in its wholeness and to the various strivings of men who live in it.

Perhaps religions will ever have two foes, those who pride themselves on their exclusive possession of the Truth and those who pride themselves on their hostility or indifference in all matters religious. As always, here the extremes play into each other's hands. Let us hope that it will not be suffering but insight which enables an increasing number of people to recognize the indigenous and unifying power in all religion. Only thus will an education be possible which is deeply religious and at the same time free from schismatic parochialism. So far as we know, never has a culture survived that has severed itself from its original roots. We are today in this danger, for one of the roots of our culture is the Judaeo-Christian form of religion, which so many of us no longer understand.

However, the analogy between culture and physical growth and, consequently, between cultural origin and the root of a plant, is misleading. The roots of a plant cannot be renewed. In contrast, the origin of a civilization is an idea or a set of ideas deeply grounded in basic human experience. Such generative ideas can ever again become part of man's inner life, provided he understands them not as a bundle of dead traditions, but as creative energies which can preserve themselves only by the continual test of action and by courageous exposure to the challenge of history.

Religion represents such an energy. It is in our hands whether we wish its wellspring to be clogged, or whether we wish to lead its refreshing waters into channels of modern life. We can, if we *will*, but whether we *all* will, or a sufficient number of us, no one can foresee.

THE MEANING AND TEACHING OF DEMOCRACY

No one doubts today that we live in a crisis not only in regard to our social, economic, and political conditions, but also in regard to our ethical convictions. We no longer have a clear concept of man either in terms of a philosophical anthropology or in terms of a transcendent metaphysics. We may be able to describe, to a degree, how man behaves in a given situation, but we have become less and less capable of developing the creative attitude which not only accepts situations, but interprets, molds, and changes them in the light of a great and far-reaching ethical vision. With this vision lacking, our minds inevitably concentrate on what is here and now. Man, losing the goal, becomes busy with details. If the history of humanity teaches us anything, it is this. To be sure, the details also should be taken seriously (who does not do so remains a lifelong amateur), but they need the illumination given by the perspective of the ideal.

But many will reply, We have a great ethical ideal on which our Western civilization and education is agreed—democracy.

No doubt, a profound value lies in the ideal of democracy, however often the term may be used for mere purposes of propaganda. We all must be grateful that the democratic ideal is the uniting factor in our schools, and, so we hope, also in our political life. But two great questions emerge.

First, is "democracy" a sufficiently strong tie, if it signifies nothing but a form of political organization, or an ideological weapon in hot and cold wars? For there are many divergences with respect to its political and economic application. Hitler's minister of propaganda also spoke of democracy and many believed him. Communism too has included the term in its vocabulary.

Second, can the deepest aspirations contained in the concept of democracy, those for which we are willing to fight, be sufficiently explained and preserved by reference to a merely secular philosophy, or to a form of humanism that holds its concepts strictly within horizontal relationships between men and men and so denies the justification of metaphysics and religious transcendence?

It is the contention of this treatise that secular humanism —despite all its merits in directing modern man's attention toward a rational interpretation of his intellectual and social obligations—is as insufficient for a complete explanation of the democratic ideal and for the vital transmission of this ideal in our schools and various institutions which serve the training of teachers, as is an intolerant and sectarian interpretation of religion.

Our schools, so we contend, must and can teach democracy in a spirit which leads man toward an understanding of its transcendent dimension, or sooner or later democracy will lose the depth which has helped it to emerge and which alone can help it to survive.

The public schools of this country, in consequence of the necessary and praiseworthy principle of the separation of State and Church, cannot attempt to indoctrinate a specific creed, Christian or otherwise. Likewise, most of our colleges and universities would reject such a demand. This, however, does not mean and has never been intended to mean, that there cannot be a religious spirit pervading our education, especially in our interpretation of democracy.

We will try to amplify this statement in the following paragraphs.

1. *The Democratic Sense of Freedom.* Democracy, in the ethical sense, feels itself to be the guardian of freedom. Of course, regard for freedom, at least to a degree, was already inherent in the civilizations of the Greeks and Romans; perhaps it existed even in the Middle Ages to a greater extent than we generally assume. For, in order to materialize his desire for freedom, man depends on the instruments available to him, and there were not too many in medieval times. Thus, if we look one-sidedly at the tangible result rather than on the motivation, we may easily misjudge our ancestors before the Renaissance. Nevertheless, freedom as a central motif of public discussion and action is a characteristic of modern or post-Renaissance culture.

When Galileo defends his cosmic theory, he consciously fights not only for the recognition of his own work, but for intellectual freedom. The term "freedom" occurs again and again in the writings of the French prerevolutionary Encyclopedists and in the thought of the German idealists. The category of freedom is almost the only one on which the modern existentialists agree. But all this, one could say, is still philosophy. To have transferred the idea of freedom into political actuality is the merit of the American Revolution. Ideal, ideological, political, economic, social, and geographical factors worked together to make this country the symbol of democratic life.

But, as in the history of every comprehensive ideal, there are strange paradoxes also in the development of political freedom. In this case the paradox lies in the relation of freedom to science. There is no doubt that science, often described as deterministic and quantitative, has contributed more to the material conditions of man's freedom than we usually recognize. But there may be something highly deceptive in the sense of physical independence which science has procured for us. A man whose airplane breaks down over the ocean may still be devoured by a shark, as were our forebears when they dared swim in dangerous waters. Nevertheless, a certain victory over the daily discomforts, the conquest of hunger, dirt, and cold, the defeat of time and space through modern inventions, a higher degree of health through modern medicine, gives man a feeling of mastery over the accidents of nature which our ancestors could not possess. It may be deceptive, but it has worked.

In a yet deeper sense science has liberated large parts of humanity. Together with philosophy it has helped to free man from magical feelings of fear and demonism. The fact that—unnecessarily from a truly religious point of view—theologians felt compelled to fight the scientists and consequently created martyrs, has but strengthened modern man's respect for science.

Both through its effects on our physical and on our mental life, science as a discipline has also contributed to man's sense of self-respect which is the twin brother to the sense of freedom. Thus, the scientific worker of today finds himself in a dilemma. On the one hand, he has to exclude the whole great world of human ethical motivations, for they only disturb the accuracy of his thought and operations. As a strict scientist, he is neither immoral, nor anti-moral, but morally neutral, or a-moral. If, on the other hand, he envisages the despair which the use of the physical power he has provided may cause to mankind, he must become one of the champions in the fight for man's ethical freedom and responsibility.

Theoretically, only a comprehensive and overarching philosophical integration can harmonize the two diverging aspects of scientific determinism and historical teleology. Practically, our greatest scientists become increasingly aware of their obligations to humanity. But along with the rest of us, they are in the position of Goethe's *Zauberlehrling* (*The Magician's Apprentice*):

> Die ich rief, die Geister,
> Werd' ich nun nicht los.
> (The spirits which I summoned,
> How can I quiet them?)

For research will go its way. As one leading scientist said to me: "We cannot cut our brains out."

Here is one of our great conflicts. As indicated, in part it will have to be solved on the level of high theoretical abstraction. On the practical level we must hope that mankind, by dint of a union of nations animated not only by utilitarian considerations but by the strongest moral motives, will turn science again into a blessing instead of into a cause of fear. Modern patriotism must no longer be confined to a single country; we must arrive at a level of historical development where loyalty to one's country and loyalty to the ideal of international solidarity are interdependent.

2. *The Sense of the Dynamic Quality of Life.* If someone would like to describe the essential difference between the mentality of medieval and modern man, he could state that the first had a static, whereas the second has a dynamic concept of life. For the medieval thinker, history centered in two great revelations, the secular coming from Aristotle, and the divine

coming from Christ. The founder of Christianity made clear
to man not only his personal nature and destiny, but also the
beginning and the end of all history, the Creation and the Day
of Judgment. All that man thought and did received its value
or its condemnation from its nearness to or distance from the
divine Center.

For modern man, on the other hand, history is evolution.
Whether he calls it revelation or not, he feels there is a chain
of significant events that have made modern civilization possible, and he hopes that he is not at the end of the chain.
Which of the many links in the chain he considers to be of
the greatest import depends on the observer's point of view.
For some Jews and Christians it may still be the Covenant,
for the scientist it is perhaps the invention of the arabic number system, for the soldier the invention of gunpowder. Optimistic societies believe that all these various occurrences inter-
lace in a meaningful order. In other words, they believe in
progress. When, in consequence of disappointing experiences,
they lose faith in progress and at the same time repudiate recourse to a transcendental salvation, modern men find themselves in the situation aptly described by Kierkegaard, Nietzsche, and the contemporary existentialists as the situation of
"anxiety," if not of despair.

However, no one completely escapes the mentality of his
society even though he may live in protest against it. Thus
the critic of modernity and its concept of progress is caught
by the dynamic spirit of our times. Either he completely with-
draws—which is no real answer—or he is bound to be excited
by the rapid succession of ideas, styles, modes of living, and
inventions, social changes, wars, displacements of peoples, and
the birth and death of nations. The final meaning of all
this restlessness—how can he know it? Whether or not we
humans want it, to a large degree the situation in which we
live determines our purposes, as also it determines our future.
If we do not want to die on the wayside, we have to share the

experiences of our fellow men, even if we would prefer to do something else.

This dynamic attitude toward life, at least for a few centuries, has made Western man the master of the earth. He will transmit his seething energy to posterity even if other cultures wrest the symbols of leadership from his hand. It is this attitude for which he has been admired and imitated, but for which he also has been hated and despised by men imbued with the profound quiet of oriental wisdom.

Unless our culture is annihilated by its own means of destruction, there is no reason to believe that the desire for continual motion characteristic of Western man will change. But the more we are the driven and no longer the drivers, the greater is the danger that the forces of motion will lose direction and turn into a whirl of contradictory activities.

This danger cannot be prevented by just confessing our faith in progress, or by profoundly showing our children the newest type of airplane. It may be the type that drops bombs into their lives and destinies. On the other hand, to tear down the hope for progress means to destroy the beacon that helps modern man orient himself on the wild waters of present-day history.

What can be done?

First, we will have to tell ourselves and the younger generation that progress, as a total human achievement, can never be partial. Indeed, nothing fails like success in one part at the expense of another significant aspect of human experiences. We may speak of making progress in theoretical knowledge, in engineering, in building a house or a road. But true historical progress is *total* progress, a continual integration of achievements of the mind, the heart, and the hand. If one of the three lags behind, the mind may be used for sophistry, the heart for sentimentality, and the hand for stealing.

In earlier times, religion at its best gave man a set of beliefs which appealed to his whole personality. Even the faith in progress, or in the Kingdom of Man, is in its origin but a secular version of the religious idea of the Kingdom of God. Today, the American's belief in progress still has the overtone of universality. He thinks of a better future for humanity as a whole, and not merely of his own personal success.

But if this faith becomes more and more depleted of its deeper inspiration, if it becomes just a desire for comfortable living, then a new depression and international conflict may plunge us into a sea of disenchantment and despair. Can we always rely on a victorious war and a boom to fish us out? Anyhow, are these the means of salvation on which man should rely?

Second, we will have to discourage the naïveté in the assumption that progress follows automatically from the accumulative flow of experiences. This doctrine, though it is a bad popularization of antimetaphysical pragmatism, has nevertheless as its motive an unconscious metaphysical conviction about ultimate reality, namely a faith in the essential goodness of nature and man. One is reminded of Whitehead's statement that if you refuse to have any metaphysics, you are bound to end in a very bad one.

We can become realistic only if we learn to see that man is neither innately good as is taught by optimistic modern thought, nor innately bad as was taught by misunderstood Christianity. Nor is he simply a "product of his environment" or a "bundle of reactions to outside stimuli." This is both bad psychology and naïve metaphysics. Man is a complicated mixture of hereditary and acquired traits which, of course, are in constant interaction with the environment. At the same time, man is constantly molded and modified by his urges, emotions and his discriminating qualities which play their role in his freedom to decide; man is more than a bundle of reflexes—he is rational and moral as well. The reactions of various people to one and the same challenge are not necessarily similar; they may be totally different. One group may turn it into a source of love and encouragement, while another group may treat it as an excuse for hatred and self-pity; one group may transform a wilderness or a desert into a community, another succumb in the same situation to misery and starvation.

To be sure, man's freedom has only a certain degree of latitude in the presence of physical power. Before a stream of lava even the freest men are not free. Yet, the realization and utilization of the latitude of freedom which may be still available even under adverse circumstances is the most important factor in human history. On it depends liberty or slavery, progress or decay, a life of hope or a life of anguish. In other words, to a large degree progress is a decision of the spirit, or a result of the conviction that man fights on the side of God and not on the side of the devil.

If we tell our students indiscriminately that this country is the land of progress and freedom in which they have the right to participate just because they have their feet on American soil, we commit the same sin of which we are guilty when we assure them that this is the land of security. Progress, freedom, and security are accomplishments and not gifts from nature. Those who take them for granted will lose them.

3. *Truth and Order.* The German philosopher and poet Lessing coined the oft-quoted statement: "If God held before my eyes a balance with Truth on the one and Search on the other scale, I would choose the latter."

This dynamic concept of truth does not express a predilection for a relativistic play of ideas or the self-enjoyment of the intellect as an end in itself. It denotes the Protestant liberal preference for the situation of spiritual freedom rather than the situation of the Truth invested in a supposedly divine institution. It signifies the hope that man may acquire deeper insights into the essence of life through participation in its surging creativeness than through placing himself in a situation of stability. In the complete shelter of the Ultimate, man would lose his freedom, and so himself.

The Protestant idea of freedom from which, at least in part, the modern notion of democracy has arisen, symbolizes not only a vague and aimless groping within a constantly changing universe, but man's chance and challenge within a world with an inner meaning to which he can relate his search. Thus we discover within freedom its complement: the idea of an Order, or Cosmos, or Logos, which gives man's groping a self-transcending and universal meaning which is both rational and ethical. According to this belief the *summum verum* and the *summum bonum*, the highest truth and the highest virtue, are the same. Man, who is actively longing for the *verum*, comes close also to the *bonum*, because he experiences the laws of creation inherent in daily life.

It is this beautiful inner polarity of freedom which gives rationality and dignity to the plurality of our endeavors, though final truth and perfection will always be beyond our reach. Through this dialectic between freedom on the one hand and truth, moral discipline and law on the other, we human beings can live a life in which analytic weighing can lead to decision, where there is responsibility and imputability despite sin and error, where loyalty balances criticism, and peace of mind does not suffer from any slight disappointment.

There is, of course, a profound ontological problem behind and within this faith. Since freedom represents the possibility of change, whereas truth represents continuity, the question arises: how can there be change within continuity, variety within unity, and the continual flux of experiences within the identity of the human person? Or, to go one step further: how can there be change, variety, and flux of experiences without resultant chaos?

Here again, the answer can be given only if we assume an ordering Logos behind all transient phenomena, something that reminds us of reason, form, structure, law, and meaningful continuity. Full insight into its essence and content is beyond the narrow scope of the human mind; in weak symbols only can we apprehend the Infinite. Indeed, prevent man from the continual revival and interpretation of these symbols, and you deprive him of life's most sublime meaning. If his mind is sufficiently dulled, he may contentedly tread on the road of habit and conventionality, but such an attitude is of no avail in times of crisis.

It has often been stated that human truth is only a lesser error. This is true. But it is not to say that the story of human search is "nothing but" error. Lesser error is also growing truth, and more truth, being a step toward the laws of reality, encourages man to adjust his conduct more adequately to the inner dynamic of reality. Here lies the deepest impetus for man's untiring quest for verity. It issues from his deep-seated feeling that the more he reasons the greater is his expectancy to overcome the threat of blind accident, i.e., the greater is his chance to survive.[1] The category of truth and the category of survival, in the most comprehensive psychophysical sense, are akin.

4. *Love and Tolerance.* As we have already indicated with reference to the relationship between truth and virtue, the origin and essence of values is probably one and the same, whatever names we may give them. Freedom, or man's capacity of weighing and choosing, would be meaningless unless it could unfold itself in an Order or a Logos. Within the compass of his understanding this Order reveals itself to man and thus makes it possible for him to direct his choice according to rational principles.

Yet, "Though I speak with the tongues of men and angels and have not charity I am become as sounding brass, or a

[1] I have dealt with this and similar problems more extensively in my book *Conditions of Civilized Living* (New York: E. P. Dutton & Co., 1946) and in The Hazen Foundation Pamphlet, *Man and Reality*, 1948.

tinkling cymbal." This verse from Chapter 13 of I Corinthians is not only a demand for "charity." It says that all power of the intellect and all earthly might may lead man away from the Lord rather than toward Him unless they are propelled by the most creative of all human motives, Love.

According to the Christian tradition, I Corinthians 13 has to be understood in connection with the various statements of the Bible that all men are brethren through their being the children of God. There is mutual respect in human brotherhood, because we know that the most precious qualities we feel in ourselves are also in our neighbors. Human brotherhood also demands tolerance, because we should feel the imperfection of our neighbor all the more painfully in ourselves. But all these virtues are but derivations from the primary virtue of love, which in turn springs from the embracing consciousness that all individual life is participation in the wonder of the divine Creation. Thus Christian love is essentially reverence, the will to help as much as possible in the mysterious unfolding of creative living.

There seems to be a paradoxical mixture of feelings in this brotherly attitude of love; on the one hand we experience dignity, on the other hand we feel humble. Our sense of dignity springs from the realization that our minds allow us to look into, and to unite ourselves with, a world far beyond our physical existence; our sense of humility results from our consciousness that all that makes us human, in the deepest meaning of that word, is not our merit, but the gift of participating in creative growth.

But there should be no false sentimentality in these feelings of love, respect, and tolerance. Those who use freedom without obligation to the Logos which gives it meaning and direction, those who try to use their fellow men's love and tolerance in order to suppress the freedom and dignity of the human person, should ask neither love, nor tolerance for their actions.

Neither love nor tolerance should open the gates to the arena
in which they might be slaughtered.

Yet, there is in freedom, truth, and love, the attitude of infinite understanding, even for the aberrations of a person. The
potential humanity in him, however deeply hidden, will be
respected. Therefore, the law of civilized nations protects
even the criminal and condemns intolerance, which is blind,
destructive, and hateful as a shame to mankind. But, to repeat, the rejection of intolerance does not prevent man from
assuming the attitude of militant self-defense and fighting tolerance if he sees the foundations of freedom, truth, love, and
mutual understanding threatened by men without sense for
these values. Christ forgave sinners of all kinds, but he in-
veighed against the Pharisees and chastised the usurers who
used the Lord's temple for cheating their fellow men.

5. *The Value of the Individual.* With the remark that in
the best of the Western tradition even love and tolerance can
become militant, but that blind intolerance against the human
person as such is a sign of barbarism, we have already touched
upon one of the basic principles of our Western tradition, the
appreciation of the individual. For how could all the values
that we have recognized be possible without this appreciation?
Collectives as such—guilds, corporations, associations, states,
and international alliances—are requisite to human development. But just as they can help, so can they also hamper it,
for they can easily become the vessels and instruments of self-
seeking power. The final moral responsibility always rests in
the human person.

This fact, however, is no excuse for the reckless individualism, actually motivated by greed for power and success, which
thrives in Western culture under the name of freedom. What
else but ruthless competition can develop in a dynamic society,
where freedom is so often misunderstood as absence from
restraint?

The counterattack against this attitude of *laissez-faire* for the privileged, without the *laissez aller* for the less fortunate fellow man, was bound to come. Unfortunately, it came at a time when the Christian churches had allied themselves more intimately with the powerful than with the poor, and had dismally failed to recognize the Christian's social responsibilities. Consequently, the opposition against the injustice of society often included hostility to any kind of religion, organized or unorganized. This opposition acquired its greatest strength in that form of Marxism which now, in the distorted form of Russian Communism, has become the main threat to the Western form of democracy.

Thus there are two central problems on the solution of which depends the survival of Western civilization. Will the followers of Marx recognize that their prophet's revolutionary protest against degenerate social relations sprang, at least in part, from the deepest motives of the Judaeo-Christian tradition with its emphasis on personal freedom and the value of the individual? Marx's concept of, and violent protest against, "exploitation" is not merely an economic and technical protest, it is a moral protest rooted in an essentially religious-idealist interpretation of man.

Second, will those who profess to defend the basic values of the Christian Western tradition against present pseudo-Marxist totalitarianism recognize that this heresy would not have sprung up and continued to grow, had there not been a shameful discrepancy between the true ethics of Christianity and the actual behavior of the so-called Christian peoples and their churches? No realistic thinker will deny the impact of our forms of production and distribution of goods on our daily lives. Hence, he will not recommend an arbitrary change or modification of these forms under the pressure of doctrinaire opinions. However, the final measure of social and economic organizations will always lie in the degree to which they help in the unfolding and realization of the inner values of man, his freedom, his progress, his search for truth, his love, and his personality. If liberal-capitalist democracy cannot stand this test, arms and police forces will not be able to save it.

Of course, it is extremely difficult to change even small details in a social structure which has lost the moral fervor of its original architects. On the other hand, if this fervor is still vital, then man will be able to make even great changes without endangering the moral nature of his society; indeed, only in this way will he be able to preserve it.

Somehow a synthesis will have to be found between the individualist and the socialist trends in the modern world. Not only because it is a threat and waste of energy to live in a "divided world," but also because the strength of each nation depends on its capacity to combine individual freedom, which in isolation easily turns into egotism, with the cooperative spirit of brotherly love.

The Responsibilities of Those Who Prepare Teachers

In the last part of this essay we may now inquire about responsibilities of the teacher, not merely as a disciplinarian and expositor of subject matter, but as an educator, acting as a trustee of the best inherent in our Western-Christian society.

1. There are certain trends in our modern intellectual world to which the teacher should not fall prey. Instead of being an admirer and imitator of "scientism," he should be its critic from a total human as well as from a truly scientific point of view. For "scientism" is a distortion of science. Needless to say, the teacher should utilize objective and scientific approaches to education, such as psychometrics, statistics, and experimental psychology, but the use of quantitative methods for the better understanding and evaluation of certain functions and achievements of man does not imply a merely quantitative and materialistic interpretation of man's total nature. The

prime obligation of the teacher is to help young people to mature, i.e., to develop intellectually, emotionally, and practically into creative and harmonious beings. For this purpose science is important, but it is not all.

2. He should resist a certain tendency on the part of learned, but essentially half-educated men, to destroy faith in permanent values by displaying their capacity for relativizing everything and anything. This technique can be learned by very crude and simple minds, which is probably why it has had so much attraction. The art of comprehensive thinking is much more difficult. Comprehensive thinking, to be sure, does not spring from an uncritical attitude; on the contrary, it cannot exist without critical power. But it realizes the deeper order within the phenomena of life; it realizes that without such a deeper order even critical thinking, in the systematic and constructive sense, would be impossible. Disciplined thought, even if—or just because—it is cruel to beloved errors, seeks and reflects the universal Logos; bad thought reflects human partiality.

3. The good teacher should understand that knowledge of psychological methods and of subject matter, though necessary, remains barren and can even become misleading without the inspiration that fills the singularity of facts and events with motive and meaning. Not that the teacher should consider himself a dogmatic preacher—what could be worse? Yet, he should open the windows of a young and waiting soul for the great wonders of life, of which freedom, the possibility of progress and truth, the urge to love, and the dignity of the individual are perhaps the greatest.

4. Nobody can inspire who does not have deep convictions. They are the results, but also the feeders of the spirit. About their basic contents we have spoken in the third part of this essay, explaining the meaning of democracy for our schools, as well as the spirit in which democracy should be taught. The moment such convictions become fixed and frozen, they be-

come their own enemies. A lecturer is much more impressive if he is not a "lecturer" in the sense of one who slavishly "reads" his prepared notes, but if, even at the risk of deviations and repetitions, he allows his listeners to participate in the struggle of creation. So also is that teacher a better guide who does not give his students the feeling that he knows all the answers, but that he has engaged in continual search and self-examination. To be ashamed of his ignorance is the sign of a dead soul. A man with such a soul radiates nothing but boredom; even the right things he says are merely correct—and mere correctness can be awfully dull for a lively young person who is trying to understand and experience the great adventure of life.

5. Much of what has been written on the training of teachers is of little avail because of a lack of realization of the difficulties with which a public secondary school system is confronted. We have in our school system about seven million youth and about three hundred thousand teachers. There are taught young people with extremes of ability (from I.Q.'s which make learning almost impossible to 140 and higher). Many of them are in school unwillingly. They have to be prepared for all kinds of vocations and professions by teachers from the most varying cultural backgrounds with highly diverse talents and interest. Often these teachers are poorly paid and must work in badly equipped buildings. In addition, many women use school work only as a transition from college to marriage.

However, certain generalities might be ventured. Our typical state teachers' colleges and just as many of our liberal arts colleges are places where the idyllic isolation of the students from practical responsibilities (a hundred years ago youth of the same age level extended our frontier to the west), as well as their isolation from the broad streams of cultural life, tends to create a dangerous state of aloofness. It is difficult in such an atmosphere to help the prospective teacher understand the deeper problems of civilization and appreciate fully the interests of our youth and their parents.

But here we already are at the frontier between the ideal and the actual. It is doubtful whether we will have a sufficient number of educators to carry through a revolution in our training of teachers and, even if they exist, whether they will have sufficient support on the part of the authorities and the taxpayers on which these authorities finally depend. Yet, even under the present conditions certain improvements might be possible. As a matter of fact, at several places they are already under way.

We need in our undergraduate and graduate preparation of teachers, both in our state teachers' colleges and in our liberal arts institutions, a better apportionment of the courses in general or liberal education in comparison with all the isolated courses in methods of teaching and psychology. Yet even here a word of caution is necessary. A large number of our teachers in secondary schools now come from liberal arts colleges; so do the large majority of students who enter the graduate schools of education in our leading universities. These graduate schools generally provide not more than one to two years for the training of advanced teachers, research workers, and administrators in our public school system. Of necessity, these graduate schools have to be "technical" to a degree, just as advanced business schools or schools of technology. For the broad liberal foundation of learning the graduate schools have to rely on the previous work of the professors in the undergraduate departments, many of whom are so apt to cast their criticism on the public school teachers and their training. If one examines this problem objectively one often discovers, even with students coming with good grades from good institutions, such an amazing lack of a truly liberal and inspiring undergraduate training that one might ask what the students and their professors have done with the four years they have had available, in comparison with the one year generally available for the graduate year in education.

In other words, the problem of the education of teachers is not just one of "teacher training" but at the same time one of liberal or general education, the joint responsibility of the liberal arts institutions and, needless to say, of our high schools also.

6. The reader might expect in this treatise a more detailed treatment of the relationship between our public schools and our various institutions for the training of teachers on the one hand, and religious institutions on the other. As has already been said, this is a country in which the majority of citizens believe in the separation of state and church, and they have good reasons to do so. However, the educational scene is now replete with discussions concerning the inclusion of religious instruction in the regular school period, the problem of denominational schools, and the problem of support of religious education by public taxation.

This is not the place for the discussion of these issues, but one of the many crucial factors may be mentioned. If all who participate in the strife of parties and opinions about religious instruction were really interested in religion and not to the same, and even to a higher degree in politics and competition, the problem would not be as difficult as it is. But, unfortunately, there is this mingling of concerns. Even if it were not of intentional character—and certainly there are many men and women with nothing but a pure interest in the religious tradition—the political consequences issuing from a modification in the relation between school and religious denominations would impress itself upon the people. For any deeper change in the spiritual life of a nation affects by necessity also its political life. Religion is not an abstract matter of learning —as ecclesiastical history may be for some university professors—rather it is "a way of life" in the most comprehensive sense of the word. It is, consequently, inevitable that through the whole history of humanity religion and politics reacted upon each other. Religion sought the help of politics, and politics the help of religion. But politics alone never could vitalize a religion that had lost its genuine vitality, just as inadequate political organizations could not survive for more than a brief time by calling religion to their succor. It is the spirit that matters; "the wind bloweth where it listeth."

Here is, therefore, the central problem of the American school, its teacher education, and to a degree, of American democracy as a whole:—

In the strife of nations this republic may still be successful because of its superior physical strength—or it may not. If among American teachers and families there is a fading away of transcendental convictions, if democracy and democratic education are conceived of in a narrow political sense, or in the manner of a merely relativist and experimental philosophy, then our republic will become but one of the several forms of organization by which men have tried and will try to order and police their societies. But certainly it will then no longer be looked upon by freedom-loving men as a source of inspiration, as a country of refuge from persecution. But if the teachers and parents of this country are still willing—and able—to convey to the younger generation its basic political and cultural concept, that of democracy, as an attempt of man to reflect in his individual and communal life the verities he discovers through the free use of his reason guided by a religious conscience, then the American culture will reflect its religious motivation and continue to make an ever growing contribution to human culture. The choice is still before us.

INDEX